MEDIEVAL WOMEN AND
THE SOURCES OF
MEDIEVAL HISTORY

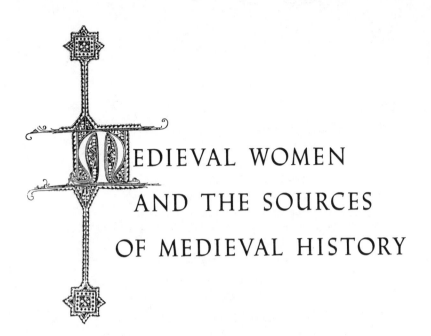

MEDIEVAL WOMEN
AND THE SOURCES
OF MEDIEVAL HISTORY

Edited by Joel T. Rosenthal

THE UNIVERSITY
OF GEORGIA PRESS

Athens and London

© 1990 by the University of Georgia Press
Athens, Georgia 30602
All rights reserved
Designed by Barbara E. Williams
Set in Trajanus and Aldus
The paper in this book meets the guidelines for
permanence and durability of the Committee on
Production Guidelines for Book Longevity of the
Council on Library Resources.

Printed in the United States of America
94 93 92 91 90   5 4 3 2 1

Library of Congress Cataloging in Publication Data
Medieval women and the sources of medieval history
/ edited by Joel T. Rosenthal.
p.   cm.
Includes bibliographical references.
ISBN 0-8203-1214-2 (alk. paper)
ISBN 0-8203-1226-6 (pbk: alk. paper)
1. Women—History—Middle Ages, 500–1500—
Sources.   I. Rosenthal, Joel Thomas, 1934–   .
HQ1143.M44   1990
305.4'09'02—dc20   89-20296
                                              CIP

British Library Cataloging in Publication Data available

CONTENTS

INTRODUCTION

Joel T. Rosenthal

inners write history. They also determine the creation, the content, and the scope of the sources. These are basic if obvious truths, and few of us fail to remind our students and scholarly colleagues of their importance when we explain the way in which our extant keys to past experience are the products of choice and intent. And yet, from the uncontested nature of these assertions, we can also arrive at another layer of questions, a set of alternate suggestions. If history reflects the winners' view, who, we are now prone to ask, were the so-called losers? What material was ignored, buried, and falsified in the sources that the winners were so careful to edit in their own favor, and to whom did it belong? ⁊ One response to this alternative question, today, is women. In the case studies and examples elaborated here, they are the women of medieval Europe, diverse as they were in terms of place, time, social level, access to power, status, and dependence or independence. An older list of answers about those pushed out of the center of historical identification might well have included other outsiders: barbarians, as seen by Gallo-Romans; Vikings, as seen by Anglo-Saxon and Carolingian monastic chroniclers; Saracens, Turks, Jews, schismatic Christians, and citizens of the Eastern Empire, as seen by the dedicated if narrow-minded travelers of the First Crusade. Or the list might have been more provincial, if hardly more broad-minded: the men of Venice, as viewed by those of Genoa; archdeacons, as viewed by parish priests and their flocks; masters of the guild merchant, as viewed by those of the countryside who had to sell their goods under rules not of their making. Why were women, as seen by men, so irrevocably in this listing? ⁊ Not that any of the answers offered below are novel ones. Our awareness of the extent to which women in the medieval world were outsiders, the other, is hardly a new perception.[1] The ideological underpinnings for their subordinate position were in place by the very beginnings of the period we cover in our undergraduate survey courses. A classroom treatment of women's social and legal status through the long medieval millennium often includes the metaphor of a line on a graph, and we can pretty easily guess the prevailing slope of such a line. Even when the effects of feudalism, the marriages of heiresses and the options of widows, the role of the Virgin in popular religion, and the taste for the literature of courtly love are all taken into account, the factors and forces that militate in women's favor never quite add up to a whole. There is little escape from the basic picture: most of those who wrote explicitly about women did so to denigrate them, and most of those who wrote for other purposes were apt to give them short shrift.

But even on this beleaguered battlefield there is the possibility of change for the better, and the current political and social consciousness and historical understanding can intertwine to enrich each other. Within the last couple of decades we have been able to congratulate ourselves upon having discovered the women of the Middle Ages. In one sense the discovery of medieval women is like Columbus's discovery of the New World: they too were there all the time, except that those who knew about them were not those who arranged the priorities and controlled the hegemonies of culture and of world view. The denizens neither wrote nor read the history that had been transmitted. For the most part, the women had indeed been hidden, and it was hardly an accident that they continued to be situated so as to remain "undiscovered" for so long.[2] From our current efforts to understand why they were relegated to the periphery, we expand and broaden our historical sympathy, our professional or academic ability to visualize how things "really happened" in the past. We also help to raise our awareness of how our own world functions: at least we can work on the conceptual framework of our students, our long-suffering friends, and our not-always-patient colleagues. And by combining our excavation for inadvertent or unintended history— material already incorporated within familiar bodies and collections of sources—with the development of a new and larger cosmos of interpretation, we can move toward a "total history" that will link together such topics as gender distinctions, the division of labor, the separation of the public and the private, and the prevalence of a sexism, an exploitation, and a fixed hierarchy that we should seek to understand but never to explain out of existence.

The interest in what we term women's history has beneficially affected most forms of historical inquiry as well as many of the inquirers. Our methods, our findings, and both our process and our substance have expanded. At the base level, we simply know more about women, and more about most forms of social interaction, because of this new focus. We have more data and more scholarship. Diversity and enrichment are yoked companions in intellectual inquiry. Whether we choose to approach women's history through "discovered" sources (Susan Mosher Stuard) or by thinking of the way in which women can be seen to constitute an invisible side to the chessboard on which men customarily play their game (John B. Freed), the tale becomes more complex and more rewarding. In the latter case, once we realize that the chessboard has this second side, the moves we usually follow in the visible game suddenly become clearer, more explicable. When we search other kinds of sources, we can even find that women sometimes had friends who were willing to take them at face value (Penny S. Gold) and that they could be accorded a level of equality beyond what is apparent at first glance (James A. Brundage). We can light upon an odd or neglected corner of medieval society, as when we examine the rich literature of remote but complex and loquacious Scandinavia and Iceland (Jenny Jochens), and we can occasionally come up with a case study or vignette so striking as to stoke our skepticism about the textbook consensus concerning sex roles and behavior (Jo Ann McNamara).

But behind these discoveries and countless others that are being made, there is always the harsh reality of the sources. In the great age of European exploration and buccaneering, new islands were not incorporated within the accepted cartographic tradition until ships sailed *and* returned. An explicit concern with sources is also a call for assessment and explanation; we have to find them and to return using them. If we wish to probe the relationship between the extant medieval sources and what we can learn about the story of women in medieval society, we probably have to accept that there are some hard knots we will perhaps never untie. In our travels—literal as well as metaphorical—we continue to look for new sources, though the odds against any major discoveries may run against us (the papers by Stuard, Helen Lemay, and Jane Tibbetts Schulenburg give some pointers on how to make an occasional breakthrough). We can reread familiar sources or, rather, reexcavate familiar sources, and many of us have been engaged in such labors—not, we hope we can add with some truth, without profit or a considerable degree of pleasure. But beneath all these brave ventures remains a layer of bedrock that will never yield much ore of distinction. Virtually all who deal with the topic, whether they concentrate on sources, social status, or ideology, quickly have to face the problems posed by the heavy bias of what they—the putative winners in the medieval battle of the sexes —chose to record about themselves and each other.

When Susan Mosher Stuard edited one of the first of the recent collections of historians' papers on women in the Middle Ages, she took a sanguine approach to the difficulties posed by the traditional sources. This was certainly a useful strategy in the mid-1970s, and Stuard's collection continues to serve us well. However, the problems remain real, and, as we see in Stuard's essay here, they cannot be explained away, or at least not beyond a certain point. They are inherent in medieval culture. They persisted through the Middle Ages; they are certainly going to persist through the maturation of our scholarship. In her detailed study of fourteenth-century English village life, Judith Bennett was moved to comment that the very listing of people in the manorial sources reflects the depth of gender-status identity: "Because a woman moved, in a sense, from one dependent status to another, it was important for the clerks . . . to specify accurately under whose authority she was at any given time."[3]

Why human society has generally been so sexist is a question whose answer is far beyond a mere medieval historian. Suffice it to say that the roots of sexism were many, and the roots went deep. Some of the phobia that men felt and expressed was obviously sexual, bespeaking some deep ambivalence about purity, potency, and fertility. In addition, women as property, both in the sexual and in the more conventional economic interpretations, constitute an ongoing theme around which much of what we call social relations was organized. This definition of social roles— mostly imposed from outside and, of course, mostly imposed by men— not only affected her role in the transmission of land and in the union or disunion of kin groups through marriage but also affected her power to act as an individual, both in this world and as a dues-paying member of Christ's Church. Apart from sometimes receiving property and what rights that might entail, what civil rights did she have? In a world where few had very many of these precious commodities, she generally had almost none.

However, we have also referred to interaction or interrelationship. Passive and active or dependent and independent are not the only conceivable categories. We do not have to think just in polarities and dichotomies. Women may have been the lesser partners in most forms of social activity, but they often were partners. They had some element of individualism, some possibility of roles (e.g., as widows or women of religion or mystics or social critics) that could give some scope for power. They could make an odd dash in the direction of self-assertion (as Alan M. Stahl and Brigitte Bedos-Rezak show), and they were often given considerable freedom and scope in some of the realms that are poorly illuminated in the written sources. The domestic environment could have been a comfortable and comforting one in many instances for both men and women, and here she may have set the tone. In addition, many men may have seen their wives' happiness as an obligation or a challenge to their own powers as homemakers and providers; a private world of joint decision making may have existed just beyond the margins of the parchment from which we usually have to draw our judgments. Decoding the sources and thinking about what they do not say are also rewarding paths, though they are narrow and some tough rules must be observed.

The papers in this collection go their own ways: some are case studies; some are surveys of sources; some are general examinations of regions or chronological periods; some are examples of how new ways of reading can shed new light on familiar texts. A number of the essays choose a particular kind of source and then test it for what it can tell us about women. This approach reminds us that a given type of record or source —recorded and preserved for whatever mix of reasons we can adduce— is a living body of data, not a quarried and polished stone upon which unyielding and irremediable material is engraved once and forever. As such, a given or discrete datum is actually a marker posted somewhere along the course of a two-way relationship: it records some episode from the lives of men and women, and it—as a genre of primary source— is likewise shaped and altered by what different people chose to enter into its record. There was a dialectical relationship *then* between those whose deeds and thoughts are recorded and the sources they themselves used and preserved. In addition, there is another such relationship *now* between the preserved record and the reading our culture and our prejudices condition us to give this text. Women on coins were the most baldly exposed among the many women who aspired to some high status and public identity. It is no wonder that, at the very top, they were destined to remain rare and exotic members of a tiny group. Alan M. Stahl guides us to where, when, and why such records came into existence. With seals, on the other hand, we have a much higher incidence of the feminine profile. There was an active record of women sealing, though here too Brigitte Bedos-Rezak warns us of the restricted roles and circumscribed context within which such activity took place.

Who among the uninitiated would expect the canon law of high medieval Europe to have been a haven of equality between the sexes? But when we remember that James A. Brundage's forceful summary can be read in conjunction with the findings of other scholars on marriage and the church's attitude toward the importance, freedom, and symmetry of sexual relations, we begin to see a wider as well as a friendlier context.[4] Brundage demonstrates how the internal logic of the canon lawyers took over and possibly left even authors and legal practitioners with a conclusion about men and women that they would have shrunk from at the outset. An internal logic can sometimes become a social dynamic.

Some types of sources reveal the way in which a society could cut different paths for men and for women, even when they were engaged in a similar line of inquiry or endeavor. In such a case our task is to gauge whether these roads are parallel, converging, or diverging and then to elaborate on the reasons for the double development. The history of medicine and of the traditions of health care and anatomy in obstetrics and gynecology furnishes an obvious topic to be treated in this fashion. Helen Lemay shows how the highbrow wisdom of the learned doctors in reality served to legitimate the lore of folk medicine and women's medicine. There was a complex pattern wherein magic and folklore and the humoral tradition of the classroom were woven together. In addition, certain myths had to be created and then taken at face value in order to cover the fact that men constantly borrowed and learned from women. Perhaps the traditions of hagiography would not seem likely to fit within this "paradigm" of male-female give-and-take. Jane Tibbetts Schulenburg shows us that they do and that by unraveling in a similar fashion the lore of the saints' lives, we can learn much about gender relationships in the early church. The tension between female creativity and male control is worked out to a different pattern in medicine and in hagiography, yet there are some basic similarities. If we could learn more of the underground tradition of midwives as well as of holy women, it is possible that many analogous points could be moved from the realms of speculation to those of relative certainty.

For some authors, the varied sources of a region or a particular regional society are useful in exploring the varieties of women's experience and testing how much we can recapture. The papers of David Herlihy and Susan Mosher Stuard complement each other. Herlihy shows the links between the social structure of Italian urban society and the reasons why certain kinds of sources were produced and used. Stuard reminds us that even the most familiar material from many political and cultural units around the great inland sea can regularly be reexamined to advantage and to the illumination of new items on our agenda. Never accept that a source has no relevance; always work from the possibility that the next archivist is guarding some buried treasure of women's history. Never accept that we have learned all we can from an old friend.

Ecclesiastical charters are mainly concerned, of course, with the recording of the landed status of regular, episcopal, or collegiate institutions. They are hardly concerned, prima facie, with gender relations or with the status of women. But even the driest of administrative transactions were carried out by living agents acting in their own interests and carrying their own histories as they went along, and both Penny S. Gold and John B. Freed show how the record can be squeezed to talk about status and activity. Two case studies, based on similar bodies of controlled data, enable Gold to demonstrate some variations in women's roles and in men's willingness to accept them in their more assertive or positive guise. Freed shows that the same story (in the setting of aristocratic families in Salzburg) is explicable in the obvious terms of men's history and then again (or simultaneously) in the much richer context that can be informed by taking the different life patterns and experiences of both sexes into account.

A favorite pedagogical tactic is to approach material through the compare-and-contrast paradigm. Jo Ann McNamara picks up this familiar line of exposition and shows that it can be used to probe the limits of some highly individualized versions of feminine sanctity, leading us to and even beyond the boundaries of permissible diversity. The attack upon what contemporaries saw as an excess of pluralism within spiritual Christianity at the turn of the fourteenth century was hardly likely to miss women, given their propensity for appearing in the vanguard of spiritual movements. When the church was in a genial or experimental mood, these women were accepted or at least permitted as brave and eager soldiers. When the mood changed, the same women were deemed dangerous misfits; some of them talked and withdrew to survive, while some of them talked and then were forced to pay the ultimate price for their commitment.

A new survey of an old but changing topic is always a welcome beacon in the twilight. In 1986 Janet Senderowitz Loengard wrote for the *Law and History Review* an article titled "Legal History and the Medieval Englishwoman: A Fragmented View." She has now expanded her comments, and she tries to balance an assessment of how recent legal and sociolegal studies have treated women in medieval England with a tea-leaf reading regarding future directions and lines of inquiry.

Jenny Jochens and I have written papers that survey the sources of a particular society or culture. Though the sources, rather than the status of women, are the point of focus, it is hard to keep our attention from wandering as we try to offer a full assessment. As Herlihy or Gold or Freed would remind us, social status and the kinds of documents created and preserved are hardly separate, unrelated topics. This is driven home when, in the papers by Jacques Berlioz and Marie Anne Polo de Beaulieu, we look at a more literary source, the *exempla,* created to categorize, to instruct, and to serve as a kind of data base for those who knew the moralistic "punch line" and who were now supplied with the long story needed to introduce it. Language (as well as the larger artifacts and structures it serves) carries its messages.

This collection of papers, though certainly of reasonable bulk, could surely have been expanded to explore many more tunnels into the past. In some cases we tried to pin down authors who would accommodate our focus to their own commitments. If some reader wishes to compile a companion volume to this collection, such obvious areas as women in art, in theological studies, and in the tradition of the narrative chronicles are awaiting their moment. Creative literature is a vast field now receiving considerable attention, and common sense, humility, and a limited dedication to the work ethic all argued for its exclusion from this collection (though the *exempla* may tread the line between creative and didactic literary sources). In addition, we clearly have been able to do little justice to those women removed from the centers of Christian thought, let alone to most of those who lived at some distance from the cultural axis that ran from Rome over the Alps to Paris and then through the Low Countries to the night boat for Dover (with only Jochens asking for a day-excursion detour). Muslims within Europe, Jews and Muslims on the outer fringes, heretics, and schismatics have been omitted: reasons of space are sufficient to explain if not to excuse. Nor, as it turns out, are there many statements about medieval views or theories of feminine inferiority or of gender relations. This is largely a function of who the authors are and of their interests. Whether it is to our credit or blame that we, by unspoken consensus, keep well away from critical theory is something to be debated elsewhere. [5]

The long myopic tradition regarding gender and historical research now stands well revealed. The studied reluctance of scholars to venture far from the study of political and mainstream social and cultural history is a story we can document today with a wealth of both positive and negative evidence. But in fairness to our forerunners and teachers of past generations, in many ways they merely accepted and in turn re-flected the way the sources of the medieval world had come down to them. Since the mid-nineteenth century, the training incorporated into academic historical research has placed great emphasis upon restoring a medieval text to its original phraseology and intent: charter research is perhaps the best example of this learned approach to unlocking the past. That such training places almost no premium upon asking why a given text or kind of text did not talk about other related topics is hardly a fair criticism of nineteenth-century empiricism. Such questions become pressing only when we think that we have exhausted the original points or when we bring a set of questions and hypotheses so different that we no longer choose to (or are able to) remain within the older framework that has been established between speaker and auditor or lector. In effect, we now seem to be on the brink of a new agenda. If it is not quite an agenda with a declaration of independence or secession, it is at least one that demands a new constitutional convention. From such a convention may come a new relationship between the voices of the past and the interpretive sensitivities of the present.

No collection of essays about any serious topic could be comprehen-sive in its coverage. Nor could any collection ask all the questions. Each new body of sources that we explore poses new queries and leads to new suggestions. Furthermore, each peculiar linkage or permutation of dif-ferent sources sparks a new series of intellectual reactions, and the same ingredients, when combined in a different order, can lead to a different result. The sources themselves work upon each other, and few would be bold enough to insist upon determining which is the inert matter, which the catalyst. The order in which we read helps to determine the way we think about the topic. To approach the study of medieval women by means of the sources makes us confront a whole range of problems cen-tering around the creation and shaping of texts. The approach we have adopted in this collection heightens our awareness of the gulf between the reasons why they wrote and the reasons why we now read. History, at best, is some shifting modus vivendi between the dead and the living. Moreover, we should be realistic about what we can accomplish. Giving proper credit and space to the "traditionally bypassed" for their long record of contributions would itself seem to be a legitimate endeavor on our part. After all, if the victors created the sources from which history has been written, we can exercise the historians' version of poetic license and decide that we too are among the winners, and can freely exercise our own proper discretion in reading the past.

This collection of essays grew from a suggestion that Alan M. Stahl, Brigitte Bedos-Rezak, and I offer a panel at the 1987 Berkshire Conference on the History of Women, held at Wellesley College. As we planned the panel on the topic of the sources and women, the idea of a larger collection on this theme began to take shape. I thank the many colleagues who helped us shape and present our panel, with special acknowledgment for the suggestions of Kathleen Biddick, our enlightened and enlightening commentator at the Wellesley College meetings. Penny Gold's paper, presented in an earlier version at the 1984 Berkshire conference, helped focus my thoughts about the ways others could be approached and recruited for our lineup. In putting together this collection, I was fortunate to find friends who were eager to help. Brigitte Bedos-Rezak spotted some corners that I had missed and some rather obvious ones that I might well have missed. Jane Tibbitts Schulenburg offered suggestions and encouragement as we stood in a dormitory lounge—the academic equivalent of the smoke-filled boardroom—at a Kalamazoo conference. Jo Ann McNamara came through one more time; she is an invariably severe critic and a friend who helps keeps faith. Elizabeth Makowski urged me, from our first communication, to force the project into the light of day, and her successors at the University of Georgia Press have continued her tradition of supportive criticism. They and all the contributors have helped guarantee that the professional isolation that threatens those who teach medieval history at American colleges and universities or who pursue research in other corridors has been held at bay by the kind of dialogue that we all once thought was the daily fare of scholarly life.

NOTES

1. Susan Mosher Stuard, ed., *Women in Medieval History and Historiography* (Philadelphia, 1987), is a good introduction to bibliography. While John B. Freed refers to some gaps in Stuard's volume, it is nevertheless a book of great value and represents perhaps the easiest way to get hold of large chunks of information readily available in English. Editors' introductions to collected essays often serve as useful summaries of the state of the research, and two topical volumes are of relevance for this purpose: Barbara A. Hanawalt, ed., *Women and Work in Preindustrial Europe* (Bloomington, Ind., 1986), pp. vii–xviii, and Mary Erler and Maryanne Kowaleski, eds., *Women and Power in the Middle Ages* (Athens, Ga., 1988), pp. 1–17.

2. Susan Mosher Stuard, ed., *Women in Medieval Society* (Philadelphia, 1976), pp. i–ix.

3. Judith Bennett, *Women in the Medieval English Countryside: Gender and Household in Brigstock before the Plague* (New York, 1987), p. 73; see also p. 43.

4. In addition to Brundage's *Law, Sex, and Christian Society in Medieval Europe* (Chicago, 1987), see Michael Sheehan, "The Influence of Canon Law on the Property Rights of Married Women in England," *Medieval Studies* 25 (1963): 109–24, and "The Formation and Stability of Marriage in Fourteenth-Century England: Evidence of the Ely Register," *Medieval Studies* 32 (1971): 228–63; see also Elizabeth Makowski, "The Conjugal Debt and Medieval Canon Law," *Journal of Medieval History* 3 (1977): 99–114.

5. For a historian's attempt to bridge the gap between women's history and gender-theory history, see Joan W. Scott, "Gender: A Useful Category of Historical Analysis," *American Historical Review* 91 (1986): 1053–75. Needless to say, her effort met with considerable controversy.

MEDIEVAL WOMEN AND
THE SOURCES OF
MEDIEVAL HISTORY

MEDIEVAL WOMEN IN FRENCH SIGILLOGRAPHIC SOURCES

Brigitte Bedos-Rezak

he creation and survival of a medieval source, or of any historical source, is determined by cultural forces informing the context wherein the source was elaborated and preserved. The specific content inherent in such a source about women, or its silence, is thus likely to say as much about the source as it does about women. But that which can be extracted and attention to the methodology that was required may allow a new reading of the general informational content of the source in question. This reciprocal process, which provides an enlarged basis for any historical analysis that follows, necessarily takes into account a feminist perspective.[1] ❡French medieval seals, one of the sources under review in this volume, have survived in large numbers; there are about 50,000 items, of which women's seals constitute perhaps 35 percent.[2] Such a broad data base encourages the possibility of formal statistical analysis; it certainly allows for the identification of trends and patterns against which to evaluate exceptions, to sense the tension within a system. Besides their survival in substantial numbers, seals were also widespread within their contemporary society. By 1230, all persons could, and many did, legally commit themselves by affixing their seals to charters recording their transactions.[3] The intensity of this cultural phenomenon was greatest in northern France, since in the south the notariate provided an effective alternative method of documentary validation.[4] As a legal tool for individual commitment, seals incorporated both a text, the legend, and an image, which further mediated the sealer's effectiveness. The abbots of Marmoutiers, for instance, surrounded the head depicted on their seal with the legend "Trust this head of Geoffroi [or Stephen, or Robert, abbot of Marmoutiers] as you would trust him."[5] The seal is a sign of and conveys specific representations of the sealer's identity within a juridical context, and it is this legal function that distinguishes it from

1

virtually all other iconographic sources. Furthermore, on seals, text and
image participate in a single discourse,[6] which has a readily interpretable
relationship to other seals of widely disparate social categories, of both
genders, across distant regions, and over some three centuries. Lastly,
these texts and images were recurrently imprinted by their owners, thus
providing a relevant basis for yet another analysis, that of a particular
representational system and its societal context.[7] To claim the expression
of a specifically female consciousness on seals used and owned by women
entails the postulate that these seals were expressly commissioned and
designed by women. There is no evidence to support such an assumption;
rather, the semiotic conventions inherent in sigillographic iconography
reveal a medieval society conforming to patriarchal views of sexual division and social order.[8] Female depictions on seals are therefore not to
be taken as direct womanly self-perceptions, but they are crucial to the
analysis of gender significance in the representational system evidenced
by seals.

Gender and methodology will be the primary concerns in considering
this sigillographic material. Drawing on the multilayered implications
of seal usage, text, and iconography, this essay will review seals used by
women and any seals where women appear as images or are specifically
referred to in the legends. Having identified a womanly sphere of action
in sealing and a semiotic system articulated around the female, I will use
the two poles of reality and myth to identify a medieval perspective on
women.

❧ The assumption of a direct correspondence between textual prescrip-
tion and actual behavior has been rightly identified as a potential pitfall in
the methodology of women's history.[9] Indeed, legal compilations, such as
Philippe de Beaumanoir's *Coutumes de Beauvaisis*, written in about 1283,
though containing numerous references to seal usage and to the juridical value of seals in connection with the social status of their owners,[10]
always refers to these owners as men.[11] To be sure, women are not infrequently referred to in this work, and several chapters are devoted to their
legal and economic prerogatives.[12] Yet in reading this text, one might get
the impression that women did not use seals. This would be incorrect,
since by the end of the thirteenth century, and especially in Beauvaisis,
women, from the aristocratic to the ranks of the non-noble landowners,
sealed commonly. [13]

I have explored elsewhere the patterns of sealing practice by women
and their implications with regard to women's position in medieval soci-

ety.[14] The analysis may be summed up as follows. In France, documentary sealing had remained an exclusively royal prerogative up to the mid-eleventh century, at which time the male aristocracy started to seal as well.[15] The practice then remained restricted to males until the early twelfth century, thereafter spreading at the same rate among both men and women through all social strata. The first French woman sealer was the dowager queen, Bertrada de Montfort, who in 1115 sealed a charter in favor of Marmoutiers.[16] She was followed by succeeding queens,[17] abbesses,[18] and women of the aristocracy and of the nobility, who prior to 1200 remained the only female sealers. During the thirteenth century, noblewomen increased their seal usage, but more remarkable still is the huge proportion of new female sealers of knightly lineage and of non-noble landowning families. Considering only data derived from the seals of women, one can make several observations about the differentiated evolution of women's legal and economic capabilities. Prior to 1200, aristocratic and noble women independently sealed transactions of various types, but by the mid-thirteenth century a regression of their seal usage had occurred after which they sealed only in concert with their fathers, husbands, or sons and only for those acts that involved their own property (personal estates, dowries, and dowers). Unmarried noblewomen did not seal at all. At this time female seals within this higher nobility are proportionally very few (5 percent) as compared with men's, indicating a male primacy that had reduced women's power and independence. By contrast, the women of knightly and non-noble landowning families seem to have acted more independently: if unmarried, they sealed acts in their own names; if married, they sealed a wide variety of deeds conjointly with their husbands, and not merely those involving disposition of their own rights or properties. The proportion of female seals is also high in this group (38 percent). Sealing therefore reflects status and capability within the family unit, and its practice offers insight into the position of women within their own kindred.[19]

To elucidate the standing of women within society as a whole, we may compare their sigillographic records to those of men. A major similarity is that the woman's seal appears to have carried as much power of authentication as that of a male.[20] To my knowledge there is no record of a document having been contested because it had been validated by a woman's seal. However, such effectiveness related only to documents issued in their own names. In contrast, male lords, by affixing their seals, often endowed the deed of a lesser person with greater security, though the lords were not themselves principals of the transaction.[21] The seals

of laywomen appear to have been confined to a strictly personal usage
and not to have possessed this public dimension of the males'.[22] This
characteristic is also perfectly exemplified by queenly seals, which were
absolutely limited to private and domestic matters and were never endowed with the symbolic value of the king's seal as representative of the
authority of the state.[23] On the other hand, seals of abbesses appear in
contexts exactly similar to those of abbots.[24] This gives further evidence
of the use of seals in defining the public versus private roles of women
and in characterizing the functional difference between lay and religious
women. Private charters reflect one aspect of public action, but use of
seals shows the various extent of women's public sphere.[25] Furthermore,
and in addition to male-only settings, many documents issued in the
names of both spouses were validated by the seal of the husband alone.[26]
As a result, male seals are far more numerous than female seals at all
social levels, though there is no reason to suppose a substantial majority
of men over women within medieval society. Thus the use of seals by
women is a later and less frequent occurrence as compared with the male
practice; it is overlooked in contemporary legal treatises; and it is limited
in its public capacity for laywomen, but not for religious women.

   In the texts of female seal legends, where patronymics and the names
and titles of husbands constitute the normal identifying formulas,[27] terms
of kinship may also be found. First appearing only in their Latin forms,
such terms are also seen in the vernacular during the second half of
the thirteenth century, but only on the seals of lesser noble and non-
noble landowning women. The most commonly used term of kinship on
women's seals is *uxor*, or *fame*;[28] mention of widowhood is much rarer
and, when not expressed by the term *relicta*,[29] is referred to with the
euphemism *uxoris quondam domini X.*[30] Much less rare than "widow"
but not quite as common as "wife" is the term *filia* or *fille.*[31] Especially
among the aristocracy, the use of *filia* could designate the sealer as an
heiress,[32] and this remark brings us to the nature and implications of the
vocabulary of kinship on female seals.

   When a male was heir to his father's patrimony, he was designated
on his seal as *primogenitus*, regardless of whether or not he had elder
sisters.[33] I have found only one, late (1333) instance in which an heiress,
that of the county of Gueldre, Marguerite, was designated as *primogenita
comitis Ghelrensis.*[34] This masculine orientation of the term *primogenitus* parallels and attests the linear devolution of birthright,[35] for, though
female heiresses were not rare, they nevertheless remained designated
on seals only as *filiae*, "daughters," if they were designated at all.[36] In

fact, whether as daughter, wife, or widow, the woman's position was consistently articulated around her male kindred, in the various economic and biological roles—heiress of the land, mother, manager of her dower—in which she was significant for the lineage or for the household.[37] I have found only two instances of a kinship articulation between women. In the first, Margaret of Flanders is designated in the legend of her seal as the sister of the countess of Flanders.[38] Joan, the elder of the two sisters, had inherited the counties of Flanders and Hainaut from their father, Baldwin, count of Flanders and Hainaut and emperor of Constantinople.[39] In identifying herself through the comital title of her sister, Margaret established her position of power on the combined bases of kinship (sisterhood) and property (the county of Flanders). This case, besides exemplifying the close connection in medieval society between kinship, power, and property, may also indicate that the usual binary construction of gender on seals resulted primarily from the property relation, property characteristically known as patrimony. In the second instance, Isabel, widow of Humbert, lord of Montpensier and constable of Beaujeu, is termed on her seal *tuttrix* of Jane, her own orphan daughter, who is labeled as the daughter of the lord of Beaujeu on this same seal. [40]

The texts of women's seals emphasize their personal, primarily marital, status, to the point where some seal legends actually read "Seal of X his wife." [41] This formulation renders the seal and its owner functionally dependent on the husband's presence, name, and seal. Such personal categorization never appears on male seals, where virtually the only terms of kinship used are those of filiation, and only in connection with their fathers.[42] A unique exception on seals is that of Jean d'Avesnes, son of the countess and heiress of the counties of Flanders and of Hainaut, who is termed on his seal Jean of Avesnes, son of Marguerite, countess of Flanders and of Hainaut.[43] Jean became count of Hainaut, while Flanders went to his half brother William of Dampierre, who, while still heir, used the equivalent Latin term *heres* on his seal, avoiding mention of the matronymic. [44]

Thus women's status was consistently defined by their position vis-à-vis male kindred; men typically identified themselves only by reference to men; and both women and men were virtually never affiliated through matronymics. Finally, seal legends of both genders never refer to parenthood.

The next question is whether kinship terminology referring to women appears on any seals other than their own or those of their male counterparts. Ecclesiastical seals, mostly those of bishops depicting the Virgin and Child, present two patterns. The first involves the use of *mater*, as in *mater Christi* or *Virgo Dei Mater*;[45] the second reads *Salve Virgo* (or *sancta*) *parens* (fig. 1).[46] In both cases parenthood is at once expressed and relates to the mother, but the context is, of course, no longer that of the natural family.

Another direct representation of kinship on seals is provided by heraldry. Heraldry is an iconographic and/or textual rhetoric that expressed the identity of a kindred in relation to other groups, to its own land, and even to its separate sub-branches. The heraldic image, through the complex grammar of its structure, allows the precise location of an individual within his kindred and within the larger social environment.[47] Three aspects of heraldry on seals are relevant for the history of women: bearings, modalities of bearing, and transmission of the device.

Originally developed to identify the medieval warrior while he was covered with armor, coats of arms initially filled a male and military function. The earliest arms still extant are recorded on seals, those of the counts of Vermandois and of Meulan in about 1130 and 1160.[48] Almost from the time of this beginning, a hereditary pattern of transmission was established in which, as with the land, the heir was privileged. He alone could inherit the full coat of arms, whereas his younger brothers had to introduce marks of cadency indicative of their cadet status.[49]

As early as 1183 in France, a female seal displayed a coat of arms,[50] and the practice grew steadily, to the point where, by 1250, most women showed arms on their seals, that is, the arms of their fathers and/or those of their husbands (fig. 2).[51] It bears emphasis that I have found no instance in which a woman introduced marks of cadency within her father's arms. If her father or husband used an already modified coat of arms, she would display it but add no further marks of cadency. A woman thus had no specific place in the heraldic grammar of her patrilineage.

Heraldry on women's seals, however, not infrequently displays matrilineal coats of arms.[52] This observation has led to an investigation of the same phenomenon on male seals. A sampling of about eight hundred male seals from 1150 to 1350 shows that the few men who retained a matrilineal coat often, though not invariably, did so in connection with matrilineal inheritance of land.[53] Still fewer men displayed the arms of their wives' families.[54] The substantial number of lineages endowed with emblems borrowed from a matrilineal heraldic device is striking. The unusual Capetian combination of or and azure was transmitted matrilineally to the Warrenne and the Beaugency;[55] the two bars of the comital house of Bar were transmitted by women to the counts of Chiny, of Clermont, and of Salm and to the lord of Nesle;[56] the garbs of the Candavène count of Saint Pol were also passed by women to the seals of the counts of Gerberoi, Chester, and Blois and of the lords of Senlis.[57] Recent scholarship has demonstrated that the identification of noble families with a single heraldic crest always reflects a horizontal and extensive structure of kinship. The principal link in such affiliations was not infrequently one or several remote female ancestors. [58]

The heraldic image, however, is but one of the iconographic categories of women on seals. The centrality of sigillographic images in assuring the effectiveness of the seal's legal function has been mentioned earlier. Seal iconography clearly shows elements of taxonomy centered less on individuality than on societal category, less on subjective consciousness than on interpersonal relationships such as kinship (heraldry) or sociopolitical function (royal, military, ecclesiastical, civic, etc.; figs. 3, 4, 5).[59] Interwoven throughout is gender. Specifically female imagery on seals falls into three categories: any iconography appearing on women's seals, female depictions on women's seals, and female depictions on other types of seals.

Female seals of lesser social status tended to show decorative vegetal motifs. These, apart from a few depictions of the distaff,[60] were not necessarily peculiar to a woman's surroundings or activities. Noteworthy, possibly unique, is the seal of Jeanne, concierge of the Parisian residence of the Artois family; her seal depicted (ca. 1303) a mother tending her child in a cradle.[61] Full-length female effigies, usually bearing a fleur-de-lis (fig. 6) or a hawk (fig. 2), are the norm on noblewomen's seals.[62] The fleur-de-lis evokes an extensive range of symbolism[63]—dynastic motherhood, as in the Tree of Jesse,[64] fertility, as in the depiction of Venus's month on calendars,[65] and, of course, the ideal of femininity as an attribute of the Virgin (fig. 7).[66] The fleur-de-lis therefore represents the importance of women in the biogenetics of lineage, though in the ambivalent terms of motherhood and virginity.[67] The hawk is also an ambivalent symbol; it represents secularity and aristocratic life, thus shifting the emphasis from Mary to Eve. In contemporary literature and miniature painting, the hawk was invested with a specific semiotic content relating to women: their beauty, their amorous conversation, and their cruelty. [68]

Both of these metaphorical attributes are set against a realistic element, clothing, which always registers the current fashion while also placing the female body in an attitude of sexual attractiveness (figs. 2, 6).[69] Significantly, this accuracy in the rendering of secular feminine

apparel serves no function other than the definition of gender.[70] This
is in contrast with male seals, where costume is normally functionally
specific: the knight in armor (fig. 4), the bishop in full episcopal array
(fig. 5),[71] the craftsman with professional equipment.[72] When women do
have a recognized function that has its equivalent in the male world,
their seals register this function. In the case of abbesses, a cross and
monastic robes indicate an equivalent status by a depiction absolutely
parallel to that on abbots' seals (figs. 8, 9).[73] This is not so for queens,
however, who may be shown on seals with crown and scepter but are not
in the enthroned posture that characterizes a king's seal (figs. 3, 10).[74]
On their seals, therefore, queens are devoid of majesty, and laywomen
are without any display of function;[75] they are stereotyped by a semiotic
convention of gender that excludes explicit references to their familial
role, affective life, or personal qualities.

It is only in turning to images of women on other than female seals
that a corpus of depictions offering a wider range of female attitudes becomes available. There are very few relating to laywomen. The lords of
Saint Aubert (1194) and of Bethune (1202) show on their seals a kneeling
knight paying homage to a lady.[76] Two officers used a seal depicting an
explicit love scene, complete in one case with physical gestures of sexual
affection.[77] But the women receiving the most varied iconographic treatment on seals are female saints, among whom the Virgin occupies the
preeminent place (figs. 7, 11, 12).

Hagiographic secular seals are mostly those of cities displaying their
local patron saints. Although the spectacular seal of Aix-la-Chapelle depicts the humility of Charlemagne offering the city to the Virgin and
Child,[78] most French city seals reflect a preference for a male saint or a
manifest disinterest in their female saints by adoption of an architectural
or other alternative device.[79] Religious institutions, chapters, and monasteries, whether for men or women, did not discriminate between male
and female saints in their seal iconography: female patrons are represented in an appropriate proportion to male patrons.[80] In assessing the
presence of female saints on the personal seals of ecclesiastical men and
women, one should note several important points. Abbesses and prioresses tended not to display the patron or indeed any saint of their institution, whether male or female.[81] Abbots, priors, archdeacons, and deans,
however, tended to display the image of the Virgin on their personal
seals whether or not she was the patron of their institution.[82] This preference became an almost invariable choice for bishops and archbishops,
especially after 1250 (figs. 1, 13).[83]

The female saint depicted on the seals of ecclesiastics of both genders is not confined to the stereotypical mode that characterizes the depiction of secular women. She may be shown simply standing together with her specific attribute, a palm, or, as in the case of Mary Magdalene, holding an ointment jar.[84] But the iconography more often involves a scene of her life wherein she is shown as a more complex individual: Saint Elizabeth washes the feet of the poor,[85] Mary Magdalene welcomes Christ and expresses deep emotion in kissing his feet.[86] Saint Catherine is presented as a scholar who argues with four doctors inspired by demons (fig. 11).[87] The courage of Saint Valery is the theme of an abbey seal on which the saint is shown being beheaded.[88] Saint Helen is recognized as discovering the Holy Cross on the seal of the dean of Orléans.[89] Bathilda, a Merovingian queen who was canonized, dreams on a seal of the ladder that will take her to paradise.[90] Another Merovingian queen, Saint Clotilde, wife of Clovis, is depicted enthroned on a seal of the Parisian abbey of Sainte Geneviève.[91] Whereas an actually reigning queen was denied this attitude of majesty on her seal, a deceased and sanctified queen might be depicted enthroned. Indeed, the representation in majesty, the prerogative of the ruler and seldom adopted by male or female ecclesiastics, is not at all unusual for the sigillographic depiction of female saints. [92]

The queen portrayed most fully on seals is the Virgin Mary (fig. 7), whose entire life cycle is a focus for attention in the sigillographic medium. Annunciation, motherhood, death and assumption, coronation —all are depicted, though Mary as queen and as mother are most emphasized.[93] Marian seals document the biological cycle of motherhood —birth (fig. 2),[94] nursing,[95] and mother/child relationship (fig. 7)[96]— though, as we have seen, none of these activities ever appeared on the seals of contemporary women. What is further noteworthy is the characteristic choice, especially after 1300, of Mary as a mother on the personal seals of male ecclesiastics in a very specifically structured image: Mary and Child occupy the upper part of the seal, while the male ecclesiastic is placed in the lower part of the seal, most often kneeling (figs. 1, 13).[97] Such a seal's legend, as already mentioned, may well refer to Mary as *parens* or *Mater* (fig. 1).[98] A further component of this composition is often the coat of arms of the seal's owner (fig. 13).[99] It is along an axis suggested by this visual structure of kinship, represented by familial heraldic emblems, and articulated around motherhood and womanhood, made explicit both iconographically and textually,[100] that the following conclusions are drawn.

❦ In medieval sigillography, woman is present both as user and as image. The seal of a secular woman, though theoretically equipotent with that of a male, was nevertheless in practice reserved for use in private and domestic matters. The seal of a religious woman, on the other hand, was unrestricted in its usage. This latter differentiation obviously reflects not gender but sexuality. A wife was a creature sexually active and ruled by man, an abbess, a creature virgin and continent, and thus recognized as fulfilling a public function within society. This dichotomy is paralleled by the visual distinction that seals establish between the "real" woman and the deceased and/or holy woman. Seal images present the following significant reversal: natural motherhood and kinship are evoked only indirectly through the emblematic system of heraldry and the metaphorical fleur-de-lis, while idealized womanhood is illustrated by naturalistic depictions of biological and affective life. On a secular woman's seal, the visual expression of her biogenetic role, by emblematic rather than naturalistic display, symbolizes an important aspect of the general social order, namely, the denial of the female personality so as to reinforce the structure of patrilineage.

For the same reason, secular men also resorted to the indirect heraldic/emblematic system whenever associating themselves with women. By contrast, clergymen did not hesitate to display a mother on their seals, albeit the Mother of God. It is true that the preference for female and Marian iconography on male ecclesiastical seals can be shown to parallel contemporary religious and symbolic uses of these themes. But a comprehensive interpretation of religious iconography on seals must be informed by these seals' function, for to be effective within the legal context, seals had to present relevant elements of identity. The comparison of lay and ecclesiastical male seals reveals that the difference in the system chosen to allude to womanhood and motherhood is of less significance than the common recourse to a single theme. Both systems, whether mediate because emblematic or immediate because naturalistic, stressed patterns of human relationships, primarily that of kinship.

Seals convey the notion that medieval perception of the self was rooted in kinship,[101] whether that of the blood or that of the spirit upon which the whole ecclesiastical institution was established. And seals also reveal that central to this governing construct was the woman whose emblematized image confirms patrilineality while also revealing the ongoing strength of matrilineality. The sigillographic transfer of natural roles, especially of motherhood, from real persons to holy females may be read as an enhancement, a sanctification of women's function within their kindreds and in society. This transfer underlines that the standard depiction of secular women on their seals is of a woman qua woman, in contrast to men, who appear on their seals only as categories such as knights, bishops, or craftsmen. Gender as function is what constituted and defined the natural woman's identity. Such an identity set her outside the order of society, where most gradations of status were in fact gradations of male status, but it also helped focus upon her necessary role in procreation. What the semantics of the female image on seals reveal is that, though part of a patrilineal, patrimonial, and patriarchal system, women, definitively identified through gender alone, were radically differentiated from males and conceptually dissociated from property, rules of succession, and other discriminations linked to paternity. Woman stood for the seamless unity of the kindred so well expressed in the maternal transmission of heraldry and emblematic crests. And when male seals display these emblems or the image of the Virgin Mother, they reveal how men in groups were bounded by the feminine, from whom they derived much of their sense, and their signs, of identity.

NOTES

An early version of this paper was presented as "Impressions of French Medieval Women: Sigillographic Evidence (Twelfth through Fourteenth Centuries)" at a session on women and the sources of medieval history during the Seventh Berkshire Conference on the History of Women, Wellesley College, 1987. I would like to thank Kathleen Biddick of Notre Dame University for her insightful comments as the session's respondent. A revised version, "The Power to Signify: French Women and Medieval Seals," was presented at a colloquium on authority and marginality in the Middle Ages, Princeton University, 1988.

1. See the remarks of Hilda Smith on the difficulties of discovering material on women in "Feminism and the Methodology of Women's History," p. 372. Susan Mosher Stuard acknowledges that a significant amount of information about medieval women has been uncovered but is concerned that some contemporary historical methods and constructs mask as well as reveal women's history; she desires that French medieval women be restored to their true role as historical agents, a rehabilitation that would also provide a broader encompassing basis for synthetic studies of social institutions (Introduction, pp. x–xi, and "Fashion's Captives," p. 75, in Stuard, *Women in Medieval History*).

2. A comprehensive bibliography on French seals can be found in Gandilhon and Pastoureau, *Bibliographie de la sigillographie française*. General introductions to medieval seals include Bascapé, *Sigillografia*; Welber, *I sigilli nella storia*; Ewald, *Siegelkunde*; Jenkinson, *Guide to Seals*; Kittel, *Siegel*; Pastoureau, *Les Sceaux*; Laurent, *Sigillographie*; Bedos-Rezak, "Seals." On women's seals and seal usage, see Deurbergue, "Les Sceaux des dames" (I wish to thank Maria

Deurbergue for allowing me to consult the full manuscript of her dissertation [Paris, Archives nationales, AB XXVIII 93]; an abstract of her work is published in *École nationale des Chartes*, pp. 29–32); Bedos-Rezak, "Women, Seals, and Power." A rapid appreciation of seals as sources for the history of women is given in Verdon, "Les Sources de l'histoire de la femme" (seals on p. 248).

The present study is based on the following inventories: Demay, *Sceaux de la Normandie*; Demay, *Sceaux de la Flandre*; Demay, *Sceaux de l'Artois et de la Picardie*; Eygun, *Sigillographie du Poitou*; Douët d'Arcq, *Sceaux*.

3. The use of seals for documentary validation, which in France had been a royal privilege from the fifth century, spread sporadically to some bishops during the ninth and tenth centuries: seals of Riculf, archbishop of Rouen (ca. 872), and of the bishop of Toul (898) in Boüard, *Manuel . . . diplomatique générale*, p. 356 n. 2; seal of Adalbéron, bishop of Metz (984–1005), in Sauer, "Sceau épiscopal messin." German nonroyal, nonimperial seals prior to the eleventh century are discussed in Kittel, *Siegel*, pp. 119–20, 246, and in Kornbluth, *Carolingian Treasure*, pp. 33–35, 42, 106–7. For early English cases, see Bedos-Rezak, "The King Enthroned," esp. pp. 54–55; Heslop, "English Seals"; Heslop, "Seals." The progressive and constant diffusion of seal usage to every stratum of medieval society began in the mid-eleventh century: see Bedos-Rezak, "Social Implications," esp. pp. 142–44, 157–58; Bedos, "Signes et insignes du pouvoir"; Bedos-Rezak, "Sceaux seigneuriaux"; Bedos-Rezak, "Les Sceaux au temps de Philippe Auguste."

4. Boüard, *Manuel . . . l'acte privé*, pp. 183–225.

5. Douët d'Arcq, *Sceaux* 3:98 nos. 8822–24 (1246, 1275, 1286); no. 8822: + *Gaufridi capiti credite sicut ei*. The thirteenth-century, two-sided seal of the English Benedictine abbey of Glastonbury shows on the obverse the Virgin and Child between Saint Catherine and Saint Margaret, with a legend that designates Mary as witness to the deed (*testis adest isti scripto Genetrix pia Christi Glastionie*); the reverse displays the three figures of Saint Dunstan, Saint Patrick, and Saint Benignus, who are said in the legend to confirm the dispositions (*confirmant has res inscripti pontifices tres*). The most recent publication and illustration of this seal is in Ellis, *Monastic Seals*, p. 36 no. 339 and pl. 1. For a more accurate dating and description, see Gray Birch, *Seals in the British Museum* 1:564 no. 3189. The Glastonbury seal raises the question of the amuletic quality of medieval seals; clearly, the legal guarantee of the seal is, through its iconography, combined with and increased by the power of holy intercessors whose presences, materialized by the image, are expected to strengthen that which has been committed to the written record. The seal legend indicates the seal's function as a mediator for the divine.

6. How a historian determines the relationship between text and image is a recurrent problem of methodology; see Miles, *Image as Insight*, pp. 12, 160 n. 38, and a rather severe review of her book, Partner, "Marianne into Battle."

7. Geertz, *Local Knowledge*, pp. 118–19, advocates that signs and symbols

be investigated in their natural habitat and career, on the assumption that their meaning arises from use.

8. Seal iconography is analyzed below. On the conventions informing the content of sigillographic themes, see Bedos, "Signes et insignes du pouvoir," pp. 55–62; Bedos-Rezak, "Social Implications," pp. 142–62; Bedos-Rezak, "Women, Seals, and Power," pp. 72–77.

9. Lerner, "Placing Women in History," p. 359.

10. See, for example, Beaumanoir, *Coutumes de Beauvaisis* 2:124–25.

11. This fact is not noted by Jean-Bernard de Vaivre in his otherwise careful study, "Sceaux selon Philippe de Beaumanoir."

12. See the "Table analytique" under "Femme" in Beaumanoir, *Coutumes de Beauvaisis* 2:535.

13. Deurbergue, "Les Sceaux des dames," abstract in *École nationale des Chartes*, pp. 30–31; Demay, *Sceaux de l'Artois et de la Picardie*; Gut, "Les Sceaux de la région du Beauvaisis" (though listing several women's seals, Gut does not comment on the fact that Beaumanoir omits all reference to use of seals by women).

14. See Bedos-Rezak, "Women, Seals, and Power," pp. 61–67, 77–80, which contains archival and bibliographical references for as well as detailed analysis of the female patterns of seal practice sketched here. Notes within this sketch will include only works not cited in "Women, Seals, and Power" and references to seals necessary for the clarity of the text.

15. See above, n. 3.

16. A drawing of her no longer extant seal can be found in Paris, Bibliothèque nationale, MS. lat. 5441/4, fol. 113, and MS. lat. 12879, fol. 24. See further references in Bedos-Rezak, "Women, Seals, and Power," p. 78 n. 5.

17. See below, n. 23.

18. See below, nn. 24, 73.

19. Lerner warns against using women's power within the family as a measure of their societal status ("Placing Women in History," pp. 360–61). Bynum points out the changing and varied nature of the "status" of medieval women (*Holy Feast and Holy Fast*, pp. 22, 315 n. 41). Various evaluations of women's "domestic" power, differentiated according to social status, can be found in Herlihy, *Medieval Households*, pp. 100–101, 121, 129; Shahar, *Fourth Estate*, pp. 176–77, 214, 217; Barthélemy, *Les Deux Âges*, pp. 209–10; Stuard, "A New Dimension?" p. 94. See further references in Bedos-Rezak, "Women, Seals, and Power," p. 79 nn. 14, 15, 18, 19.

20. Demay, *Sceaux de la Normandie*, p. 39 no. 340, quotes a document in which the seal of a woman is declared authentic. Douët d'Arcq, *Sceaux* 1:xxxi, gives examples of male seals declared to be authentic.

21. Examples of deeds to which a lord affixed his seal to convey greater authority are published in Newman, *Les Seigneurs de Nesle en Picardie* 2:127 no. 55 (ca. 1171–78), p. 265 no. 165 (April 1233).

22. Bedos-Rezak, "Women, Seals, and Power," p. 66.

23. There is still no published comprehensive catalog of French queenly seals. Bosredon, *Sceaux des rois et des reines,* is outdated and incomplete. Deurbergue's most recent compilation in her dissertation "Les Sceaux des dames" includes only extant seal impressions, thus suggesting that some queens actually never sealed. In an ongoing project on royal seals, I have found textual references to the seals of some of these queens in records given in their names and from which the seal has since disappeared (seal of Ingeborg, consort of Philip Augustus: Paris, Archives nationales, JJ 26, fol. 125, August 1223: *Carta regine Isamburgis super compositione facta inter regem Ludovicum et ipsam . . . Que omnia ut perpetue stabilitatis robur obtineat, sigilli nostri auctoritate presentem paginam fecimus roborari;* seal of Jeanne de Bourbon, consort of Charles V: Paris, Archives nationales, P 1362²/1084, November 1375: *Jehanne par la grace de Dieu royne de France . . . en signe de verité nous avons fait mettre notre seel a ces lettres*). The very circumstances of queenly seals' state of preservation indicate that they sealed documents of a transitory nature and not worth preserving; this archival evidence points to the marginal role of queens in state affairs. For references on other French queenly seals, see above, n. 16, and Bedos-Rezak, "Women, Seals, and Power," p. 78 nn. 9–12.

A catalog of French kings' seals is soon to appear: Martine Dalas Garrigues, *Corpus des sceaux français du moyen âge: Les Sceaux des rois.* Studies on royal seal usage and iconography can be found in Bedos-Rezak, "Mythes monarchiques et thèmes sigillaires"; Bedos-Rezak, "Suger and the Symbolism of Royal Power"; Bedos-Rezak, "Les Sceaux au temps de Philippe Auguste," pp. 722–25; Bedos, "Signes et insignes du pouvoir," pp. 47–55.

24. A good survey of French monastic seals is given in Coulon, "Sigillographie ecclésiastique française," esp. pp. 142–45 (abbots' seals), 145–47 (abbesses' seals). Examples of abbesses' seals can be found in Douët d'Arcq, *Sceaux,* vol. 3, nos. 9183–9270. A sampling of records sealed by abbesses are published in *Layettes du Trésor des Chartes:* see, for instance, vol. 1, nos. 315 (1182), 461 (June 1197); vol. 2, no. 2217 (1232); vol. 4, nos. 5528 (November 1266), 5351 (1267–68). Compare these with records sealed by abbots' seals in *Layettes du Trésor des Chartes,* vol. 1, nos. 445 (April 1195–96), 1154 (ca. 1215); vol. 3, nos. 4218 (October 1255), 4588 (April 1259–60). To the state of the question and pertinent bibliography on religious women given in Bynum, *Holy Feast,* pp. 13–22, 311–15, should be added the comments of Allen, *Concept of Woman,* pp. 252, 279–81, 439–40.

25. On the issue of women's public versus private roles, see Stuard, Introduction to *Women in Medieval History,* p. 4; Stuard, "A New Dimension?" p. 94.

26. For the modalities of women's participation in medieval French records, see Herlihy, "Land, Family, and Women," esp. pp. 28–31; Hajdu, "Position of Noble Women"; Gold, *The Lady and the Virgin,* pp. 116–44.

27. See Bedos-Rezak, "Women, Seals, and Power," pp. 68–71, where the patterns of name usage are detailed.

28. See, for example, the seal (1246) of Philippette de Dammartin, wife of Ralf, count of Eu: *sigillum Philippe uxoris Radulfi comitis Augi*, in Eygun, *Sigillographie du Poitou*, p. 204 no. 306; the seal (1286) of Isabel, wife of Arnoul de Lesdain, armiger: *seel Isabiel, feme Ernoul de Lesdaing*, in Demay, *Sceaux de la Flandre* 1:150 no. 1213.

29. See examples in Demay, *Sceaux de la Normandie*, p. 71 no. 652 (1271), p. 142 no. 1390 (1257), p. 171 no. 1672 (1276); no. 1672 describes the seal of Aline, widow of Philip Eustache, burgher of Caen: *sigillum Aeline relicte Philippe Extacii*. An interpretation concerning the fact that these seals belong to non-noble landowning and bourgeois women appears in Bedos-Rezak, "Women, Seals, and Power," p. 81 n. 36.

30. Seal (1320) of Jeanne de Flandre, widow of Enguerran of Coucy: *sigillum Johanne de Flandria, uxoris quondam domini Couciaci*, in Douët d'Arcq, *Sceaux* 1:583 no. 2169.

31. Seal (1290) of Marguerite de Flandre, countess of Gueldre: *sigillum Margharete filie comitis Flandrie comitisse Ghelrensis*, in Demay, *Sceaux de la Flandre* 1:31 no. 186. Seal (1322) of Mary, wife of Amauri, lord of Meulan: *seel Marie fille au seigneur de Cantaing*, in Demay, *Sceaux de la Flandre* 1:162 no. 1322.

32. The use of the terms *filia*, *primogenitus*, or *primogenita* also signals the fact, though not its systematic occurrence, that the sealers thus designated were sealing within the lifetimes of their fathers. When heirs, male or female, had assumed control of their patrimony, their seals no longer included mention of filiation. See, for instance, the seal (1178) of Agathe, daughter and heiress of her father, Dreux de Pierrefonds (d. 1160), and wife of Conon, count of Soissons: *sigillum domine Petripuntis*, in Demay, *Sceaux de la Flandre* 1:47 no. 301; Agathe, however, did not adopt the title of her husband, an occurrence most frequently found on heiresses' seals. See also the seal (ca. 1183) of Constance, daughter and heiress of her father, Conan IV, count of Brittany (d. 1167), and wife of Geoffrey of England: *Constancia ducissa Britannie comitissa Richemundie*, in Demay, *Sceaux de la Normandie*, p. 5 no. 29. Further cases of the use of *filia* on women's seals are discussed in Bedos-Rezak, "Women, Seals, and Power," pp. 68, 80 n. 29.

33. See an example in Douët d'Arcq, *Sceaux* 1:292 no. 187 (1267): Philip was heir to the French king Louis IX but not his firstborn child, who was Isabelle, wife of Thibaut, count of Champagne and king of Navarre; Philip's seal, before his accession to the throne, reads *sigillum Philippi domini regis francorum primogeniti*; the counterseal of his elder sister (as queen of Navarre, 1255) reads, *Ysabellis filie regis Francie* (Douët d'Arcq, *Sceaux* 3:463 no. 11378 bis).

34. Demay, *Sceaux de la Flandre* 1:32 no. 192.

35. The literature on patrilineage is rather extensive; states of the question

and further references can be found in Bloch, *Etymologies and Genealogies*, pp. 64–74; Herlihy, *Medieval Households*, pp. 82–88, 92–98; Guerreau-Jalabert, "Sur les structures de parenté," esp. pp. 1042–43; Duby, *Le Chevalier, la femme, et le prêtre*, pp. 107–8; Duby, "Structures de la parenté et noblesse"; Werner, "Liens de parenté et noms de personne," esp. p. 27.

36. See above, n. 32.

37. Bynum, *Holy Feast*, p. 415 n. 28, concludes from her analysis of chapter 23 of Saint Francis of Assisi's rule that "women are categorized by sexual or marital status whereas men are not." Shahar, *Fourth Estate*, pp. 2–3, 5, draws exactly the same conclusions from her analysis of the *Livre des Manières* of Etienne de Fougères and of medieval registers and censuses. Guerreau-Jalabert, "Sur les structures de la parenté," pp. 1031, 1040, notes from her analysis of medieval genealogies that women are not designated under their own names but by the terms *filia* or *soror* of such and such male member of their family.

38. Douët d'Arcq, *Sceaux* 1:362 and bis no. 623 (1236); the seal published by Douët d'Arcq is fragmentary, with a partially missing legend. See a complete drawing of the seal in Vredius, *Sigilla comitum Flandriae*, p. 35: *sigillum Margarete sororis comitisse Flandrensis;* seal in use since 1225. The legend of Margaret's seal continues on her counterseal and includes her patrilineal filiation, *filie comitis Flandrie.*

39. When Joan died (1244), she was succeeded by Margaret, who immediately changed her seal to include her new title of countess of Flanders and Hainaut (Douët d'Arcq, *Sceaux* 1:362 no. 624 and bis [1244]: *sigillum Margarate comitisse Flandrie et Hainonie*); her counterseal reads, *secretum meum michi.* Joan had had a daughter, Mary, from her marriage to Ferrand of Portugal. Mary did not survive her mother, but she was alive when Margaret was using her "sisterly" seal; it is therefore inaccurate to assume that Margaret titled herself *soror comitisse Flandrie* to express her status as heiress.

40. The seal reads, *sigillum Isabellis de Melloto, tuttricis Johanne, filie . . . domini Montis Pacerii* (Demay, *Sceaux de la Flandre* 1:36 no. 221 [1287]); the seal (1271) of the late Humbert of Montpensier, constable of Beaujeu, is published in Douët d'Arcq, *Sceaux* 1:294 no. 194.

41. See several examples in Demay, *Sceaux de la Normandie*, p. 134 no. 1302 (1260); Douët d'Arcq, *Sceaux* 2:149 no. 4170 (1271), p. 162 no. 4286 (1298). All such seals belong to non-noble landowning women. For further examples and discussion of their sociological and gender implications, see Bedos-Rezak, "Women, Seals, and Power," pp. 68, 71, 80 n. 35.

42. So far I have found only one, rather obscure seal that lacks a filial construct—that of William, uncle of Baldwin IX, count of Flanders and Hainaut: *sigillum Willelmi avonculi comitis Flandrie et Hainonie* (Demay, *Sceaux de la Flandre* 1:25 no. 144 [1204]). The seals belonging to the sons of Gui, count of Flanders (1278–1305), consistently display filiation with the father. The eldest son and heir, Robert, is titled *primogenitus* (Demay, *Sceaux de la Flandre* 1:26

no. 149 [1275]); see the whole series of his seals as heir (1265–1305) in Vredius, *Sigilla comitum Flandrie*, pp. 48–52. The seals of the younger sons are published in Demay, *Sceaux de la Flandre* 1:27 nos. 153 (1290), 154 (1292), 155 (1298), 156 (1298); no. 155, for instance, reads, *sigillum Johannis filii Guidonis comitis Flandrie et marchionis Namurcensis.*

For titles in charters from southern France that associate males with their mothers, see Herlihy, "Women in Continental Europe," pp. 22–23.

43. Douët d'Arcq, *Sceaux* 1:362–63 nos. 625 (1245), 626 (1256). This use of matronymics may relate to the fact that the marriage of Marguerite of Flanders to Bouchard d'Avesnes, father of Jean, had not received a necessary papal dispensation and had been considered illegitimate. It also echoes the exceptional use, discussed above in n. 38, by Margaret, Jean's mother, of a seal legend mentioning her sisterly relation to the countess of Flanders. For Jean, as for Margaret, identifications through combined kinship and property were channels to power and status, regardless of gender discrimination. For a different position, sensitive to gender terminology, see below, in n. 44, the case of William of Dampierre, half brother of Jean. On use of matronymics, see Herlihy, "Women in Continental Europe," pp. 22–23.

44. The seal is published in Douët d'Arcq, *Sceaux* 1:363 no. 628 (1246), with a damaged legend. A complete drawing of the seal may be seen in Vredius, *Sigilla comitum Flandrie*, p. 38: *sigillum Guillelmi domini de Dampetra heredis Flandrie.*

45. See, for instance, Douët d'Arcq, *Sceaux* 2:527 no. 6740 (1174), p. 534 no. 6787 bis (1224). The terminology discussed here and below in n. 46 is not specific to French ecclesiastical seals. For English cases, see Ellis, *Monastic Seals*, p. 7 no. 61 (1279), p. 58 no. 551 (1279): *mater Dei memento mei.*

46. Douët d'Arcq, *Sceaux* 2:589 no. 7165 bis (thirteenth century), p. 515 no. 6661 bis (1221), with a slight variation: *salve sancta Parens* (see fig. 1).

47. Most useful treatises on heraldry include Galbreath and Jéquier, *Manuel du Blason*; Pastoureau, *Les Armoiries*; Pastoureau, *Traité d'héraldique.* Studies on the social and cultural implications of medieval heraldry have been conducted by Bloch in *Etymologies and Genealogies*, pp. 28, 75–78, and by Pastoureau, whose numerous essays are now collected in two volumes, *L'Hermine et le sinople* and *Figures et couleurs.*

48. Galbreath and Jéquier, *Manuel du Blason*, pp. 17–25; Pastoureau, *Traité d'héraldique*, pp. 24–36; Pastoureau, "L'Apparition des armoiries en Occident" and "La Genèse des armoiries," in *L'Hermine et le sinople*, pp. 51–70, 84–95; Bedos-Rezak, "L'Apparition des armoiries sur les sceaux."

49. Bouly de Lesdain, "Les Brisures d'après les sceaux," with multiple references to seals with marks of cadency slightly updated in Pastoureau, *Figures et couleurs*, pp. 101–2.

50. For general studies on women's heraldry, see Bouly de Lesdain, "Les Armoiries de femmes"; Franklyn, *Bearing of Coat-Armour by Ladies.* The oldest

extant female seal displaying a coat of arms is that of Agnès de Saint Verain (1188), in Douët d'Arcq, *Sceaux* 2:70 no. 3551. The earlier seal of 1183 belonged to Yseult de Dol, wife of Asculphe of Soligné, and is documented by an eighteenth-century drawing, which is reproduced and discussed in Pastoureau, *L'Hermine et le sinople*, pp. 183–84. The earliest heraldic female seal is British and belonged to Rochaise of Saint Clare, countess of Lincoln (d. 1156); see Gray Birch, *Catalogue of Seals* 3:444 no. 13048.

Quite remarkably, the seal of Agnès de Saint Verain's husband does not display a coat of arms; see Douët d'Arcq, *Sceaux* 2:70 no. 3550 (1188). This case is not isolated, as evidenced by the seal of Catherine of Clermont, countess of Blois: her seal displays heraldic devices, whereas her husband's seal does not (Douët d'Arcq, *Sceaux* 1:418 nos. 956 [1201] and 957 [1211]).

51. Bouly de Lesdain, "Les Armoiries de femmes"; Bouly de Lesdain, "Quelques changements d'armoiries," p. 82, discusses the apparently unique case (1314) of a woman displaying on her seal the coats of the two husbands she had in successive marriages. I examine the patterns in women's selection of heraldic devices in "Women, Seals, and Power," pp. 71–72 (figs. 3, 4, 8) and p. 81 nn. 39–42.

52. Bedos-Rezak, "Women, Seals, and Power," pp. 72, 81 nn. 43–44; Bedos-Rezak, "L'Apparition des armoiries sur les sceaux," pp. 31–32; Bedos-Rezak, "An Image from a Medieval Woman's World." Further examples of women's seals displaying matrilineal coats can be found in Eygun, *Sigillographie du Poitou*, p. 220 no. 428 (1276); Demay, *Sceaux de l'Artois*, p. 193 no. 1794 (1268), discussed in Bouly de Lesdain, "Les Armoiries de femmes," p. 182; Demay, *Sceaux de la Picardie*, p. 10 no. 62 (1335), discussed in Bouly de Lesdain, "Les Armoiries de femmes," p. 188, together with several other cases analyzed on pp. 195–96 and in Bouly de Lesdain, "Quelques changements d'armoiries," p. 110; Bony, "Cistercian Seals," esp. p. 209.

53. The sampling was conducted from Douët d'Arcq, *Sceaux*, and would require further research before risking statistics; as it is, 0.03 percent of male seals in the current sampling displayed maternal coats (i.e., maternal grandfathers' coats); see examples in Douët d'Arcq, *Sceaux* 1:321 no. 367 (1270), p. 322 nos. 368 (1289) and 370 (1300), p. 440 no. 1093 (1269). More cases are discussed in Bouly de Lesdain, "Quelques changements d'armoiries," pp. 71, 80–81, 87; Pastoureau, *L'Hermine et le sinople*, pp. 88–90, 92–94; Pastoureau, *Figures et couleurs*, pp. 89–113, esp. pp. 110–11; Loutsch, "Origine des armes de la maison de Luxembourg," esp. pp. 367–68; and Schlumberger, *Sigillographie de l'Orient Latin*, pp. 45–46.

Matrilineal inheritance of lands did not systematically entail the display of a maternal coat; Matilda inherited the county of Boulogne from her mother, Ida, but displayed on her seal (1239, Douët d'Arcq, *Sceaux* 1:435 no. 1061) the coat of her father, Renaud de Dammartin; Matilda's second husband, Alphonse de Portugal, count of Boulogne through his marriage, displays the Dammartin coat as well (1241, Douët d'Arcq, *Sceaux* 1:435 no. 1063 bis). The Boulogne heraldic device used by Ida (1201, Douët d'Arcq, *Sceaux* 1:434 no. 1058) was not passed along with the land.

The prestige associated with the matrilineal descent, rather than matrilineal inheritance, might have induced men to adopt their maternal coats and thus boast of membership within an illustrious lineage; see relevant remarks in Shahar, *Fourth Estate*, pp. 136–37, and in Guerreau-Jalabert, "Les Structures de la parenté," p. 1043 (on the strategy of attributing names from illustrious maternal lineages). I have discussed this aspect in "Women, Seals, and Power," pp. 71–72, but have since then come across an astonishing case in which a stepson, John II, count of Roucy and heir to the county through his mother, Eustachie, retained on his seal (1227, Douët d'Arcq, *Sceaux* 1:429 no. 1022) the coat of his stepfather, Enguerran III of Coucy, whose marriage to Eustachie had been annulled. The Coucy lineage evidently meant more than the descent of Robert de Pierrepont, natural father of John. And feudal alliances probably dictated siding with the Coucy in a pattern of extended family symbolized by the sharing of a similar heraldic device, which might explain why the Roucy coat was simply abandoned. On the regional power exercised by the Coucy and their connections with the Roucy, see Barthélémy, *Les Deux Âges*, esp. pp. 408, 413.

54. This is, of course, in contrast to their wives' custom of displaying both father's and spouse's coat, as discussed above and in nn. 50 and 51. Current percentages (see above, n. 53) are very low for male seals showing wife's coats: 0.01 percent. The reasons for so doing are identical to those examined above in n. 53 (case of the husband of Matilda, countess of Boulogne). For instance, Charles de Blois became count of Brittany through his wife and displayed on his seal the coat of Brittany (1345, Douët d'Arcq, *Sceaux* 1:349 no. 542). Ida, countess of Boulogne in her own right, married several times, bringing the county of Boulogne to her spouse each time; her first husband, Gerard, count of Gueldre, displayed the Boulogne coat (before 1181, Demay, *Sceaux de l'Artois*, p. 6 no. 26); her last husband, Renaud, count of Dammartin, displayed only the coat of Dammartin (1204, Douët d'Arcq, *Sceaux* 1:434 no. 1059).

55. Pastoureau, *L'Hermine et le sinople*, p. 93.

56. Ibid., pp. 71–83, esp. pp. 80–81.

57. Galbreath and Jéquier, *Manuel du Blason*, pp. 244–45.

58. See the detailed study by Wagner, "The Swan Badge and the Swan Knight," and the more general synthesis of Pastoureau in *Figures et couleurs*, pp. 139–54, esp. pp. 148–49.

59. Bedos-Rezak, "Social Implications"; Bedos, "Signes et insignes du pouvoir"; Bedos-Rezak, "Sceaux seigneuriaux"; Bedos-Rezak, "Suger and the Symbolism of Royal Power"; Bedos-Rezak, "Les Sceaux au temps de Philippe Auguste," pp. 725–29, 731–33; Bedos, *Les Sceaux des villes*; Pedrick, *Borough Seals*; Pedrick, *Monastic Seals*; Coulon, "Sigillographie ecclésiastique française," pp. 121–83; Diederich, "Zum Quellenwert und Bedeutungsgehalt mittelalterlicher Städtesiegel."

On the general reading of medieval visual images, see Miles, *Image as Insight*, pp. 35–36; Shapiro, *Words and Pictures;* Turner and Turner, *Image and Pilgrimage,* pp. 140–71. Pastoureau discusses the structure and function of medieval emblematic systems in *Figures et couleurs,* pp. 51–57, 115–22. On the awareness of role and group in the definition of self and individual identity, see the chapter "Did the Twelfth Century Discover the Individual?" in Bynum, *Jesus as Mother,* pp. 82–109.

60. See Bedos-Rezak, "Women, Seals, and Power," pp. 72–73, 81 n. 46, for references and illustrations (figs. 10, 11) of seals showing vegetal motives and distaff.

61. Demay, *Sceaux de l'Artois,* p. 232 no. 2194.

62. I have dealt in detail with the interpretation of these attributes in "Women, Seals, and Power," pp. 75–77.

63. The polysemous symbolic content of the fleur-de-lis throughout the ages has been the subject of numerous studies and interpretations. States of the question and further references are found in Pastoureau, "La Fleur-de-lis"; Pastoureau, *Traité d'héraldique,* pp. 160–62; Pastoureau, *Figures et couleurs,* pp. 107–11; Pinoteau, "La Création des armes de France"; Koch, "The Fleur-de-lis and the *Lilium Candidum*"; Bedos-Rezak, "Suger and the Symbolism of Royal Power," pp. 100, 103 n. 56.

64. On the relationship between the constitution of the family as lineage and the appearance of the Jesse tree pictorial theme, see Bloch, *Etymologies and Genealogies,* pp. 87–91; Ladner, "Medieval and Modern Understanding of Symbolism," esp. pp. 250–51. The association between the Jesse tree, Mary, and the fleur-de-lis is discussed in Johnson, "Tree of Jesse Window of Chartres," esp. pp. 3, 9; Koch, "The Fleur-de-lis and the *Lilium Candidum*," pp. 118–19; Watson, *Tree of Jesse;* Bedos-Rezak, "Suger and the Symbolism of Royal Power," p. 100.

65. Venus's month, April, is springtime and the renaissance of nature; it is illustrated on calendars with a female flower bearer: Fowler, "Medieval Representations," esp. p. 210 n. 39; Le Sénéchal, "L'Iconographie du moyen âge," esp. pp. 60, 91; Webster, *Labors of the Months,* pp. 102–3; Morgan, *Early Gothic Manuscripts,* p. 60 no. 14 (1190–1200), p. 62 no. 15 (1190–1200), p. 84 no. 35 (1210–20), p. 113 no. 68 (1230–40); Heslop, "Seals," esp. p. 306 no. 337, where he discusses the iconography of the seal of Isabella, countess of Gloucester (1189–1217).

66. On the fleur-de-lis as a Marian attribute, see references given above in nn. 63 and 64. Marian iconography on seals is discussed below.

67. On the ambiguous consequences for medieval women of the elevation of the Virgin Mary, see Gold, *The Lady and the Virgin,* pp. 70–71, 73, 74, with further references in n. 86; Warner, *Alone of All Her Sex,* pp. xxi, 49, 77, 148; Kraus, *Living Theatre of Medieval Art,* pp. 41–62 (reprinted as "Eve and Mary"); Miles, *Image as Insight,* pp. 79–80, 88–89. See below, n. 81, on the nature and implications of women's devotion to Mary.

68. Cadart-Ricard, "Le Thème de l'oiseau," esp. pp. 215–17; Benoist, "La

Chasse au vol," esp. p. 124; Harris-Stäblein, "La Sémiologie de la chasse," esp. pp. 447–49; Rowland, *Birds with Human Souls*, p. 58; Shahar, *Fourth Estate*, p. 152 (the last two both quote John of Salisbury: "Women were better at hawking than men because the worst people were always the most predatory"). See also this seal belonging to Jean Arsi, squire (Douët d'Arcq, *Sceaux* 1:456 no. 1210 bis in 1290), inscribed with the legend *Je vis d'amours* and depicting a bird of prey holding an animal in his beak.

69. On the gender and sociocultural implications of clothing, see Casey, "Cheshire Cat," esp. pp. 237–38; Stuard, *Restoring Women to History*, p. 140. A detailed survey of female garments as depicted on seals is given in Demay, *Le Costume au moyen âge*, pp. 91–108.

70. There are a few exceptions to this remark; I have found two women's seals depicting them as equestrian knights, which I discuss in "Women, Seals, and Power," pp. 73, 75, 81 n. 50. Both seals, which belong to a countess of Provence (1220) and to Galberge of Serres (1256), are published, respectively, in Blancard, *Iconographie des sceaux et bulles conservés* 1:11 no. 12, and vol. 2, pl. 5, no. 2; vol. 1, pl. 53, no. 13, and vol. 2, pl. 27, no. 3. These cases relate to a specific status: heiresses with recognized feudal obligations.

71. The iconography of male noble and ecclesiastical seals is discussed, analyzed, and illustrated in the works cited above in nn. 23, 24, 59, and below in nn. 82, 83, and 97. A good survey is also given in Demay, *Le Costume au moyen âge*, pp. 109–85 (knightly seals), 267–305 (ecclesiastical seals).

72. A good sampling of craftsmen's seals is provided in Demay, *Sceaux de la Flandre* 1:520–27 nos. 4776–4857.

73. For instance, the two contemporary seals of the abbot of Notre-Dame-du-Val (twelfth century, Douët d'Arcq, *Sceaux* 3:144 no. 9150) and of Elisabeth, abbess of Montmartre (1182, Douët d'Arcq, *Sceaux* 3:156 no. 9233, display remarkably similar seated figures holding crosiers. Sigillographic depictions remain identical for both abbots and abbesses throughout the Middle Ages; see the later examples of Peter, abbot of Saint-Yved of Braine (1372); and Agnes, abbess of Montivilliers (1369) (Douët d'Arcq, *Sceaux* 3:63 no. 8572, p. 155 no. 9232).

74. References to male and female royal seals are given above, n. 23. Medieval Germany offers many examples of empresses depicted in majesty: Matilda, wife of the emperor Henry V (Borrie, "Sealed Charter of the Empress Matilda"); her seal (1125), together with those of other enthroned empresses, are published in Posse, *Die Siegel der deutschen Kaiser*, vol. 1: pl. 19 no. 4, pl. 24 no. 1, pl. 26 no. 1, pl. 32 nos. 1–2, pl. 33 nos. 1–2, pl. 34 no. 7, pl. 35 no. 5, pl. 42 no. 7, etc.; vol. 5 (descriptions): pp. 24, 26, 27, 30, 31, 33, etc.

Alix of Lusignan, as widowed queen of Cyprus, displays a majesty type on her seal (1234): Douët d'Arcq, *Sceaux* 3:516 no. 11802, and Richard, "La Diplomatique Royale," esp. pp. 83–84. French queens are never depicted enthroned on their seals, but there are a few instances of French women in majesty. Constance, as countess of Toulouse, used a seal of majesty (from 1172 on, Douët d'Arcq, *Sceaux* 1:381 no. 741), which, significantly, was retained by her descendants both male and female (Douët d'Arcq, *Sceaux* 1:381–83 nos. 742–48, and Evans, "Le Sceau de Jeanne Plantagenet," p. 50). Constance, a daughter of the French king Louis VI, had also first been married to Eustace of Boulogne, heir to the English king Stephen of Blois. Through this alliance, Constance was in direct competition for the throne of England with the Empress Matilda, whose seal, bearing an orb and enthroned (discussed above), she later imitated. Alix, heiress of the county of Burgundy and wife of Philip, duke of Savoie, is also depicted enthroned on her seal (1276), which is discussed and published in Galbraith, *Sceaux vaudois*, p. 20 no. 2 (pl. 11, 1); Douët d'Arcq, *Sceaux* 1:340 no. 490; Bascapè, "I sigilli delle signorie e dei principati," esp. pp. 67–68.

75. Medieval sources indicate that women were not accommodated within the functional social schema of the three *ordines,* which articulated gradations of male status, but that they were at least characterized according to their female or biological status: virgin, married, mother, widow; see discussion on women not fitting medieval statuses in Casey, "Cheshire Cat," p. 239; Bynum, *Holy Feast,* p. 286; Corti, "Models and Antimodels," esp. pp. 340–41; Shahar, *Fourth Estate,* p. 2; Flori, *L'Essor de la chevalerie,* p. 233.

Female images on women's seals may therefore be seen as radical in excluding categorization by sexual (motherhood) role.

76. Demay, *Sceaux de la Flandre* 1:187 nos. 1556, 1557 (Gérard de Saint-Aubert), p. 80 no. 580 (Conon de Béthune).

77. Demay, *Sceaux de l'Artois,* p. 204 no. 1897 (1297), p. 227 no. 2146 (1376).

78. Demay, *Sceaux de la Flandre* 1:420 no. 3840 (1404, matrix from the fourteenth century).

79. Bedos, *Les Sceaux des villes,* p. 412 no. 546: Poitiers, for instance, ignores its local Saint Radegonde; on the saint, see Briand, *Histoire de Ste Radegonde.* For Brussels's seal, which shows Saint Michel rather than Saint Gudule, the patron of the city, see Laurent, *Sigillographie,* pp. 129–31, pl. 37 no. 66.

80. For instance, the abbey seals of Vezelay (a male institution) consistently display Mary Magdalene (Douët d'Arcq, *Sceaux* 3:44 no. 8436 [1205], p. 45 no. 8437 [1469]; Coulon, *Sceaux de la Bourgogne,* p. 228 no. 1297 [1354]). The abbey seal (1271) of Saint Laurent of Cordeillon (a female institution) depicts Saint Lawrence (Douët d'Arcq, *Sceaux* 3:47 no. 8450).

81. See, however, in Douët d'Arcq, *Sceaux* 3:159 no. 9260, the seal of Emeline, abbess of Saint-Cyr-de-Berchères (bishopric of Chartres, 1268), on which the mother of Saint Cyr, Saint Julita, is specifically depicted, though not part of the abbey's dedication.

On the fact that one group of women, namely, monastic women, did not use female imagery to any significant extent, see Miles, *Image as Insight,* pp. 88, 178 n. 92; Bynum, *Jesus as Mother,* p. 162; Bynum, *Holy Feast,* pp. 26, 269, 318 n. 57, 409 n. 43; Tavormina, "Of Maidenhood and Maternity," esp. p. 387

(Tavormina points out that English and Continental ceremonies during which a nun made her permanent vow of dignity do not refer to Mary).

I also gathered very few lay female seals including saints; these, however, consistently refer to the Virgin Mary, showing the laywoman kneeling at her feet (Douët d'Arcq, *Sceaux* 1:670 no. 2828 [1284]). Bynum, *Holy Feast*, as quoted above and in contrast to Warner, *Alone of All Her Sex*, denies that women laid special emphasis in their devotion to the Virgin and states that any reverence for Mary was for a "representative woman." The recurrence of a Marian attribute, the fleur-de-lis, on many women's seals has been discussed above and at n. 67 as referring to dynastic motherhood. Again, the symbol refers less to women's personal consciousness than to a cultural consensus probably integrating patriarchal visions of social order.

82. This display of the Virgin occurs on counterseals between 1200–1250, for the seals' obverses retain the depiction of a standing figure in ecclesiastical vestments; see, for instance, the seals of the abbots of the Chaise-Dieu in Douët d'Arcq, *Sceaux*, 3:67 no. 8604 (1231), p. 68 nos. 8605 (1256), 8606 (1307). After 1250 the Virgin appears on the obverse of male ecclesiastical seals; see Douët d'Arcq, *Sceaux* 3:79 no. 8681 (1258, seal of Peter, abbot of Coulombs), p. 60 no. 8545 (1325, seal of Noel, abbot of the Bourg-Moyen of Blois).

83. Episcopal seals present an interesting evolution in their display of hagiographic themes. Early items show only the standing or seated figure of the bishop in vestments (see, for instance, the twelfth-century seals of the archbishops of Sens in Douët d'Arcq, *Sceaux* 2:471–72 nos. 6382–89). After 1200 the emphasis on function was accompanied by such expressions of piety as kneeling and praying postures, which indicate a desire for grace and intercession. Between 1200–1250, these new forms involved male saints and God as well as the Virgin Mary, who appears on a significant number of episcopal counterseals. Requests for intercession during this period, however, were primarily addressed to male saints or to God: see, for instance, Guillaume de Seignelay, bishop of Auxerre (1212), whose counterseal displays an *Agnus Dei* and a legend that reads, *miserere mei deus* (Douët d'Arcq, *Sceaux* 2:486 no. 6478); Hugues de Montreal, bishop of Langres (1226), whose counterseal displays a kneeling figure with the legend *conserva me Dominus* (Douët d'Arcq, *Sceaux* 2:508 no. 6618); Guillaume de Brosse, bishop of Sens (1259), whose counterseal depicts the stoning of Saint Stephen with the legend *sancte Stephane ora pro me* (Douët d'Arcq, *Sceaux* 2:473 no. 6393).

Between 1250 and 1300, the depiction of Mary increasingly appeared on the obverse of episcopal seals. After 1300, the great majority of episcopal seals displayed Marian iconography on both sides. Depictions of male saints occur virtually only on counterseals from 1200 through 1350, never appearing on the obverse; after 1350, male hagiographic iconography significantly regressed in favor of Marian themes on episcopal seals. This pattern is based on the data in Douët d'Arcq, *Sceaux*, and is further analyzed below and at nn. 97 and 98.

84. Coulon, *Sceaux de la Bourgogne*, p. 229 no. 1297 bis (1345).

85. Demay, *Sceaux de la Flandre* 2:325 no. 7565 (1263).

86. Douët d'Arcq, *Sceaux* 3:257 no. 9974 (1366); Demay, *Sceaux de la Normandie*, p. 354 no. 3133 (1249).

87. Douët d'Arcq, *Sceaux* 3:184 no. 9430 (fourteenth century). See also a depiction of Mary Magdalene reading in Demay, *Sceaux de l'Artois*, p. 309 no. 2848 (1328). Evidence of this activity is not documented on laywomen's seals, unless the rare type of a female effigy carrying a book is taken into consideration, such as those on the seals of Agnes de Neauphle (1243) (Douët d'Arcq, *Sceaux* 2:316 no. 5314) and of Agnes d'Ablon (1258), (Douët d'Arcq, *Sceaux* 1:444 no. 1115) (Douët d'Arcq does not mention the book, but it is visible on the original impression appended to a document in Paris, Archives nationales, S 2082 n. 39/dossier 27).

88. Douët d'Arcq, *Sceaux* 3:8 no. 8181 bis (thirteenth century).

89. Douët d'Arcq, *Sceaux* 2:645 no. 7561 (1274).

90. Douët d'Arcq, *Sceaux* 3:150 no. 9194 (1301); on Saint Batilda, see Folz, "Tradition hagiographique et culte de sainte Bathilde," and Dubois, "Sainte Bathilde."

91. Douët d'Arcq, *Sceaux* 3:161 no. 9275 (1269).

92. See, for instance, ibid., p. 12 no. 8207 (1215, Saint Foy, wrongly described by Douët d'Arcq as the Virgin [Framont, *Sceaux rouergats du moyen âge*, p. 372 no. 491]), p. 29 no. 8330 (1224, Saint Geneviève); Demay, *Sceaux de la Flandre* 2:224 no. 6769 (1167, Saint Rictrude), p. 231 no. 6831 (twelfth century, Saint Aldegonde).

93. As citations of these seals would run into the hundreds, see convenient surveys of sigillographic depictions of the Virgin in Demay, *Le Costume au moyen âge*, pp. 379–97; Bony, "Cistercian Seals"; Heslop, "Virgin's Regalia"; Isla, "La Imagen de la Virgen." A particularly interesting seal (1302) of the Chapter Notre-Dame d'Auxerre displays the Assumption of the Virgin, Coulon, *Sceaux de la Bourgogne*, p. 185 no. 1055; a superb scene of Mary's coronation is shown on the counterseal of Antoine, bishop of Durham (1298), in Douët d'Arcq, *Sceaux* 3:298 no. 10224.

94. Two scenes of the Nativity, including details of Mary's bed and Jesus' cradle, over which oil lamps hang, can be seen on the seal (1271) of the abbey of Grandchamp (fig. 12) and on the seal of the abbess of the Clarisses of Aix (fourteenth century) (Douët d'Arcq, *Sceaux* 3:16 no. 8236, p. 237 n. 9827).

95. For instance, see a depiction of a lactating Virgin on the seal and counterseal of Moutier-Saint-Jean (1202) in Coulon, *Sceaux de la Bourgogne*, pp. 225–26 nos. 1282 and bis.

96. A vivid and sensual evocation of the mother-child relationship is evoked on the seal of la Charité-sur-Loire (1203), in Douët d'Arcq, *Sceaux* 3:178 no. 9391; also on the seal of Notre-Dame of Chartres (twelfth century), in Douët d'Arcq, *Sceaux* 2:587 no. 7150, and Bedos, "Le Sceau du chapitre Notre-Dame de Chartres," pp. 132–35.

97. The fact that the Virgin Mother became the preferred motif on ecclesiastical male seals did not preclude rarer cases in which a prelate is shown kneeling in front of a female (1316, Eygun, *Sigillographie du Poitou*, p. 437 no. 1631) or a male saint (1282, Douët d'Arcq, *Sceaux* 2:473 no. 6396 bis).

See also instances of abbots' seals displaying the Virgin and Child with kneeling abbot in Douët d'Arcq, *Sceaux* 3:58 no. 8535 (1307), p. 59 no. 8544 bis (1325), p. 68 no. 8606 bis (1307). For episcopal seals on which this iconographic program appears slightly earlier (after 1250), see Douët d'Arcq, *Sceaux* 2:470 no. 6374 (1333), p. 621 no. 7387 (1280), p. 628 no. 7436 (1269), p. 629 no. 7439 (1271), and Bony, "Cistercian Seals," p. 208 and figs. 3/13, 5/20. For the increasing depiction of Marian themes on episcopal seals, see above, n. 83.

See various interpretations, mostly political and sociological, for the depiction of a prostrate ecclesiastical male figure in front of Mary with the Child in Miles, *Image as Insight*, pp. 31–32. The pictorial association between male supplicant and Mary as mother is discussed in Francastel, *Le Droit au trône*, p. 319.

98. See above, nn. 45, 46. Explicit references to the physical motherhood of Mary with kneeling male ecclesiastics are found on some English seals. The abbot's seal (ca. 1300) of the Tironian abbey of Kelso has a legend that reads *Virgo tuum natum lactans fac me sibi gratum;* in the upper part of the seal, the Virgin nurses the Child, and below the abbot is kneeling in prayer before an altar on which is a chalice (Ellis, *Monastic Seals*, p. 44 no. 415 and pl. 25). This seal illustrates male spirituality that associated the flesh of Christ with Mary and assimilated Mary's milk with the blood of the Eucharist; Robert Grosseteste (d. 1253) wrote to the monks of Peterborough: "In your monastery continually dwells the King of Heaven, not only by his divinity but also, in the sacrament of the Eucharist, by the true substance of the flesh, which he took from the Virgin." This passage is quoted and discussed in Bynum, *Holy Feast*, pp. 267–68, 271; Bynum also points out the place of honor occupied by Mary on tabernacles. On the seal of the Gilbertine priory of Sixhills, a monk kneels in front of the Virgin, while the legend reads, *lactans Virgo Deum protege.* . . . (Ellis, *Monastic Seals*, p. 82 no. 779 [fourteenth century]).

99. See, for instance, the seals of Jean de Vienne, bishop of Avranches (1317), of Hugues, bishop of Orange (1326), and of Barthélémy, abbot of Aleth (1317), in Douët d'Arcq, *Sceaux* 2:489 no. 6495, 2:530 no. 6757, 3:52 no. 8491.

100. On family imagery, the metaphor of the family in a devotional context, and spiritual kinship as a system buttressing the institutional structure of the church, see Warner, *Alone of All Her Sex*, p. 288; Guerreau-Jalabert, "Les Structures de parenté," pp. 1036–38; Miles, *Image as Insight*, pp. 35–36, 79; Herlihy, *Medieval Households*, pp. 113, 118, 120–24.

In *Holy Feast*, and especially in chapter 10, Bynum analyzes the symbolic reversal religious men accomplished when using the image of woman to express a sense of religious self: "The priest was female; he was Mary, for in his hands, as in her womb, Christ was incarnate" (p. 285). She further demonstrates (pp. 288–94) that women's religious self-images were not inverted but "profoundly

deepenings of what 'woman' is" (p. 289). Thus the preference for female and
Marian iconography on male ecclesiastical seals and the relative scarcity of such
depictions on religious women's seals parallel contemporary religious and symbolic use of these themes. On the other hand, the interpretation of religious seal
iconography should be informed by an awareness of these seals' function: they
had to be effective within a legal context and therefore had to present elements
of identity relevant to that context. By comparing these elements with those
displayed on lay seals, I established that the dialectical kinship was the most
significant depiction, rather than the identification between Mary and the male
ecclesiastic.

101. On the role of kinship both as a system and as a concept in medieval society, see Guerreau-Jalabert, "Les Structures de parenté," pp. 1028–1149;
Pastoureau, *Figures et couleurs*, pp. 54–56.

BIBLIOGRAPHY

Inventories

Beaumanoir, Philippe de. *Coutumes de Beauvaisis*. 2 vols. 1894–1900. Reprint.
     Paris, 1970.
Bedos, Brigitte. *Corpus des sceaux français du moyen âge*. Vol. 1, *Les Sceaux des
     villes*. Paris, 1980.
Blancard, Louis. *Iconographie des sceaux et bulles conservés dans la partie an-
     térieure à 1790 des Archives départementales des Bouches-du-Rhône*. 2 vols.
     Marseille, 1860.
Bosredon, Philippe de. *Repertoire des sceaux des rois et des reines de France et des
     princes et des princesses*. Périgueux, 1893.
Coulon, Auguste. *Inventaire des sceaux de la Bourgogne*. Paris, 1912.
Demay, Germain. *Inventaire des sceaux de la Flandre*. 2 vols. Paris, 1873.
———. *Inventaire des sceaux de l'Artois et de la Picardie*. 2 vols. Paris, 1877.
———. *Inventaire des sceaux de la Normandie*. Paris, 1881.
Deurbergue, Maria. "Les Sceaux des dames jusqu'en 1350, spécialement en Ile-
     de-France." Ph.D. diss., École nationale des Chartes, 1966. Paris, Archives
     nationales, AB XXVIII 93. An abstract of her work is published in *École
     nationale des Chartes: Positions des thèses soutenues par les élèves de la promo-
     tion de 1966 pour obtenir le diplôme d'archivistique-paléographe*, pp. 29–32.
     Paris, 1966.
Douët d'Arcq, Louis. *Collection de sceaux*. 3 vols. Paris, 1863–68.
Ellis, Roger H. *Catalog of Seals in the Public Record Office*. Vol. 1, *Monastic Seals*.
     London, 1986.
Eygun, François. *Sigillographie du Poitou jusqu'en 1515*. Poitiers, 1938.
Framont, Martin de. *Sceaux rouergats du moyen âge*. Rodez, 1982.

Galbraith, Donald Lindsay. *Inventaire des sceaux vaudois.* Lausanne, 1937.

Gray Birch, Walter de. *Catalogue of Seals in the Department of Manuscripts in the British Museum.* 6 vols. London, 1887–1900.

Layettes du Trésor des Chartes. Ed. Alexandre Teulet, Joseph Delaborde, Elie Berger, and Henri-François Delaborde. 5 vols. 1863–1909. Reprint. Nendeln, 1977.

Posse, Otto. *Die Siegel der deutschen Kaiser und Könige von 751 bis 1913.* 5 vols. 1909–13. Reprint. Leipzig, 1981.

Schlumberger, Gustave. *Sigillographie de l'Orient Latin.* Paris, 1943.

Vredius, Olivarius. *Sigilla comitum Flandriae.* Bruges, Flanders, 1639.

Studies

Allen, Prudence. *The Concept of Woman: The Aristotelian Revolution, 750 BC– AD 1250.* Montreal, 1985.

Barthélémy, Dominique. *Les Deux Âges de la seigneurie banale: Coucy (XIe–XIIIe siècles).* Paris, 1984.

Bascapè, Giacomo C. "I sigilli delle signorie e dei principati." In *Studi in onore di Carlo Castiglioni Profetto dell'Ambrosiana,* pp. 49–82. Milan, 1957.

———. *Sigillografia: Il sigillo nella diplomatica, nel diritto, nella storia, nell'arte.* Vol. 1, *Sigillografia generale.* Milan, 1969. Vol. 2, *Sigillografia ecclesiastica.* Milan, 1975.

Bedos, Brigitte. "Le Sceau du chapitre Notre-Dame de Chartres témoin d'une antique tradition mariale." *Bulletin du Club français de la médaille* 64 (1979): 132–35.

———. "Signes et insignes du pouvoir royal et seigneurial au moyen âge: Le Témoignage des sceaux." In *Actes du cent cinquième congrès national des sociétés savantes,* pp. 47–62. Paris, 1984.

Bedos-Rezak, Brigitte. "An Image from a Medieval Woman's World: The Seal of Jeanne de Châtillon, Countess of Alençon (1271)." In *The Worlds of Medieval Women,* ed. C. Berman, C. W. Connell, and J. Rice Rotschild, pp. xi–xiii. Morgantown, W. Va., 1985.

———. "The King Enthroned, a New Theme in Anglo-Saxon Royal Iconography: The Seal of Edward the Confessor and Its Political Implications." In *Medieval Kings and Kingship,* ed. Joel T. Rosenthal, pp. 53–88. ACTA, no. 11. Binghamton, N.Y., 1986.

———. "L'Apparition des armoiries sur les sceaux en Ile-de-France et en Picardie (v. 1130–1230)." In *Actes du IIe Colloque international d'héraldique: Les Origines des armoiries,* ed. Hervé Pindeau, Michel Pastoureau, and Michel Popoff, pp. 23–41. Paris, 1983.

———. "Les Sceaux au temps de Philippe Auguste." In *La France de Philippe Auguste,* ed. Robert-Henri Bautier, pp. 721–36. Colloque International du CNRS, no. 602. Paris, 1982.

————. "Mythes monarchiques et thèmes sigillaires: Du sceau de Louis VII aux sceaux de Charles VII." In *XV Congreso internacional de las ciencias genealogica y heraldica,* pp. 199–213. Madrid, 1982.

————. "Sceaux seigneuriaux et structures et sociales en Dauphiné." In *Actes du cent huitième congrès national des sociétés savantes,* pp. 23–50. Paris, 1985.

————. "Seals." In *Dictionary of the Middle Ages,* ed. Joseph Strayer, 11:123–31. New York, 1988.

————. "The Social Implications of the Art of Chivalry: The Sigillographic Evidence (1050–1250)." In *The Medieval Court in Europe,* ed. Edward Haymes, pp. 142–75. Houston German Studies, no. 6. Munich, 1986.

————. "Suger and the Symbolism of Royal Power: The Seal of Louis VII." In *Abbot Suger and Saint-Denis,* ed. Paula L. Gerson, pp. 95–104. New York, 1986.

————. "Women, Seals, and Power in Medieval France, 1150–1350." In *Women and Power in the Middle Ages,* ed. Mary Erler and Maryanne Kowalewski, pp. 61–82. Athens, Ga., 1988.

Benoist, J.-O. "La Chasse au vol: Techniques de chasse et valeur symbolique de la volerie." In *La Chasse au moyen âge,* pp. 117–31. Nice, 1980.

Bloch, R. Howard. *Etymologies and Genealogies.* Chicago, 1983.

Bony, Pierre. "An Introduction to the Study of Cistercian Seals: The Virgin as Mediatrix, then Protectrix, on the Seals of Cistercian Abbeys." *Studies in Cistercian Art and Architecture* 3 (1987): 201–40.

Borrie, Michael A. "A Sealed Charter of the Empress Matilda." *British Museum Quarterly* 34, nos. 3–4 (1970): 104–7.

Boüard, Alain de. *Manuel de diplomatique française et pontificale: Diplomatique générale.* Paris, 1929.

————. *Manuel de diplomatique française et pontificale: L'Acte privé.* Paris, 1948.

Bouly de Lesdain, Louis. "Les Armoiries de femmes d'après les sceaux." *Annuaire du Conseil héraldique de France* 11 (1898): 176–205.

————. "Les Brisures d'après les sceaux." In *Études d'héraldique* 2:1–39. Paris, 1983.

————. "Notes sur quelques changements d'armoiries aux 12ème et 13ème siècles." *Études héraldiques* 2:61–117. Paris, 1983.

Briand, E. *Histoire de Ste Radegonde, reine de France, et des sanctuaires et pélerinages en son honneur.* Paris, 1898.

Bynum, Caroline Walker. *Holy Feast and Holy Fast: The Religious Significance of Food to Medieval Women.* Berkeley, 1987.

————. *Jesus as Mother: Studies in the Spirituality of the High Middle Ages.* Berkeley, 1982.

Cadart-Ricard, O. "Le Thème de l'oiseau dans les comparaisons et les dictons chez onze troubadours de Guillaume IX à Cerveri de Girone." *Cahiers de civilisation médiévale* 21 (1978): 205–30.

Casey, Kathleen. "The Cheshire Cat." In *Liberating Women's History,* ed. Bernice Carroll, pp. 224–49. Urbana, Ill., 1976.

Corti, M. "Models and Antimodels in Medieval Culture." *New Literary History* 10 (1979): 339–66.

Coulon, Auguste. "Éléments de sigillographie ecclésiastique française." In *Introduction aux études d'histoire d'ecclésiastique locale*, ed. Victor Carrière. Vol. 2, *L'Histoire locale à travers les ages*, pp. 109–215. Paris, 1934.

Demay, Germain. *Le Costume au moyen âge d'après les sceaux*. 1880. Reprint. Paris, 1978.

Diederich, Toni. "Zum Quellenwert und Bedeutungsgehalt mittelalterlicher Städtesiegel." *Archiv für Diplomatik* 23 (1977): 269–85.

Dubois, J. "Sainte Bathilde (vers 625–680), reine de France 641–655, fondatrice de l'abbaye de Chelles." *Fédération des sociétés historiques et archéologiques de Paris et de l'Ile-de-France* 32 (1981): 13–30.

Duby, Georges. *Le Chevalier, la femme, et le prêtre*. Paris, 1981. This work has been translated by Barbara Bray as *The Knight, the Lady, and the Priest*. New York, 1983.

———. "Structures de la parenté et noblesse dans la France du Nord aux XIe et XIIe siècles." In *Hommes et structures du moyen âge*, pp. 267–85. Paris, 1973. An English version of this essay, "The Structure of Kinship and Nobility," translated by Cynthia Postan, is in *The Chivalrous Society*, pp. 135–48. Berkeley, 1977.

Evans, J. "Le Sceau de Jeanne Plantagenet, reine de Sicile et comtesse de Toulouse." *Bulletin de la Société archéologique du Midi*, 1897, p. 50.

Ewald, Wilhelm. *Siegelkunde*. 1914. Reprint. Munich, 1975.

Flori, Jean. *L'Essor de la chevalerie*. Geneva, 1986.

Folz, R. "Tradition hagiographique et culte de sainte Bathilde, reine de France." *Comptes-rendus de l'Académie des inscriptions et belles-lettres*, 1975, pp. 369–84.

Fowler, J. "On Medieval Representations of the Months and Seasons." *Archaeologia* 44 (1873): 137–224.

Francastel, Galienne. *Le Droit au trône: Un Problème de prééminence dans l'art chrétien d'Occident du IVe au XIIe siècle*. Paris, 1973.

Franklyn, C. A. *The Bearing of Coat-Armour by Ladies*. 1923. Reprint. Baltimore, 1973.

Galbreath, Donald Lindsay, and Léon Jéquier. *Manuel du Blason*. Lausanne, 1977.

Gandilhon, René, and Michel Pastoureau. *Bibliographie de la sigillographie française*. Paris, 1982.

Garrigues, Martine Dalas. *Corpus des sceaux français du moyen âge: Les Sceaux des rois*. Forthcoming.

Geertz, Clifford. *Local Knowledge*. New York, 1983.

Gold, Penny Schine. *The Lady and the Virgin*. Chicago, 1985.

Guerreau-Jalabert, Anita. "Sur les structures de parenté dans l'Europe médiévale." *Annales: Économies, sociétés, civilisations* 36 (1981): 1028–49.

Gut, Marie-Josèphe. "Recherches sur les sceaux de la région du Beauvaisis à l'époque de Beaumanoir." In *Actes du colloque scientifique international orga-nisé pour la commémoration du VIIe centenaire des "Coutumes et Usages de Beauvaisis" de Philippe de Beaumanoir*, pp. 53–57. Beauvais, 1983.

Hajdu, Robert. "The Position of Noble Women in the *Pays des coutumes*, 1100–1300." *Journal of Family History* 5 (1980): 122–44.

Harris-Stäblein, P. "La Sémiologie de la chasse dans la poésie de Bertrand de Born." In *La Chasse au moyen âge: Actes du Colloque de Nice*, pp. 447–62. Nice, 1980.

Herlihy, David. "Land, Family, and Women in Continental Europe, 701–1200." In *Women in Medieval Society*, ed. Susan Mosher Stuard, pp. 13–45. Phila-delphia, 1976.

————. *Medieval Households*. Cambridge, Mass., 1985.

Heslop, T. A. "English Seals from the mid-Ninth Century to 1100." *Journal of the British Archaeological Association* 133 (1980): 1–16.

————. "Seals." In *English Romanesque Art*, ed. George Zarnecki, Janet Holt, and Tristram Holland, pp. 298–319. London, 1984.

————. "The Virgin's Regalia and Twelfth-Century English Seals." In *Studies Presented to Christopher Hohler*, ed. A. Borg and A. Martindale, pp. 53–62. British Archaeological Reports, International Series, no. 3. Oxford, 1981.

Isla, B. F. "La Imagen de la Virgen en los sellos." *Revista de Archivos* 43 (1922): 495–526; 44 (1923): 153–95, 320–49.

Jenkinson, Hilary. *A Guide to Seals in the Public Record Office* 2d ed. London, 1968.

Johnson, J. R. "The Tree of Jesse Window of Chartres: *Laudes Regiae*." *Speculum* 36 (1961): 1–22.

Kittel, Erich. *Siegel*. Brunswick, 1970.

Koch, Robert A. "The Origin of the Fleur-de-lis and the *Lilium Candidum* in Art." In *Approaches to Nature in the Middle Ages*, ed. Lawrence D. Roberts, pp. 109–30. Binghamton, N.Y., 1982.

Kornbluth, Genevra. *Carolingian Treasure: Engraved Gems of the Ninth and Tenth Centuries*. Ann Arbor, Mich., 1987. Microfilm.

Kraus, Henry. "Eve and Mary: Conflicting Images of Medieval Women." In *Feminism and Art History: Questioning the Litany*, ed. N. Broude and M. D. Garrard, pp. 79–99. New York, 1982.

————. *The Living Theatre of Medieval Art*. Philadelphia, 1967.

Ladner, Gerhart. "Medieval and Modern Understanding of Symbolism: A Com-parison." *Speculum* 54 (1979): 223–56.

Laurent, René. *Sigillographie*. Brussels, 1985.

Lerner, Gerda. "Placing Women in History: A 1975 Perspective." In *Liberating Women's History*, ed. Berenice A. Carroll, pp. 357–67. Urbana, Ill., 1976.

Le Sénéchal, J. "Les Occupations des mois dans l'iconographie du moyen âge." *Bulletin de la Société des antiquaires de Normandie* 35 (1921–23): 1–218.

Loutsch, Jean-Claude. "Origine des armes de la maison de Luxembourg." In

Recueil du 11e congrès international des sciences généalogiques et héraldiques, pp. 365–68. Liège, 1972.

Miles, Margaret R. *Image as Insight.* Boston, 1985.

Morgan, N. *Early Gothic Manuscripts, 1190–1285.* 2 vols. London, 1982.

Newman, William Mendel. *Les Seigneurs de Nesle en Picardie (XIIe–XIIIe siècles).* 2 vols. Paris, 1971.

Partner, Peter. "Marianne into Battle." Review of *Image as Insight,* by Margaret R. Miles. *New York Review of Books,* 10 April 1986, pp. 38–40.

Pastoureau, Michel. *Figures et couleurs.* Paris, 1986.

———. "La Fleur-de-lis, emblème royal, symbole marial ou thème graphique." In *Monnaie miroir des rois,* pp. 251–71. Paris, 1978.

———. *L'Hermine et le sinople.* Paris, 1982.

———. *Les Armoiries.* Brepols-Turnhout, 1976.

———. *Les Sceaux.* Brepols-Turnhout, 1981.

———. *Traité d'héraldique.* Paris, 1979.

Pedrick, Gale. *Borough Seals of the Gothic Period.* London, 1904.

———. *Monastic Seals of the Thirteenth Century.* London, 1902.

Pinoteau, Hervé. "La Création des armes de France au XIIe siècle." *Bulletin de la Société nationale des antiquaires de France.* 1980–81, pp. 87–99.

Richard, Jean. "La Diplomatique Royale dans les royaumes d'Arménie et de Chypre (XIIe–XVe siècles)." *Bibliothèque de l'Ecole des Chartes* 144 (1986): 69–86.

Rowland, B. *Birds with Human Souls.* Knoxville, Tenn., 1978.

Sauer, E. "Notice sur un sceau épiscopal messin." *L'Austrasie: Revue de Metz et de Lorraine* 6 (1858): 227–29.

Shahar, Shulamit. *The Fourth Estate: A History of Women in the Middle Ages.* London, 1983.

Shapiro, Meyer. *Words and Pictures: Approaches to Semiotics 11.* Ed. Th. Sebeok. The Hague, 1973.

Smith, Hilda. "Feminism and the Methodology of Women's History." In *Liberating Women's History,* ed. Berenice A. Carrol, pp. 368–84. Urbana, Ill., 1976.

Stuard, Susan Mosher. "Fashion's Captives: Medieval Women in French Historiography." In Stuard, *Women in Medieval History and Historiography,* pp. 59–80.

———. "A New Dimension?: North American Scholars Contribute Their Perspective." In Stuard, *Women in Medieval History and Historiography,* pp. 81–99.

———, ed. *Restoring Women to History: Materials for Western Civilization.* Bloomington, Ind., 1983.

———, ed. *Women in Medieval History and Historiography.* Philadelphia, 1987.

Suleiman, Susan Rubin, ed. *The Female Body in Western Culture.* Cambridge, 1986.

Tavormina, T. "Of Maidenhood and Maternity: Liturgical Hagiography and the Medieval Ideal of Virginity." *American Benedictine Review* 31 (1980): 384–99.

Turner, Victor, and Edith Turner. *Image and Pilgrimage in Christian Culture.* New York, 1978.

Vaivre, Jean-Bernard de. "Valeur et hiérarchie des sceaux selon Philippe de Beaumanoir (fin du XIIIe siècle)." In *Mélanges offerts à Szabolcs de Vajay,* ed. Pierre Brière, pp. 585–603. Braga, 1971.

Verdon, Jean. "Les Sources de l'histoire de la femme en Occident aux Xe–XIIIe siècles." *Cahiers de civilisation médiévale* 20 (1977): 219–51.

Wagner, Anthony. "The Swan Badge and the Swan Knight." *Archaeologia* 97 (1959): 127–38.

Warner, Marina. *Alone of All Her Sex.* New York, 1983.

Watson, Arthur. *The Early Iconography of the Tree of Jesse.* London, 1934.

Webster, J. C. *The Labors of the Months.* Princeton, N.J., 1938.

Welber, M. *I sigilli nella storia del diritto medievale italiano.* Vol. 3 of *Sigillografia: Il sigillo nella diplomatica, nel diritto, nella storia, nell'arte.* Milan, 1984.

Werner, Karl-Ferdinand. "Liens de parenté et noms de personne." In *Famille et parenté dans l'occident médiéval,* ed. Georges Duby and Jacques Le Goff, pp. 13–18, 25–34. Rome, 1977.

1. Guillaume de Pont-de-l'Arche, bishop of Lisieux. 1221. The Virgin Mary with Child; below, a kneeling man in prayer; surrounded with the legend *salve sancta parens*. Douët d'Arcq, *Sceaux*, no. 6661 bis.

2. Alix de Nemours, wife of Gautier de Nemours, marshal of France. 1265. Full-length depiction of a woman bearing a hawk and standing between the coats of her husband (shields bearing three bars gemel). Douët d'Arcq, *Sceaux*, no. 3045.

3. Louis VII, king of France. 1141. The king enthroned, with regalia. Douët d'Arcq, *Sceaux*, no. 36.

4. Gautier de Nemours, marshal of France.
1260. Equestrian in arms, with shield bearing
three bars gemel (Nemours). Douët d'Arcq,
Sceaux, no. 216.

5. Garin, bishop of Senlis. 1217. The
full standing figure of a bishop in
vestments, with miter, crosier in the
left hand, right hand uplifted in
benediction. Douët d'Arcq, *Sceaux*,
no. 6856.

6. Lucie de Montigny. 1266. The
standing figure of a woman holding a
fleur-de-lis. Demay, *Sceaux de la
Flandre*, no. 1352.

7. Notre-Dame de Mantes, chapter. 1210. The enthroned and crowned Virgin Mary, with Child and fleur-de-lis. Douët d'Arcq, *Sceaux*, no. 7215.

8. Elisabeth, abbess of Montmartre. 1182. Seated abbess, with book and crosier. Douët d'Arcq, *Sceaux*, no. 9233.

9. Abbot of the Val-Notre-Dame. Twelfth century. Seated abbot with book and crosier. Douët d'Arcq, *Sceaux*, no. 9150.

10. Constance of Castille, wife of Louis VII, king of France. Ca. 1154. The standing figure of the queen, crowned, with fleur-de-lis and short scepter. Douët d'Arcq, *Sceaux*, no. 151.

11. Priory of Saint-Catherine-Du-Val-
des-Ecoliers. 1375. Saint Catherine
crowned, veiled, and with nimbus,
seated holding a book, and arguing with
two scholars, inspired by two demons.
Douët d'Arcq, *Sceaux*, no. 9430.

12. Abbey of Grandchamp. 1271.
Nativity: the Virgin Mary seated in
bed; above, the Child in a hanging
cradle. The scene is lit by oil lamps.
Douët d'Arcq, *Sceaux*, no. 8236.

13. Hugues, bishop of Orange. 1326.
The crowned figure of the Virgin Mary
with Child, within a niche. Below, the
bishop kneeling in prayer, between two
shields of arms bearing an eagle with a
baton. Douët d'Arcq, *Sceaux*, no. 6757.

EXEMPLA: A DISCUSSION
AND A CASE STUDY

I. *Exempla* as a Source for
the History of Women

Jacques Berlioz

The Definition
and Evolution
of the Genre

Though *exempla* have not been adequately utilized by historians, they stand ready as a valuable source for the study of women in medieval society. Exemplary material was long considered to be of secondary importance among our extant sources, largely suited to a history of the picturesque and noted for their stock of anecdotes. Literary specialists read and used the tales but accorded them only grudging toleration because of their clumsy and unpolished form. That they were referred to in the nineteenth century as *anecdotes, historiettes* (short tales), or *contes moraux* (moral tales) gives an indication of their peripheral status as guides to medieval society.[1] In addition, there is still a lack of critical editions, though efforts are now under way to rectify this shortcoming.[2] ❡ Despite these difficulties, the literature on *exempla* is not entirely terra incognita. Since the second half of the nineteenth century a considerable amount of work—crowned by the thesis of J. Th. Welter in 1927—has enabled scholars to consult and profit from these exemplary tales.[3] Furthermore, in recent years the inquiries and publications of historians using these materials have begun to move the focus away from the folkloric content of the sources. ❡ Our goal here is not to pursue a full

Editor's note: The papers of Jacques Berlioz and Marie Anne Polo de Beaulieu were planned and written as a complementary presentation. The first essay is a general discussion of *exempla* as a source, with special reference to the material they contain for and about women. The second is a detailed case study of the language and terminology pertaining to women and how they were presented in the *Scala celi* of Jean Gobi (1322–30). The two articles are independent in presentation and in authors' views. A common bibliography is offered after the second article.

history of women by means of the *exempla* but rather to present, in a summary fashion, what historians may expect to gather from the *exempla* when they turn to write such a history. Because a fascicle on *exempla* was published in 1981 in the series Typologie des Sources du Moyen Âge Occidental, we need neither survey the source, as such, nor provide a comprehensive bibliography for earlier studies. [4]

In the Middle Ages the term *exemplum* had a variety of related meanings. The most common usage—directly in keeping with the models of antiquity—was "an example to follow" or "a model for behavior or for virtue." In technical terms an *exemplum* also had a rhetorical function as a particular type of tale or story[5] used by preachers or authors of moral works for persuasion. It was one of the basic materials of the moral work (*ouvrages moraux*).

The rhetorical *exemplum* is a direct descendant of classical models. As medieval writers and preachers evoked the model, their definition is drawn directly from the *Rhetorica ad herennium*, which they attributed to Cicero: the *exemplum* is a presentation of factual material or an edifying saying from the past, now cited by a character worthy of faith ("Exemplum est alicuis facti aut dicti praeteriti cum certi auctoris nomine proposito"). Such an *exemplum* is meant to persuade, as it was thought by classical and medieval readers to do in Cicero's judicial discourses.[6] This rhetorical device runs through much medieval literature, and we know it particularly as it was developed in the "mirror of princes" genre. It generally took the form of a citation or a saying borrowed from a situation or a reference in classical history or literature.[7] As an illustrative story in its own right, the *exemplum* was systematically developed in the context of the sermon literature of the twelfth and thirteenth centuries (though it had appeared in Western Christian writings since patristic times). Jacques Le Goff has defined it as "a brief tale offered as true and intended for use in a speech (generally a sermon) that aims to convince a listener through a salutary lesson."[8] Though this definition is provisional and cannot be expected to cover every instance we encounter, it gives us a concise point around which to begin our discussion.

Exempla became widely diffused, as part of Western homiletics, because of their use by the mendicant orders in the thirteenth century. The tales were soon gathered into collections compiled for the use of preachers, and the earliest one we have is the *Treatise on Various Subjects for Preaching* (*Tractatus de diversis materiis predicabilibus*). In this compendium the Dominican Étienne de Bourbon brought together nearly three thousand tales and comparisons (*similitudines*), not to speak of biblical

citations and snippets culled from the patristic writers and the arguments and expositions of the scholastics. Other compendia followed. At
first such works were arranged in some sort of logical or thematic order,
but by the end of the thirteenth century they were usually arranged
alphabetically, according to their rubrics or key words.[9] As a further
indication of their popularity, many were translated into various vernacular tongues, and by the fifteenth century they had reached a secular
or lay audience that certainly embraced the aristocracy in many parts of
Europe. [10]

Nor were *exempla* confined to collections intended to aid preachers
working to prepare their sermons. We also know them from sermons
transcribed after the fact (of delivery) and then translated from the vernacular into Latin. Such sermons could be taken up again and reedited
so as to provide the bulk of treatises, such as those delivered by Jacopo
Fassavanti in his Lent sermons of 1354 and gathered under the title of
Specchio di vera penitenza. We have other such collections, such as those
offered by the Franciscan Iacobus de Marchia (1394–1476).[11] Sometimes
the scribes who worked on the sermons that had already been delivered encountered long *exempla* amidst the text; they might choose to
abridge or even omit such materials.[12] But they also might be scrupulous
about writing down the material as they received it, and often the extant
sermon volumes contain their full share of the *exempla* that had been
incorporated in the original oral delivery. [13]

Many of the exemplary tales used by preachers make their way into
the moral treatises that were written in (or translated into) the vulgar
languages of Europe, particularly in the works intended for the edification of women. We see their role and their influence in such works as *The
Book of the Knight of La Tour Landry* of the second half of the fourteenth
century and *Le Menagier de Paris* from about the same time.[14] These examples remind us of the way in which the *exempla*, once translated and
incorporated into literature that reached far beyond their homiletic point
of origin, became familiar to a wider and wider audience.

Modern Scholarly Use of the *Exempla*

In this discussion we are principally guided
by the usage of homiletic *exempla* as defined
by Le Goff in his contribution to the Typolo-
gie des Sources. There are difficulties concerning both the accessibility
and the reliability of the *exempla* available to us.[15] However, a considerable amount of work has been done, and many paths are well cleared.
J. Th. Welter's dissertation (1927) offers a detailed index of the principal

collections. The *Index exemplorum* of F. C. Tubach catalogs approximately 5,400 themes from *exempla:* it is based on a scrutiny of the main published collections, and it classifies key words in alphabetical order and follows them with a short analysis. Though this catalog is obviously useful, it has some serious shortcomings. There is no precise criterion for the choice of entries. In addition, the cross-reference index merely repeats the principal listing.[16] There are numerous typographical errors and omissions, and some relatively recent editions of collections have not been taken into account. Nor have older printed editions (including incunabula) been adequately combed, and some handwritten collections have been consulted only in a cursory fashion.[17] So while one is certainly inclined to use Tubach's *Index*, one should do so only with considerable caution.

But the situation should change for the better. Soon the *New Index of Medieval Exempla* will appear, compiled by the Group for Western Medieval Anthropology (Le Groupe d'Anthropologie Historique de l'Occident Médiéval) at the École des Hautes Études en Sciences Sociales and the Centre National de la Recherche Scientifique in Paris. The first fascicle, almost ready for publication, will present a critical cross-reference index of the collections already cataloged by Tubach. For a tale found in a collection that he took into account, one will be immediately able to locate the number of the corresponding rubric of the *Index exemplorum*. Subsequent fascicles of the *New Index* will be devoted to indexes of collections not covered by Tubach.

Le Goff has recently explicated many of the basic rules to be followed when the *exempla* are being subjected to criticism and analysis.[18] Nevertheless, dilemmas persist, given the nature of this kind of source and of earlier scholarly efforts. When an editor or author cites no sources for a given *exemplum*, how can we tell whether a given tale is the recorded version of an oral tradition, or whether it is a retranscription of an earlier written text? And even when an oral source has been cited, how can we tell whether or not it is based on an earlier written text? Jean Gobi clearly illustrates this in his use of an *exemplum* under the rubric "crusaders" (*croisés*), concerning the efficacy of relying upon *exempla* when preaching in favor of the Crusades. In his *exemplum* a simple priest persuades a group of peasants to make the sign of the cross, an enterprise in which a legate had failed miserably.[19] Though Gobi gives no source, the same material is found in the *Compilatio singularis exemplorum*, a collection compiled by a monk and preacher from Angers in the late thirteenth century. The *Compilatio singularis exemplorum*, in turn, gives no source for its tale. How, then, can one tell when the tale originated?[20] One must proceed with caution when attempting to pin down the period in which the "events" of a specific *exemplum* took place and the *exemplum* took its original shape.

The question of the transmission of particular tales is tied to the question of the spread of the collections and compendia. Each collection of *exempla* may have been broken up and pilfered to contribute to a succeeding collection. For example, the *Tractatus de diversis materiis predicabilibus* by Étienne de Bourbon is transcribed, almost word for word, into the *Speculum morale* attributed to Vincent de Beauvais. Again, much of the *Compilatio singularis exemplorum* finds its way into Jean Gobi's *Scala celi*, a work widely propagated in the late Middle Ages.

There is also the question of how the tales within the compendia were spread through Europe. Were they transmitted by means of the pulpit and sermons, as one might suppose? If this was the case, is it not reasonable to study *exempla* "as testimony of the culture of the people," as Bronislaw Geremek suggests?[21] There is perhaps no global answer. The fact remains that even in the sermons that have been preserved—despite their large number—we can make few assumptions regarding whether or not they are accurate reflections of the exact words of pulpit antecedents. Perhaps they barely reflect the content of what was preached. Nevertheless, it is probable that *exempla* were largely employed in sermons addressed especially to the common people.[22]

Women and *Exempla*

As Le Goff has reminded us, historians' interest in the study and use of *exempla* is twofold.[23] First, they supply important information on the day-to-day material, mental, and social life of the people. The recovery of such "realistic details" is today among the historian's high priorities, provided that such materials are understood and interpreted with some trepidation. Second, the *exempla* furnish valuable testimony about the structures, methods, and intentions of religious personnel and their policies as they were put into operation upon the mass of believers.[24] How do women fit into the story of the production and reception of the exemplary literature?

As with the overwhelming bulk of medieval literature, men generally produced the *exempla*. Though only clerics were empowered to preach in public, the laity (including women) had a right to preach in private.[25] However, we suspect that private lay sermons were usually a mere echo of the official (public) sermons of the church. This is confirmed by a

passage from a sermon by Saint Bernardin of Sienna, delivered there
in 1427: "Women, starting tomorrow I would like to make all of you
preachers. How will this be possible? Because today you will hear the
elucidation from my mouth; your souls will be enlightened and all of
you will be able to truly become purveyors of the word."[26] Readings
from religious texts could also foster this version of the art of "preaching": in this way, at age sixteen, Jeanne Marie de Maillé (1331–1414)
was able to recite to her young spouse several *exempla et miracula* from
the lives of saints, presumably read to her at some earlier time by her
own confessor.[27] Furthermore, when we assess the preaching of women
—even when they were carrying out this activity in private—we are
dealing with a form of religious expression that was likely to have been
strictly regulated.[28]

Can we see women as the sources of *exempla*? Probably only in the
sense that they can be depicted as the heroines of exemplary tales. In this
limited sense they play a considerable role in the total import and weight
of this body of literature, and further studies should take account both
of their appearances in the collections and of the rubrics under which
they appear. On the other hand, women are rarely cited by editors of
the collections as sources of the information contained in the *exempla*.
Exceptional cases are usually ones where the woman possesses very high
social status. When Étienne de Bourbon cites a woman as the source of
an *exemplum* concerning the blessed Alpais de Cudot, she turns out to be
none other than Sybille de Beaujeu, sister-in-law of Philippe Auguste,
king of France.[29] Though this is probably typical, there is no systematic
cataloging of the female sources.

To appreciate fully the reception of homiletic *exempla* by the medieval
public, we must keep in mind the size and the visibility of the female
audience. Details on the importance of women as recipients (and con-
sumers) of sermons should be among the information we hope to derive
from editions of sermon texts now under way. In this regard Ranulphe
de la Houblonnière, bishop of Paris (1280–88), was very attentive to his
female constituency. In fact, such a group made up virtually all of his
nonuniversity audience, as best we can judge from the preponderantly
feminine examples he gives with respect to confession.[30] There are also a
significant number of model sermons that include a great many *exempla*
and that are addressed to various categories of female listeners; those
of Jacques de Vitry (d. 1240) and of the Franciscan Guibert de Tournai
(d. 1284) readily come to mind.[31]

Furthermore, sermons offer valuable information about their listeners

—specifically for us, about women's reactions to the words of the preacher. It is not uncommon to have a preacher vigorously disputed. In an unpublished sermon Jacques de Vitry declares: "I see that the women present today are angered by what I say about the malice of women. I have said enough about the evil woman. You want me to speak about the good woman? I will speak about her then."[32] *Exempla* themselves often give an indication of behavior during the sermon. We have glimpses of the old woman who has fallen asleep and must be awakened by a vigorous pin prick, along with the young girls who disrupt the sermon with songs and dances; a nun inadvertently reveals, in her chatter, that the preacher was the son of a priest. [33]

We can gain even more information about women's image, from our sources, than we can about behavior. We are always confronted by barriers when we confront medieval sources: as Carla Casagrande and Silvana Vecchio have remarked, "The history of women in the medieval western world necessarily passes as well through the series of feminine images that populate the texts of the men of the church."[34] Of course, a problem we must worry about but cannot solve relates to the relationship between the representation of women in sermons and *exempla* and their "real" activities and image. We have models, presented in sermons and stories, that mediate between their daily lives and the view the preacher or author chose to present. The representations of women conveyed in *exempla* should be understood as daily referents for actual women, but beyond that it is hard to go with any assurance.

The first step toward establishing an ideological system of representations might well consist of undertaking a systematic study of the various designations of women as presented in the collections of *exempla*. A basic task, with which we might begin, is to analyze the rubrics and the alphabetical ordering of key words around which the collections were structured, particularly those that bear directly on women.[35] We soon see that certain rubrics appear only in certain collections and nowhere else; real distinctions and variations among different authors' views can be uncovered in this fashion.[36] Such an approach will reveal the general picture of women held by the collection's author or final compiler and editor, and it opens the way for comparative analysis.

Let us look at some examples. We can take the *Speculum laicorum,* composed at the end of the thirteenth century. There are rubrics such as "adulterer," "carnal love," "chastity," "priests' concubines," "dancers," "lust," "bodily ornaments," "beauty," and so forth. A collection such as the *Compilatio singularis exemplorum* is equally of value for its different arrangement; it presents women listed by precise types or groups, ordered according to social standing or roles: abbesses, nuns, beguines, queens, countesses, ladies (*dames*), maidens, common women, match-makers, magicians, and witches are among the categories. However, this latter scheme of presentation is generally not the case; to study a definite social type in a given collection, one must usually expect to examine all of the rubrics, not just those with explicit references to women.[37] Even works composed in a "theological" order, such as Étienne de Bourbon's *Tractatus de diversis materiis predicabilibus*, are complicated due to the dilution and scattering of the subject matter on any given topic or class of women.

Needless to say, the image of women conveyed in the collections of *exempla* as well as in the moral treatises is largely negative. The female body is a prime target for male moralizing. Innumerable tales condemn women's seductive clothing, their makeup—that "artificial extension of a natural object," as Casagrande puts the matter—or their care for their hair.[38] Women's idle talk is equally condemned, along with dancing, seen as essentially feminine and inspired by the Devil. Women are frequently accused of following superstition and of encouraging heresy. The *exempla* offer a ready guide to clerical reproaches of women, and they, along with the moral tales, can be read as a *vade mecum* to this aspect of medieval consciousness and of the male (clerical) predilection for denigration.[39]

Not all views are hostile, and the *exempla* also present images of the ideal woman. Such favorable anecdotes and models are found not only in the action of the stories, as in the tale of the wife nursing her imprisoned husband or that of the noble woman who, while on the verge of death, reserved her body to help fill in the moat surrounding the evil tower at the siege of Acre.[40] Women could be held up as more general models. It is no surprise to find complimentary tales about Judith, Esther, Madeleine, the virgin martyrs, and such pagan heroines as Pauline or Lucretia (especially as models of conjugal fidelity). The status of the Virgin is ambiguous: she seems to appear more as an effective mediator than as an exemplary individual figure in her own right. However, she is depicted in her direct relations with pious women who invoked her name for such typically feminine miracles as special protection during pregnancy and an easier time when giving birth. How far we can go toward erecting a positive image of women and womanhood on the basis of the *exempla* is a topic worthy of more study and discussion. The *Scala celi* shows women who were concerned for the religious education of their children—a woman teaching her young daughters the value of religious fasts, a wife doing penance while her husband is absent, and so forth. There was also an emphasis on familial piety, alms giving, and the need to welcome pilgrims and to care for the sick, especially lepers. [41]

When we assess the weight of the positive comments, we must strike a balance with views that are more critical. If we look at the *Lamentations of Matheolus*, a vigorous critique of women from the late thirteenth century, we find a wealth of negative comments. However, we also discover that many of the unkindest exemplary tales in this compendium (and the morals drawn from them) were refuted a century later by the volume's translator, Jean Le Fevre, in his *Book of Leesce*. For Le Fevre, most of the stories told by Matthew are treated as jokes and barely warrant serious discussion. Le Fevre stresses that it is illogical and unfair to extend to all women a flaw that applies only to a single woman, and he thus rejects the inductive argument or logic underlying the weight of generalizations based on using an *exemplum*. [42] Christine de Pizan takes the same view in her rejection of the *Lamentations*, and her *Book of the City of Ladies* is filled with deliberate counter-*exempla*. [43] Once again we see that it is important to study how the images of women in *exempla* were actually received, both at the time of writing and subsequently, as well as how they were first produced and what the original compiler tried to say to his auditor or reader.

No medieval source makes a statement and then rests, forever, as a closed book. Le Goff reminds us that "against their own will *exempla* furnish us with information that calls into question the finality which was their original intent." [44] The tales often depict dramatic or historical situations peculiar to the period of their production, if only to hold the contemporary reader's attention. Although they do not simply reflect the structures of their society and of daily behavior, they still contain realistic features and details that we can cull for our purposes. But in this endeavor it is important to exercise strict chronological control over the subject matter; an *exemplum* reported by a fifteenth-century source that paints a vivid picture of current morals and customs may very well have been excerpted from a thirteenth-century collection.

Keeping this caveat in mind, we can find valuable information in the *exempla* about the daily lives and routines and rituals of women. There is material about their life-style: the house is woman's privileged place, and the tales reflect this.[45] In that arena she enjoys undeniable power and prestige, even though obedience to the husband is the first rule of family life. Women are often represented as the administrators of domestic affairs and of relations with the servants. Their meeting places are, in many instances, the washhouse or the church. And while condemning their manner of dress, many authors provide choice information and minute descriptions of hairstyles and attire. Even anathema and censure can bring a precious lot of useful information for us. [46]

A good example of the way in which we can turn contemporary moralizing with a strongly negative flavor to our ends is provided by a sermon of Jacques de Vitry, who attacks the conduct of mothers who fail to chastise their daughters:

> When they see their daughters seated between two young men, one of whom places his hand on their breast, while the other clasps their hand or embraces them about the waist, the wretches exult with joy and say, "You see how honorably my daughter is seated? She is esteemed and loved by these young men." And because they do not punish their daughters' behavior, their joy and laughter will change to suffering when, after six months, their bellies begin to swell; and then—too late —starting to blush, they will say, "Blessed are the infertile women who have borne no children and the breasts that have given no milk." [47]

Other aspects of parent-child relations emerge from other tales. From the works of Étienne de Bourbon and the *Tabula exemplorum* (composed at the end of the thirteenth century) we learn about the "barbo" or bogeyman invoked by nurses to frighten their charges into obedience, a droll insight into family life that has not been transmitted by other sources.[48] In fact, people of all ages find favor in the *exempla*—from the young child to the old woman, often portrayed as either the witch or the matchmaker, along with the young woman, the married woman, and the widow. *Exempla* reinforce the value of desirable practices, that is, attending mass, confession, and prayer, just as they come down hard on undesirable ones, that is, singing, dancing, and mixing with profane persons. [49]

As I have tried to show in this brief paper, *exempla* offer a choice resource for the history of medieval women. Unfortunately, though the sources are very numerous, they still remain poorly understood because of the lack of critical editions. We hope that in the near future works such as Étienne de Bourbon's *Tractatus de diversis materiis predicabilibus*, Jean Gobi's *Scala celi*, or Arnold de Liege's *Alphabetum narrationum* will be made available for modern study and analysis. When such texts, among others, are available we will recognize the *exempla* as an exceptionally rich source by means of which we can catch details both of everyday life and of the medieval consciousness in the portrayal of gender and gender relations.

NOTES

This article was translated by Stephen Michelman and revised and edited by Joel T. Rosenthal.

1. In 1888 Albert Lecoy de la Marche, graduate of the École des Chartes, published an anthology of exemplary tales, *L'Esprit de nos aïeux*, with a long chapter on women (pp. 223–72).

2. On the reaction of French scholars to the appearance, in 1887, of Lecoy de la Marche's partial edition of Étienne de Bourbon's *exempla*, see Berlioz, "Le Récit efficace." Such great philologists as Gaston Paris (1839–1903) and Paul Meyer (1840–1917) did recognize the full value of *exempla*.

3. On the history of the study of *exempla*, see Schenda, "Stand und Aufgaben der Exempla Forschung"; Berlioz and David, "Introduction bibliographique"; Delcorno, "Nuovi studi sull *exemplum*."

4. We use the terminology proposed by Leopold Genicot: see Brémond, Le Goff, and Schmitt, *L'Exemplum*.

5. Moos, "Sulla retorica dell'exemplum nel Medioevo"; I warmly thank the author for sharing his text prior to publication. See also Le Goff's chapter in Brémond, Le Goff, and Schmitt, *L'Exemplum*, pp. 28–38.

6. *Rhetorica ad herennium* 4.49.62; David, "Maiorum exempla sequi."

7. Moos, "Use of *Exempla*," and his *Geschichte als Topik*.

8. Brémond, Le Goff, and Schmitt, *L'Exemplum*, pp. 37–38. On the question of definition, see the fundamental article by Rudof Schenda, "Stand und Aufgaben der Exempla Forschung." For an older treatment, see Crane, *"Exempla" or Illustrative Stories*, p. xviii. On women and their role—a topic still not systematically covered—see Moos, "Use of *Exempla*," p. 235.

9. Though the evolution of the genre is too large a tale to deal with here, see Schmitt, *Prêcher d'exemples*, pp. 16–20; Brémond, Le Goff, and Schmitt, *L'Exemplum*, pp. 37–68 (covering both definition and evolution).

10. To take but one example, this was the case with the *Dialogus creaturarum*, which was attributed to Mayno de Maynari from Milan of the fourteenth century and was the source of two French translations in 1482: see Ruelle, *Le Dialogue des créatures*, and my review in *Romania*.

11. Iacobus de Marchia, *Sermones dominicales*.

12. On *exempla* and their reflection of sermon materials, see Bataillon, "Similitudines et *exempla*," and Bériou, *La Prédication de Ranulphe de la Houblonnière*, pp. 106–21.

13. One of these fifteenth-century collections (Florence, MS. Riccardiana 2894) has recently been studied by Rosamaria Dessi (at the École des Hautes

Études en Sciences Sociales, Paris): see "Prédication, _exempla_, et réception par le public à Florence au XVe siècle."

14. "Si les devoit l'en tout au commencement prendre a chastier courtoisement par bonnes exemples et par doctrines" (Montaiglon, _Le Livre du chevalier de La Tour Landry_, p. 3). For an example from Catalan literature, see _Llibre de les dones_, written in 1392 by the Franciscan Francesc Eiximenis (d. 1409). There are excerpts, in Italian, in Eiximenis, _Estetica medievale dell'eros, della mensa, della citte_, pp. 41–90.

15. Brémond, Le Goff, and Schmitt, _L'Exemplum_, pp. 71–78.

16. Ibid., pp. 75–76.

17. Because of these problems, not even Gobi's _Scala celi_, which has been printed in various editions, has been treated exhaustively by F. C. Tubach, _Index exemplorum_. The bibliography attached to this paper includes various printed editions of _exempla_.

18. In Brémond, Le Goff, and Schmitt, _L'Exemplum_, especially chap. 4, "Rules for Criticism," pp. 69–70. Because of the need for brevity, this fascicle deals only briefly with rhetorical _exempla_; see, instead, Peter von Moos's work cited in the bibliography.

19. The text has been translated into French by Marie Anne Polo de Beaulieu: see Schmitt, _Prêcher d'exemples_, pp. 135–36.

20. On this _exemplum_, see Berlioz, "L'Auditoire des prédicateurs."

21. Geremek, "L'_Exemplum_ et la circulation de la culture au moyen âge," esp. p. 177.

22. Berlioz, "Le Récit efficace," pp. 115–18.

23. Brémond, Le Goff, and Schmitt, _L'Exemplum_, chap. 6, "Historical Value," pp. 79–84.

24. As Le Goff has written, "The historical value of _exempla_ seems to us to reveal itself above all in their testimony about the presuppositions and the conscious and unconscious goals of the catechism of this period: about the relationships between speech and writing, rhetoric and history, the strategies of persuasion that lie at the heart of the production, diffusion and reception of _exempla_" (Brémond, Le Goff, and Schmitt, _L'Exemplum_, p. 79).

25. Bériou, _La Prédication de Ranulphe de la Houblonnière_ 1:9 n. 2.

26. Cited in Schmitt, _Prêcher d'exemples_, p. 188.

27. Vauchez, "Influences franciscaines et réseaux aristocratiques," p. 96.

28. Casagrande and Vecchio, _I Peccati della lingua_.

29. Lecoy de la Marche, ed. (Paris, 1877), no. 19, p. 26. (Étienne de Bourbon borrows yet another _exemplum_ from him, on the death of Philippe Auguste, _idem_, no. 322, pp. 271–72).

30. Bériou, _La Prédication de Ranulphe de la Houblonnière_ pp. 141–42. Though a full bibliography would be too elaborate here, see Zefarana, "Per la storia religiosa di Firenze nel Quattrocento."

31. See Casagrande and Vecchio, *I Peccati della lingua*, pp. 53–67, for a French translation of a sermon to married couples by Jacques de Vitry.

32. Jacques de Vitry, *Sermo ad conjugatos*, fols. 137–39; we thank Madame Marie Claire Gasnault (École des Hautes Études en Sciences Sociales, Paris) for making a copy available. Albert Lecoy de la Marche devotes many pages to this issue: see *La Chaire française*, pp. 193–213; though old, this work is still indispensable.

33. Jacques de Vitry, cited by Lecoy de la Marche, *La Chaire française*, p. 202; also, Étienne de Bourbon, as given by Lecoy de la Marche, *L'Esprit de nos aïeux* no. 185 (pp. 161–62); ibid., no. 175 (pp. 229–30); *Compilatio singularis exemplorum* (MS. Upsalla University Library, C. 523, fol. 99). See Berlioz, "L'Auditoire des predicateurs."

34. Casagrande and Vecchio, *I Peccati della lingua*, p. ix.

35. See the list of rubrics of the *Alphabetum narrationum* of Arnold of Liège, in Le Goff, "Le Vocabulaire des *exempla*." The "woman" (*mulier*) rubric is second, of 537 rubrics, with 64 *exempla* (of which 17 are furnished under the *mulier* rubric itself). Others are given by reference, e.g., "The demon is gladdened by women's appearance." This is in the "appearance" rubric, translated into French in Schmitt, *Prêcher d'exemples*, pp. 109–20.

36. The "old woman" (*vetula*) rubric appears only in the *Tabula exemplorum* and in Bibliothèque Municipale d'Auxerre, MS. 35 (from the thirteenth century); the *meretrix* rubric appears only in the *Sertum florum moralium* (fourteenth century).

37. See Michel Parisse's use of *exempla* for a history of nuns in *Les Nonnes au moyen âge*, pp. 250–55 ("[In *exempla*] nuns are not represented very often . . . The subject most often treated is the chastity of nuns" [p. 251]). This study is confined to the works of Étienne de Bourbon and Jacques de Vitry, and a wider search would reveal a tale with more nuances.

38. Schmitt, *Prêcher d'exemples*, p. xix; Polo de Beaulieu, "La Condamnation des soins de beauté," pp. 297–309. Étienne de Bourbon takes great care to specify the social status and age of his heroines: see Flüry-Hérard, *L'Image de la femme dans les exempla*, pp. 87–90. Also see the texts collected by Lecoy de la Marche, *L'Esprit de nos aïeux*, pp. 223–72, and in *La Chaire française*, pp. 396–415.

39. It would be interesting to make a study of women's image in the collection of Frère Sachet, J. Th. Welter, "Un Recueil d'*exempla* du XIIIe siècle," in *Études franciscaines*, 1913, p. 646–55. In this long series of tales—a true cycle of feminine wiles and ruses—her way of acting and the very lure of her flawed nature enable women to outwit men.

40. The latter *exemplum* is found in the works of Guiard de Laon (first half of the thirteenth century). See Boeren, *La Vie et les oeuvres de Guiard de Laon*, p. 176.

41. *Scala celi*, nos. 689 (marriage rubric), 260 (confession), 573 (hospitality), 749 (*mulier*: woman), 946 (vainglory), as taken from the numbering in the edition being prepared by Marie Anne Polo de Beaulieu. Also, nos. 683–84, 686 (Virgin Mary).

42. Van Hamel, *Les Lamentations de Matheolus*, p. cxcix. For metonymy, see Brémond, Le Goff, and Schmitt, *L'Exemplum*, pp. 115–16.

43. The most recent French edition of Christine de Pizan's *Book of the City of Ladies* is that of Hicks and Moreau; see pp. 13–24 for a short but valuable introduction.

44. Brémond, Le Goff, and Schmitt, *L'Exemplum*, pp. 79–80.

45. We are dealing here with laywomen. For religious, see the material cited above, n. 37.

46. See the texts provided by Lecoy de la Marche, in *L'Esprit de nos aïeux*, no. 47, pp. 221–72, and Polo de Beaulieu, "La Condamnation des soins de beauté," p. 47.

47. Schmitt, *Prêcher d'exemples*, p. 59. On the conception of the erotic self in the Middle Ages, see Berlioz, "Il seno nel Medioevo tra erotismo e maternita," pp. 40–44.

48. Berlioz, "Masques et croquemitaines."

49. See the comments of Schmitt in Brémond, Le Goff, and Schmitt, *L'Exemplum*, pp. 85–107.

II. *Mulier* and *Femina*: The Representation of Women in the *Scala celi* of Jean Gobi

Marie Anne Polo de Beaulieu

To study the use of the word *mulier* in a collection of *exempla* is a good way of analyzing the representation of women presented by a work that belongs, in its polished written form, to the "learned" culture. In addition, such a study enables us to look at some of the themes and messages incorporated within popular preaching as it was offered both to clerics, who made use of such texts in the preparation of their own sermons, and to the lay audience that listened to them. [1]

The *Scala celi* is a collection of lively *exempla*, rarely original and with many well-worn stories filled with stereotypes. It was composed or compiled between 1322 and 1330 by Jean Gobi the Younger at the Dominican house of Saint Maxim in Provence.[2] It enjoyed long-lasting success: forty manuscript copies of the work have been preserved and are scattered throughout Europe. In addition, there are no less than five incunabula editions. Our study deals with material as presented in the incunabulum edition of Ulm (1480), of which we are preparing a critical edition. [3]

Thanks to various indexes and a concordance, we have traced the word *mulier* (and its various declensions) through the *Scala celi*'s 972 *exempla*, which are divided into 121 rubrics, alphabetically arranged from *abstentia* to *usura*. [4] We have taken no account of the context of such pronouns as *que, qua, illa,* or *ipsa* that are directly tied to *mulier,* mainly for reasons of clarity and simplicity in classifying our words. We have chosen, rather, to highlight the key expressions—in which *mulier* figures prominently —that play a powerful mnemotechnic role. The relations between the various terms that form these key expressions are associative relations in the sense defined by Ferdinand de Saussure: "Outside of discourse, words that have something in common are associated with each other in memory and, thus, form groups ordered by very diverse relations. We shall call them associative relations."[5]

Our first idea was to center this study on the opposition *mulier/femina.* These rubrics do in fact exist in the *Scala celi;* they are clearly distinguished by the preacher in the introduction to the *femina* rubric.[6] Such a distinction is based on a deep semantic distinction or opposition, which is revealed by the various dictionaries we have consulted.[7] *Mulier* and *femina* are the two most common designations of women. *Mulier* is a term that first surfaces in imperial Roman usage. Though Isidore of Seville derives it from *mollitia,* its origins are unknown.[8] It is used to designate what is proper and specific to women—one woman, a group of women, or women in general. It is never used to designate female animals, in contrast to *femina.* Until the end of the empire *mulier* refers exclusively to a female member of the human species: *vir* and *mulier* are the two subcategories of the genus *Homo.* Gradually the use of *mulier* in the sense of "spouse" appears. It is used as an equivalent of *uxor,* and it connotes a woman who has had sexual relations, as opposed to *virgo.*

Femina is an ancient word derived from the Indo-European root *tdhe,* meaning "to suckle, suck, milk, or draw milk."[9] It seems to correspond to the ancient present participle "giving milk." Despite a brief popularity among poets in imperial times, *femina* retains fairly pejorative connotations from its animal associations. In the Vulgate, the term is used only 16 times to refer to sexual relations or physiological phenomena proper to women, as opposed to 487 instances of the word *mulier*.

As a good and orthodox cleric, raised in Jerome's tradition, Jean Gobi employs *mulier* and *femina* in a comparable way. Although it is retained as the title of an important rubric (comprising fifteen *exempla*, one of exceptional length), *femina* is a rare term. It occurs but five times: *femina*, 1 (within its own rubric), 1 (outside); *feminae*, 3 (outside). *Femina* only appears once in a neutral sense (to designate the inhabitants of a castle, *feminae et viri: ex.* 926, fol. 159v). The other four occurrences of the word are clearly pejorative. In fact, they refer to women impassioned by an evil dance (*ex.* 342, fol. 61v) and to a woman, damned as an adulteress, who appears one night to a coal seller (*ex.* 626, fol. 109v). More general designations insist on the sinful nature of women, as in the introduction to the *femina* rubric (cited above) and in the expression *deditus corruptinibus feminarum* (*ex.* 647, fol. 113v).

Other senses of *femina*, as servant or dependent or as spouse, prostitute, or witch do not appear in our collection.[10] Moreover, a distinct opposition between *mulier* and *femina* is not always maintained by Jean Gobi. In *exemplum* 626 (fol. 113v), on the infernal or diabolical hunt, *femina* is replaced by *mulier*. Furthermore, the word *mulier* is far from invariably positive in its connotation or context.

The semantic field of *mulier* has a twofold structure. On the one hand, there are unilateral equivalencies with more exact or precise terms; on the other, there are usages that float between equivalence with and opposition to other feminine terms. The former elements of this semantic approach are designations of women in specific situations or relationships, either in the family or in society. We can begin with some kinship links and the words used to express them.

Uxor. A univocal designation of "spouse" and a frequent choice, it is often set against or in place of *mulier* as a virtual synonym. We see this in *exempla* 183 (fol. 31r), 184 (fol. 31r), 520, line 295 (fol. 89r) and line 544 (fol. 92r), 615 (fol. 107v), 626 (fol. 109v), and 742 (fol. 132r).

Mater. Mother, in relation to her children, appears in ten *exempla*: *exempla* 183 (fol. 31r), 250 (fol. 43r), 446 (fol. 76v), 474 (fol. 81r), 514 (fol. 86r), 537 (fol. 97r), 641 (fol. 112r), 679 (fol. 121r), 688 (fol. 123r), and 944 (fol. 163v).

We also find *concubina sacerdotum* in *exemplum* 307 (fol. 53v) and *socia*, used to designate a cleric's concubine, in *exemplum* 517 (fol. 86v).

As well as kinship or family relations, there are social ranks, bonds, and roles that have to be identified and labeled. We find *domina* used quite often, and in its primary usage it means "head of a household" or "owner" of possessions, that is, slaves. It carries a sense of power and authority, which helps explain its gradual transformation into a term with titular or honorific weight, until eventually it took on a connotation of civility or politeness. In the *Scala celi* the *domina* appears as the head of a household of fairly high social standing: *exempla* 181 (fols. 28–29), 222 (fol. 38r), 478 (fol. 82r), 508 (fol. 85v), 520 (fol. 92r), and 744 (fol. 132r). We also find *comitissa* (*ex.* 784, fol. 136v), *regina* (*ex.* 184, fol. 31v), and *imperatrix* (*ex.* 184, fol. 31v).

The above terms were all fairly fixed. But there is a floating relationship between *mulier* and some terms that ranges from equivalence to opposition. *Puella* offers an example of this more flexible or ambiguous relationship. *Puella* is the feminine form of *puer*, and thus conveys the idea of a young girl (now) of an age to be married—whether maiden or member of a convent. It is equivalent to *mulier* in *exemplum* 182 (fol. 30r) and opposed to it in *exemplum* 129 (fol. 20r).

Another term that appears in this fashion is *virgo*, a virgin. It is equivalent to *mulier* in four *exempla*: 182 (fol. 30r), 186 (fol. 32r), 633 (fol. 110v), and 961 (fol. 166r). In these instances it designates a member of a convent. It appears in opposition or contrast to *mulier* in *exempla* 182 (fol. 30r) and 474 (fol. 78r). Du Cange offers a broad spectrum of meanings, some contradictory, for *mulier*, including both "married woman" and "virgin to be married," and Jean Gobi plays with such varying senses in different sections of his compilation.

Other examples of varying linguistic usage are not hard to come by. In *exemplum* 181 (fols. 27–28) we have the tale of "the chaste girl of the Count of Poitou," wherein we find a multitude of feminine terms. They run in a chronological or life order, with marriage and the birth of children as the major dividing point. Before marriage one speaks of *filia, puella, domicella* (*ex.* 516, fol. 86r) as roughly synonymous with *mulier*. Afterward, the terms are *uxor, sponsa, mater, consors*, and *domina*. All the same, at the very end of the tale the term *juvencula* is used for our married heroine, while in two other tales it clearly refers to an unmarried woman (*ex.* 520, line 544, fol. 92r, and 538, fol. 97v).

While some of these distinctions may seem a bit fragile, they do show the existence (and understanding) of three levels of meaning for *mulier*:

(1) a general meaning, where it is employed alone or in opposition to *homo* (as in *ex.* 181, fols. 28–29; *ex.* 249, fol. 42r; *ex.* 437, fol. 75r); (2) a more particular meaning, "spouse," as opposed to *vir* (as in *ex.* 181, fols. 28–29; *ex.* 182, fol. 30r; *ex.* 282, fol. 48v); (3) the various specific meanings.

As Jacques Berlioz observes above, usages regarding the Virgin Mary are often less than clear-cut. Twice the Virgin is referred to as *mulier* in a quote from the Bible. *Exemplum* 807 (fol. 141r), quotes from John 19:26 ("Mulier ecce filius tuus, ecce mater tua . . ."). Then, from the mouth of a Jewish child, who is awkwardly describing the Virgin, "Referabat quod mulier illa in cuius basilica panem acceperat, sedens in cathedra cum parvulo filio" (*ex.* 368, fol. 65v). Blaise's dictionary underscores the paradox of using *mulier* for Mary, since the term normally refers to women in general and to married women in particular. On the other hand, Jean Gobi often refers to the Virgin Mary as *virgo* and *domina.*

It comes as no surprise to find that *mulier* is the most frequently employed term among the *Scala celi*'s references to women. Of the one hundred nouns used to name living beings, *mulier* is sixth in overall usage: *filiuus,* 404; *miles,* 292; *rex,* 292; *homo,* 277; *pater,* 232; *mulier,* 229; *juvenis,* 221; *dominus,* 212; *frater,* 204.[11] Of the other words used to designate women, the frequency distribution is as follows: *uxor,* 190; *mater,* 129; *filia,* 105; *domina,* 79; *juvencula,* 30; *puella,* 30; *domicella,* 24; *soror,* 19.

In total frequency distribution, the first five places belong to masculine terms. However, comparing masculine and feminine forms of usage is a delicate matter, because such terms as *dominus, pater,* and *frater* may be used in both familial and religious contexts. Still, we can offer a few comparisons. The index reveals Jean Gobi's emphasis on the family role of women, that is, women as spouses (*uxor,* 190 uses) and as mothers (*mater,* 129). Masculine family roles are not specified as frequently, and *pater* (232 uses) has religious as well as secular meanings. *Vir* (160 uses) and *maritus* refer to the male spouse or husband. In other female kinship ties (and terms), vertical relations are more common: *filia* is used 105 times (as against the 404 appearances of *filius*), while *soror* is used but 19 times (as against 204 instances of *frater,* though the latter word also carries its share of religious connotations).

Feminine designations that connote power are less commonly found, as we might expect. There are 79 uses of *domina* against 212 uses of *dominus,* 16 of *imperatrix* against 131 of *imperator,* and 16 of *regina* against 292 of *rex.* There is a marked absence of terms designating feminine social status or typical female occupations, just as there are few mentions of female religious orders or of their members. For men, on the other hand, such terms are common. *Miles*, for example (292 uses), and *sacerdos* (189), *episcopus* (118), *clericus* (125), and *monachus* (77) make regular appearances. Terms used for very young or very old women are quite rare: *vetula* (19 uses), *juvencula* (30), *puella* (30), and *domicella* (24) hardly make a great impact. In the *Scala celi* women are most frequently represented as middle-aged wives and mothers.

We proceed now to examine the rubrics that contain the term *mulier*. The originality of Jean Gobi's collection lies in its classification of all the defects of women under the rubric *femina* and of all their positive qualities under *mulier*. Other collections that are ordered alphabetically do not follow this bold distinction. The thirteenth-century *Tabula exemplorum* offers but one rubric, *mulier* (*ex.* 186–91), combining both sides of the coin. The *Speculum laicorum*,[12] under the rubric *de mulierum cohabitatione fugienda* (*ex.* 399–403), represents women only as sinners. Its other rubrics for the particular status of women are equally negative: *de concubinis sacerdotum* (cap. 18) and *de coreatricubus* (cap. 21) follow in the same vein. It is only in the fourteenth century, in the *Alphabetum narrationum* of Arnold of Liege, that we find a pair of rubrics classifying women according to two fairly broad categories, *mulier* and *uxor*.[13] Neither rubric is totally devoted to either defense or attack, and vices and virtues are mixed in varying proportions. Of course, the total balance is invariably unfavorable to women.[14]

Jean Gobi clearly separates the rubric of feminine virtues (*mulier*, fols. 132–33) from that of feminine vices (*femina*, fols. 85–94). The latter category contains almost twice as many tales as the former (15 against 8). Still, both rubrics are marked by the same number of theological or moral lessons that are offered to introduce the *exempla*, and the lessons are opposed to each other almost word for word. Their confrontation is very revealing of Jean Gobi's conception of women and of how to present them and to moralize from and about them. We can look at some comparisons that amplify this theme.

Femina	*Mulier*
1. *Primo est virorum deceptiva.*	*Primo est sponsi sui dilectiva.*
6 *exempla* (fols. 85–86): no. 506, philosopher brought down on fours by a woman; no. 507, the stirred-up snake; no. 508, woman who skimps	1 *exemplum* (fol. 132r): no. 742, husband who wants to buy wife an old coin.

on husband's funeral shroud; no.
509, ruse by wife helps lover escape;
no. 510, same ruse by pilgrim's wife;
no. 511, drunken husband placed in
convent.

2. *Secundo est jurgiorum provocativa.*
   2 *exempla* (fol. 86r): no. 512,
Socrates' disputes with wife; no.
513, Georgias cannot keep peace at
home.

Secundo mulier est pacis vocitativa.
   1 *exemplum* (fol. 132r): no. 743,
exemplary wife converts thieving
husband.

3. *Tercio est immundicie amativa.*
   2 *exempla* (fols. 86–86v): no.
514, young man senses woman's
perversion in his mother; no. 515, a
vetula's strategies to awaken the love
of a virtuous woman.

Tercio mulier est immundicie oditiva.
   2 *exempla* (fols. 132v–132r): no.
744, virtue of wife coveted by a
knight; no. 745, 3 women's thoughts
on vanity of the world.

4. *Est cupiditatis augmentative.*
   2 *exempla* (fol. 86v): no. 516,
Atalanta's cupidity; no. 517, the
woman who ruins a cleric.

Est hospicium reformativa.
   1 *exemplum* (fol. 132v): no. 748,
Virgin Mary takes place of woman
whose husband wanted to sell her to
the Devil.

5. *Est omnium preceptorum contraria
operative.*
   2 *exempla* (fol. 86v): no. 518,
drowned woman who is searched for
upriver; no. 519, woman who goes
into the oven.

Est orationis continuativa.

   1 *exemplum* (fol. 132v): no. 746,
widow who marries Christ.

6. *Est omnis malicie inventiva.*
   1 *exemplum* (fols. 86–94): no.
520, romance of the 7 sages, particularly their misogynous tales.

Est bonitatis conservativa.
   1 *exemplum* (fol. 132v): no. 747, a
woman's thoughts about a sermon.

7. *Est infirmantium consolativa.*
   no *exempla.*

The term *mulier* is employed not only in these two outstanding rubrics
but also in nearly half of all the rubrics (57 of 121, or 47 percent).
(See Table 1.) Table 1 reveals some points of interest. *Mulier* occurs
frequently under the *ad status* rubric (60 percent), giving an image of
women as more engaged in the world than our frequency of usage analy-

Table 1.   Distribution of Rubrics and *Exempla* with the Word *Mulier*

	Total Rubrics	Rubrics with *Mulier*	Total *Exempla*	*Exempla* with *Mulier*
Vice	41	20 (49%)	257	42 (16%)
Virtue	20	9 (45%)	144	16 (11%)
Theology	35	13 (37%)	347	43 (12%)
Status	25	15 (60%)	224	32 (14%)
Total	121	57 (47%)	972	133 (14%)

sis might have indicated. Also, *mulier* occurs almost as often under the rubrics that denounce a vice (49 percent) as under those that present a virtue (45 percent). It occurs less frequently under the rather abstract theological rubrics (37 percent). In raw numbers, *mulier* appears most often under the rubrics and *exempla* that deal with vices, followed by rubrics on status, theology, and the virtues. Clearly, women's virtues were not considered their most prominent characteristic!

We also note that the size of the *exempla* may play a role in our analysis. The longer rubrics (both in terms of *exempla* and words) naturally have a better chance of containing more occurrences of *mulier*. For example, the *confessio* rubric (with 24 *exempla*) and the rubrics on *crux* (20), *cruce signatus* (23), *oratio* (17), *prelatus* (19), and *peregrinacio* (13) support this. The rubric *Virgo dei genitrix* combines two factors: size (with 55 *exempla*) and feminine themes. This latter factor should be compared to the *femina* rubrics (12 of 15 *exempla*), as well as *mulier* (6 of 7 *exempla*), *castitas* (7 of 10 *exempla*), *ornatus vanus* (7 of 11 *exempla*), and *luxuria* (5 of 12 *exempla*). What is more, we shall see below that women do not invariably play positive roles in either the theological or the status rubrics.

In analyzing the stories of these *exempla* we have come up with a new classification, one according to the type of images of women presented therein. We have selected five types according to the characteristics or evolution of the story's main female character: (1) positive image of women—33 *exempla*; (2) negative image of women—70 *exempla*; (3) neutral image of women—13 *exempla*; (4) image of women who improve—15 *exempla*; and (5) image of women who decline or are degraded —2 *exempla*. Clearly, the preponderance is of *exempla* that offer negative images. Nonetheless, if we add those with positive images (33) and those with images of women who improve (15), we have the respectable total of 48 *exempla* of a more positive sort. The small number of *exempla* that concentrate on women who fall is not peculiar to stories about women and is often within a genre that teaches that all can be saved. Finally, the 13 neutral images of women refer to women in general or to texts where women have but a minor or passive role never developed in much detail.

We can also look at the syntactical usage of *mulier* in Jean Gobi's text. The different declensions of *mulier* break down according to this frequency distribution:

	Singular	Plural
Nominative	*mulier*, 124	*mulieres*, 9
Accusative	*mulierem*, 19	*mulieres*, 9
Genitive	*mulieris*, 27	*mulierum*, 18
Dative	*mulieri*, 7	*mulieribus*, 1
Ablative	*muliere*, 11	*mulieribus*, 4
Total	188	41

In the *Scala celi*, *mulier* appears much more often in the singular than in the plural and in the active mode (133 nominatives). In the nominative case *mulier* is qualified 36 times by the indefinite article *quedam*. In 52 occurrences it has no qualifier, and in its other occurrences it is qualified in various ways. Sometimes it is qualified by demonstrative adjectives such as *illa, ista* (in a deprecatory sense, *ex.* 626, fol. 109v), and *haec*. Then there are qualifying adjectives referring to appearance: *nigerrima* (*ex.* 289, fol. 49v), *pulcerrima* (*ex.* 464, fol. 79v; *ex.* 516, fol. 86v; *ex.* 538, fol. 98r). There are terms that indicate social status: *simplex* (*ex.* 768, fol. 134v); *pauper* (*ex.* 433, fol. 74v); *paupercula* (*ex.* 415, fol. 71v; *ex.* 688, fol. 123v); *paupercula et nuda* (*ex.* 478, fol. 82v); *vidua* (*ex.* 304, fol. 52); *nobilis sed pauper* (*ex.* 686, fol. 123r); *nobilis* (*ex.* 147, fol. 22r; *ex.* 282, fol. 48r); *alienigena* (*ex.* 182, fol. 30r). Some of the terms carry moral and religious values: *christiana* (*ex.* 660, fol. 116r); *infelix* (*ex.* 165, fol. 24r); *honesta* (*ex.* 183, fol. 31r; *ex.* 706, fol. 126r); *castissima corpore tamen immunda mente* (*ex.* 220, fol. 38r); *sancta* (*ex.* 237, fol. 40r; *ex.* 568, fol. 102r); *summe devota* (*ex.* 746, fol. 132); *nepharia* (*ex.* 944, fol. 163v). There are some participial adjectives that are occasionally added to the qualifying terms: *mortua* (*ex.* 309, fol. 54r); *maledicta* (*ex.* 249, fol. 42). These last two terms are rather somber compared to most of the adjectives referring to a woman's health in the tales of improvement. Such terms run as follows: *compucta* (*ex.* 309, 310, fol. 54r); *confessa* (*ex.* 249, fol. 42v); *conversa* (*ex.* 202, fol. 35v; *ex.* 241, fol. 41r); *curata* (*ex.* 925, fol. 159r); *compatientes* (*ex.* 222, fol. 38r); *vivens* (*ex.* 520, line 550, fol. 92r).

Whether used with or without a qualifying term, in two declensions *mulier* is pejorative in itself (11 of 18 occurrences): in the nominative and the accusative plural—*mulieres*. This is exemplified in Father Assenech's address to his daughter: "Saluta fratrem tuum qui odit omnes mulieres sicut tu omnes viros" (*ex.* 182, fol. 30v). We find this pejorative connotation once more in two expressions in the ablative plural: "Nec corea placabilis est sine mulieribus," for example, comes after a discussion of the diabolical origin of dancing (*ex.* 616, fol. 108r). It also occurs when *mulier* is placed beside other despised creatures: "De ribaldariis, de mulieribus, de immundiciis" (*ex.* 616, fol. 108r). [15]

There are also some terms used by Gobi as nouns, juxtaposed to *mulier* and summarizing women's major sins. These include *sortilega* (*ex.* 323, fol. 56v), *peccatrix* (*ex.* 660, fol. 117r), and *meretrix* (*ex.* 633, fol. 110v).

We can look at some terms used to complement *mulier* and strengthen our impression of the values that lurk behind the usage. Such terms refer to women's appearance: *aspectus, habitus, pulcritudo, decor, ornatus, ornamenta,* and *vestes.* They refer to women's bodies, often in a vague or general way: *caro, cor.* They also refer to the symbolic parts of the body: *manus, venter, os et ventrem, facies, brachia.* Such terms sometimes allude to the Devil's guiles, practiced as he assumed a woman's form: "Multitudo demonum in specie juvenum et mulierum" (*ex.* 341, fol. 61r; *ex.* 587, fol. 104r; *ex.* 948, fol. 164r). We also have "Princeps demonum in specie mulieris virginis" (*ex.* 371, fol. 66r). We are warned against keeping company with women: *multitudo, familiaritas* (used in the singular or plural: *ex.* 506, fol. 85r; *ex.* 520, line 306, fol. 89v; *ex.* 629, fol. 110r); *consortia* (*ex.* 203, fol. 35v), and *amplexus* (*ex.* 170, fol. 24v). They can allude to women's living places: *pratum, domum, hospicium, habitacium.* But above all, they refer to women's sins, "male conditiones mulierum," and the list includes *immunditia, libido, cupiditas, verbum falsum, fecunditas verborum, dolositas,* and *diffamatio.*

These remarks indicate the many levels of Jean Gobi's text when we consider the negative portrayal of women. But we should remember that Gobi does devote a whole rubric to the virtues of women, and he does portray some remarkable heroines. Still, one cannot forget his radical distrust of women, often brought into sharp focus by his use of allegorical images that embellish certain tales: "carnis complacent que sunt mulieres" (*ex.* 538, fol. 98r); "hec mulier est suggestio diabolica" (*ex.*

774, fol. 135r); "portaria inferni" (*ex.* 289, fol. 50r); "vanitas mundi" (*ex.* 464, fol. 79v).

I will conclude this brief study with two suggestions. In this study of *exempla* women are represented as narrowly tied to the world through their homes and their families. We see this in the importance of the vocabulary of family relations and of the rubrics and terms pertaining to social status. Women are seen as being caught—as are men—between the poles of Christian life, between sin and damnation on the one hand and virtue and salvation on the other. The woman's margins of mobility are relatively narrow, as is her permissible life-style. For a woman to achieve salvation, Jean Gobi recommends a life of virtue and piety; note the importance of his rubrics emphasizing confession, prayer, alms, and chastity. The life of heroic saintliness is basically reserved for men. In this way a woman who fiercely defends her sense of virtue can be compared to a man: "Illa autem in castitate et in mundicia confirmata non tanquam mulier, sed sicut vir, repulit maliciam patris," and "illa clamat viriliter" (*ex.* 180, fol. 27r).

On the other hand, Gobi cannot find enough harsh words to denounce women's vices that stem not from passing temptations but from her sinful nature. This is attested by the preponderance of female characters under the rubrics of *luxuria* and *ornatus vanus* as well as by the frequency of appearances of the Devil in female guise and form. More globally, women maintain particular relations with the beyond: the female souls who return from purgatory or from hell to give voice to their grief to the living are described with an abundance of detail bordering on the sadistic or voyeuristic (*ex.* 785, fol. 137r; *ex.* 792, fol. 139r). Male souls that return from the dead are much closer to neutral. A young cleric describes the appearance of his damned mother: "De capite ejus exibant lacerte multe et maxime que sugebant cerebrum eius, in oculis eius scorpiones stabant et in auribus eius crudelissimi mures, symea stabat ante eam et cum crudelissimo lapide comminuebat et frangebat labia, os, dentes eius. Serpens maximus cingebat collum eius et sugebat ubera" (*ex.* 785). Might we not see this sort of representation of women—beyond Jean Gobi's method of pedagogy by fear[16]—as indicating, simultaneously, a fascination and a repulsion for the being who, in her procreative function, holds both the power of life and the power of death?

NOTES

1. Charland, *Artes predicandi;* Welter, *L'Exemplum dans la littérature didactique.*

2. *Dictionnaire de spiritualité, d'ascétique, et de mystique,* v. "Jean Gobi"; Langlois, *Histoire littéraire de la France* 31:47–65, 35:532–56; Quetif and Échard, *Scriptores ordinis praedicatorum* 1:63, 633; Welter, *L'Exemplum dans la littérature didactique,* pp. 319–35.

3. Polo de Beaulieu, "Édition et étude d'un recueil *d'exempla* du XIVème siècle: La *Scala celi* de Jean Gobi." Forthcoming. We refer to our own enumeration of the *exempla* and to their references in the Ulm incunabula edition of 1480.

4. In this task we have used the word-processing program Wordstar and the lexicometric programs Aline, Sainchef, and Jeudemo.

5. Saussure, *Cours de linguistique général,* p. 7. The quotation has been translated by Steve Michelman.

6. "Notandum hic quod ponuntur omnes male conditiones mulierum, sed postea ubi tangitur de ista dictione 'mulier,' ponantur omnes bone conditiones earum."

7. A historical account of this opposition has been given by Grisay, Lavis, and Dubois-Stasse, *Les Dénominations de la femme.*

8. Isidore de Sevilla, *Etymologies,* 11, orig.: "Mulier a mollitia, tanquam mollier, detracta littera et mutata, appellata est mulier."

9. Benveniste, *Le Vocabulaire des institutions indo-européenes* 1:32.

10. In regard to women who are witches, Du Cange's dictionary cites an excerpt from the *Decretum* of Burchard of Worms and specifies that prostitutes are called *femina peccati* or *femina vitae.*

11. We have coded our text of the *Scala celi* to obtain indexes separated according to grammatical categories (verbs, adjectives, adverbs, etc.) and semantic categories (nouns that name inanimate things, nouns that name animate things, place names, names of persons, names of works and authors). We then ordered the indexes according to lemmas in order to obtain synthetic figures of usage frequency, ready to be used for particular studies of this sort.

12. Welter, *Tabula exemplorum.* See also Welter's partial edition of the *Speculum laicorum.*

13. Ribeaucourt, ed. "*L'Alphabetum narrationum:* Un Recueil d'*exempla.*" The *mulier* rubric is translated in Schmitt, *Prêcher d'exemples,* pp. 109–20.

	Mulier Rubric		*Uxor* Rubric	
	References	*Exempla*	References	*Exempla*
Positive	9 (29%)	4 (23.5%)	4 (36%)	0
Negative	22 (71%)	13 (76%)	7 (63%)	4 (100%)
Total	31	17	11	4

14. Rubrics from the *Scala celi* that contain one or more occurrences of *mulier*:

Vice	Vertu	Theologie	Ad Status
Adulterium, 1	Caritas, 1	Communio, 4	Advocatus, 1
Amor, 3	Castitas, 7	Confessio, 3	Balivus, 1
Aspectus, 4	Compassio, 1	Consolatio, 3	Bellum, 1
Avaricia, 1	Elemosina, 3	Contritio, 4	Clericus, 3
Blasphemia, 1	Misericordia, 2	Conversio, 1	Consiliarius, 1
Cantus, 2	Perseverancia, 2	Corpus Xi, 2	Femina, 12
Cogitatio, 2		Cruce sign., 3	Filii, 2
Consuetudo, 1		Crux, 2	Histrio, 1
Corea, 2		Diabolus, 1	Mercator, 1
Delicie, 3		Eukaristia, 1	Mulier, 6
Discursus, 1		Incarnatio, 1	Prelatus, 1
Divicie, 1		Oratio, 2	Questor, 1
Ira, 1		Passio Xi, 2	Sacerdos, 1
Locutio, 2		Peregrinacio, 1	
Luxuria, 5		Verbum Dei, 1	
Ornatus, 7		Virgo D.G., 12	
Rapina, 1			
Sortilega, 1			
Tactus, 1			
Testimonium, 1			
Vana gloria, 1			

15. In Paris, Bibliothèque nationale, MS. 3506, *mulieribus* is replaced by *meretricibus*, an edifying variation.

16. Delumeau, *La Peur en Occident*.

BIBLIOGRAPHY

A Joint Bibliography for the Papers of Berlioz and Polo de Beaulieu

Primary Sources

Bériou, Nicole, ed. *La Prédication de Ranulphe de la Houblonnière: Sermons aux clercs et aux simples gens à Paris qu XIIIe siècle*. 2 vols. Paris, 1987.

Casagrande, Carla, trans. *Prediche alle donne del secolo XIII: Testi di Umberto da Romans, Gilberto da Tournai, Stefano di Borbone*. Milan, 1978.

Christine de Pizan. *Le Livre de la cité des dames*. Trans. Eric Hicks and Thérèse Moreau. Paris, 1986.

Crane, Thomas Referick, ed. *The "Exempla" or Illustrative Stories from the "Sermones Vulgare" of Jacques de Vitry.* London, 1890.

Eiximenis (Ximenez), Francesc. *Llibre de les dones.* Ed. Fr. Naccarato. Barcelona, 1981.

———. *Llibre de les dones.* In *Estetica medievale dell'eros, della mensa, della citte,* trans. Gabriella Zanoletti, pp. 41–90. Milan, 1985.

Iacobus de Marchia, ed. Renato Lioi. *Sermones dominicales.* 3 vols. Falconara, 1978. Supplement, 1982.

Jacques de Vitry. *Sermo ad conjugatos* (no. 67). Paris, Bibliothèque nationale, MS. lat. 17509, fols. 137–39.

Lecoy de la Marche, Albert, ed. *Anecdotes historiques, lègendes et apologues tirés du Recueil inedit d'Étienne de Bourbon.* Paris, 1877.

Lecoy de la Marche, Albert. *L'Esprit de nos aïeux: Anecdotes et bons mots tirés des manuscrits du XIIIe siècle.* Paris, 1888.

Montaiglon, Anatole (Corde de Montaiglon), ed. *Le Livre du chevalier de La Tour Landry.* Paris, 1854.

Polo de Beaulieu, Marie Anne, ed. "Édition et étude d'un recueil d'*exempla* du XIVe siècle: La *Scala celi* de Jean Gobi." "troisième cycle" thesis, École des Hautes Études en Sciences Sociales, 1984.

Quetif, Jacques, and J. Échard. *Scriptores ordinis praedicatorum.* 2 vols. Paris, 1719–21.

Ribeaucourt, Colette, ed. "*L'Alphabetum narrationum:* Un Recueil d'*exempla* compilé au début du XIVe siècle." Ph.D. diss., University of Paris, 1985.

Ruelle, Pierre, ed. *Le Dialogue des créatures.* Trans. Colart Mansion (1482) du *Dialogus creaturarum (XIVe siècle).* Brussels, 1985.

Schmitt, Jean-Claude, ed. *Prêcher d'exemples: Récits de prédicateurs du moyen âge.* Paris, 1985.

Van Hamel, A. G., ed. *Les Lamentations de Matheolus et le livre de leesce de Hejan Le Febre, de Ressons.* Paris, 1905.

Welter, J. Th., ed. *Speculum laicorum.* Paris, 1914.

———. *Tabula exemplorum.* Paris-Toulouse, 1927: Slatkine Reprint, 1973.

Zefarana, Zelina. "Per la storia religiosa di Firenze nel Quattrocento: Una raccolta privata di prediche." *Studi medievali* 9 (1968): 1017–1113. Republished in *Da Gregoria VII a Bernadino da Siena: Saggi di storia medievala,* pp. 279–377. Quaderni del Centro per il Collagamento degli Studi Medievale e Umanistic nell'Universita di Perugia, no. 17. Perugia, 1987.

Secondary Sources

Bataillon, Louis-Jacques. "*Similitudines* et *exempla* dans les sermons du XIIIe siècle." In *The Bible in the Medieval World: Essays in Memory of Beryl Smalley,* ed. K. Walsh and D. Wood, pp. 191–215. Oxford, 1985.

Benveniste, Émile. *Le Vocabulaire des institutions indo-européennes.* 2 vols. Paris, 1969.

Berlioz, Jacques. "Il seno nel medioevo tra erotismo e maternita." *Storia e dossier* 2, no. 12 (November 1987): 40–44.

———. "L'auditoire des prédicateurs dans la littérature des *exempla* (XIII–XIVe siècles)." In *Dal pulpito alla navata: La predicasione medievale nella sua recezione da parte degli ascoltatori (secc. xiii–xv).* International conference in memory of Zelina Zefarana, Florence, 5–7 June 1986. Forthcoming.

———. "Le Récit efficace: L'*exemplum* au service de la predication (XIII–XVe siècles)." *Mélanges de l'École française de Rome* 92 (1980/1): 113–14.

———. "Masques et croquemitaines: A propos de l'expression 'Faire barbo' au moyen âge." In *Le Monde alpin et rhodanien* (1982): 221–34.

———. Review of P. Ruelle, ed., *Le Dialogue des créatures. Romania* 106 (1985): 273–85.

Berlioz, Jacques, and Jean-Michel David. "Introduction bibliographique." *Mélanges de l'École française de Rome* 92 (1980/1): 15–31.

Boeren, Peter C. *La Vie et les oeuvres de Guiard de Laon (ca. 1170–1248).* The Hague, 1956.

Brémond, Claude, Jacques Le Goff, and Jean-Claude Schmitt. *L'Exemplum.* Typologie des Sources du Moyen Âge Occidental, no. 40. Turnhout, 1982.

Casagrande, Carla, and Silvana Vecchio. *I Peccati della lingua: Disciplina ed etica della parole nella cultura medievale.* Rome, 1987.

Charland, Th. M. *Artes predicandi: Contributions à l'histoire de la rhetorique au moyen âge.* Paris, 1936.

David, Jean-Michel. "*Maiorum exempla sequi:* L'*Exemplum* historique dans les discours judiciares de Ciceron." *Mélanges de l'École française de Rome* 92 (1980): 67–86.

Delcorno, Carlo. "Nuovi studi sull *exemplum.*" *Lettere italiane* 36 (1984): 49–69.

Delumeau, J. *La Peur en Occident.* Paris, 1978.

Dessi, Rosamaria. "Prédication, *exempla,* et réception par le public à Florence au XVe siècle." Master's thesis, École des Hautes Études en Sciences Sociales, 1987.

Flury-Hérard, E. *L'Image de la femme dans les exempla, XIIIe siècle.* Paris, 1975.

Geremek, Bronislaw. "L'*Exemplum* et la circulation de la culture au moyen âge." *Mélanges de l'École française de Rome* 92 (1980/1): 153–79.

Grisay, A., G. Lavis, and M. Dubois-Stasse. *Les Dénominations de la femme dans les anciens textes littéraires français.* Gembloux, 1969.

Langlois, Charles Victor. *Histoire littéraire de la France.* Vol. 31. Paris, 1893.

Lecoy de la Marche, Albert. *La Chaire française au moyen âge, spécialement au XIIIe siècle.* Paris, 1869.

Le Goff, Jacques. "Le Vocabulaire des *exempla* d'après l'*Alphabetum narrationum.*" In *La Lexicographie du latin medieval et ses rapports avec les recherches actuelles sur la civilisation du moyen âge,* ed. Yves Lefèvre, pp. 97–103. Paris, 1981.

Moos, Peter von. *Geschichte als Topik: Das Rhetorische Exemplum von der Antike*

zur Neuzeit und die historiae im Policraticus Johannis von Salisbury. Ordo:
Studien zur Literatur und Gesellschaft des Mittelalters und der fruhen Neuzeit. Hildesheim, 1988.

————. "Sulla retorica dell'exemplum nel Medioevo." In *Retorica e poetica tra
xii e xiv secolo,* ed. C. Leonardi. In press.

————. "The Use of *Exempla* in the *Policraticus* of John of Salisbury." In *The
World of John of Salisbury,* ed. Michael Wilks, pp. 207–61. Oxford, 1984.

Parisse, Michel. *Les Nonnes au moyen âge.* Le Puy, 1983.

Polo de Beaulieu, Marie Anne. "La Condamnation des soins de beauté par les
prédicateurs du moyen âge." In *Les Soins de beauté: Moyen âge, debut des
temps modernes,* pp. 297–309. Nice, 1987.

Saussure, Ferdinand de. *Cours de linguistique général.* Paris, 1975.

Schenda, Rudof. "Stand und Aufgaben der Exempla Forschung." *Fabula* 10
(1969): 69–85.

Tubach, Frederic C. *Index exemplorum: A Handbook of Medieval Religious Tales.*
Helsinki, 1969.

Vauchez, Andre. "Influences franciscaines et réseaux aristocratiques dans le Val
de Loire: Autour de la Bienheureuse Jeanne-Marie de Maillé (1331–1414)."
In *Mouvements franciscains et Société française, XIIe–XXe siècles,* ed. Andre
Vauchez, pp. 95–105. Paris, 1984.

Welter, J. Th. *L'Exemplum dans la littérature didactique et religieuse du moyen
âge.* 1927. Reprint. Geneva, 1973.

————. "Un Recueil d'*exempla* du XIIIe siècle." *Études franciscaines* (1913):
646–55; (1914): 194–213, 312–30.

SEXUAL EQUALITY IN
MEDIEVAL CANON LAW

James A. Brundage

quality of persons was not an ideal to which medieval society generally subscribed. Despite occasional assertions by theologians that everyone was equal in the eyes of God, medieval discussions of the social order almost always assumed that society both was and ought to be hierarchically structured and that individuals or groups could best be described in terms of their relationships to superiors and inferiors.[1] Medieval discussions of the status of women, in particular, often assumed that the position of any given woman in the social hierarchy was inferior to that of every male of the same social rank or class.[2] ❡ These theoretical principles, however, did not necessarily reflect social realities. David Herlihy has shown, for one thing, that the property rights of women varied greatly, not only among different social classes but also among different regions and periods of time. Noblewomen in southern France and Spain, for example, enjoyed considerable freedom in disposing of property, and the social distance between noblemen and noblewomen of this region was consequently far narrower than that among the middle or lower classes or their counterparts in northern Italy.[3] ❡ Despite such variations, however, to be a woman was, by and large, to be socially disadvantaged in comparison with males, and the legal systems of medieval Europe reflected that fact. Canon law in particular has a notorious reputation as a bastion of inegalitarian political and social views, and canonists did much to merit this reputation.[4] In his authoritative exposition of the *Liber extra*, for instance, Bernard of Parma (d. 1266) expounded the law on female incapacity: "A woman, on the other hand, should not have [jurisdictional] power . . . because she is not made in the image of God; rather man is the image and glory of God and woman ought to be subject to man and, as it were, like his servant, since man is the head of the woman and not the other way around."[5]

This was no personal idiosyncrasy of Bernard of Parma; rather, it reflects quite accurately the policies embedded in the law.[6] It is surprising, therefore, to find that in one important area of ordinary experience the canonists flatly rejected the postulate of female inferiority and insisted instead that men and women had precisely equal rights and obligations.

This exceptional matter, in which the canonists adopted equality, not subordination, as a guiding principle, was sex, both within marriage and outside of it. Surprising as it may seem, the canonists' attachment to the principle of equality in sexual matters remained firm and unwavering at least from the twelfth century, when canon law first blossomed into a distinct and well-organized juridical system. Gratian, the twelfth-century Bolognese scholar who has been styled the father of canon law, was quite clear about this principle.[7] "A [married] man does not have power over his body; rather, his wife does," Gratian declared, paraphrasing a Pauline injunction (1 Cor. 7:4), and he repeatedly affirmed this idea in his treatment of the law of marriage. [8]

Tension between two conflicting views ran throughout Gratian's whole discussion of marital sex. On the one side, there was a distrust of, indeed, an active hostility to, pleasure, especially sexual pleasure, as a lure of the Devil and a source of both spiritual and physical impurity. On the other side, Gratian assumed that married persons usually indulged in sexual relations; he acknowledged that this was necessary for procreation; and he therefore concluded that somehow the nastiness of sex must have a role in the divine plan.

Gratian and his expositors were convinced that sexual pleasure was evil or was at best a morally suspect means to achieving admirable goals.[9] The canonists also observed, moreover, that men and women seemed equally prone to committing sexual offenses.[10] Writers on canon law insisted that the standards for dealing with sexual misbehavior by women should be the same as those applied to men.[11] Canonists adopted this principle from Saint Augustine, who held that men should be penalized just as severely as women for adultery and other sexual offenses.[12] For this reason, canon law maintained what is often called the clean-hands rule. This meant that, for example, an adulterous husband was legally unable to charge his wife with adultery, no matter how she flaunted her extramarital affairs. [13]

In general, the canonists viewed sex, even within marriage, with suspicion and often with loathing. Gratian cited with approval Saint Jerome's verdict that a man who loves his wife too passionately is an adulterer.[14] Yet at the same time, Gratian and other canonists treated sex as a normal element of married life, if not an absolutely necessary one. Indeed, because sexual congress was essential for procreation, which medieval Christians accepted as a fundamental purpose of marriage, it seemed necessary to admit that married couples had a right to coitus—if not necessarily to sexual enjoyment.

Pleasure in the sexual union was at the center of the problem that vexed the lawyers. They saw no way to accept pleasure as a good in itself without opening the door to moral consequences that they rejected.[15] When pleasure resulted from some action, as it commonly did from sexual intercourse, then that pleasurable experience needed to be justified or excused by some higher and more worthy purpose, to which pleasure was annexed as a secondary and unfortunate effect.

This aversion to pleasure informed the canonists' whole treatment of marriage.[16] The canonists saw marriage as a consensual contract and adopted the Roman law rule that "consent, not coitus, makes a marriage." On this basis they succeeded in constructing a matrimonial law in which sexual pleasure could be restricted severely or even eliminated altogether.[17] Although coitus and its accompanying pleasure normally played a role in marriage, the consensual theory of marriage that the canonists arrived at ensured that consummation was unnecessary for valid marriage. This was theologically useful, for it could then be maintained that the Virgin Mary and Saint Joseph were married (and it seemed unthinkable to hold that they were not), despite the fact that dogmatic theologians insisted that they never had intercourse.[18] Thus marriage without sex was legally possible and, many felt, morally laudable, though admittedly not usual or common.

Some lawyers in the generations following Gratian wanted to diminish still further the role of sex in marriage. One notably influential law professor, Huguccio (d. 1210), taught that sexual relations were invariably sinful, even within marriage, "since there is always pleasure in the emission of sperm." The sin inherent in the sex act might be mitigated by the good aims of marriage, he believed, but it was nonetheless sinful, even if only venially, for married persons to enjoy coitus. Of course, if they could manage to have joyless sex, coitus without pleasure, then perhaps the act itself would cease to be sinful. Huguccio noted that sex in paradise before man's fall from grace would not have been sinful because it would not have been intensely pleasurable.[19] But the fall from grace had transformed the human frame in such a way that sexual intercourse in the postlapsarian world was a source of both great pleasure and grave sin. Therefore, God-fearing men and women should avoid it

Cor 7:3

Let the husband render unto
the woman due benevolence
also the woman unto her husband.

benevolence -
    disposition to do good
    an act of kindness
    generous gift

eunoia
good mind

render-
apodidomi

to give away
deliver
give again
pay

NIV

The husband should fulfill his marital duty to his wife, and likewise the wife to her husband.

as far as possible and, when they lapsed from grace by having sexual relations, should forthwith confess their sin and do penance for it. Fortunately for medieval married couples, however, most canon lawyers rejected Huguccio's position, and some even wondered if it might not be heretical. [20]

Still, most people married; virtually all who did so had sexual relations, and it is fair to assume that they frequently enjoyed the experience.[21] Given the moral scruples of medieval intellectuals (such as lawyers and theologians) about sexual pleasure even in marriage, it is not surprising that their theory of sexual relations in marriage distinguished between the roles of the parties in marital intercourse. For this purpose, Saint Paul provided a crucial metaphor. Paul had spoken of marital sex as a debt: "Let the man pay the debt to his wife, and likewise the wife to her husband" (1 Cor. 7:3).[22] Lawyers found this construct congenial, for debt was a familiar and comfortable juristic category. What canonists did, then, was to treat the law of debt as a model for the sexual rights and duties of husband and wife.

The canonists classified the conjugal debt, that is, marital coitus, as a mutual obligation.[23] Each party owed this obligation to the other, and each had the right to payment on demand. Now, it is obviously possible to distinguish, both morally and legally, between the person who demands fulfillment of an obligation and the person who responds to that demand by rendering what is required. The debt itself is impersonal and morally neutral, simply the object of an obligation, something that creates an obligatory bond between debtor and creditor. But the actions of the person who asks for payment and of the person who responds by paying what is owed may carry quite different moral and legal consequences. Evaluation of the actions of creditor and debtor will depend on their roles in the transaction, the circumstances and motives that prompt the creditor to call the debt, the willingness and speed with which the debtor pays up, the circumstances under which the debtor may delay or deny payment, and so forth.

Canonists pursued this analysis of marital relations with enthusiasm. Because the conjugal debt was a mutual obligation, it followed that neither party could withhold payment without the consent of the partner.[24] Thus, even such worthy and pious enterprises as entering the religious life, vowing continence, or going on crusade might infringe the right of one spouse to collect the conjugal debt from the other. For this reason, popes and canonists up to the time of Pope Innocent III (1198–1216) held that no married person could unilaterally make any of these commitments without the consent of the marital partner.[25] Canonists also found that the debt concept of marital relations furnished a useful tool for penal law. Thus they held that an excommunicated man, for example, could not lawfully demand payment of the conjugal debt from his wife, but he nonetheless remained bound to pay if she required it of him.[26] Married persons guilty of adultery could be penalized in similar fashion for their illicit adventures. [27]

Obviously, the workability of the debt construct of marital relations depended upon the willingness of married persons to observe the rules. While qualms of conscience might deter conscientious persons from gross infractions, the penitential system of the church was also available to advise parties of the moral dangers of disregarding the law's require- ments and to punish those who ignored these warnings. The courts had to devise mechanisms to cope with more hardened sinners who could not be kept in line by the informal sanctions of conscience and the moral suasion of confessors. For this reason the canonists contrived actions at law to compel payment of the conjugal debt by unwilling spouses. The action to enforce payment of marital debt proved in fact to be a very useful juristic device, and it was often employed to compel deserting spouses to return to their marital partners and to bring to justice—or at least into court—third parties who interfered with the conjugal rights of married couples. [28]

In all of this the canonists asserted that husbands and wives had equal rights to demand and participate in marital intercourse, although they also believed that women might prove less likely than men to insist on their sexual rights.[29] In the field of sexual relations within marriage, their guiding principle was Saint Paul's statement (Gal. 3 : 28) that within the Christian community there is neither Jew nor Gentile, bond nor free, man nor woman, but that all are spiritually equal in the sight of God. Although other Pauline statements seemed to contradict this principle of the equality of all believers, the medieval canonists embraced the prin- ciple of equal sexual rights within marriage as a fundamental tenet of matrimonial law.[30] In so doing they found support from many of the leading theologians of their age. [31]

One is entitled to wonder, however, just how important this conces- sion of female equality in marital sexual relations actually was. Did it have any real significance, either for individual women or for society as a whole?

I would argue that the medieval canonists' notion of sexual equality was important for three rather different reasons. First, the doctrine of sexual equality in some sense legitimized female sexuality itself, even if only within narrow limits. The canonists' doctrines implicitly conceded not only that it was natural for women to have sexual desires, just as men did, but also that their right to satisfy these desires within marriage was just as important as the satisfaction of men's sexual urges. This was an important principle both for married women and for society as a whole. Even if one harbors reservations about the adequacy of the conventional drive-reduction model of sexuality—the notion, in other words, that sexual desire is one of the most basic and powerful human drives, whose frustration or radical sublimation often results in neurosis, psychosis, and other undesirable consequences [32]—it would be hard to deny that sexual desires are common and important to a good many people, men and women alike. It is also evident that many societies, including Western Christian societies, have tried to deny or to minimize the legitimacy of female sexual desire, while accepting male libidinous urges as normal, natural, and, indeed, unavoidable. The canonists' assertion that on this score there is no difference between the rights of men and those of women was important because it meant that female sexuality was legally as important as male sexuality and thus extended legal legitimacy to the sexual feelings of women.

Second, the legitimation of female sexuality within marriage seems to have been a critical factor in the growth of the idea that marriage ought to be something more than a physical union of two partners for the breeding of children and the transmission of property. The acceptance by canonists of the parity of male and female sexuality was arguably significant for the growth of ideas about the emotional content of married love. Noonan has shown how the canonists came to think of marriage as a union characterized by "marital affection." [33] They borrowed this phrase (along with many others) from Roman law. As they did with several of these borrowings, the canonists invested this term with meanings rather different from those that Roman jurists had assigned to it. Recognition of the sexual equality of spouses was almost certainly connected with the growth of the idea that an emotional bond between the partners ought to be an essential constituent of any marriage. Union without love was not something that society ought to legitimate by granting it recognition as a marriage. Development of this belief, which is quite foreign to Roman and other ancient doctrines about marriage, reflected noteworthy changes in social attitudes toward both sexuality and emotional bonding in late medieval society. [34]

Finally, the development among the canonists of notions of sexual equality may have been symptomatic of the beginning of a breakdown of the ambivalence that earlier Christian authorities had shown toward the position of women in society.[35] If we assume that women are men's equals in the sexual domain but are inferior to males in all other respects, then we might reasonably infer that a society that accepts this assumption considers sexuality to be less important than most other aspects of human life. Acknowledgment of female equality in this area, in other words, might have resulted from a low valuation of sexuality itself. If, on the other hand, we accept the notion that marital affection (in the canonists' sense of the phrase) is an essential attribute of marriage and that women have the same rights as men to expect sexual expression of that affection, then our theory would allow us to infer that men and women might reasonably enjoy equal rights in aspects of the marital relationship other than the purely sexual ones.

Medieval canonists did not share many of the values that modern liberal social thought takes for granted. Both the canonists' anthropological assumptions and the principles that underlay their value systems differed radically from those cherished by most people in our own society. The canonists' ideas about the legal structure of human relationships nevertheless contained suggestive insights for later generations. Canon law was, after all, a learned profession, or at least it was rapidly becoming one by about 1250. It was also an intricate and formidable intellectual enterprise. The canonists of each generation not only passed on to their students a considerable body of technical professional lore but also speculated about the values, ideals, and insights that informed the law. As lawyers in general and canon lawyers in particular emerged during the late Middle Ages as powerful members of a ruling elite, their views played a significant role in shaping social thought and public policy. Medieval canonists' opinions about the sexual equality of married men and women formed an integral part of the process that slowly led to a grudging recognition that equity requires that men and women be treated equally in other spheres of life as well.

NOTES

I should like to acknowledge my deep obligation to Elizabeth Makowski, whose work on the law of conjugal debt first focused my attention on the issues discussed in this paper.

1. Walter Ullmann, in particular, stresses the pervasiveness of this hierar-

chical ideal; see, for example, Ullmann, *Principles of Government and Politics,* pp. 32–56; Ullmann, *History of Political Theory,* pp. 100–129; Ullmann, *Law and Politics,* pp. 31, 130–31, 230, 233, 282–83; and the concluding chapter of Ullmann, *Growth of Papal Government.* A well-known medieval example of the theological importance of the hierarchical principle is Saint Thomas Aquinas's axiomatic use of hierarchy in his fourth and fifth proofs for the existence of God (*Summa theologica* [hereafter cited as *ST*] la q. 2 a. 3).

2. For a theologian's view, see Thomas Aquinas, *ST* la q. 92 a. 1–3. The ideas of the lawyers were similar; see Gratian, *Decretum* C. 33 q. 5 c. 12–20 and d.p.c. 11. References to the *Decretum* and other texts of the *Corpus iuris canonici* are to the standard work edited by Friedberg, while references to the *Glossa ordinaria* to the various parts of the *Corpus* are to the Venice 1605 edition. References to the Roman law texts are to the definitive edition of the *Corpus iuris civilis* edited by Mommsen et al. For the *Digest of Justinian* (hereafter cited as *Dig.*), I have also consulted the translation by Watson et al.

3. Herlihy, "Land, Family, and Women," pp. 110–11.

4. This characterization is a commonplace in general histories of the Middle Ages; see, for example, Artz, *Mind of the Middle Ages,* pp. 293–94; Heer, *Medieval World,* pp. 54–55, 346; Previté-Orton, *Shorter Cambridge Medieval History* 2:943, 946–47.

5. Bernard of Parma, *Glossa ordinaria* to X 1.33.12 v. *iurisdictionis;* cf. Hostiensis, *Commentaria* to X 1.43.4 §§ 5–6, and Joannes Andreae, *In quinque decretalium libros novella commentaria* to X 1.33.12 § 6 (hereafter cited as *Novella*).

6. This attitude was common, of course, throughout classical antiquity. Papinian, a third-century Roman jurist, summed up the situation when he observed that "in multis iuris nostri articulis deterior est condicio feminarum quam masculorum" (*Dig.* 1.5.9). Medieval canonists were well aware of Papinian's observation and assumed that the same policy of gender discrimination applied in canon law as in Roman civil law. As the rubric to C. 33 q. 5 c. 17 of Gratian's *Decretum* put it, "Nulla est mulieris potestas, sed in omnibus viri dominio subsit." One anonymous twelfth-century commentator went so far as to claim that women were only equal to each other. Despite their differences in social class, he asserted, all women share the same lowly status, "quia omnes vero funguntur officio, omnes aequaliter mereri" (*Summa Parisiensis* to C. 32 q. 1 c. 11 v. *non in sola,* pp. 240–41).

7. There is a vast literature on Gratian. For good, brief introductions, see Kuttner, *Harmony from Dissonance,* and his "Father of Canon Law," pp. 2–19. See also LeBras, Lefebvre, and Rambaud, *L'Âge classique,* pp. 51–129; Noonan, "Gratian Slept Here," pp. 145–72; Mesini, "Postille sulla biografia del 'Magister Gratianus,'" pp. 509–37.

8. Gratian, *Decretum* C. 27 q. 2 d.p.c. 18 and d.p.c. 28, C. 33 q. 5 c. 2.

9. Joannes Teutonicus, *Glossa ordinaria* to C. 32 q. 1 c. 11 v. *usus mali.*

10. Huguccio, *Summa* to D. 1 c. 7 v. *ut viri et femine coniunctio,* Vat. lat. 2280, fol. 2va, and BN lat. 3892, fol. 2va; see also John of Salisbury, *Policraticus* 8.11, 2:301.

11. Rolandus, *Summa* to C. 32 q. 6 c. 4, p. 182; Rufinus, *Summa* to C. 32 q. 6 pr., p. 491, followed almost verbatim by Joannes Faventinus's comments on the same passage in his *Summa,* in the British Library (hereafter cited as BL), MS. Royal 9.E.VII, fol. 144vb. Ulpian had observed much earlier (Dig. 48.5.14[13].5) that it seemed unjust for men to require a standard of sexual conduct from women that they did not observe themselves. See also Brundage, *Law, Sex, and Christian Society,* pp. 146, 306–7.

12. Saint Augustine, *Sermones* 492.4, PL 39:1711.

13. Rufinus, *Summa* to C. 32 q. 1 d.a.c. 11 v. *publice iudicis,* pp. 477–78; *Summa "Elegantius"* 4.7, 2:4; Sicard of Cremona, *Summa* to C. 32 q. 6, in BL MS. Add. 18367, fol. 60ra; and Joannes Faventinus, *Summa* to C. 33 q. 1 d.p.c. 10 v. *hoc in mulieribus,* in BL MS. Royal 9.E.VII, fol. 142ra (for the last two texts, see Brundage, *Law, Sex, and Christian Society,* pp. 320–21). Similarly, the grounds for divorce were supposed to be the same for men as for women, a view that Roman authorities had arrived at centuries before (*Novellae leges* 127.4). Inconsistently enough, however, it long remained true that a husband could base an action against his wife on suspicion alone, whereas a woman who sought to bring an adultery charge against her husband was obliged to furnish full legal proof (Rufinus, *Summa* to C. 32 q. 1 c. 2 v. *suspitio,* p. 476, followed verbatim by Joannes Faventinus in BL MS. Royal 9.E.VII, fol. 141vb; Stephen of Tournai, *Summa* to C. 2 q. 1 c. 13 v. *suspicionis arbitrio,* pp. 160–61; Sicard of Cremona, *Summa* to C. 32 q. 6, in BL MS. Add. 18367, fol. 60rb; anonymous gloss to C. 32 q. 1 c. 2 v. *suspicio,* in BL MS. Stowe 378, fol. 174vb [for the texts of Sicard and the Stowe gloss, see Brundage, *Law, Sex, and Christian Society,* p. 321]). This inconsistency disturbed canonists, however, and views on this matter began to change by the beginning of the thirteenth century (see *Decretales Gregorii IX* 2.16.2, as well as Joannes Teutonicus, *Glossa ordinaria* to C. 32 q. 1 c. 2 v. *suspicio* and d.p.c. 10 v. *accusationem,* as well as C. 33 q. 2 c. 1 v. *probabiliter*).

14. Gratian, *Decretum* C. 32 q. 4 c. 5; see also *Summa Parisiensis* to C. 32 q. 2 rubr. ad c. 2 v. *immoderatus* and C. 32 q. 4 c. 5 v. *deformis,* pp. 241, 243, and Rufinus, *Summa* to C. 32 q. 4 c. 5, p. 486.

15. This ambivalence about the morality of sexual pleasure is not, as is sometimes supposed, uniquely Christian. Several leading Greek philosophers of the classical age, for example, rejected autonomous pleasure as a worthy goal, and the orators of ancient Athens thought poorly of those who spent much time, trouble, or expense in the pursuit of sensual joys (see Dover, "Classical Greek Attitudes," pp. 59–73 at 63–64, and Brundage, *Law, Sex, and Christian Society,* pp. 12–21). Many Christian writers acknowledged that, at least in theory, sexual desire formed part of natural law, even though they felt constrained to restrict the outlet for that desire quite severely (thus, e.g., Isidore of Seville, quoted in Gratian, *Decretum* D. 1 c. 7).

16. Thus Gratian, *Decretum* D. 5 c. 2, reiterated in the *Summa "Elegantius"* 1.35, 1:9.

17. *Dig.* 24.1.32.13; Gratian, *Decretum* C. 27 q. 2 c. 1–5, and C. 30 q. 2 c. 1.

18. Fransen, "La Formation du lien matrimonial," pp. 106–26 at 118; Bailey, *Sexual Relation in Christian Thought,* p. 138; Gold, "Marriage of Mary and Joseph," pp. 102–17.

19. Huguccio, *Summa* to D. 13 pr., in Cambridge, Pembroke College, MS. 72, fol. 124vb, and Vat. lat. 2280, fol. 12ra; a slightly different version of this text, taken from Munich and Bamberg manuscripts, appears in Lindner, *Der Usus matrimonii,* p. 96 n. 20. See also Weigand, "Die Lehre der Kanonisten," pp. 443–78 at p. 472 n. 141.

20. Huguccio, *Summa* to C. 32 q. 2 c. 4 v. *set et alia plura sunt,* quoted by Weigand, "Die Lehre der Kanonisten," p. 472 n. 142; but cf. Joannes Teutonicus, *Glossa ordinaria* to C. 33 q. 4 c. 7 v. *voluptate.*

21. At least the canonists thought that they enjoyed it; legal writers also maintained that marriage for pleasure was valid, even if no good (i.e., nonpleasurable) goal was intended (C. 32 q. 2 d.p.c. 5 and c. 6).

22. Patristic writers, and Saint Augustine in particular, found the debt metaphor congenial and considerably enlarged on Saint Paul's treatment of it; see especially Augustine, *De bono coniugali* 7.6.

23. Gratian, *Decretum* C. 27 q. 2 d.p.c. 18.

24. Vaccari, "La tradizione canonica," pp. 535–47; Makowski, "Conjugal Debt," pp. 99–114.

25. Gratian, *Decretum* C. 33 q. 5 c. 4, 11, and 16 deal with the problem of married persons who entered religion and took vows of continence. For the crusade and conjugal rights, see my "Crusader's Wife," pp. 427–41.

26. Joannes Teutonicus, *Glossa ordinaria* to C. 11 q. 3 c. 103 v. *de uxoribus;* Joannes Andrea, *Novella* to X 5.39.31; Vodola, *Excommunication,* pp. 64–65.

27. C. 32 q. 1 c. 5–6.

28. Joannes Teutonicus, *Glossa ordinaria* to C. 32 q. 1 c. 5 v. *sub cautela* and to C. 33 q. 2 pr. v. *sed queritur;* Brundage, *Law, Sex, and Christian Society,* pp. 505–6. For the formulas used in these cases, see Herde, *Audientia litterarum contradictarum* 2:299–305.

29. Joannes Teutonicus, *Glossa ordinaria* to C. 32 q. 1 c. 4 v. *non ad imparia* and C. 32 q. 6 c. 2 v. *intactam.*

30. E.g., 1 Cor. 11:3, 7–11; Eph. 5:21–24; Col. 3:18; on canonistic treatments of these passages, see Metz, "Recherches," pp. 92–99.

31. Børresen, *Subordination et équivalence,* pp. 86–89, 204–5, 258–60; Zeimentz, *Ehe nach der Lehre der Frühscholastik,* p. 220.

32. For criticism of the drive-reduction model, see Gagnon and Simon, *Sexual Conduct,* p. 285.

33. Noonan, "Marital Affection," pp. 479–509. This idea also had important implications for nonmarital unions, as I earlier indicated in "Concubinage and Marriage," pp. 1–17.

34. There is, of course, no necessary relationship between sex itself and the emotional involvement that society ascribes to sexual relations. The degree of affective investment is, however, related to the normative significance that a society attaches to sexual relations. Thus, the growth of the notion that "marital affection" (in the sense of emotional bonding) is an essential element of marriage affirms the social importance of sexual activity (see also Gagnon and Simon, *Sexual Conduct*, pp. 306–7).

35. On this ambivalence, see Zeimentz, *Ehe nach der Lehre der Frühscholastik*, p. 236; see also Leibbrand and Leibbrand, *Formen des Eros* 1:570–71.

BIBLIOGRAPHY

Primary Sources

Andreae, Joannes. *In quinque decretalium libros novella commentaria.* 1581. Reprint (5 vols. in 4). Turin, 1963.

Augustine, Saint. *De bono coniugali.* Ed. Joseph Zycha. Corpus scriptorum ecclesiasticorum Latinorum, vol. 41. Vienna, 1900.

———. *Sermones.* In *Patrologiae cursus completus . . . series Latina,* ed. J.-P. Migne, 38:23–1484, 39:1493–1736. Paris, 1844–64.

Bernard of Parma. *Glossa ordinaria in Decretales Gregorii IX.* In *Corpus iuris canonici* (Venice, 1605), vol. 3.

Codex Iustinianus. Ed. Paul Krueger. In *Corpus iuris civilis,* vol. 2.

Corpus iuris canonici. Ed. Emil Friedberg. 2 vols. 1879. Reprint. Graz, 1959.

———. 4 vols. Venice, 1605.

Corpus iuris civilis. Ed. Theodor Mommsen, Paul Krueger, Rudolf Schoell, and Wilhelm Kroll. 3 vols. Berlin, 1872–95.

Decretales Gregorii IX. In *Corpus iuris canonici,* ed. Emil Friedberg, vol. 2.

Gratian. *Decretum Gratiani.* In *Corpus iuris canonici,* ed. Emil Friedberg, vol. 1.

Hostiensis. *In quinque decretalium libri commentaria.* 1581. Reprint (5 vols. in 2). Turin, 1965.

Huguccio. *Summa.* Cambridge, Pembroke College, MS. 72.

———. *Summa.* Vatican City, Biblioteca Apostolica Vaticana, MS. 2280.

———. *Summa.* Paris, Bibliothèque nationale, MS. lat. 3892.

Joannes Faventinus. *Summa.* London, British Library, MS. Royal 9.E.VII.

———. *Summa.* London, British Library, MS. Add. 18369.

Joannes Teutonicus. *Glossa ordinaria in Decretum Gratiani.* In *Corpus iuris canonici* (Venice, 1605), vols. 1–2.

John of Salisbury. *Policraticus, sive de nugis curialium et vestigiis philosophorum libri VIII.* Ed. C. C. J. Webb. 2 vols. 1909. Reprint. Frankfurt am Main, 1965.

Justinian. *Digest of Justinian.* Ed. Theodor Mommsen and Paul Krueger, trans. Alan Watson et al. 4 vols. Philadelphia, 1985.

——— . *Digest of Justinian.* In *Corpus iuris civilis*, vol. 1.

Liber extra. See *Decretales Gregorii IX.*

Monumenta iuris canonici. Vatican City, 1965–. Series A, Corpus collectionum, 7 vols. to date; Series B, Corpus glossatorum, 5 vols. to date; Series C, Subsidia, 8 vols. to date.

Novellae leges. Ed. Rudolf Schoell and Wilhelm Kroll. In *Corpus iuris civilis*, vol. 3.

Rolandus. *Die summa magistri Rolandi nachmals Papstes Alexander III.* Ed. Friedrich Thaner. Innsbruck, 1874.

Rufinus. *Summa decretorum.* Ed. Heinrich Singer. 1902. Reprint. Aalen, 1963.

Sicard of Cremona. *Summa.* London, British Library, MS. Add. 18367.

Stephen of Tournai. *Die summa des Stephanus Tornacensis über das Decretum Gratiani.* Ed. Johann Friedrich von Schulte. 1891. Reprint. Aalen, 1965.

Stowe glosses. London, British Library, MS. Stowe 378.

Summa "Elegantius in iure diuino" seu Coloniensis. Ed. Gérard Fransen and Stephan Kuttner. In *Monumenta iuris canonici*, Corpus glossatorum, vol. 1. Vatican City, 1969–.

Summa Parisiensis on the Decretum Gratiani. Ed. Terence P. McLaughlin. Toronto, 1952.

Thomas Aquinas, Saint. *Opera omnia ut sunt in indice Thomistico.* Ed. Roberto Busa. 7 vols. Holzboog, 1980.

Secondary Sources

Artz, Frederick B. *The Mind of the Middle Ages, 200–1500.* 3d ed. New York, 1962.

Bailey, Derrick S. *Sexual Relation in Christian Thought.* New York, 1959.

Børresen, Kari Elisabeth. *Subordination et équivalence: Nature et rôle de la femme d'après Augustin et Thomas d'Aquin.* Oslo, 1968.

Brundage, James A. "Concubinage and Marriage in Medieval Canon Law." *Journal of Medieval History* 1 (1975): 1–17.

——— . "The Crusader's Wife: A Canonistic Quandary." *Studia Gratiana* 12 (1967): 425–42.

——— . "The Crusader's Wife Revisited." *Studia Gratiana* 14 (1967): 241–52.

——— . *Law, Sex, and Christian Society in Medieval Europe.* Chicago, 1987.

Bullough, Vern L., and James A. Brundage, eds. *Sexual Practices and the Medieval Church.* Buffalo, N.Y., 1982.

Dover, J. K. "Classical Greek Attitudes to Sexual Behavior." *Arethusa* 6 (1973): 59–73.

Fransen, Gérard. "La Formation du lien matrimonial au moyen âge." *Revue de droit canonique* 21 (1971): 106–26.

Gagnon, John H., and William Simon. *Sexual Conduct: The Social Sources of Human Sexuality.* Chicago, 1973.

Gold, Penny S. "The Marriage of Mary and Joseph in the Twelfth-Century Ideology of Marriage." In *Sexual Practices and the Medieval Church*, ed. Vern L. Bullough and James A. Brundage, pp. 102–17. Buffalo, N.Y., 1982.

Heer, Friedrich. *The Medieval World*. New York, 1963.

Herde, Peter. *Audientia litterarum contradictarum: Untersuchungen über die päpstlichen Justizbriefe und die päpstliche Delegationsgerichtsbarkeit vom 13. bis zum Beginn des 16. Jahrhunderts*. 2 vols. Tübingen, 1970.

Herlihy, David. "Land, Family, and Women in Continental Europe, 701–1200." *Traditio* 18 (1962): 89–120.

Kuttner, Stephan. "The Father of the Science of Canon Law." *Jurist* 1 (1941): 2–19.

———. *Harmony from Dissonance: An Interpretation of Medieval Canon Law*. Latrobe, Pa., 1960.

LeBras, Gabriel, Charles Lefebvre, and Jacqueline Rambaud. *L'Âge classique, 1140–1378: Sources et théorie du droit*. Histoire du droit et des institutions de l'église en occident, vol. 7. Paris, 1965.

Leibbrand, Annemarie, and Werner Leibbrand. *Formen des Eros: Kultur- und Geistesgeschichte der Liebe*. 2 vols. Orbus academicus: Problemgeschichten der Wissenschaft in Dokumenten und Darstellungen, vol. 31. Freiburg, 1972.

Lindner, Dominikus. *Der Usus matrimonii: Eine Untersuchung über seine sittliche Bewertung in der katholischen Moraltheologie alter und neuer Zeit*. Munich, 1929.

Makowski, Elizabeth M. "The Conjugal Debt and Medieval Canon Law." *Journal of Medieval History* 3 (1977): 99–114.

Mesini, C. "Postille sulla biografia del 'Magister Gratianus,' padre del diritto canonico." *Apollinaris* 54 (1981): 509–37.

Metz, René. "Recherches sur le statut de la femme en droit canonique: Bilan historique et perspectives d'avenir; problèmes de méthode." *Année canonique* 12 (1968): 85–113.

Noonan, John T., Jr. "Gratian Slept Here: The Changing Identity of the Father of the Systematic Study of Canon Law." *Traditio* 35 (1979): 145–72.

———. "Marital Affection in the Canonists." *Studia Gratiana* 12 (1967): 479–509.

Previté-Orton, C. W. *The Shorter Cambridge Medieval History*. 2 vols. Cambridge, 1952.

Ullmann, Walter. *The Growth of Papal Government in the Middle Ages: A Study in the Ideological Relation of Clerical to Lay Power*. 2d ed. London, 1962.

———. *A History of Political Theory: The Middle Ages*. Harmondsworth, 1965.

———. *Law and Politics in the Middle Ages*. London, 1975.

———. *Principles of Government and Politics in the Middle Ages*. London, 1961.

Vaccari, Pietro. "La Tradizione canonica del 'debitum' coniugale e la posizione di Graziano." *Studia Gratiana* 1 (1953): 533–47.

Vodola, Elizabeth. *Excommunication in the Middle Ages.* Berkeley, 1986.

Weigand, Rudolf. "Die Lehre der Kanonisten des 12. und 13. Jahrhunderts von den Ehezwecken." *Studia Gratiana* 12 (1967): 443–78.

Zeimentz, Hans. *Ehe nach der Lehre der Frühscholastik: Eine moralgeschichtliche Untersuchung zur Anthropologie und Theologie der Ehe in der Schule Anselms von Laon und Wilhelm von Champeaux, bei Hugo von St. Viktor, Walter von Mortaigne und Petrus Lombardus.* Moraltheologische Studien, vol. 1. Düsseldorf, 1973.

GERMAN SOURCE COLLECTIONS

The Archdiocese of Salzburg as a Case Study

John B. Freed

lthough German historians, particularly before World War I, contributed greatly to the study of medieval women through their investigations of such topics as women's legal rights, their social and economic position in the late medieval city, and their involvement in medieval religious movements, women's history as such has until very recently attracted little attention in the German-speaking world. As Martha Howell points out, there has been even less interest in "the larger questions of gender, sexuality, socio-economic structure, ideology, and historical change that inform feminist historical scholarship elsewhere." She attributes this to the Rankean tradition in German historiography, with its preoccupation with national history and its emphasis upon the primacy of politics.[1] ❡ Edith Ennen's *Frauen im Mittelalter* reveals, as Howell suggests,[2] the strengths and weaknesses of German scholarship. While it is not a study of medieval German women per se, the work draws heavily upon German examples. As one might expect of a distinguished urban historian, Ennen is at her best when talking about women in the area of her expertise, the late medieval German city. The rest of the book is largely a synthesis of the secondary literature, much of it anecdotes about famous queens. The weakest part of Ennen's book is the section on the High Middle Ages, the period from 1050 to 1250, to which she devotes only 43 of the 243 pages of text and which includes 2 pages on the Fair Maid of Kent, who died in 1385; in contrast, there are 53 pages about the status of women in the late medieval German city. Ennen discusses the formation of the patrilineal lineage in a short paragraph,[3] but she appears to have been unfamiliar with Georges Duby's contention that the emerging patrilineal lineages deliberately limited after 1000 the inheritance rights of women and tried to prevent younger sons from marrying.[4] She thus overlooks the possible connection be-

[margin handwritten note:] focus on political aspects of women instead of social

tween this change in family structure and strategy and the proliferation of convents during the High Middle Ages. As Suzanne Fonay Wemple concludes in her review of Ennen's book, "This book gives much information on women over a span of one thousand years but, except for city dwellers in Germany, it does not offer detailed and deep historical insights. It can best serve as a textbook on women's lives in the Middle Ages, to be read by those interested in German historiography on women. The section on the participation of German women in urban life is commendable but, even in this area, new observations are beginning to be published by scholars."[5] Nevertheless, Ennen's bibliography is undoubtedly the best available guide to German historiography about medieval women.[6]

Although we will never know as much as we would like to know about high medieval German women, we can obtain more information than appears in Ennen's book from the vast collections of documents that German, Austrian, and Swiss scholars have been publishing since the eighteenth century. Most pre-1300 documents have been reproduced by now in some form, and a good many late medieval documents are also available in print. Since temporal institutions of government that preserved records developed very slowly in Germany, most of the surviving documentation from the High Middle Ages is of ecclesiastical provenance. The most complete listing of these source collections can be found in Dahlmann-Waitz, *Quellenkunde der deutschen Geschichte: Bibliographie der Quellen und der Literatur zur deutschen Geschichte.*[7] Regrettably, very few American university libraries possess a copy of Dahlmann-Waitz, but any book that deals with a general topic in medieval German history—for instance, Benjamin Arnold's *German Knighthood, 1050–1300,* or my own *The Friars and German Society in the Thirteenth Century*—is likely to contain a fairly extensive bibliography of source collections.

The collections are generally organized in accordance with the boundaries of the German states of the nineteenth century; for instance, the *Wirtembergisches Urkundenbuch* contains documents written before 1300 that pertain to the area that belonged to the Napoleonic kingdom of Württemberg, a state that bore no resemblance to any medieval political entity. Many of the late medieval documents from Württemberg were published in the *Württembergische Geschichtsquellen* and in the *Württembergische Regesten von 1301 bis 1500.* This is a good example of the vast extent of these collections. It was the most important German states —Austria, Bavaria, Brandenburg, and Saxony—that took the lead in publishing their sources, and it is precisely these collections that are in the greatest need of revision. The older collections—for instance, the *Monumenta Boica*—tend to be organized by provenance; that is, a specific volume contains the documents from a specific institution. This is useful if one wishes to examine, say, a particular monastery, but it is less helpful if one wishes to study, say, the nobles of a particular area who are likely to have been mentioned in the records of different institutions. More recent collections like the *Wirtembergisches Urkundenbuch* have therefore generally followed a chronological approach; that is, all the documents from the prescribed area and time period, regardless of provenance, are contained in a specific volume.

The best way to discuss the organization and content of the collections is to cite a specific example. I have selected the archdiocese of Salzburg because it is the area with which I am most familiar. The archdiocese stretched from the Inn River and its tributary, the Isen, in southeastern Bavaria, across the modern Austrian provinces of Salzburg, Carinthia, and Styria, to as far south as the Drava, in what is now northern Yugoslavia. The ecclesiastical principality comprised not only the present-day province of Salzburg but also the Rupertiwinkel, a strip of territory on the left bank of the Salzach between the Saalach and Tittmoning that was ceded to Bavaria in 1816, and the Ziller valley, which was assigned to the Tyrol in 1810. The archbishops had extensive holdings throughout the archdiocese and were also the temporal rulers of Mühldorf in Upper Bavaria, Friesach, Carinthia, and Pettau, Styria (now Ptuj, Yugoslavia). In addition, they were the lords of a territory of approximately three hundred square kilometers surrounding the city of Rann (Brezice) on the Sava, more than four hundred kilometers from the city of Salzburg. This lordship in what was until 1919 Lower or Southern Styria was under the spiritual jurisdiction of the patriarch of Aquileia. The area under the archbishop's spiritual and temporal jurisdiction was thus situated in three modern nations and four Austrian provinces.

Because the source collections are generally organized in accordance with modern rather than medieval boundaries, anyone interested in the archdiocese is forced to employ several collections. The chief source is the *Salzburger Urkundenbuch*. Abbot Hauthaler of St. Peter's in Salzburg published the first part of the first volume in 1898. It contains two eighth-century summaries of Salzburg's rights and holdings; the *Traditionsbücher* of five archbishops who presided over the church between 923 and 1060; the codex of traditions of St. Peter's, which contains 681 entries dating from 987 to 1297; the 373 entries in the *Traditionsbuch* of the cathedral chapter, which date from 1058 to 1264; 169 notices recorded between 1072 and 1459 (only a handful is from later than 1267) in the *Traditionsbuch* of the small Benedictine monastery of Michael-beuern; 19 notices, written between 860 and 1263, that have been reconstructed from the lost *Traditionsbuch* of the Benedictine abbey and collegiate church of Mattsee; and 27 notices, made between the eighth and twelfth centuries in the *Traditionsbuch* of the Benedictine abbey of Mondsee in the diocese of Passau, that pertain to the Austrian province of Salzburg. The entire collection of Mondsee traditions was published in the Upper Austrian collection *Urkundenbuch des Landes ob der Enns*, volume 1, which also contains the traditions of Reichersberg and Suben, archiepiscopal proprietary churches of Augustinian canons situated in the diocese of Passau.

The *Traditionsbücher* are a major source for the study of Austro-Bavarian history between the eighth and thirteenth centuries. Some of the entries are summaries of charters, most of which are now lost, and were made either when the charter was written or at some later date. In most cases, however, no formal written document was ever drafted. The notices were simply devices to record the identity of individuals who had witnessed a particular transaction that was summarized in the *Traditions-buch* and who could be summoned to testify if the proceedings were ever challenged; the *Traditionsbücher* themselves had no legal standing. Most ecclesiastical institutions gradually ceased making entries in their *Traditionsbücher* sometime in the thirteenth century, when charters became the preferred form of proof.[8] While women could not serve as witnesses, they were frequent participants in the transactions described in the notices. The *Traditionsbücher* are thus probably the best source for studying the status of women in the Austro-Bavarian area before 1300.

Volumes 2 and 3 of the *Salzburger Urkundenbuch* contain 1,100 charters or entries from *Traditionsbücher*, not published in the first volume, that pertain to the archbishop or the modern province of Salzburg in the period between 790 and 1246. Half of these (vol. 3) are from the archiepiscopate of Eberhard II (1200–46), the creator of the ecclesiastical principality. Virtually all of the extant documentation prior to the interregnum that directly concerns the archbishop and modern province of Salzburg has thus been published. The volumes are meticulously indexed, and all places are identified as carefully as possible. The fourth volume contains Franz Martin's selection of 390 important or representative documents dating from 1247 to 1343. In addition, Martin summarized approximately 4,000 documents in *Die Regesten der Erzbischöfe und des Domkapitels von Salzburg, 1247–1343*. The vast increase in the surviving documentation from the period after the Interregnum necessitated this change in format.

The documents from the Bavarian portion of the archdiocese are not as accessible. In some cases (for instance, the *Traditionsbücher* of the Augustinian collegiate churches of Baumburg and Herrenchiemsee), it is still necessary to rely on the eighteenth-century editions in the *Monumenta Boica*, though a new edition of the Herrenchiemsee traditions is being prepared. The texts of the notices are incomplete, dated only approximately, and poorly indexed. The *Quellen und Erörterungen zur bayerischen und deutschen Geschichte* contains better texts of much of the material in the *Monumenta Boica*. The edition of the *Schenkungsbuch* of Berchtesgaden in the first volume of the old series needs to be redone, but later volumes in the new series that contain material pertaining to the archdiocese are excellent: the codex of traditions of the Cistercian abbey of Raitenhaslach; the charters of Raitenhaslach; the twelfth-century *Codex Falkensteinensis*, the only *Traditionsbuch* from a secular lordship; and the codex of traditions, charters, and manorial register of the Augustinian canons of Gars, an archiepiscopal proprietary house. An edition of the *Traditionsbuch* of Au, another archiepiscopal proprietary house of Augustinian canons, appeared in 1880,[9] but work is under way on a new edition. [10]

The documents of the duchy of Carinthia have been published in the *Monumenta historica ducatus Carinthiae*. The first four volumes were published by August von Jaksch between 1896 and 1906. The first two contain the documents pertaining to the Carinthian bishopric of Gurk, an archiepiscopal proprietary bishopric situated within the archdiocese, from the period between 864 and 1269. More than 3,000 other Carinthian documents from the period before the end of Spanheimer rule in 1269 appear in the third and fourth volumes. Publication of the Carinthian documents resumed in 1956 under the leadership of Hermann Wiessner, the provincial archivist. Volumes 5 through 9 cover the period between the end of Spanheimer rule in 1269 and the accession of the Hapsburgs in 1335; the remaining two volumes include material from 1335 to 1500. Regrettably, there is a notable decline in the quality of the later volumes. The documents are usually merely summarized, often incompletely, and the indexes are not as complete as those in the earlier volumes prepared by Jaksch. The sheer quantity of the material may be partly responsible for this.

The first three volumes of the *Urkundenbuch des Herzogtums Steiermark*, which were published between 1875 and 1903, contain material from 798 to the end of Hungarian control of Styria in 1260. The fourth volume, which appeared in installments only between 1960 and 1975, contains 606 documents dating from 1260 to 1276, when King Ottokar II of Bohemia was the ruler of the duchy. Styria is defined in this documentary collection in accordance with its pre-1919 boundaries. The *Urkundenbücher* thus include material from the southern portion of Styria, an area of more than five thousand square kilometers, which was under the spiritual jurisdiction of the archbishop of Salzburg and the patriarch of Aquileia. Once again, the increase in documentation from the late Middle Ages has necessitated a change in format: documents written after the murder of King Albrecht I in 1308 are summarized rather than reproduced in their entirety. The first volume in this new undertaking, the *Regesten des Herzogtums Steiermark*, which covers the period from 1308 to 1319, is difficult to use because it lacks an index, but this deficiency should be remedied in a later volume. At present, Friedrich Hausmann is also working on a new edition of the first three volumes of the *Urkundenbuch des Herzogtums Steiermark*. Hausmann has been able to find and to reconstruct many more of the traditions and charters of the Benedictine abbey of Admont that were destroyed in a fire at the beginning of the nineteenth century.[11] Their reconstruction may alter our understanding of twelfth-century Styrian history.

One other source collection that concerns the archdiocese needs to be mentioned. The second volume of the meticulously indexed *Necrologia Germaniae* contains the books of remembrance and necrologies from the archdiocese. Karl Schmid and his students have demonstrated that these long-neglected sources are a gold mine for the study of medieval social and political history.[12] It remains to be seen how these necrologies can be exploited as a source for studying medieval women.

I have described in some detail the collections that pertain to the archdiocese of Salzburg, but it should be stressed that there are similar collections for most of the German-speaking world. The only way a reader can familiarize himself or herself with a specific collection is by using it.

How, in fact, can any of these collections be employed to study family history and the history of women in particular? The collections are, after all, the product of German particularism, assembled in large part to provide historical legitimacy for the regnant houses and to arouse local patriotism. (For instance, the traditions of Au, Gars, and the Falkensteins were published in 1880 to commemorate the seven-hundredth anniversary of Wittelsbach rule in Bavaria.)[13] This is one of the reasons why nationalistic German historians have been so reluctant to study local history and to investigate topics (such as family history) that lend themselves to such an approach. The documents themselves, except for an occasional oddity like the *Codex Falkensteinensis,* are largely the records of ecclesiastical corporations and their property acquisitions and losses, disputes, privileges, and so forth, not the records of secular institutions of government, let alone of families.

Nevertheless, the collections can be used to reconstruct the history of a particular lineage or group of lineages from a specific stratum of society in a given area. The indexes to the collections are the starting point. A file is created on every toponymic surname—such surnames were adopted in the archdiocese in around 1100—and a subfile is created on every individual who employed the name. Then every reference to the lineage and its members is noted. Special attention has to be paid to references to unnamed individuals—for example, passing references to unnamed children or, conversely, to children who might yet be born. Of course, as the case of the Pettaus will show, lineages could change their surnames with remarkable rapidity when a family acquired a notable maternal inheritance. Nevertheless, it becomes possible in this way to reconstruct not only the genealogies and property holdings of families but also such things as approximate age of marriage and life expectancy. For instance, one can note when an individual first appeared as a witness with his father and when he in turn served as a witness with his son. Sometimes there is only a single reference to an individual who employed a particular toponym, but other lineages can be followed for generations. All such studies must be prosopographical because of the gaps in the evidence and the variations in family strategies. Inevitably, the documentation provides much more information about men than women because only men served as witnesses and men normally represented the lineage in public, but there is also information about women.

I will apply this methodology to a model case study of the female members of one lineage of archiepiscopal ministerials, the Pettaus and their cadet branches, during the twelfth and thirteenth centuries and raise some questions suggested by the history of the Pettaus about the status of medieval German women in general in the hope that other scholars will be inspired to undertake similar investigations.[14] The Pettaus were for three hundred years the hereditary burgraves of Pettau and were before their extinction in 1438 the second most powerful noble family in Styria.[15] Presenting the material in this fashion inevitably overstresses the patrilineal character of medieval family structure. As we shall see, surnames could also be transmitted by women from one lineage to another—in the case of Montpreis, from the older Montpreises, via the Pettaus, to the Scharfenbergs, some of whom then became the newer Montpreises. We will need many more such studies of individual families before we will be able to generalize about the status of medieval German women, and all such generalizations will have to take into account chronological, regional, and social differences. My purpose here is simply to suggest what can be gleaned from the sources about the women who were associated by birth or marriage with one ministerial lineage.

❦ The archbishops established themselves in the former Roman city of Poetovio, the modern Ptuj, Yugoslavia, during the ninth century. Emperor Otto II confirmed in 982 a forged charter of Arnulf of Carinthia, in which the king had allegedly granted Salzburg the church and tithes in Pettau, two-thirds of the city, and the court, tolls, and bridge. Thereafter, the archbishops exercised sole jurisdiction in Pettau.[16] Upon his return from exile in 1121, Archbishop Conrad I built a new castle on the Schlossberg in place of a ruined older castle to protect the Drava valley from Hungarian incursions.[17] The history of the lineage began with the construction of this castle.

There are two references to a Frederick of Pettau in the 1130s (see *Genealogical Chart of the Pettaus*).[18] Because the next reference to a Frederick of Pettau occurs only in 1153[19] and because a Frederick of Pettau was not a member of the archiepiscopal entourage between 1139 and 1146 during Archbishop Conrad I's nearly yearly visits to Carinthia and Styria,[20] the best guess is that Frederick I died in the late 1130s and left behind a son, Frederick II, who was still a minor. We have some clues about the ancestry of Frederick I, the founder of the Pettau lineage. Frederick III was in 1215 the lord of the castle of Stein, five kilometers northeast of the monastery of St. Paul's in the Lavant valley in Carinthia, and in 1245 Frederick III's sons, Frederick IV and Hartnid I, surrendered to St. Paul's their patronage of and all their other rights to the chapel of St. Georgen, two kilometers south of Stein.[21] A Frederick of Petra, that is, Stein, witnessed in the 1120s three documents that involved St. Paul's.[22] Moreover, Hans Pirchegger, who studied the Pettau lineage, observed that Frederick was a rare name in the eastern Alps before 1122 and that Frederick I might have accompanied Archbishop Conrad I (1106–47) from Bavaria to Salzburg.[23] As it happens, a Frederick of Bavaria witnessed an entry in the *Traditionsbuch* of St. Paul's in 1106.[24] Fred-

GENEALOGICAL CHART OF THE PETTAUS

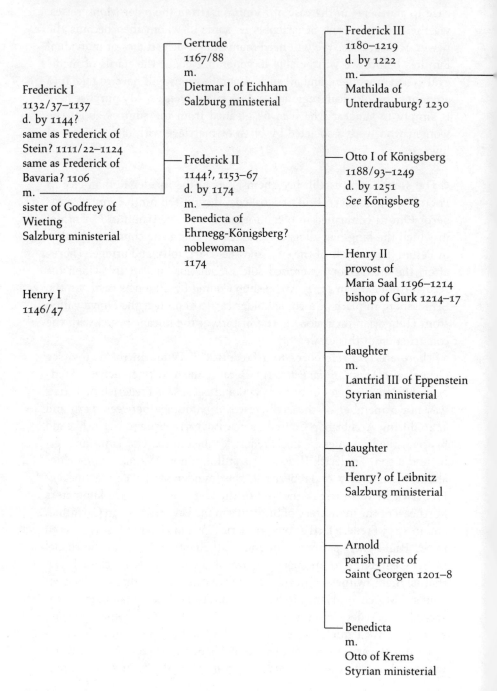

Frederick I
1132/37–1137
d. by 1144?
same as Frederick of
Stein? 1111/22–1124
same as Frederick of
Bavaria? 1106
m. ——————————
sister of Godfrey of
Wieting
Salzburg ministerial

Henry I
1146/47

—— Gertrude
1167/88
m.
Dietmar I of Eichham
Salzburg ministerial

—— Frederick II
1144?, 1153–67
d. by 1174
m. ——————————
Benedicta of
Ehrnegg-Königsberg?
noblewoman
1174

—— Frederick III
1180–1219
d. by 1222
m. ——————————————
Mathilda of
Unterdrauburg? 1230

—— Otto I of Königsberg
1188/93–1249
d. by 1251
See Königsberg

—— Henry II
provost of
Maria Saal 1196–1214
bishop of Gurk 1214–17

—— daughter
m.
Lantfrid III of Eppenstein
Styrian ministerial

—— daughter
m.
Henry? of Leibnitz
Salzburg ministerial

—— Arnold
parish priest of
Saint Georgen 1201–8

—— Benedicta
m.
Otto of Krems
Styrian ministerial

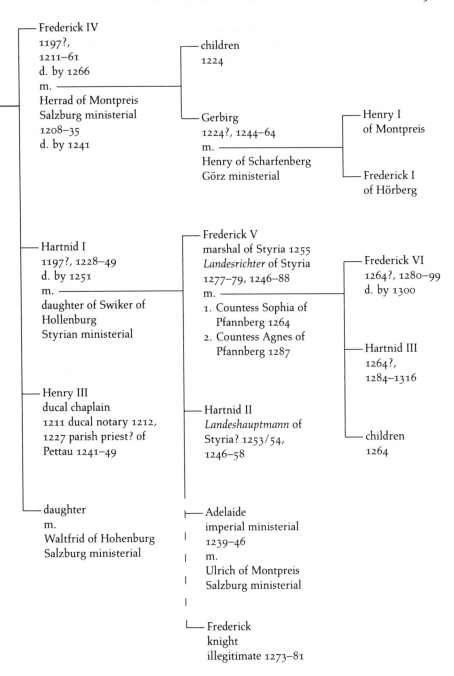

Frederick IV
1197?,
1211–61
d. by 1266
m.
Herrad of Montpreis
Salzburg ministerial
1208–35
d. by 1241

children
1224

Gerbirg
1224?, 1244–64
m.
Henry of Scharfenberg
Görz ministerial

Henry I
of Montpreis

Frederick I
of Hörberg

Hartnid I
1197?, 1228–49
d. by 1251
m.
daughter of Swiker of
Hollenburg
Styrian ministerial

Frederick V
marshal of Styria 1255
Landesrichter of Styria
1277–79, 1246–88
m.
1. Countess Sophia of
   Pfannberg 1264
2. Countess Agnes of
   Pfannberg 1287

Frederick VI
1264?, 1280–99
d. by 1300

Hartnid III
1264?,
1284–1316

Henry III
ducal chaplain
1211 ducal notary 1212,
1227 parish priest? of
Pettau 1241–49

Hartnid II
Landeshauptmann of
Styria? 1253/54,
1246–58

children
1264

daughter
m.
Waltfrid of Hohenburg
Salzburg ministerial

Adelaide
imperial ministerial
1239–46
m.
Ulrich of Montpreis
Salzburg ministerial

Frederick
knight
illegitimate 1273–81

Dates included in the chart refer either to specific dates of office or to first and last
appearances in the source material.

erick I may thus have been a Bavarian who settled initially in Stein in the Lavant valley and who then became in the 1130s the burgrave of the newly built archiepiscopal castle of Pettau in southern Styria at the fringes of German settlement in southeastern Europe.

His son Frederick II served as a witness between 1153 and 1167 and was dead by 1174.[25] Frederick II became embroiled in a bitter dispute with his uncle, the Carinthian archiepiscopal ministerial Godfrey of Wieting, about the latter's disposition of his property. Shortly before Archbishop Conrad's death on 9 April 1147, the childless Godfrey and his wife, Adela, gave Admont their property situated in Muggenau, eight kilometers northwest of Leibnitz, Styria, and conferred their other alods to St. Peter's. If there was sufficient property to endow a monastery, an abbey was to be built on their chief alod, Wieting, after their deaths. [26]

In making these arrangements, Godfrey did not pay any attention to the potential claims of his nephews Frederick II of Pettau and Frederick I of Deutsch-Landsberg. Godfrey and his nephews appeared together as witnesses until 25 December 1161,[27] but Archbishop Eberhard I reported on 20 December 1163 that the Devil had incited Godfrey's nephews against him and St. Peter's. They had rejected all of Godfrey's offers of compensation, which he had made to them in the archbishop's presence, and had burned and pillaged Godfrey's land. They had finally renounced their claims to Wieting only after Eberhard had admonished and excommunicated them. To preserve the peace, Abbot Henry enfeoffed Frederick of Pettau on the archbishop's advice with eight hides and gave twenty marks to Frederick of Deutsch-Landsberg.[28] Frederick II's descendants continued until 1240 to trouble St. Peter's about the Wieting inheritance. [29]

Frederick II's claims to Wieting provide the only evidence about the identity of his mother; his mother and the mother of Frederick I of Deutsch-Landsberg presumably were the sisters of Godfrey of Wieting. Since the father of Frederick of Deutsch-Landsberg, Poppo of St. Ulrich, appears to have been a younger son who came from the Chiemgau in Upper Bavaria,[30] it would appear that both Frederick I of Stein-Pettau and Poppo established themselves in Carinthia and Styria, respectively, by marrying the sisters of one of the most powerful archiepiscopal ministerials in Carinthia. We do not know precisely what lands, if any, these Bavarian emigrants acquired through their marriages, but it is worth noting that Stein is situated about thirty-five kilometers southeast of Wieting as the crow flies and that there is an Ulrichskirche, the probable source of Poppo's toponym, in Frauenthal, three kilometers east of Deutsch-Landsberg, the toponym adopted by Poppo's son, and sixteen kilometers west of Muggenau, which Godfrey of Wieting gave to Admont. Frederick I and Poppo may thus have acquired Stein and St. Ulrich, respectively, from their Wieting wives. Marriage was one way that ambitious men from the German heartland, especially younger sons, could establish themselves on the southeastern German frontier.

Maternal uncles like Godfrey, who have been called "a kind of 'male mother,'"[31] often played a large role in the education of the fatherless sons of their sisters. It was only natural that a widow would turn to her brother for assistance. The mutual devotion of Charlemagne and Roland in *The Song of Roland* is the classic literary example, but such bonds between maternal uncles and their nephews can also be found among the archiepiscopal ministerials during the twelfth century.[32] A similar relationship may have existed between Godfrey of Wieting and Frederick II of Pettau. Godfrey and his nephew Frederick witnessed an archiepiscopal charter in Leibnitz in May 1144.[33] While we cannot be absolutely certain which Frederick was meant—Frederick II or Frederick of Deutsch-Landsberg—Frederick II's cousin accompanied his father on this occasion to Leibnitz.[34] It would appear, therefore, that Godfrey served as Frederick II's guardian after the death of Frederick I in the late 1130s, and the two men continued to witness documents together after Frederick II attained his majority. The appearance of nephews with their maternal uncles can thus serve as a gauge for measuring the continued importance of enates, even after the establishment of patrilineal lineages.

In spite of these apparently close ties between Godfrey and Frederick II, Godfrey left his lands to Admont and St. Peter's rather than to his nephews; nor was he the only maternal uncle who acted in this fashion. Henry of Seekirchen, the first archiepiscopal ministerial to serve as the burgrave of Hohensalzburg, bequeathed in 1139 his alods to St. Peter's, the cathedral chapter, and the Nonnberg, the Benedictine convent in the city of Salzburg, rather than to his sister's son, Henry of Högl, with whom the burgrave had been closely associated for years. The ensuing dispute dragged on for a century.[35] Archbishops Conrad I and Eberhard I, who were involved in both the Wieting and Seekirchen inheritance disputes, were seemingly unconcerned about any possible claims by Godfrey's and Henry's nephews. The only possible explanation is that sisters' sons, at least among the archiepiscopal ministerials in the mid–twelfth century, had no legal right to the alods and fiefs of their maternal uncles, though Frederick II of Pettau, Frederick of Deutsch-Landsberg, and Henry of Högl clearly felt that they did. Inheritance customs and what they reveal about kinship structure and family identity in specific regions in a given time period need to be studied in more detail.

As the Wieting inheritance dispute shows, property disputes often provide the only indication of a connection between lineages. We do not know even the names of Godfrey of Wieting's sisters, who married Frederick I of Pettau and Poppo of St. Ulrich. In some cases the fate of a piece of property offers the only clue about the identity of a married woman's family of origin. For instance, the subsequent history of Kirchberg, four kilometers northeast of Wieting, supplies us with the name of a likely sister of Frederick II of Pettau. In 1266 Frederick V of Pettau granted St. Peter's the patronage of the church in Kirchberg, which he and his fellow heirs had inherited from their ancestors, presumably the Wietings.[36] In 1167/88 G. (Gertrude?) had given to St. Peter's her alod situated in Kirchberg. Her husband, the archiepiscopal ministerial and marshal Dietmar I of Eichham, was listed among the witnesses, but there is no indication that Dietmar gave his consent.[37] The best explanation for why a woman who lived in Bavaria could dispose freely of alodial property located in Carinthia is that it formed part of her own inheritance. The subsequent history of Kirchberg suggests that Gertrude was a Pettau and, judging by the date of her gift, the sister of Frederick II.

If this identification is correct, it is worth noting that Gertrude's share of the Pettau inheritance consisted at least in part of land that had formed part of her mother's Wieting inheritance (that is, the Pettaus tried to minimize the losses entailed by Gertrude's marriage by providing her with land marginal to the lineage's main interest) and that Gertrude's marriage to Dietmar had involved considerable geographical mobility on her part, namely, relocation from southern Styria to Bavaria. Such far-flung marriages point to the role that women (and not only queens like Eleanor of Aquitaine or Beatrice of Burgundy) could play in the diffusion of culture and in the maintenance of a common identity in a specific group in society—in this case, the archiepiscopal ministerialage.

As we have already seen, Frederick II was named for the last time in 1167 and was dead by 1174; Frederick III first served as a witness in 1180, when he was called a boy.[38] Frederick II's widow, Benedicta, acted as the head of the lineage during the interim. She was mentioned on two occasions. Before his death, Frederick II had seized five hides in Werbno, near Mahrenberg (Radlje), that Countess Kunigunde of Marburg had given to Admont. The hides formed part or all of the dowry that the widowed Benedicta gave on behalf of her unnamed daughter to the Styrian ministerial Lantfrid III of Eppenstein,[39] who was mentioned for the first time in 1172 and who died on the Third Crusade.[40] Marrying a daughter to an Eppenstein made sense because Eppenstein is situated on the Lavant, north of the Pettaus' ancestral castle of Stein. From the perspective of a patrilineal lineage, the marriage of a daughter was a liability because it involved the loss of property, though the connections that the marriage established with another lineage were a partial compensation. Including stolen property in the girl's dowry was one way to minimize the loss. It is worth noting that, as head of the Pettau lineage, Benedicta did not hesitate to employ such tactics to preserve her son's patrimony.

The second reference to Benedicta occurs in a tale worthy of Sir Walter Scott. In June 1174 Provost Otto of Rottenbuch wrote to his brother, Abbot Rupert of Tegernsee in Bavaria, that a certain H., who had kidnapped their niece, had decided to return her to her family with appropriate compensation. The girl was unharmed because H. had neither seen nor spoken to her; instead, he had entrusted their niece on the day of her abduction to his noble kinswoman, the widow of Frederick of Pettau, who had protected the girl's honor.[41] In 1177 Patriarch Ulrich II of Aquileia advised his kinsman Provost Otto of Rottenbuch to give his consent to the marriage of his niece, the daughter of Otto's late brother, to the patriarch's vassal, the Friulian nobleman Henry of Villalta, presumably the H. of the earlier letter. Henry had previously implored the patriarch for permission to marry her but had desisted after she had been betrothed to the son of a count. When Henry had learned that it was unlikely that this marriage would occur, he had renewed his entreaties to the patriarch on a daily basis. The patriarch recommended that Otto accept the offer because Henry would be satisfied with a modest dowry.[42] It looks as if Otto and his relatives had tried to thwart a medieval romance and that Benedicta had helped Henry to plan the abduction of Otto's niece, who may herself have been a willing accomplice.

Otto's reference to Benedicta as a noblewoman indicates that Frederick II, like several other prominent archiepiscopal ministerials in the twelfth century, had married a woman of higher social status than himself. Although the children of such mésalliances were legally ministerials, such marriages between ministerials and noblewomen were one factor in the gradual acceptance of the ministerials as nobles. Since most of the old noble lineages in the archdiocese had been extinguished or had themselves become ministerials by 1200, a noblewoman who wished to marry often had little choice but to consent to such a match or to enter a convent.[43] The frequency with which men married women of higher legal and social status than their own and the effect that such marriages had on the status of the men's families need to be studied in more detail.

Benedicta's family of origin remains, however, uncertain. She was, as we have seen, a kinswoman of Henry of Villalta, but Otto's description of her as Henry's *cognata* rather than, say, his sister suggests that Benedicta was not a member of Henry's immediate family. There have been several attempts to deduce Benedicta's family of origin from the Pettaus' extensive holdings in the Lungau, the southeastern corner of the modern province of Salzburg. The ancestral property of Benedicta's grandsons, Frederick IV and Hartnid I, in the Lungau in the 1240s included the castle in St. Michael and the church in Tamsweg.[44] Pirchegger identified Benedicta, therefore, as a member of an Upper Austrian noble family, the Machlands, who had owned until 1147 the church in St. Michael;[45] but Ernst Klebel thought that the Pettaus might have acquired Tamsweg from the Draus because the Carinthian nobleman Eberhard of Drau conferred an alod in Tamsweg to the cathedral canons in 1165.[46] Eberhard probably resided, according to Klebel, in Drauhofen, near Tainach, eight kilometers southwest of Völkermarkt, Carinthia, and, significantly enough, thirty-two kilometers southwest of the Pettaus' castle in Stein.[47] The Pettaus would presumably have found a union with a noble family who lived in Carinthia more advantageous than an Upper Austrian connection.

However, Pirchegger and Klebel overlooked another clue to Benedicta's identity. Frederick III had a younger brother, Otto of Königsberg (today Kunšperk, eighteen kilometers northeast of Rann [Brežice], Yugoslavia), the founder of the cadet line of the Pettaus.[48] An Otto of Königsberg had already appeared as a witness in 1178 and was the first witness in charters of Duke Otakar of Styria in 1182 and 1185.[49] Since it is highly unlikely that the younger brother of a man who was called a boy in 1180 would have been the first witness in a ducal charter two years later, there is general agreement that we are dealing here with two different Ottos of Königsberg: an older man and the man who was identified in 1201 as Frederick III's brother.[50]

The older Otto was almost certainly the same person as Otto of Ehrnegg. According to the *Chronicon Gurcense*, Bishop Henry I of Gurk (1167–74) had destroyed the castle of Königsberg and had captured an Otto and a Reimbert, over whom he had triumphed magnificently.[51] A charter issued jointly by Bishop Henry and Duke Hermann of Carinthia in 1173 indicates that the culprits had been Otto of Ehrnegg and the Styrian ministerial, Reimbert of Mureck. Frederick Barbarossa, Duke

Henry of Austria, Duke Hermann, Provost Roman of Gurk, and the bishop's vassals and ministerials had interceded for the release of Otto, who had seized church property. Out of respect for the individuals who had interceded on Otto's behalf, Bishop Henry restored to Otto the fief that had belonged to his father, Reginhard. To indemnify Gurk for its losses, Otto swore that he would surrender to the bishop through the hand of his mother, Gisela (an indication that a widowed matriarch could continue to represent her family in public even after her son attained his majority), and his brother, Rapoto, the use and lordship of his alods situated in Ehrnegg, ten kilometers northeast of Völkermarkt, Carinthia, and in the Jauntal, the name given to the Drava valley between the Stein situated southwest of Völkermarkt and Unterdrauburg. If Otto died without legitimate and free heirs, both properties would belong to Gurk; if Otto had legitimate heirs, they would hold the property in the Jauntal in fief from Gurk, but Ehrnegg would revert to Otto's children as an alod.[52] There is no other reference to an Otto of Ehrnegg, but there is general agreement that the Otto of Ehrnegg, who was mentioned in the Gurk chronicle in conjunction with the destruction of Königsberg and who was forced to surrender Ehrnegg to Bishop Henry in 1173, was the same person as the older Otto of Königsberg who appeared for the first time in 1178.[53] The fact that the emperor and the dukes of Austria and Carinthia intervened on Otto's behalf is a good indication of his status.

Klebel speculated that Otto of Ehrnegg-Königsberg, like Benedicta of Pettau, belonged to the house of the lords of Drau and that his father, Reginhard, was the nobleman Reginhard of Donawitz, a stepson of Dietmar of the Lungau, whose property the older Otto of Königsberg inherited.[54] It seems likely that Otto of Ehrnegg was a member of the Drau clan, because Drau is located eight kilometers southwest of Völkermarkt, while Otto owned property in Ehrnegg, northeast of Völkermarkt, and in the Jauntal. Klebel did not comment on the relationship between Otto of Ehrnegg and Benedicta, whose younger son succeeded Otto of Ehrnegg as the lord of Königsberg. Otto could not have been Benedicta's father because his 1173 agreement with the bishop of Gurk indicates that Otto was a relatively young man without a legitimate heir, whereas Benedicta was by 1167/74 the widowed mother of several children. The most likely guess is that Benedicta was Otto's sister.

Three pieces of circumstantial evidence support this conclusion. First, men were often given the first name of a maternal uncle or grandfather whose lands they hoped to inherit[55]—that is, the name of Benedicta's younger son Otto was itself a claim to Königsberg. Second, Ehrnegg is situated only fourteen kilometers southwest of the Pettaus' castle in Stein. Finally, Benedicta's third son, Henry, became the provost of Maria Saal, a house of Augustinian canons situated only fifteen kilometers west of Drauhofen, and then became bishop of Gurk. Frederick II's marriage to Benedicta was thus of crucial importance to the Pettaus: it provided the senior line of the lineage with its extensive rights in the Lungau, derived ultimately from Dietmar of the Lungau, and enabled the Pettaus to establish a cadet line in Königsberg, which Bishop Ulrich I of Gurk called in 1251 one of the five principal fiefs of his church.[56] Königsberg, it should be stressed, is located outside the archdiocese, about four hundred kilometers from Salzburg. The marriage of Frederick II and Benedicta reveals the importance of the "right" marriage in the rise of a lineage.

Their son, Otto I of Königsberg, married Richza of Rohitsch (today Rogatec, Yugoslavia, twenty-five kilometers south of Pettau), whose family members were the lords of another of the five principal fiefs of the church of Gurk (see Genealogical Chart of the Königsbergs).[57] The Rohitsches were the founders of the Dominican nunnery of Studenitz (Studenice, ten kilometers northwest of Rohitsch). Richza announced in 1237 that she was giving twenty hides that she had inherited from her father, the Styrian ministerial Albert of Rohitsch, to the church and hospital that her sister Sophia was planning to found and that she was renouncing her rights to whatever property Sophia would give to the planned foundation. Otto I and the couple's unnamed children gave their consent, and Otto sealed the document for his wife.[58] A dozen years later Sophia's brother Henry announced that she had used her inheritance to found Studenitz and that he and his relatives, including his sister Richza and her children, Otto II, Henry, and Katherine, had consented.[59]

Otto I was still alive on 15 May 1249,[60] but he must have been dead by 6 August 1251, when the boys Otto II (Otlinus) and Henry of Königsberg sealed Frederick IV's reconciliation with Bishop Ulrich of Gurk.[61] Since Otto, even if he was born after Frederick II's death, must have been at the very least seventy-five years old in 1249 (his father died in 1167/74), it is striking that his sons were called "pueri," or boys, in 1251. We should probably not take this designation too literally because Otto's unnamed children were already alive in 1237 and were obviously old enough to seal a document in 1251. Still, their comparative youth explains why their mother played an active role in the affairs of the Königsberg lineage for several years after her husband's death. In 1256, for instance, arbiters, who included Richza's brother and Frederick IV of Pettau, settled a dispute that she and her unnamed son, presumably Otto II, had waged

GENEALOGICAL CHART OF THE KÖNIGSBERGS

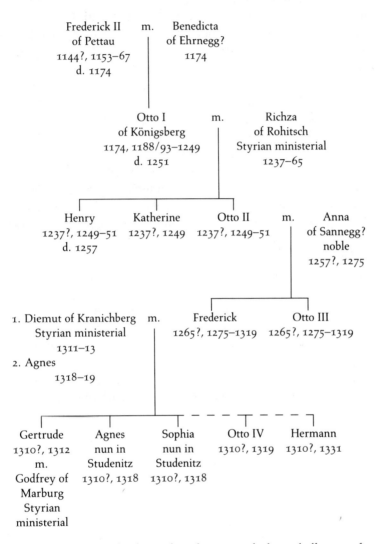

Dates included in the chart refer either to specific dates of office or to first and last appearances in the source materials.

with one of their vassals about a village located near Königsberg. Interestingly enough, she was to give the vassal ten marks and to forgive the injuries he had caused her, while her son was to enfeoff the vassal with the village, perhaps because only a man could carry out this formal act.[62] In 1257 the Benedictines of Oberburg (Gornji Grad), thirty-five kilometers west of Cilli (Celje), settled their quarrel with the Königsbergs by giving Otto II thirteen marks and Richza five.[63] She was still alive in 1265, when she arranged for a pittance to be served on her anniversary to the nuns of Studenitz.[64] Richza, whose children could be called boys in 1251 and who outlived Otto I by at least fifteen years, must have been considerably younger than her husband. While we do not know if Richza was Otto's first wife, the histories of other noble and ministerial lineages in the archdiocese suggest that many men in the twelfth and early thirteenth centuries were in their thirties or even forties when they married for the first time.[65] Men's late marriages explain why so many widows like Richza and Benedicta assumed positions of leadership and outlived their husbands by so many years.

When Otto II settled his differences with Oberburg in 1257, his brother Henry was dead and Otto was married but childless. Otto II's marriage at a relatively young age may have been prompted by his brother's death, which left Otto II as the last male Königsberg. Both Otto's unnamed wife and Richza gave their consent.[66] We know that Otto was a father by 1265, when Richza arranged for Studenitz to celebrate her anniversary, because Otto gave the Dominican nuns on this occasion a hamlet with the consent of his unnamed wife and children.[67] It is noteworthy that the family unit consisted of a married couple, their children, and the husband's widowed mother and that Otto sought the consent of his wife and minor children. Otto II was last mentioned in 1273.[68] Two years later, Anna of Königsberg and the brothers Otto III and Frederick of Königsberg, presumably Otto II's widow and sons, were reconciled with the bishop of Gurk.[69] Once again, a widow headed the lineage. Is it an accident that Anna was identified by name only after her husband's death, when she had to represent the lineage in public? The pattern in supplying the names of married women and widows ought to be investigated.

The Königsbergs retained their close ties to Studenitz after Richza's death. Her grandson Frederick gave to the convent in 1318 an annual income of eight marks on behalf of his daughters Agnes and Sophia (had the latter been named after the founder of Studenitz?). Since Frederick's second wife, Agnes, gave her consent, it is possible that Agnes and Sophia, judging by Agnes's name, were the very young children of Frederick's second marriage (his first wife was still alive in 1313). He gave the nuns an additional rent of one mark to provide a perpetual light over the graves of his saintly aunt (*hailigen mumen*), Sister Sophia, and his beloved grandmother (*meiner lieben anen*), Sister Richza.[70] Patrilineal lineages tended to emphasize their male ancestry, as can be seen in the repetition of a lineage's distinctive leading names (for example, Otto among the Königsbergs and Frederick among the Pettaus), but the Königsbergs were clearly proud of Sophia and Richza, who had founded what was in effect the dynastic monastery of the Königsbergs.

Placing daughters in a convent was considerably cheaper than providing a daughter with a dowry. The Styrian ministerial Godfrey of Marburg (Maribor) announced in 1312 that his father-in-law, Frederick of Königsberg, had given to his daughter Gertrude a dowry of five hundred Graz pounds, in accordance with Styrian territorial law. Godfrey promised to invest the money in properties within Styria, which were to revert to Frederick and his heirs if Godfrey and Gertrude's marriage was childless. If Godfrey failed to do this and if the couple had no heir, then Frederick and his descendants were to have a lien of five hundred pounds on the castle of Marburg. The duke or his representative were to see to the enforcement of the latter provision.[71] While the family of origin lost its proprietary rights to a daughter's dowry only if she had children, it clearly cost far less to place a daughter in a convent—eighty marks (£160) for two daughters if we employ a ten-to-one ratio for the value of a rent—than to marry her off.

This must have been an important consideration for the Königsbergs, who were, like many other lineages of archiepiscopal ministerials, in financial difficulty by 1300. In 1299 Otto III and Frederick sold to Archbishop Conrad IV for 412½ Graz marks their mining rights and tithes in the parish of Pettau;[72] in 1305 Frederick pledged the castle of Königsberg with its appurtenances to the bishop of Gurk;[73] in 1311 Frederick sold to his brother-in-law, the Styrian ministerial Siegfried of Kranichberg, for 70 Graz marks various properties that had belonged to the dowry of Frederick's first wife, Diemut, and she and their unnamed children gave their consent;[74] and in 1313 Frederick sold four hides with Diemut's and his children's consent to the Benedictines of Oberburg for 40 marks as they were calculated in the Sann valley (Savinska dolina).[75] Providing two more daughters with dowries as large as Gertrude's would have been nearly impossible for a family in the Königsbergs' straitened circumstances. The family foundation of Studenitz was the only respectable alternative.

Harald Bilowitzky's study of 475 late medieval Styrian marriages (only 10 predate 1300) indicates that the terms of Gertrude's marriage contract were in accordance with Styrian law and custom. The woman's family provided the bride with a dowry (*Heimsteuer*), the amount of which was fixed by custom and depended on the family's estate. It was usually paid in cash and invested in land; an annual return of 10 percent was considered normal. The husband administered the property and enjoyed the income but could not alienate the property without his wife's express consent. If the couple were childless and the wife died first, the husband would receive the lifelong income; the property would then revert, as Gertrude's marriage contract shows, to her relatives unless she had made other arrangements. A woman's dowry was not the same as her share of the family inheritance, though the amount of the dowry could be deducted from her share of the inheritance. However, in the fifteenth century it became customary for a woman's inheritance to be limited to her dowry.

The groom or his family was required to designate the lands that would form her widow's dower (*Widerlage*). The designated land could not be alienated without the wife's consent, and her claims to her widow's dower took precedence over all other claims to her husband's estate. If the couple had been childless, the property reverted to the husband's family after her death. In addition, a woman who married for the first time also received a *Morgengabe*. A woman could dispose of her *Morgengabe* in whatever way she wished. In the thirteenth century, the *Heimsteuer* equaled the combined *Widerlage* and *Morgengabe*. Thereafter, the amount of the *Heimsteuer* declined relative to the groom's contribution, so that in 84 percent of the marriages in the second half of the fifteenth century, the bride's contribution was less than the groom's. The purpose of these arrangements was to provide a newly married couple or a widow, especially a childless one who had no further claim upon her own family, with the income to live in accordance with their estate. [76]

Bilowitzky's findings raise a number of questions. First, how widespread were such arrangements? Second, is it only a function of the extant documentation that most of his evidence comes from after 1300, or do the contracts also reflect a change in family strategy in the late Middle Ages? Bilowitzky argues that his couples married at a relatively early age, about twenty years for a woman and between twenty-five and thirty years for a man.[77] My own work has suggested that men (for instance, Otto I of Königsberg) usually married at a later age during the High Middle Ages and that usually only one son married in each generation to prevent a fragmentation of the family's patrimony. Were the marriage contracts, therefore, a device to arrange for the marriage of more than one son in each generation and during the father's lifetime by providing the young couple with the means to establish a separate household? Such a system would presumably have reduced the chances of a family dying out in the male line because the designated heir had failed to sire a son. Third, as we have seen, wives and children usually gave their consent when their husband and father alienated property. When a document specifies that a wife had given her consent to her husband's alienation of property, are we justified in assuming that the property in question was part of the wife's inheritance, dowry, or dower?

The main line of the Pettau lineage descended from the brother of Otto I of Königsberg, Frederick III. Frederick, who had been called a boy in 1180, was a father by 1197[78] and died sometime between 1219 and 1222.[79] The Dominicans remembered in the fifteenth century that his widow, Mathilda, had founded in 1230 their priory in Pettau,[80] which served as the repository of the family archives.[81] Mathilda may thus have introduced the Dominicans to her brother-in-law, Otto of Königsberg, and his wife, Richza of Rohitsch, the cofounder of Studenitz.

Mathilda's son Frederick IV, who was mentioned for the first time by name in 1211,[82] married Herrad, the daughter of the archiepiscopal ministerial Ortolf of Montpreis, in the castle of Hörberg on 17 December 1213 in the presence of Archbishop Eberhard II (see Genealogical Chart of the Montpreis-Hörbergs).[83] Montpreis (today Planina) and Hörberg (today Podsreda), which are situated between Cilli and Rann, were two more of the five principal fiefs of the church of Gurk.[84] Eberhard's presence at a wedding so far from Salzburg attests to the importance of the union of these two powerful lineages.

In 1208 Bishop Walter of Gurk had granted Ortolf's fief, presumably the castles and lordships of Montpreis and Hörberg, to his wife, Lady Gerbirg, and their daughter, Lady Herrad. Any additional children, sons or daughters, that the couple might yet have would possess the same rights. If Ortolf died without an heir and if Gerbirg outlived him, she was to retain the lifelong use of the fief, except for one village. In return for this favor, Ortolf, Gerbirg, and Herrad had given Gurk an annual rent of five marks in St. Stefan, Carinthia, a rent of fifty pennies in the Lungau, and a village in southern Styria.[85]

This agreement was modified when Herrad married Frederick IV in 1213. Ortolf gave to Gerbirg the castle of Hörberg, with all its appurtenances and servile retainers, as well as several individuals who lived in Montpreis. If Ortolf and Gerbirg did not have a male heir, the castle and people were to belong to the nearest heir in Ortolf's lineage. Six men, including Frederick III of Pettau and his brothers Otto I of Königsberg and Provost Henry of Maria Saal, who subsequently became the bishop of Gurk, swore that Ortolf's new son-in-law, Frederick IV, would not in the future disturb Gerbirg's possession of Hörberg.[86] The purpose of this so-called marriage contract was thus not to regulate Herrad's inheritance but to provide for her mother's maintenance if she were widowed.

GENEALOGICAL CHART OF THE MONTPREIS-HÖRBERGS

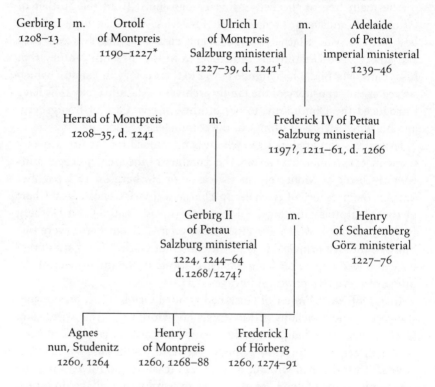

Gerbirg I m.   Ortolf   Ulrich I   m.   Adelaide
1208–13   of Montpreis   of Montpreis   of Pettau
            1190–1227*   Salzburg ministerial   imperial ministerial
                            1227–39, d. 1241†   1239–46

        Herrad of Montpreis   m.   Frederick IV of Pettau
         1208–35, d. 1241   Salzburg ministerial
                                        1197?, 1211–61, d. 1266

                Gerbirg II   m.   Henry
                of Pettau   of Scharfenberg
             Salzburg ministerial   Görz ministerial
                1224, 1244–64   1227–76
                d.1268/1274?

        Agnes   Henry I   Frederick I
    nun, Studenitz   of Montpreis   of Hörberg
      1260, 1264   1260, 1268–88   1260, 1274–91

Dates included in the chart refer either to specific dates of office or to first and last appearances in the source materials.

*Same as Ortolf II of Katsch? Salzburg ministerial 1180
†Same as Ulrich of Katsch? 1221

Herrad's rights are less clear. Are we to surmise that she was to obtain Montpreis immediately after her father's death but Hörberg only if her parents did not have a son? The problem is complicated by the existence of the archiepiscopal ministerial Ulrich of Montpreis, who was mentioned for the first time in 1227 and who died sometime between 1239 and 1241.[87] Klebel thought that Ulrich was Ortolf's son,[88] but this is almost certainly wrong because by 1227 Ortolf and Ulrich had divided the lordship of Montpreis between them.[89] Since any son of Ortolf could have been born only after 1213, when Ortolf was still hoping for a male heir, I find it highly unlikely that Ortolf would have divided his lands with a boy who would have been, at best, fourteen years old in 1227. Ulrich was probably, therefore, Ortolf's brother, nephew, or cousin. [90]

Whoever Ulrich was, the Pettaus were determined to bring Montpreis within their sphere of influence; and Ulrich was married by 1239 to Frederick IV's niece, the daughter of Hartnid I of Pettau.[91] In the end, the descendants of Herrad of Montpreis and Frederick IV possessed both Montpreis and Hörberg.[92] The Pettaus had thus acquired by the 1240s three of the five principal fiefs of Gurk—Montpreis, Hörberg, and Königsberg—and the family of Otto I's wife, the Rohitsches, were the lords of the fourth. The importance the Pettaus attached to acquiring the Gurk fiefs explains why Frederick IV, contrary to the prevailing custom in the archdiocese, married in his father's lifetime. Herrad was too important an heiress to pass up. [93]

The 1213 agreement between the Montpreises and the Pettaus provides the best clue to the identity of Frederick IV's mother, Mathilda, the founder of the Dominican priory in Pettau. As we have seen, six men, including Frederick IV's father and paternal uncles Otto I of Königsberg and Provost Henry of Maria Saal, swore that Frederick IV would not disturb his mother-in-law, Gerbirg, in her possession of Hörberg. The Pettaus were the last three; the first three were the Styrian ministerials, Otto of Krems and the brothers Otto and Albert of Unterdrauburg (today Dravograd). Pirchegger thought that Ortolf of Montpreis was the son of Ortolf of Trixen-Unterdrauburg,[94] that is, the first cousin of Otto and Albert of Unterdrauburg. Klebel has demonstrated rather convincingly, however, that Ortolf of Montpreis was the same person as Ortolf II of Katsch.[95] Besides, it is not obvious why Ortolf's relatives should have guaranteed Frederick IV's good conduct.

A better guess is that Otto and Albert of Unterdrauburg were Frederick IV's kinsmen—let us say, for argument's sake, his maternal uncles. There are several pieces of circumstantial evidence that support such a conclusion. First, both Otto's and Albert's mother, the daughter of the Bavarian count Conrad I of Valley, and one of Otto's daughters were named Mathilda.[96] It seems plausible to surmise that Otto and Albert might also have had a sister named Mathilda, namely, the wife of Frederick III. Second, the Styrian ministerial Liutold of Wildon referred to Mathilda's younger son, Hartnid I of Pettau, as his kinsman.[97] This genealogical connection stumped Pirchegger,[98] but Liutold's wife, Agnes, was the daughter of Otto of Unterdrauburg.[99] If I am right about Mathilda of Pettau's family of origin, she would have been the paternal aunt of Agnes of Wildon. Third, Albert's widow and son, Geisla and Siegfried of Mahrenberg—that is, if I am right, Mathilda's sister-in-law and nephew —founded in 1251 the Dominican nunnery in Mahrenberg.[100] As we have already seen, Mathilda was the founder of the Dominican priory in Pettau, and her husband's sister-in-law was the cofounder of Studenitz.

The latter fact suggests that Mathilda was the central figure among the Dominicans' patrons in southern Styria, a group in which women were particularly prominent, and that these women played a major role in shaping the religious sensibilities of their families. The role of women in the expansion of the new religious orders during the High Middle Ages —for example, in the proliferation of Dominican nunneries in Germany —ought to be investigated from this perspective.

Frederick III had thus married a woman who belonged to a powerful lineage of Styrian ministerials who lived in Unterdrauburg, upstream from Pettau. It is another example of the Pettaus' ability to make the "right" marriage. The example of Mathilda of Pettau shows not only how difficult it can be to determine a woman's family of origin but also how such a determination can shed new light on many points—in this case, on the expansion of the Dominicans in Styria. Furthermore, if Mathilda was indeed an Unterdrauburg-Mahrenberg, we can surmise that there was a connection between the execution of her nephew Siegfried of Mahrenberg in the winter of 1271–72 by King Ottokar II of Bohemia and the fact that the name of her grandson Frederick V of Pettau headed the list of Styrian and Carinthian magnates of ministerial rank who pledged their support to Rudolph of Hapsburg against Ottokar in 1276 in the decisive sequence of events that led to the establishment of the Hapsburgs in Austria and Styria.[101] Determining a woman's family of origin can thus add a new perspective to events.

We have yet to explain why Otto of Krems (three kilometers southeast of Voitsberg, Styria) headed the list of six men who guaranteed that Frederick IV would not challenge Gerbirg's possession of Hörberg.

According to the book of confraternity of the Augustinian canons of
Seckau, Otto's wife was named Benedicta.[102] Since Frederick III's mother
had been named Benedicta, I suspect that the wife of Otto of Krems was
the sister of Frederick III and that Otto, as the husband of Frederick IV's
paternal aunt, was asked to guarantee Frederick IV's good conduct. As
this example shows, books of remembrance and necrologies, combined
with documentary evidence, can provide clues to a woman's family of
origin.

The repetition of the name Frederick in the Pettau lineage shows that
the Pettaus had a clearly defined patrilineal identity, but when Frederick IV married Herrad of Montpreis, the Pettaus called upon Frederick IV's paternal and maternal relatives to provide surety for his behavior. As David Herlihy points out, in the High Middle Ages a patrilineal
kinship system had simply been superimposed upon an earlier, bilateral
kinship structure. [103]

Frederick IV's and Herrad's pious donations were a joint affair. In
1224 Frederick gave to the church of St. Michael's in Zosen, Carinthia, a
hide in Zosen. Since Zosen is ten kilometers north of Wieting, the hide
was probably part of the Pettaus' Wieting inheritance. Frederick's unnamed wife and children consented.[104] In 1233 Frederick and Herrad gave
to the Cistercians of Sittich (Stična), southeast of Ljubljana (Laibach),
twelve hides situated near Hörberg.[105] Herrad may have been specifically named on this occasion because the hides were presumably part of
her inheritance. In 1235 the couple conferred to the Teutonic Knights the
patronage of the church in Gross-Sonntag (today Velika Nedelja), eighteen kilometers east of Pettau.[106] Herrad was not identified by name in
this document, perhaps because Frederick had acquired Gross-Sonntag
from his father.[107] Can we conclude from these examples that scribes
were most likely to mention the wife's name if the property in question
belonged to her inheritance? The question requires further scrutiny. In
any case, Herrad was dead by 1241, when Archbishop Eberhard II indicated that Frederick had given to Sittich in Herrad's memory twelve
hides, apparently the same hides that the couple had already given to the
Cistercians in 1233.[108] Frederick IV, who was still alive in 1261,[109] was
dead by 1266;[110] there is no evidence that he remarried.

Although Frederick had referred in 1224 to his unnamed children, he
had only one surviving daughter, Gerbirg II, who had obviously been
named after her maternal grandmother (we need to investigate whether
women were more likely to be named after their paternal or maternal
ancestors). She married Henry of Scharfenberg (Svibno, Carniola), a

ministerial of the count of Görz,[111] sometime between 1235 and 1244.[112] In 1244 Henry renounced with the consent, hand, and will of his wife, Gerbirg, all his proprietary rights in the Lungau, in particular to the castle situated near St. Michael, and Frederick IV granted his assent. Frederick's brother Hartnid I and his heirs acquired sole possession of the property.[113] It is not clear whether the Pettaus obtained their rights in St. Michael from Frederick IV's paternal grandmother, Benedicta, or from Gerbirg's maternal grandfather, Ortolf of Montpreis.[114] In the latter case, Frederick IV would merely have been exercising his residual rights as Herrad's widower, but the charter's emphasis upon Gerbirg's consent indicates that Henry of Scharfenberg had acquired his rights to St. Michael through his wife.

This was also true in the case of Montpreis and Hörberg. Henry's 1250 reconciliation with the Cistercians of Landstrass (Kostanjevica) in Carniola stressed that he could not alienate Herrad's property without her express participation and consent. To obtain absolution for burning monastic property, Henry agreed to give the monks five hides that belonged to Herrad. Since the hides were part of his wife's patrimony, Henry pointed out that his donation had no validity unless she herself conferred it to the monks ("Verum cum hec donatio preter manum coniugis mee cuius fuit hereditas et patrimonium nullum robur firmitatis habere potuit"). He therefore summoned the subprior of Landstrass to Montpreis, and Gerbirg voluntarily and freely repeated the donation on the altar of the castle's chapel. To compensate Gerbirg, Henry gave her a village that he had inherited.[115] This transaction indicates that a husband's and wife's properties were kept separate and shows why the documents placed so much importance on the wife's consent. In general, neither a husband nor a wife appears to have been able to alienate property in the archdiocese in the thirteenth century without the approval of the other.

In 1251 Bishop Ulrich I of Gurk settled his lengthy dispute with Gerbirg's father and husband, Frederick IV of Pettau and Henry of Scharfenberg, and enfeoffed them jointly with the castles of Montpreis and Hörberg.[116] Henry gave to the Augustinian nuns of Michelstetten in the diocese of Aquileia a serf in 1260 with the consent of his unnamed wife and children; Henry's sister Agnes executed the transaction on his behalf.[117] While staying in Montpreis in 1264, Henry gave twelve hides to the Dominican nuns of Studenitz, the foundation of Gerbirg's Königsberg relatives and the convent of choice for the Pettaus and their kinsmen, because his daughter Agnes was taking the veil there. Gerbirg and Henry's other children consented. [118]

Henry the Younger of Scharfenberg was mentioned for the first time by name in 1268,[119] and he was presumably the same person as the Henry of Montpreis who made his appearance in 1274.[120] Frederick I of Hörberg sold in 1274 his share of the upper castle of Pettau to Frederick V of Pettau, Gerbirg's first cousin.[121] Henry's and Frederick's adoption of the surnames Montpreis and Hörberg, respectively, around 1274 suggests that Gerbirg had died sometime between 1268, when Henry was still known as Henry the Younger of Scharfenberg, and 1274, when her sons had divided their maternal inheritance between them. Montpreis and Hörberg had passed through two successive heiresses, Herrad of Montpreis and Gerbirg of Pettau, to two new lineages. Henry and Frederick clearly identified with their maternal rather than their paternal ancestors, the Scharfenbergs, a toponym that their father's relatives continued to employ. We must be careful not to exaggerate the patrilineal structure of thirteenth-century society. It is also worth noting that Gerbirg had inherited rights from her father, Frederick IV, in Pettau itself.

The male line of the Pettaus was continued by Frederick IV's brother Hartnid I. While Frederick had been mentioned for the first time by name in 1211, Hartnid made his first appearance only in 1228,[122] fifteen years after his brother's marriage. It may be that Hartnid had originally been intended for a clerical career and that he resumed lay status only when it became clear that his older brother would have no son. He too married an heiress, the daughter of the Styrian ministerial, Swiker III of Hollenburg. Through this marriage the Pettaus obtained the castles of Hollenburg, nine kilometers south of Klagenfurt, Carinthia, on the north bank of the Drava, and Wurmberg (today Vurperg), ten kilometers northwest of Pettau.[123] We do not know when Hartnid married or even his wife's name, but his daughter Adelaide was married by 1239 to the archiepiscopal ministerial Ulrich of Montpreis, Ortolf's brother, nephew, or cousin.[124] Hartnid fathered at least one illegitimate son, the knight Frederick of Pettau.[125] There is no indication whether he was born before or after his father's marriage.

Hartnid's legitimate son Frederick V, who supplied Rudolph of Hapsburg with two hundred men in 1276,[126] was the most important member of the lineage. Frederick was named for the first time in 1246, when his father promised Archbishop Eberhard II that Frederick would marry an archiepiscopal ministerial within two months after Eberhard II or his successor ordered Frederick to marry. If Frederick died before this occurred, Hartnid's second son, presumably Hartnid II, would be obligated to marry an archiepiscopal ministerial or the Pettaus would forfeit their archiepiscopal fiefs.[127] There is no evidence that Frederick married a Salzburg retainer; instead, he was married by 1264 to Sophia, the sister of the Styrian counts Bernard and Henry of Pfannberg, who promised that she and her unnamed children would renounce their claims to the castle of Albeck, north of Feldkirchen, Carinthia, which belonged to Gurk.[128] Frederick's great-grandmother Benedicta had been a noblewoman, and his grandmother Mathilda was in all probability the granddaughter of the count of Valley, but Frederick V was the first Pettau to marry a woman who belonged to the high aristocracy. It was a good indication of how far the Pettaus, who were technically of servile legal status, had risen.

Frederick V claimed in 1280 that Archbishop Frederick II owed him money for the marriage that Archbishop-Elect Philip (1247–57), Eberhard II's successor, had arranged for him.[129] There is no record of such a marriage, but on 1 June 1250 the counts Bernard and Henry of Pfannberg, Frederick's future brothers-in-law, had agreed to serve Philip and his successors against everyone except the ruler of Styria.[130] Two weeks earlier, Philip had made a similar agreement with the Styrian ministerial Ulrich I of Liechtenstein, who promised to serve the archbishop and his successors with one hundred armed men. Philip's agreement with the Liechtensteins included the provision that Ulrich's son would marry the daughter of the archiepiscopal ministerial Conrad I of Goldegg. Philip agreed to give the couple an annual rent of ten pounds from the archiepiscopal saltworks in Hallein until they could be enfeoffed with a comparable rent as well as nine hundred pounds, payable over three years, which were also to be invested in rents.[131] My guess is that the elect's agreement with the Pfannbergs included a similar provision and that instead of marrying an archiepiscopal ministerial, as had been stipulated in 1246, Philip promised to subsidize Frederick V's marriage to the counts' sister. The Pettaus had always arranged their marriages with the utmost care and to their considerable advantage, but Frederick V's marriage to Sophia of Pfannberg had been turned into an instrument in the archbishop's battle against the Hohenstaufen.

During the first years of their marriage, Frederick V and Sophia may have lived in Hollenburg, the castle he had inherited from his unnamed mother, because his uncle Frederick IV was still the head of the lineage. Frederick settled a dispute in Hollenburg in 1252 and stressed that he was the lord of Hollenburg by hereditary succession.[132] A generation later, in 1286, that is, when Frederick V was still alive, his and Sophia's son Frederick VI was identified as Frederick of Hollenburg the Younger of Pettau.[133] The future head of the Pettau lineage appears thus to have established a separate household in Hollenburg, probably after his marriage. We need to find out if other lineages made similar arrangements when a son married in his father's lifetime. If they did, it would suggest that a household was expected to have only one dominant couple.

When Frederick V settled his differences with Archbishop Frederick II in 1280, the archbishop specified that the castellany of the castles and city of Pettau was an indivisible office, heritable only in the direct male line of the Pettaus.[134] This provision may have been included in the settlement because questions had arisen about the respective rights of Gerbirg of Pettau, the daughter of Frederick IV, and of Hartnid I, Frederick IV's brother, and their descendants to the castellany. As we have already seen, Gerbirg's son Frederick of Hörberg sold his share of the upper castle to Frederick V in 1274.

Frederick's wife, Sophia of Pfannberg, was not mentioned after 1264, perhaps because Frederick, like his father, Hartnid, was not noted for his gifts to churches, which involved the type of document in which women and minor children were most likely to be named. Frederick remarried near the end of his life. On 24 June 1287 Archbishop Rudolph authorized Frederick to give to his wife, Countess Agnes of Pfannberg, a dower ("in donationem propter nuptias") of five hundred Graz or Friesach marks that he held in fief from the archbishop under the condition that any sons born of this marriage would marry only women who belonged to the family of the church of Salzburg. If she died without a son, this rent was to revert to the sons of Frederick's previous marriage, Frederick VI and Hartnid III. The archbishop promised to enfeoff her with the rents as soon as he came to Pettau or to Styria, whereupon she was to give the archbishop a document listing the rents by name.[135] Frederick V died in 1288. [136]

The most obvious conclusion that can be drawn from this history of the Pettau women in the twelfth and thirteenth centuries is the impor-tance of marriage in the rise of the Pettaus. Frederick I had been in all probability a Bavarian emigrant to Carinthia; Frederick V was one of the great lords of southeastern Germany. Each of the Pettaus married well: Frederick I's unnamed wife was the sister of one of the most powerful archiepiscopal ministerials in Carinthia, Godfrey of Wieting; Benedicta of Ehrnegg, Frederick II's wife, brought to the Pettaus their extensive lands and rights in the Lungau and the castle and lordship of Königsberg; Frederick III's wife, Mathilda of Mahrenberg, was the granddaughter of a Bavarian count; Frederick IV married an heiress, Herrad of Mont-preis and Hörberg; Hartnid I's unnamed wife inherited the lordships of Hollenburg in Carinthia and Wurmberg in southern Styria; and Fred-

erick V married two countesses. Conversely, the Pettaus tried to limit
the losses to the family patrimony entailed in a daughter's marriage by
providing their daughters with property that was of only marginal interest to the lineage or even, in one case, property that had been stolen
from a monastery.

Still, marriages to women of free-noble ancestry could not overcome
the remaining barriers that separated the ministerials from the old German nobility. In spite of the Pettaus' great wealth, power, and noble
blood, Archbishop Rudolph agreed to enfeoff Frederick V's second wife,
Countess Agnes of Pfannberg, with her widow's dower only if the sons
of that marriage married women who belonged to the archiepiscopal *fa-
milia*, that is, only if they acknowledged their servile status. Bilowitzky
points out that while the Pettaus married countesses for the next four
generations, no Pettau woman married a count. It was only in the fifth
and last generation after Frederick V that the two sisters of Frederick IX
married counts, one of whom was a younger son. Men could marry up,
but women married down because comital houses refused to dilute their
own blue blood.[137] The role of marriage in medieval social mobility needs
to be studied very carefully.

The second conclusion is that the Pettau women retained considerable
control of their property after their marriages. This was stated most explicitly in Henry of Scharfenberg's reconciliation with the Cistercians
of Landstrass, but husbands in general did not alienate property without the consent of their wives and children, especially if it belonged to
the wife's dowry or dower, let alone her inheritance. Marriage was a
union of two lineages that was not completely consummated until there
were surviving children who joined the blood and property of both their
parents.

Finally, the history of each family is in some way unique and sheds
some light on a different aspect of medieval society. The Pettaus are an
example of a ministerial family, probably of Bavarian origin, that moved
to the southeastern frontier of medieval Germany and became the second most powerful family in Styria (only the counts of Cilli, who were
of free-noble status and who became imperial princes, surpassed the Pettaus). Few ministerial lineages were so successful. However, the Pettaus
were not the only family in the twelfth century to seek its fortune on the
borders of German settlement. The nobleman Otto of Ehrnegg, whom I
have identified as the brother of Benedicta of Pettau, shifted his interests
from the area around Völkermarkt in Carinthia to the Sotla valley, west
of Zagreb; and the archiepiscopal ministerial Ortolf of Montpreis, the

father-in-law of Frederick IV of Pettau, was probably the same person as Ortolf of Katsch, who lived in Rauchenkatsch, fourteen kilometers south of St. Michael in the Lungau, and who built Montpreis in the 1180s.[138] These families received some of their holdings in fief from the archbishops of Salzburg or the bishops of Gurk (for instance, the castellany of Pettau or the castles of Königsberg, Montpreis, and Hörberg), but Frederick IV also stressed that his father had seized from the Hungarians the vacant and uninhabited land he gave to the Teutonic Knights in Gross-Sonntag.[139] One wonders how life on the frontier affected the status and position of women. At the very least, the close ties between the Dominicans and such women as Mathilda of Pettau and Richza of Königsberg suggest that the women were concerned about the spiritual welfare of their families in a newly settled region.

❡ I do not wish to suggest that my study of the Pettau women offers the last word about the status of women during the High Middle Ages in the archdiocese of Salzburg, let alone in medieval Germany. Rather, my purpose has been to acquaint readers with the vast published collections of medieval German documents, the type of material they contain, and some examples of how these sources can be exploited to learn more about medieval German women. We will need many more regional monographs and prosopographical studies of different strata of German society before we will be able to generalize. Such studies will have to take into account chronological, regional, and social differences. For instance, the Pettaus were a lineage of ministerial status who rose into the ranks of the upper nobility in a border area of the German-speaking world, but would a noble lineage, say, one in Westphalia, have treated its women in the same fashion? Frederick V provided his second wife with a large dower, an annual rent of fifty marks (one hundred pounds); but was he being unusually generous because he, a ministerial, was eager to marry a woman who belonged to the high aristocracy? Did the fact that he had two grown sons by a previous marriage force him to provide especially well for a second wife, who was likely to survive him by many years? Much work is required before we can answer such questions, but it should then be possible to write more than these few pages about the history of women during the High Middle Ages in Germany.

NOTES

I would like to thank my colleague, Roy A. Austensen, for his critical comments about an earlier draft.

1. See Howell, with the collaboration of Wemple and Kaiser, "A Documented Presence," pp. 101–31; the quotation is on p. 101. For similar comments about German historiography on women in the modern period, see Sheehan, "What Is German History?" p. 20.

2. Howell, with Wemple and Kaiser, "A Documented Presence," p. 124.

3. Ennen, *Frauen im Mittelalter*, p. 81.

4. Duby, "Lineage, Nobility, and Knighthood," pp. 71–75; Duby, *Medieval Marriage*, pp. 9–12.

5. Wemple, review of *Frauen im Mittelalter*, by Edith Ennen, p. 924.

6. Ennen does, however, omit a number of relevant books and articles in English from her bibliography, including Leyser, *Rule and Conflict* (chaps. 5 and 6 deal with the women of the Saxon aristocracy); McDonnell, *Beguines and Beghards*; Phillips, *Beguines in Medieval Strasburg*; Stuard, *Women in Medieval Society*; and my own "Urban Development." Some relevant French studies that are missing include: Dollinger, *L'Évolution des classes rurales* (especially useful for its discussion of *censuales*, or altar dependents, a group composed predominantly of women); and Simon, *L'Ordre des Pénitentes de Ste. Marie-Madeleine*. Some important German works are also missing: Busse-Wilson, *Das Leben der heiligen Elisabeth von Thüringen*; Decker, *Die Stellung des Predigerordens*; Greven, *Die Anfänge der Beginen*; Maurer, "Zum Verständnis der hl. Elisabeth von Thüringen"; Schuller, "Dos—Praebenda—Peculium"; and Wauer, *Entstehung und Ausbreitung*.

7. Volume 1, which deals with the discipline of history in general, ancillary disciplines, general German history, and the individual German-speaking territories and states, contains a subsection about women by Thomas Nipperdey (titles 664 to 764 of section 35); it was published, however, in 1969. Volume 2 deals with the Merovingian and Carolingian periods, volume 3 with the period from 911 to 1254, and volume 4 with the late Middle Ages.

8. For information about the *Traditionsbücher*, see Erben, "Untersuchungen zu dem Codex traditionum Odalberti," pp. 454–80; Fichtenau, *Das Urkundenwesen*, pp. 73–87, 100–106, 174–79; Hauthaler and Richter, "Die Salzburgischen Traditionscodices," pp. 63–95, 369–85; Redlich, "Über bairische Traditionsbücher und Traditionen," pp. 1–82; and Widemann, "Die Traditionen der bayerischen Klöster," pp. 225–43.

9. "Codex traditionum Augiensium," pp. 87–152.

10. *Die Traditionen, Urkunden und Urbare des Stiftes Gars*, p. 9*.

11. Dopsch, "Die Ministerialität des Herzogtums Steiermark," p. 33 n. 28.

12. See, for instance, Schmid's articles in the section "Gebetsgedenken," which are reprinted in Schmid, *Gebetsgedenken und adliges Selbstverständnis im*

Mittelalter, pp. 469–644; see also Althoff, "Unerforschte Quellen aus quellen-armer Zeit (IV)," pp. 37–71.

13. The traditions of Au, Gars, and the Falkensteins appear in *Drei bayerische Traditionsbücher aus dem XII.*

14. For information about the Salzburg ministerialage, see Dopsch, *Ge-schichte Salzburgs* 1/1:367–403; Dopsch, "Ministerialität und Herrenstand," pp. 3–31; Dopsch, "Probleme," pp. 207–53; Freed, "Crisis of the Salzburg Minis-terialage"; Freed, "Diemut von Högl," pp. 581–657; Freed, "Formation of the Salzburg Ministerialage," pp. 67–102; and Freed, "Nobles, Ministerials, and Knights," pp. 575–611.

15. Pirchegger, "Die Herren von Pettau," p. 3.

16. Dopsch, *Geschichte Salzburgs* 1/2:975–76; Pirchegger, *Die Untersteier-mark,* pp. 57–68.

17. *Vita Chunradi archiepiscopi,* pp. 74–75.

18. *Salzburger Urkundenbuch* (hereafter cited as *SUB*), 2:230–31, no. 154; *SUB* 2:258–59, no. 175.

19. *SUB* 2:426–28, no. 305.

20. *SUB* 2:284ff., nos. 196, 199, 203, 204, 206, 218, 219, 220, 224, 225, 226, 229, 239, 240, 247.

21. *Monumenta historica ducatus Carinthiae* (hereafter cited as *MC*), 4/1:79–80, no. 1720; *MC* 4/1:333–34, no. 2321.

22. *MC* 3:221, no. 543; *MC* 3:240, no. 590; *MC* 3:248–49, no. 608.

23. Pirchegger, "Die Herren von Pettau," pp. 3–5.

24. *MC* 3:211, no. 525.

25. *SUB* 2:426–28, no. 305; *SUB* 2:531–33, no. 384; and *Urkundenbuch des Herzogthums Steiermark* (hereafter cited as *UB Steiermark*), 1:531–32, no. 559.

26. *SUB* 1:399–400, no. 278; *SUB* 2:336–37, no. 234; *SUB* 2:377–78, no. 267; *SUB* 2:378–80, no. 268a. For additional information, see Höck, *Geschichte der Propstei Wieting,* pp. 15–30.

27. *SUB* 2:426ff., nos. 305, 313, 363.

28. *SUB* 2:523–25, no. 375.

29. *SUB* 2:663–64, no. 489; *SUB* 3:505–6, no. 955.

30. Bracher, "Lassnitz-Sulm," pp. 135–48.

31. McLaughlin, "Survivors and Surrogates," p. 178 n. 217.

32. Freed, "Diemut von Högl," pp. 638–40.

33. *SUB* 2:326–28, no. 226.

34. *SUB* 2:324–25, no. 224.

35. Freed, "Diemut von Högl," pp. 592–631.

36. *MC* 4/2:639–40, no. 2905.

37. *SUB* 1:465–66, no. 390b.

38. *SUB* 2:584–85, no. 424a.

39. *MC* 3:330–31, no. 848II. On the location of the hides, see Pirchegger, *Die Untersteiermark,* p. 157.

40. *UB Steiermark* 1:516–17, no. 548; *Necrologia Germaniae* 2:416, 23/6.

41. *UB Steiermark* 1:531–32, no. 559.

42. *MC* 3:467, no. 1234. On Henry's status, see *MC* 3:469, no. 1238. For additional information, see Tyroller, "Abstammung und Verwandschaft," pp. 117–20.

43. Freed, "Diemut von Högl," pp. 595–97, 641–47.

44. *SUB* 3:601, no. 1054; *SUB* 3:640–42, no. 1096; *SUB* 3:644, no. 1098.

45. Pirchegger, "Die Herren von Pettau," pp. 5–7; *Urkundenbuch des Landes ob der Enns* 2:227, no. 155. On Otto of Machland and his other possessions in the Lungau, see *SUB* 2:284–89, no. 196, and *SUB* 2:621–22, no. 458. Pirchegger, *Die Untersteiermark*, p. 241, subsequently indicated that Frederick III's brother might have been the nephew of the older Otto of Königsberg, but Pirchegger did not pursue the issue.

46. *SUB* 1:663, no. 166.

47. Klebel, *Der Lungau*, pp. 151–53, 160–63.

48. *SUB* 3:8–10, no. 540.

49. *MC* 3:470–71, no. 1242; *UB Steiermark* 1:585–89, nos. 619, 620, and pp. 620–21, no. 644.

50. Klebel, *Der Lungau*, p. 164.

51. *Chronicon Gurcense*, p. 9.

52. *MC* 1:211–14, no. 279.

53. *MC* 1:212, headnote to no. 279.

54. Klebel, *Der Lungau*, pp. 164–65.

55. Freed, "Diemut von Högl," pp. 638–40; Freed, *The Counts of Falkenstein*, p. 51.

56. *MC* 2:57–58, no. 602.

57. Ibid.

58. *UB Steiermark* 2:472–73, no. 363. Sophia was called the daughter of Albert of Rohitsch in *UB Steiermark* 3:106–8, no. 49. He was identified as a Styrian ministerial in *UB Steiermark* 2:134–35, no. 87.

59. *UB Steiermark* 3:106–8, no. 49.

60. *UB Steiermark* 3:110–11, no. 51.

61. *MC* 2:55–56, no. 600.

62. *UB Steiermark* 3:293–94, no. 207.

63. *UB Steiermark* 3:328–30, no. 248.

64. *MC* 2:112–13, no. 665.

65. Freed, *The Counts of Falkenstein*, pp. 65–66; Freed, "Diemut von Högl," pp. 654–55.

66. *UB Steiermark* 3:328–30, no. 240. Pirchegger, *Die Untersteiermark*, p. 190, suggests that a Königsberg might have married before 1257 a Sannegg, one of the ancestors of the later counts of Cilli. Since Otto I's wife was a Rohitsch, Otto II's wife, Anna, is the most likely candidate.

67. *MC* 2:112–13, no. 665.

68. *MC* 2:126–27, no. 683.

69. *UB Steiermark* 4:337, no. 562.

70. *Regesten des Herzogtums Steiermark* (hereafter cited as *Regesten Steiermark*), 1:260, no. 981.

71. *Regesten Steiermark* 1:121, no. 435. See also *Regesten Steiermark* 1:128, no. 461.

72. *Die Regesten der Erzbischöfe und des Domkapitels von Salzburg, 1247–1343* (hereafter cited as *Regesten Salzburg*), 2:52, no. 418. On the ministerials' financial problems, see Freed, "Crisis of the Salzburg Ministerialage."

73. *MC* 7:106, no. 271.

74. *Regesten Steiermark* 1:79, no. 282. The document does not explicitly state that the properties had been part of Diemut's dowry, but they were situated in and around Mureck. The Kranichbergs had been one of the Mureck heirs. See *SUB* 3:624–26, no. 1079.

75. *Regesten Steiermark* 1:158, no. 581.

76. Bilowitzky, "Heiratsgaben," esp. pp. 27–34, 69, 75. For a more generalized discussion of the *Heiratsgabensystem*, see Brauneder, *Die Entwicklung des Ehegüterrechts in Österreich.*

77. Bilowitzky, "Heiratsgaben," p. 40.

78. *UB Steiermark* 2:43–44, no. 21.

79. *SUB* 3:269–70, no. 744a; *UB Steiermark* 2:292–93, no. 203.

80. *UB Steiermark* 2:369, no. 271.

81. Pirchegger, "Die Herren von Pettau," p. 12.

82. *SUB* 3:146–49, no. 645.

83. *SUB* 3:174–76, no. 669.

84. *MC* 2:57–58, no. 602.

85. *MC* 1:310–12, no. 418.

86. *SUB* 3:174–76, no. 669. On the identification of Provost Henry as Frederick III's brother, see *MC* 1:346, no. 451, and *Annales sancti Rudberti Salisburgenses*, p. 700.

87. *UB Steiermark* 2:335–38, no. 245; *SUB* 3:495–96, no. 943; *SUB* 3:519–20, no. 969.

88. Klebel, *Der Lungau*, p. 89.

89. *UB Steiermark* 2:335–38, no. 245 (see esp. p. 336).

90. Pirchegger, *Die Untersteiermark*, p. 243, thinks that Ulrich might have been Ortolf's nephew. Franz von Krones identifies Ulrich as Ortolf's brother or cousin (cited by Klebel, *Der Lungau*, p. 89 n. 349).

91. *SUB* 3:495–96, no. 943. Emperor Frederick II referred to Adelaide of Pettau as an imperial ministerial. Hartnid I's wife, an unnamed Hollenburg, was a Styrian ministerial. The couple's children had presumably been divided, as was customary in such cases, between the archbishop and the duke of Styria; Adelaide had presumably been assigned to the duke. Since Frederick II had confiscated the duchy of Styria, Adelaide was technically in 1239 an imperial ministerial.

92. *MC* 2:55–56, no. 600.

93. For another example of a young man, Meginhard of Siegsdorf, marrying an heiress in his father's lifetime, see Freed, "Diemut von Högl," pp. 603–5, 655.

94. Pirchegger, *Landfürst und Adel*, vol. 1, genealogical chart after p. 205.

95. Klebel, *Der Lungau*, pp. 89–92.

96. MC 3:402–3, no. 1073; MC 4/1:129–30, no. 1847. See Pirchegger, *Landfürst und Adel* 1:153–55 and genealogical chart after p. 205.

97. *UB Steiermark* 3:103–5, no. 47.

98. Pirchegger, "Die Herren von Pettau," genealogical chart after p. 199.

99. *MC* 4/1:163, no. 1930.

100. Dopsch, *Geschichte Salzburgs* 1/2:1049; Pirchegger, *Die Untersteiermark*, p. 159.

101. *Ottokars österreichische Reimchronik*, vol. 1, lines 11900–980; *UB Steiermark* 4:356–57, no. 600.

102. *Necrologia Germaniae* 2:361, no. 35.

103. Herlihy, "The Making of the Medieval Family," p. 123.

104. *UB Steiermark* 2:316, no. 223.

105. *Urkunden- und Regestenbuch des Herzogtums Krain* (hereafter cited as *UB Krain*), 2:61, no. 83.

106. *UB Steiermark* 2:427–28, no. 324.

107. *UB Steiermark* 2:292–93, no. 203.

108. *SUB* 3:516–17, no. 967.

109. *UB Steiermark* 4:38, no. 58. Frederick V was still identified here as Frederick the Younger.

110. *MC* 4/2:639–40, no. 2905.

111. *SUB* 3:531–32, nos. 982, 983.

112. Henry was still married in 1235 to a sister of the Carinthian ministerial Henry of Greifenfels (*MC* 4/1:225, no. 2100).

113. *SUB* 3:601, no. 1054.

114. Klebel, *Der Lungau*, pp. 151–53.

115. *UB Krain* 2:130–32, no. 168.

116. *MC* 2:55–56, no. 600.

117. *UB Krain* 2:213–14, no. 273.

118. *UB Krain* 2:250–51, no. 331.

119. *MC* 4/2:687–88, no. 2974.

120. *MC* 5:107–8, no. 154.

121. *UB Steiermark* 4:307, no. 509.

122. *UB Steiermark* 2:354, no. 257.

123. *MC* 4/1:336–37, no. 2327; MC 4/1:363, no. 2381; MC 4/1:412–13, no. 2504; and *SUB* 3:640–42, no. 1096. On the Hollenburgs' status, see Fräss-Ehrfeld, *Geschichte Kärntens* 1:189–90. On Wurmberg, see Pirchegger, *Die Untersteiermark*, pp. 76–79.

124. *SUB* 3:495–96, no. 943.

125. *UB Steiermark* 4:298, no. 494; *MC* 5:274–75, no. 428; *Regesten Salzburg* 1:123, no. 959; *Regesten Salzburg* 1:126, no. 981.

126. *Ottokars österreichische Reimchronik*, vol. 1, lines 14587–97.

127. *SUB* 3:640–42, no. 1096.

128. *MC* 2:111–12, no. 664.

129. *Regesten Salzburg* 1:123, no. 959.

130. *Regesten Salzburg* 1:15, no. 101.

131. *Regesten Salzburg* 1:14–15, nos. 98, 99.

132. *MC* 3/1:412–13, no. 2504.

133. *MC* 6:20–21, no. 29.

134. *Regesten Salzburg* 1:123, no. 959.

135. *Regesten Salzburg* 1:164–65, no. 1276.

136. Pirchegger, "Die Herren von Pettau," p. 17.

137. Bilowitzky, "Heiratsgaben," pp. 51–52. Bilowitzky talks about the last generation of the Pettaus as the seventh generation after Frederick V, but Pirchegger's genealogical chart, "Die Herren von Pettau," after p. 199, indicates that there were only five generations after Frederick V.

138. Klebel, *Der Lungau*, pp. 89–92.

139. *UB Steiermark* 2:292–93, no. 203.

BIBLIOGRAPHY

Primary Sources

Annales sancti Rudberti Salisburgenses a. 1–1286. Ed. Wilhelm Wattenbach. MGH SS 9:758–810. Hannover, 1851.

Chronicon Gurcense. Ed. Wilhelm Wattenbach. MGH SS 23:8–10. Hannover, 1874.

Codex diplomaticus Brandenburgensis: Sammlung der Urkunden, Chroniken und sonstigen Quellenschriften für die Geschichte der Mark Brandenburg und ihrer Regenten. Ed. Adolf Friedrich Riedel. 41 vols. Berlin, 1838–69.

Codex diplomaticus Saxoniae Regiae. 24 vols. Leipzig, 1864–1909.

Codex Falkensteinensis: Die Rechtsaufzeichnungen der Grafen von Falkenstein. Ed. Elisabeth Noichl. Quellen und Erörterungen zur bayerischen Geschichte, n.s., 29. Munich, 1978.

"Codex traditionum Augiensium." Ed. Johann Mayerhofer. In *Drei bayerische Traditionsbücher aus dem XII. Jahrhundert: Festschrift zum 700 jährigen Jubiläum der Wittelsbacher Thronbesteigung*, ed. Hans Petz, Hermann Grauert, and Johann Mayerhofer, pp. 87–152. Munich, 1880.

Drei bayerische Traditionsbücher aus dem XII. Jahrhundert: Festschrift zum 700 jährigen Jubiläum der Wittelsbacher Thronbesteigung. Ed. Hans Petz, Hermann Grauert, and Johann Mayerhofer. Munich, 1880.

Fontes rerum Austriacarum: Österreichische Geschichtsquellen. I. Abteilung: *Scriptores.* 9 vols. Vienna, 1855–. II. Abteilung: *Diplomataria et acta.* 78 vols. Vienna, 1849–. III. Abteilung: *Fontes iuris.* 4 vols. Vienna, 1953–.

Monumenta Boica. 60 vols. Munich, 1763–1956.

Monumenta historica ducatus Carinthiae. Ed. August von Jaksch and Hermann Wiessner. 11 vols. 1896–1972. Reprint of vols. 1–4. Klagenfurt, 1976–78.

Necrologia Germaniae. Vol. 2, *Dioecesis Salisburgensis.* Ed. Sigismund Herzberg-Fränkel. Monumenta Germaniae Historica. 1904. Reprint. Munich, 1983.

Ottokars österreichische Reimchronik. Ed. Joseph Seemüller. 2 vols. MGH Deutsche Chroniken, no. 5. 1890–93. Reprint. Dublin and Zürich, 1974.

Quellen und Erörterungen zur bayerischen und deutschen Geschichte. 9 vols. Munich, 1856–64. New series, 31 vols. Munich, 1903–.

Die Regesten der Erzbischöfe und des Domkapitels von Salzburg, 1247–1343. Ed. Franz Martin. 3 vols. Salzburg, 1926–34.

Regesten des Herzogtums Steiermark. Vol. 1, *1308–1319.* Ed. Annelies Redik. Quellen zur geschichtlichen Landeskunde der Steiermark, no. 6. Graz, 1976.

Salzburger Urkundenbuch. Ed. Willibald Hauthaler and Franz Martin. 4 vols. Salzburg, 1910–33.

Schenkungsbuch der ehemaligen gefürsteten Probstei Berchtesgaden. Ed. Karl August Muffat. Quellen und Erörterungen zur bayerischen und deutschen Geschichte, o.s., no. 1, pp. 225–364. Munich, 1856.

Die Traditionen, Urkunden, und Urbare des Stiftes Gars. Ed. Heiner Hofmann. Quellen und Erörterungen zur bayerischen Geschichte, n.s., no. 31. Munich, 1983.

Urkundenbuch des Herzogthums Steiermark. Ed. Joseph von Zahn and Gerhard Pferschy. 4 vols. Graz and Vienna, 1875–1975.

Urkundenbuch des Landes ob der Enns. 11 vols. Vienna and Linz, 1852–1956.

Die Urkunden des Klosters Raitenhaslach, 1034–1350. Ed. Edgar Krausen. Quellen und Erörterungen zur bayerischen Geschichte, n.s., no. 17. 2 vols. Munich, 1959–60.

Urkunden- und Regestenbuch des Herzogtums Krain. Ed. Franz Schumi. 2 vols. Ljubljana, 1882–87.

Vita Chunradi archiepiscopi. Ed. Wilhelm Wattenbach. MGH SS 11:62–77. Hannover, 1854.

Wirtembergisches Urkundenbuch. 11 vols. 1849–1913. Reprint. Aalen, 1972.

Württembergische Geschichtsquellen. 25 vols. Stuttgart, 1894–1956.

Württembergische Regesten von 1301 bis 1500. 3 pts. Stuttgart, 1916–40.

Secondary Sources

Althoff, Gerd. "Unerforschte Quellen aus quellenarmer Zeit (IV): Zur Verflechtung der Führungsschichten in den Gedenkquellen des frühen zehnten Jahrhunderts." In *Medieval Lives and the Historian: Studies in Medieval Prosopog-*

raphy, ed. Neithard Bulst and Jean-Philippe Genet, pp. 37–71. Kalamazoo, Mich., 1986.

Arnold, Benjamin. *German Knighthood, 1050–1300.* Oxford, 1985.

Bilowitzky, Harald. "Die Heiratsgaben in der Steiermark während des späten Mittelalters unter stände- und wirtschaftsgeschichtlichem Aspekt." Ph.D. diss., University of Graz, 1977.

Bracher, Karl. "Lassnitz-Sulm: Zur mittelalterlichen Geschichte der Zwischenflusslandschaft." *Zeitschrift des Historischen Vereines für Steiermark* 59 (1968): 135–69.

Brauneder, Wilhelm. *Die Entwicklung des Ehegüterrechts in Österreich: Ein Beitrag zur Dogmengeschichte und Rechtstatsachforschung des Spätmittelalters und der Neuzeit.* Salzburg and Munich, 1973.

Busse-Wilson, Elisabeth. *Das Leben der heiligen Elisabeth von Thüringen: Das Abbild einer mittelalterlichen Seele.* Munich, 1931.

Dahlmann-Waitz. *Quellenkunde der deutschen Geschichte: Bibliographie der Quellen und der Literatur zur deutschen Geschichte.* Ed. Hermann Heimpel and Herbert Geuss. 4 vols. 10th ed. Stuttgart, 1965–83.

Decker, Otmar. *Die Stellung des Predigerordens zu den Dominikanerinnen (1207–1267).* Quellen und Forschungen zur Geschichte des Dominikanerordens in Deutschland, no. 31. Leipzig, 1935.

Dollinger, Philippe. *L'Évolution des classes rurales en Bavière depuis la fin de l'époque carolingienne jusq'au milieu du XIIIe siècle.* Publications de la Faculté des lettres de l'Université de Strasbourg, no. 112. Paris, 1949.

Dopsch, Heinz. "Die Ministerialität des Herzogtums Steiermark zur Zeit der Georgenberger Handfeste: Ihre rechtliche, gesellschaftliche und politische Stellung." In *800 Jahre Georgenberger Handfeste: Lebensformen im Mittelalter. Ausstellung im Museum Lauriacum Enns 15. Mai. bis 26. Oktober 1986,* pp. 29–44.

———. *Geschichte Salzburgs: Stadt und Land.* Vol. 1, *Vorgeschichte, Altertum, Mittelalter.* 3 pts. Salzburg, 1981–84.

———. "Ministerialität und Herrenstand in der Steiermark und in Salzburg." *Zeitschrift des Historischen Vereines für Steiermark* 62 (1971): 3–31.

———. "Probleme ständischer Wandlung beim Adel Österreichs, der Steiermark und Salzburg vornehmlich im 13. Jahrhundert." In *Herrschaft und Stand: Untersuchungen zur Sozialgeschichte im 13. Jahrhundert,* ed. Josef Fleckenstein, pp. 207–53. Veröffentlichungen des Max-Planck-Instituts für Geschichte, no. 51. Göttingen, 1977.

Duby, Georges. "Lineage, Nobility, and Knighthood: The Mâconnais in the Twelfth Century—a Revision." In *The Chivalrous Society,* trans. Cynthia Postan, pp. 59–80. Berkeley, 1977.

———. *Medieval Marriage: Two Models from Twelfth-Century France.* Trans. Elborg Forster. Johns Hopkins Symposia in Comparative History, no. 11. Baltimore, 1978.

Ennen, Edith. *Frauen im Mittelalter.* Munich, 1984.

Erben, Wilhelm. "Untersuchungen zu dem Codex traditionum Odalberti." *Mitteilungen der Gesellschaft für Salzburger Landeskunde* 29 (1889): 454–80.

Fichtenau, Heinrich. *Das Urkundenwesen in Österreich vom 8. bis zum frühen 13. Jahrhundert.* Mitteilungen des Instituts für österreichische Geschichtsforschung, suppl. vol. 23. Vienna, 1971.

Fräss-Ehrfeld, Claudia. *Geschichte Kärntens.* Vol. 1, *Das Mittelalter.* Klagenfurt, 1984.

Freed, John B. *The Counts of Falkenstein: Noble Self-Consciousness in Twelfth-Century Germany.* Transactions of the American Philosophical Society, 74/6. Philadelphia, 1984.

———. "The Crisis of the Salzburg Ministerialage, 1270–1343." *Studies in Medieval and Renaissance History* 11 (1989). In press.

———. "Diemut von Högl: Eine Salzburger Erbtochter und die erzbischöfliche Ministerialität im Hochmittelalter." *Mitteilungen der Gesellschaft für Salzburger Landeskunde* 120/21 (1980/81): 581–657.

———. "The Formation of the Salzburg Ministerialage in the Tenth and Eleventh Centuries: An Example of Upward Social Mobility in the Early Middle Ages." *Viator* 9 (1978): 67–102.

———. *The Friars and German Society in the Thirteenth Century.* Publications of the Mediaeval Academy of America, no. 86. Cambridge, Mass., 1977.

———. "Nobles, Ministerials, and Knights in the Archdiocese of Salzburg." *Speculum* 62 (1987): 575–611.

———. "Urban Development and the 'Cura Monialium' in Thirteenth-Century Germany." *Viator* 3 (1972): 311–27.

Greven, Joseph. *Die Anfänge der Beginen: Ein Beitrag zur Geschichte der Volksfrömmigkeit des Ordenswesen im Hochmittelalter.* Vorreformationsgeschichtliche Forschungen, no. 8. Münster, 1912.

Hauthaler, Willibald, and Eduard Richter. "Die Salzburgischen Traditionscodices des X. und XI. Jahrhunderts." *Mittheilungen des Instituts für österreichische Geschichtsforschung* 3 (1882): 63–95, 369–85.

Herlihy, David. "The Making of the Medieval Family: Symmetry, Structure, and Sentiment." *Journal of Family History* 8 (1983): 116–30.

Höck, Josef. *Geschichte der Propstei Wieting im Görtschitztal, Kärnten (1147–1848).* Salzburg, 1979.

Howell, Martha, with the collaboration of Suzanne Wemple and Denise Kaiser. "A Documented Presence: Medieval Women in Germanic Historiography." In *Women in Medieval History and Historiography,* ed. Susan Mosher Stuard, pp. 101–31. Philadelphia, 1987.

Klebel, Ernst. *Der Lungau: Historisch-politische Untersuchung.* Salzburg, 1960.

Leyser, Karl J. *Rule and Conflict in an Early Medieval Society: Ottonian Saxony.* London and Bloomington, Ind. 1979.

McDonnell, Ernest W. *The Beguines and Beghards in Medieval Culture: With Special Emphasis on the Belgian Scene.* 1954. Reprint. New York, 1969.

McLaughlin, Mary Martin. "Survivors and Surrogates: Children and Parents from the Ninth to the Thirteenth Centuries." In *The History of Childhood,* ed. Lloyd deMause, pp. 101–81. New York, 1975.

Maurer, Wilhelm. "Zum Verständnis der hl. Elisabeth von Thüringen." *Zeitschrift für Kirchengeschichte* 65 (1953–54): 16–64.

Phillips, Dayton. *Beguines in Medieval Strasburg: A Study of the Social Aspects of Beguine Life.* Palo Alto, Calif. 1941.

Pirchegger, Hans. "Die Herren von Pettau." *Zeitschrift des Historischen Vereines für Steiermark* 42 (1951): 3–36.

―――. *Die Untersteiermark in der Geschichte ihrer Herrschaften und Gülten, Städte und Märkte.* Buchreiche der Südostdeutschen Historischen Kommission, no. 10. Munich, 1962.

―――. *Landfürst und Adel in Steiermark während des Mittelalters.* 3 vols. Forschungen zur Verfassungs- und Verwaltungsgeschichte der Steiermark, nos. 12, 13, 16. Graz, 1951–58.

Redlich, Oswald. "Über bairische Traditionsbücher und Traditionen." *Mittheilungen des Instituts für österreichische Geschichtsforschung* 5 (1884): 1–82.

Schmid, Karl. *Gebetsgedenken und adliges Selbstverständnis im Mittelalter: Ausgewählte Beiträge. Festgabe zu seinem sechzigsten Geburtstag.* Sigmaringen, 1983.

Schuller, Helga. "Dos—Praebenda—Peculium." In *Festschrift Friedrich Hausmann,* ed. Herwig Ebner, pp. 453–87. Graz, 1977.

Sheehan, James J. "What Is German History?: Reflections on the Role of the Nation in German History and Historiography." *Journal of Modern History* 53 (1981): 1–23.

Simon, André. *L'Ordre des Pénitentes de Ste. Marie-Madeleine en Allemagne au XIIIe siècle.* Fribourg, 1918.

Sonnleitner, Käthe. "Die Stellung der Kinder von Unfreien im Mittelalter in Salzburg, Steiermark und Kärnten." *Mitteilungen der Gesellschaft für Salzburger Landeskunde* 123 (1983): 149–66.

Stuard, Susan Mosher. *Women in Medieval Society.* Philadelphia, 1976.

Tyroller, Franz. "Abstammung und Verwandschaft des Abtes Rupert I. von Tegernsee († 1186)." *Studien und Mitteilungen zur Geschichte des Benediktiner-Ordens und seiner Zweige* 65 (1953/54): 116–45.

Wauer, Edmund. *Entstehung und Ausbreitung des Klarissenordens besonders in den deutschen Minoritenprovinzen.* Leipzig, 1906.

Wemple, Suzanne Fonay. Review of *Frauen im Mittelalter,* by Edith Ennen. *Speculum* 61 (1986): 923–25.

Widemann, Josef. "Die Traditionen der bayerischen Klöster." *Zeitschrift für bayerische Landesgeschichte* 1 (1928): 225–43.

THE CHARTERS OF
LE RONCERAY D'ANGERS

Male/Female Interaction in Monastic Business

Penny S. Gold

onastic charters survive by the hundreds for many medieval religious communities. These documents were drawn up and preserved in order to provide a permanent record of a community's rights and privileges; they were commonly recopied into collections called cartularies. The two most common sorts of charters are <u>records of gifts</u> or sales to the community and <u>records of disputes</u> regarding monastic property or privileges and their dispositions. Although the intention with which these records were made may have centered on the provision of a business and legal archive, the charters unintentionally reveal to the historian much information regarding social, political, and religious history as well. The wealth of information available in these documents may be divided into information about the secular context external to the monastery and information about the internal institutional setup of the monastery. Both types of information are available in sufficient amounts to be analyzed by quantitative as well as by qualitative methodologies. ❡ The quantitative analysis of information regarding the secular environment has yielded much significant information regarding the <u>position of women</u> within medieval social structures—information regarding, for example, the extent of women's control over property and how it changed over time.[1] Less work has been done to exploit these documents for information about the lives of the religious women within the communities. This essay will explore one particular area of monastic life that is richly documented: the institutional structures governing the administration of a monastery's temporal holdings. In particular, I have wanted to know in what ways and to what extent nuns controlled and participated in such administration and to what extent male personnel connected with female communities shared or directed such administration. What was the extent of power and authority exercised by women in their communities, and how did this compare with the power of secular women?

Information about male/female interaction in the administrative workings of monastic communities is best gained by combining a systematic quantitative analysis with a more traditional exploitation of particular details of institutional life, which are scattered through the charters. A quantitative approach is useful for the general picture it can provide of persistent patterns of interaction, while an anecdotal approach helps to fill out details and to give a sense of particular situations. The present study will illustrate the possibilities for such analysis by using the case of Le Ronceray d'Angers, a community of Benedictine nuns in western France.[2] Some comparison will be made to the community of Fontevrault, whose rule was a modification of Saint Benedict's.[3] For both communities I have focused the analysis on the first half of the twelfth century. [4]

The charters were coded using the following categories of information.

Personnel. What people associated with the community participated in transactions? If male, were they clerics or laymen, and what official function did they have in the community? If female, did they hold a monastic office (and which one), or were they simple members of the community?

Role. What role did each individual play in the transaction? Was the person named as having initiated an action or as having seen to its being carried through? Who received *in manu* (in hand) the symbol of the gift or agreement? Who was present as witness to the transaction? (The great majority of participants were present as witnesses. It was those few individuals who were in charge of transactions who participated in the first two roles.)

Type of action. Does the charter record a donation or sale, or does it record a settlement reached after a claim or other disagreement? If the latter, was the disagreement with a layperson, or was it a dispute with another religious community?

Location of action. Was the transaction done within the monastery? If so, where—in chapter, in the church, or in the abbess's chamber? If done outside the community, was it in someone's home, at another monastic community, or in the bishop's court or the count's court?

From a combination of the data on personnel, roles, and context, we can discern patterns of participation in the charters and thereby determine to what extent and under what conditions male and female personnel acted separately and together.

❧ Le Ronceray was founded in 1028 by Fulk Nerra, count of Anjou, and his wife, Hildegarde. At the time of the foundation, Fulk and Hildegarde also established four priests to serve the nuns (R1). By the middle of the twelfth century, two clerical communities were associated with Le Ronceray: the canons (*canonici*), who were to take care of the liturgical needs of the abbey itself, and a number of chaplains (*capellani*), who were to serve the parish church adjacent to the abbey.[5] We usually cannot ascertain the precise number of canons and chaplains associated with Le Ronceray at any one time, but a charter of about 1130 mentions four chaplains (R42), and a charter of 1160 mentions four canons and two chaplains, the six appearing to make up the entire clerical staff at that time (R31).

Among the male clerical personnel, the canons appear the most prominently in the charters of the community. Over the course of the fifty-year period, fifteen canons participated in various transactions. Most appear several times or more, with one canon serving as witness no fewer than thirty-five times and five others serving ten or more times. Other clerical personnel mentioned include four priests (*sacerdos, presbiter*), four chaplains, two clerics (*clericus*), five deacons (*diaconus, archidiaconus, subdiaconus*), and two sacristans (*sacrista, secretarius*).[6] This diversity of personnel was probably due to the parish church associated with Le Ronceray.

Fontevrault, in contrast, was a community without a parish church, and it was in a rural area, unlike Le Ronceray, which had close by the numerous other monastic and ecclesiastical foundations of Angers. Yet the number of clerical personnel in service to Fontevrault was larger than that at Le Ronceray. Charters from the period 1100–1149 include at least seventy-nine different male (clerical) witnesses, as opposed to about thirty for Le Ronceray. In the case of Fontevrault, the men were monks from the male community resident at Fontevrault. The pattern of clerical participation is also different in the two communities: at Le Ronceray, a small number of clerics, mostly canons, are visible in a large number of transactions; at Fontevrault, no monk appears more than once or twice, the function of witness being spread more widely through the larger group of clerical personnel.

In addition to its clerics, Le Ronceray was also served by a variety of laymen, of whom about half a dozen appear frequently among witnesses (one as many as forty-five times). Most prominent were men in two administrative positions, those of vicar (*vicarius* or *villicus*) and of provost (*prepositus* or *prefectus*). Other officials or servants appearing regularly were cellarers, seneschals (*siniscallus, dapifer*), cooks (*cocus*), and bakers (*pistor*). A certain Engelbaudus, identified simply as *villanus* or *rusticus*, witnessed thirty charters, and appearing occasionally were various other men, including shoemakers, a fisherman, carpenters, farriers, millers, preparers of skins, foresters, and others identified only as servants of Le Ronceray (*famuli, servientes*).

All these men served as witnesses in the charters, but the provost also occasionally played a more central role in the transaction of business. Rainaudus Fossardus, one of the most prominent of the ten or so provosts, gave testimony on behalf of Le Ronceray in the bishop's court (R181) and also was the recipient of an oath of fidelity to the community (R248). Mainus Bacheloth went to the neighboring monastery of Saint-Aubin to negotiate a settlement with the monks (R123) and handled other disputes as well (R107, R205). A provost named Hugo saw to it that some needed ditches were dug (R202); Garinus was sent out to obtain a concession to a gift made to the community (R195); and Bernardus participated in the symbolic gesture of receiving a gift to the community "in his hand" (*in manu*), a role usually played by the abbess of the community (R204). Thus the provost, in addition to serving in the ancillary role of witness, had the capacity to serve as an official representative of the community.

Important as was the participation of provost, other laymen, and clerical personnel, what is most striking is the extent to which these men acted in conjunction with women of the community. The abbess was the most active and central participant, but other nuns holding monastic office also appear, including five prioresses, six almoners (*elemosinaria*), five sacristans (*sacrista*), five deans (*decana*), nine cellarers, and one *grammatica*. More than thirty other nuns not identified by any office also participated, with a total of about seventy different nuns appearing in the charters from this fifty-year period. In most instances they served as witnesses, although the nuns holding office—especially the abbess, but also the almoner, the cellarer, and the sacristan—played other roles as well. The abbess was clearly in charge of most of the transactions in which she appears. It is common to see her named as the person initiating settlement, and the abbess normally received in hand the token symbolizing a gift or settlement. She represented the community in the courts of bishops, counts, and abbots, and she herself held court, at which some disputes were settled. There was little or nothing done by men that was not also done, and done more frequently, by the abbess or by other nuns holding office.

This constellation of participation contrasts sharply with that found at Fontevrault. While the abbess's role was the same and the prioress figured prominently as well, virtually no other nuns served as witnesses in the charters of Fontevrault, nor are they seen carrying out any other business role. Thus, the administrative control in both Le Ronceray and Fontevrault was in the hands of the abbess, but at Fontevrault the tasks of dealing with the outside world were restricted to two female officials and spread widely over a large group of monks, whereas at Le Ronceray these tasks were spread widely over a large group of nuns, with extensive participation by a smaller group of male personnel, both clerical and lay.

A few examples drawn from the cartulary of Le Ronceray will illustrate the procedures usually followed in the transaction of business and the extent to which success in this business rested upon the close interaction of men and women. At the community, business was usually carried out in the nuns' chapter and in the church. Commonly, a gift to the community was confirmed in the chapter, in the presence of the whole congregation of nuns, and a ceremony was performed at the altar of the church, with a ritual transfer of an object symbolizing the gift. Witnesses might be recorded for either or both of these events, which could be attended by people from outside the community. One gift, for example, was confirmed in chapter "in the presence of Theburgis abbess, Imberga cellerar, Orieldis sacristan, Anna almoner, and the whole convent, in the hearing of the clerics and servants of this church . . . and in the presence of a big crowd of people gathered there" (R101). The way in which men and women of Le Ronceray were recorded as witnesses may represent both the closeness of association—in that they were both present at the transaction—and the separation of the sexes —in that men and women were always grouped separately in the lists, never intermixed. Sometimes the list is marked off into groups tagged "from the nuns" and "from the men [or servants or clerics] of Sancta Maria"; sometimes there is just one list, but the men and women of the community are always grouped by sex.

Formal actions performed at the community were handled by the abbess, commonly with the participation of some nuns and male personnel. Actions carried out away from the community were often handled in a similar fashion but were sometimes handled by the female cellarer or almoner (R296, R118) and sometimes by male personnel only.[7] A typical trip included the abbess, a couple of nuns, and a variety of men from the community, both clerical and lay. For example, in 1126 a man made a gift to Le Ronceray on the occasion of his sister becoming a nun. The ceremony was held in the cathedral church of Angers, across the river from Le Ronceray. Listed as "present" at the ceremony were the bishop of Angers, the abbess, and two nuns of Le Ronceray. Listed as "seeing and consenting" to the act were seventeen men, including a canon and the vicar (*vicarius*) of Le Ronceray (R356). In 1143, the settlement of a dispute between the monks of Saint-Aubin of Angers and the nuns was first confirmed in the chapter of Le Ronceray in a ceremony attended by three monks and a servant from Saint-Aubin. "Then, on the same day, the venerable lady abbess Hamelina came to the chapter of Saint-Aubin with two nuns, the deaconess [*diaconissa*] Petronilla and the cellarer Osanna, and there the settlement was confirmed by Abbot Robert." The witnesses listed "on the part of the nuns" were a canon, vicar, seneschal, farrier, cook, and baker (R111).[8] The division of ritual role in these and other cases suggests that the abbess and nuns were the official representatives of the community and that they were accompanied by an appropriate retinue of men. It was important and expected that the abbess be accompanied in her travels by men.[9] The duties of a servant of the community might include going with the abbess wherever she wanted to go (R290). One agreement states that a man who had been given a house by the nuns was to go with them on their journeys for whatever cause, and if fear kept him from doing so, he was to lend two horses to the nuns, who were not responsible if anything happened to them on the way (R70).

The closeness of association between the nuns and their canons is highlighted by the language used to describe the bringing of several suits (*calumpniae*) by the community: the claims were made conjointly by the nuns and canons or by the abbess, nuns, and canons.[10] The canons were not just "employees" but members of the community—not in the same way nuns were, yet they were more integrally involved in community identity and community affairs than one might suspect.

The nuns thus interacted with men in substantial ways in the ordinary course of the community's business. In addition to whatever interaction there might have been in connection with religious ceremony, the nuns worked together with men in seeing that the community's interests were being protected and extended. It was expected that women and men would travel together; in fact, the rule of Fontevrault established that no nun was to go outside the community without at least two men, one religious and one secular.[11] The clerical personnel at a female community lived in close proximity to women and had frequent contact with them. In contrast, their male peers in a cathedral chapter or male monastery had more limited contact with women. For example, female servants at a male community certainly were not asked to attend the abbot in his travels or to serve as witnesses to gifts or settlements. These monks and clerics experienced a world that was more homosocial than that of their brothers among the personnel of nuns' communities or that of the nuns.

Attention should also be given to the extent to which the administration of temporal affairs at Le Ronceray, as well as at Fontevrault, was in the hands of the abbess. Comparative study of other communities and at other periods is much needed. The abbess at a community more strictly cloistered than either of these Benedictine communities might have had to rely more heavily on her male personnel. But at least in these two cases, the authority and power exercised by the abbess was different from that possible for most medieval women, who, as daughters, wives, and mothers, usually acted through men, except in unusual circumstances or perhaps in widowhood.[12] The frequent presence of nuns as witnesses, at least at Le Ronceray, is also important in this regard, as it is in striking contrast with the rarity of secular women among witnesses.

Yet despite the similarity of the abbess's role at Le Ronceray and Fontevrault, there was also an important difference in the relationship between the abbess and the clerical personnel at these two communities. At Fontevrault, the abbess was in complete charge of the whole community of men, and, according to the rule of Fontevrault, the male members of the community, both clerical and lay, promised to serve under a bond of obedience to the nuns.[13] But at Le Ronceray, the abbess's authority over the resident clerics was not so absolute. The noble founders of Le Ronceray anticipated possible problems in the foundation charter. Fulk and Hildegarde insisted that the four priests were to "personally serve zealously in this church, not having substitutes, and . . . [were] to remain continually in this church; lest, on account of their neglect or inconstancy some negligence will occur in the service of God in this church" (R1). Although I have found no evidence of such neglect in the charters, there is scattered evidence of discord between the abbess and her canons or priests over more mundane matters. In 1160, for example, the nuns and the two chaplains of their parish church argued over the distribution of offerings received at Easter and at masses for the dead. This dispute was settled at Chinon in the court of Henry II (in his capacity as count of Anjou). Included in his ruling was the decision that after the death of the current two chaplains and four canons, the abbess and nuns were to have control over the choice of clerical personnel and were also to have the authority to fix their income (R31). A similar dispute over clerical income occurred at a priory of Le Ronceray (R167). Such occurrences were less likely at Fontevrault, where the abbess's authority over the men had been more fully spelled out.

❡ The above analysis of the charters of the monastery of Le Ronceray d'Angers illustrates both the strengths and weaknesses of a local study based on detailed analysis of the corpus of documents from one community. By combining quantitative and qualitative approaches, we can gain an understanding both of the makeup of monastic personnel in a women's community and of the patterns of interaction between men and women in the carrying out of official business. By comparing local studies, we can see the diversity of arrangements that female communities made for the provision of spiritual and economic service. Some of the differences undoubtedly derive from the differences in monastic rules among various communities, but my suspicion is that local situations also had a prominent effect on particular arrangements. We need many more local studies in order to gauge these differences and to assess their causes. Gathered together, local studies will eventually enable us to generalize about the type and extent of power exercised by women within a monastic context.

But other sorts of information about the relationship of women and men within a religious community are not available in the charters. These documents are by their nature records of interaction with the world outside the community. There is little surviving evidence of the internal workings of a community or, more particularly, of the everyday interaction between men and women within the community. It is therefore difficult to know the nature or extent of such interaction or to understand the emotional content of the relationships between men and women within the same community. Some sense of the affective side of this interaction may be gained from hagiographical and epistolary documents, but one is unlikely to be able to match up analysis of such documents with an analysis of charter evidence from the same communities.

Finally, I would like to note some of the technical problems involved in the exploitation of these documents. Monastic charters are not the uniform, precise, and complete records that are most suitable for quantitative analysis. Any such analysis of monastic charters must be done

—and read—with an acknowledgment that completeness and precision cannot be attained. The most serious problem for the study presented here was the difficulty in ascertaining with precision the particular men associated directly with Le Ronceray. Since people are commonly identified by a first name only, and since different individuals may have the same name, I may have underestimated the number of individuals by counting two or more individuals with the same name as only one person. It was also difficult to know precisely which participants are actually directly associated with Le Ronceray as members or servants of the community and which are at the ceremony for other reasons. Although I counted all witnesses listed *ex parte Sancte Marie* as being associated with Le Ronceray, there is at least one example where that list includes an abbot and monks from another community (R228). And while I usually relied on a specific notation of office or position to identify an individual associated with the community (thus judging individuals identified by their name alone as *not* being associated with the community, unless they were identified in a witness list), there were many charters in which an individual familiar to me as, say, a provost of Le Ronceray because of identification in other charters appeared without such identification. [14]

While these problems may blur the details of a study, they are not serious enough to invalidate the general picture of institutional structures at a given community and of the pattern of interaction between men and women in these structures. For this subject there is no better source than the multitude of monastic charters at our disposal.

NOTES

An earlier version of this paper was presented at the Sixth Berkshire Conference on the History of Women, 1984. I would like to thank Penelope Johnson for her comments and suggestions.

1. The pioneering study of this type was David Herlihy's "Land, Family, and Women in Continental Europe, 701–1200." For a review of more recent scholarship and for a sample analysis of charters from Anjou, see Gold, *The Lady and the Virgin*, pp. 116–44.

2. *Cartulaire de l'abbaye du Ronceray d'Angers (1028–1184).* Individual charters will be referred to by the letter *R* followed by the number of the charter in this edition.

3. The cartulary of Fontevrault, of which less than half still exists, is in two pieces: Paris, Bibliothèque nationale, MS. nouv. acq. lat. 2414, and Archives départementales de Maine-et-Loire 101H225.

4. This period yielded 253 charters from Le Ronceray and 242 charters from Fontevrault. For a detailed analysis of the institutional structure of Fontevrault, see Gold, *The Lady and the Virgin*, pp. 93–113.

5. See R42 for information on the chaplains' responsibilities for the parish church. For an analysis of the structure of the clerical staff, see Avril, "Le Diocèse d'Angers," p. 39.

6. I have included in this count only the clerics clearly identified as being directly associated with the nuns' community: for example, "Giraudus Sancte Marie sacerdos" (R195; Le Ronceray was dedicated to Mary) and witnesses who are identified as *de hominibus* (or *clericis, famulis, servientibus*) *Sancte Marie* or as *ex parte abbatisse* (or *ex parte monialibus*). Other clerics (for example, eighteen additional priests) are not so identified. Some may in fact have been in service to Le Ronceray, but others were probably visitors, neighbors, or those in some other relationship to one or the other of the parties in the transaction. See below for my discussion of identification as a methodological problem.

7. See, for example, R53, which records the attempts by two canons of Le Ronceray to negotiate a settlement to a long-standing dispute (over burial rights) with the monks of Saint-Nicholas.

8. The order of ceremonies could also be reversed. Another dispute with Saint-Aubin (from before 1120) was settled at Saint-Aubin by the male provost of Le Ronceray, who was accompanied by five men from the community. After the agreement was reached, the abbot and some monks from Saint-Aubin came to the chapter of Le Ronceray and confirmed the settlement in the presence of "the congregation of ladies" (R123).

9. In this respect, the abbess was like Chaucer's prioress, who traveled to Canterbury with a nun and three priests.

10. For example: "Quod postquam sanctimoniales et canonici B. Marie audierunt, in presentia domni Raginaldi episcopi calumpniati sunt" (R50). See also R46 and R54.

11. *Patrologiae cursus completus* (hereafter cited as *PL*) 162:1079.

12. For a comparison of religious women with secular women, see Gold, *The Lady and the Virgin*, chap. 4.

13. *PL* 162:1084.

14. For example, Rainerius and Hylarius are identified as *canonici S. Marie* in R50 but are listed by their names only in R49.

BIBLIOGRAPHY

Primary Sources

Cartulaire de l'abbaye du Ronceray d'Angers (1028–1184). Ed. Paul Marchegay. Paris, 1900.

Cartulary of Fontevrault. Paris, Bibliothèque nationale, MS. nouv. acq. lat. 2414, and Archives départementales de Maine-et-Loire 101H225.

Patrologiae cursus completus: Series latina. Ed. J.-P. Migne. 221 vols. Paris, 1844–64.

Secondary Sources

Avril, Joseph. "Les Fondations, l'organisation, et l'évolution des établissements de moniales dans le diocèse d'Angers (du XIe au XIIIe siècle)." In *Les Religieuses en France au XIIIe siècle,* ed. Michel Parisse, pp. 27–67. Nancy, 1985.

Gold, Penny Schine. *The Lady and the Virgin: Image, Attitude, and Experience in Twelfth-Century France.* Chicago, 1985.

Herlihy, David. "Land, Family, and Women in Continental Europe, 701–1200." *Traditio* 18 (1962): 89–121.

Parisse, Michel. *Les Nonnes au moyen âge.* Le Puy, 1983.

WOMEN AND THE SOURCES
OF MEDIEVAL HISTORY

The Towns of Northern Italy

David Herlihy

n the history and civilization of northern Italy in the Middle Ages, towns hold a special prominence. Even the violence and tumult of the early medieval centuries only
weakened and did not erase a significant urban presence.
The economic revival from about 1050 carried with it a
full rebirth of urban life. From the late thirteenth century to the end of
the Middle Ages, towns included within their walls probably one in five
or one in four northern Italians.[1] Throughout the central and late Middle Ages, towns dominated the political and cultural life of the Italian
north, and their residents produced a prodigious amount of records and
documents, many of which have survived. For the historian of women
in the Middle Ages, these historical sources hold a special interest. What
do the sources of these vigorous communities reveal about women?[2]
❡ The great strength of the Italian medieval documentation associated
with cities is its sheer volume.[3] Several factors made urban dwellers
prolific producers of records. The traditions of Roman law gave to the
written instrument a special priority in determining what the law was
and in proving facts in dispute. Perhaps the supreme expression of this
respect for writing was the notarial act, the exact nature of which I shall
presently consider. More than six hundred notaries were practicing at
Florence in 1336–38.[4] In the late Middle Ages, notaries typically represented a large and often the largest profession in the Italian cities. ❡ The
urban milieu, in which roughly a quarter of the population lived, supported a highly literate culture. According to the manuals that guided
him, the mark of a good merchant was "to write everything . . . almost
always to have pen in hand."[5] He should keep a record of "everything,
every purchase, every sale, every remembrance and contract, every gain

and loss, in the shop and outside the shop . . . And this is necessary, since by failing to write it and entrusting it to the pen, things are forgotten and grow stale."[6] After all, he could never predict what items of information would later prove of value. So important were literacy and arithmetical ability in the urban economies that some towns maintained public schools, where the young could learn the vital skills. According to the Florentine chronicler Giovanni Villani, some 8,000 to 10,000 children, both boys and girls, were learning to read in the city grammar schools in 1336–38. Older boys learning the abacus in six schools numbered 1,000 to 1,100 (girls did not continue formal education beyond grammar school). Some 550 to 600 other boys were studying Latin and logic in four schools in preparation for the university.[7] The community nurtured a large pool of educated persons, from which the urban governments drew scribes and clerks, to staff their big bureaucracies. The active merchants and the busy officials in turn generated massive documentation.

But in spite of their abundance, the records of these urban communities scrutinize women much less thoroughly than they do men. There are several reasons for this. The legal traditions imposed on women numerous disabilities that made it difficult for them to act independently of male tutelage.[8] The Lombard law, which prevailed in most of the north, placed the woman under a permanent wardship, called the *mundium*. Initially under the authority of her father, she passed at marriage into the *mundium* of her husband. The woman without a living father or husband remained in the wardship of the king. No other code of Germanic law was as restrictive on women as the Lombard. But even Roman law required that a woman live under the *tutela* of a male, although this was in practice often fictional and there were legal ways by which she could become a person *sui iuris*. Still, the common practice of the cities required that any woman entering into contract must obtain the express approval of a male relative. This limited women's initiative, and they do not appear as independent actors as often as their numbers would lead us to expect.

A second institutional obstruction to the visibility of women in Italian medieval documentation was the republican form of government under which the free communes principally lived. In areas of Europe, principally in the north, where a hereditary nobility dominated politically and socially, women often gained offices and influence through the play of inheritance or through service as regents for minor sons or absent husbands. These routes to preferment were closed to female residents in the republican communes, for only males served in communal offices. Even the public ceremonies associated with the city governments were closed to women. Not until late in the Middle Ages, with the emergence in Italy of princely lines and a flourishing court life, did women acquire the social visibility and influence they had long held within the northern nobility.

Still another institution that obstructed women's active participation in public affairs, and therefore their appearance in medieval sources, was the guild. In many cities guilds were central to the economic and even the political systems. The guild almost everywhere limited the participation of women in the trade it represented; usually, it grudgingly allowed only the widows and daughters of masters to practice the art. And women were altogether excluded from guild offices. As a result, it is difficult to judge the exact economic role of women under the free communes. [9]

Finally, Italy and other Mediterranean lands nurtured a strong cultural prejudice against feminine participation in all forms of public life. About 1420, Christine de Pisan, a native of Italy though living in France, asked the allegorical figure Reason why women did not appear in courts as lawyers or advocates. Reason explained that women could not exercise force or coercion and that public roles would at all events give them a "brazen appearance." [10] In Italy, virtuous girls past the age of puberty were expected to limit their contacts with the world beyond the household. When Catherine of Siena reached the age of twelve, she was kept at home "according to the local custom, for at Siena it is exceptional that single girls of that age are allowed to leave their homes." [11] But even married women were repeatedly admonished against unnecessary contacts with persons outside their immediate families. Women did not move easily through Italian urban societies.

In sum, men and women in the medieval towns operated within widely separate social spheres. Men held a near monopoly over public affairs, and the formal acts of governments—the promulgating of laws and statutes, the imposing of taxes, the making of peace and war—were almost always the work of males. Women, on the other hand, presided over the activities that were carried on within or were centered upon the household. To be sure, even in domestic affairs males decided how resources should be allocated and made the important decisions that affected the family fortunes and the marriages and careers of offspring, but women still directed the household in all its quotidian activities. They supervised the early education of the young, of boys as well as girls. They set the tone of domestic culture, and they took leading roles in the rituals of the home and in the practice of charity and private devotions. Although these activities were rooted in the home, they sometimes opened for women access to a wider world. This is especially noticeable in regard to religious practices. In medieval urban Italy, there were few women statesmen but many women saints.

The levels of visibility that women attained in medieval sources therefore differed radically according to the type of record and the person or institution that produced it. The typology that I use in the following survey of Italian medieval documentation is as follows: prescriptive literature; administrative records; account books, memoirs, and correspondence; narrative accounts (chronicles and biographies); and imaginative literature. The sources may further be classified according to the entities that produced them: the church, to which we owe the oldest documents; governments; and private individuals. Finally, some of the categories admit a further division into literary or statistical documents, depending on whether the information they contain is principally verbal or numerical.

❡ Prescriptive literature either commanded or counseled people how to behave. The church, of course, was the chief source of moral exhortation, but large numbers of persons, authorized or unauthorized, spoke in the name of religion. Women were often targeted. They may have been only half citizens in a political sense, but they were fully and completely moral persons, the agents or objects of moral or immoral acts. They had souls to save and were involved in the salvation of others—family members, lovers, friends.

Much church legislation (chiefly expressed in conciliar enactments) and many works in moral theology refer to women in both the religious and the secular life. But the genre that contains perhaps the richest materials on women is the sermon.[12] The rise of the mendicant orders from the early thirteenth century lent a powerful stimulus to preaching, which the mendicants construed as a major part of their mission.[13] A series of great preachers—Giordano da Rivalto (or da Pisa), Iacopo Passavanti, Bernardino da Siena, Cherubino da Siena, Girolamo Savonarola, Bernardino da Feltre, and others—addressed big congregations in which women constituted a large, perhaps often the largest, part. Some sermons were addressed directly to women.[14] The preachers often dwell on the moral failings they regarded as common among women: vanity, immodesty, bickering and nagging, and sexual sins, such as contraception and abortion. And they sometimes congratulate women for the virtues in which, in their estimation, women were superior to men: modesty, compassion, charity, and piety itself.

Bernardine of Siena (1380–1444) was probably the most outspoken of all the great preachers. Before his time, preachers allegedly spoke in vague and abstract terms about the moral ills of the day.[15] Bernardine, in contrast, called a spade a spade, and his frank and clear messages attracted and enraptured huge crowds.[16] Once, he directed mothers to come to the church with their daughters alone so that he could talk to them frankly about sexual abuses in marriage. He addressed many social issues: the reluctance of men to marry; the confinement of unwilling girls into convents, as if they were "the scum and vomit of the world"; homosexuality and contraception; and the duties and claims of various family members, including wives and mothers. Finally, he often made concrete and colorful references to daily life. He described the inept bachelor, who left his quarters in squalor, and the good wife, who maintained the cleanliness of her home and the physical and moral health of her family. [17]

Women were not supposed to preach in churches, but they could and did serve as sages and spiritual counselors. A French scholar, André Vauchez, speaks of the feminization of piety in late medieval Italy.[18] (We shall return to this when we consider hagiography.) In Italy late medieval women saints were not only numerous but also influential. None was more influential than Catherine of Siena (1349–80), who wrote devotional tracts, letters, and sermons or at least dictated them to her male secretaries, as she had never learned to read. In her letters to women, she warns them against an excessive commitment to their husbands, children, and families; they had their own souls to save. Catherine Vigri of Bologna (1413–63), a Poor Clare and a renowned mystic, wrote a book entitled *The Seven Spiritual Arms*.[19] Catherina Fieschi Adorno, known as Catherine of Genoa (1446–1510), who entered the religious life after the death of her husband, composed a vivid meditation on purgatory.[20] Concern for the suffering of others, in this life and after, was a mark of the period's feminized piety. These tracts from Italy are exceptional sources for investigating the cultural world of women in the late Middle Ages; no part of Europe offers richer materials. In religious matters, Italian urban women spoke with exceptional strength and clarity, perhaps because they were silenced in almost every other cultural sphere.

In contrast to the religious literature prescribing modes of behavior for women, the public legislation of the town governments is singularly poor in what it tells us about women. This is true in spite of its volume. Every free town had its statutes, many of which have survived and have been published, sometimes in repeated revisions. The enactments of the urban governments, usually called *provvisioni*, are still lengthier. The governments legislated on many matters affecting women—ages of marriage, amounts of the dowry, crimes of abduction and rape, and prostitution.[21] But they tell more of the legal constraints on behavior than of behavior itself. As a great historian of the Italian family, Nino Tamassia, wrote, they illuminate very well the *mala vita* of the conjugal couple but say little of its good life, the contentment with which probably most husbands and wives passed their days.[22]

One kind of legislation did have a special relevance to women. These were the sumptuary laws, which were multiplied over Europe from about 1300. The laws were directed against the supposed waste embodied in lavish social events (weddings and funerals) and expensive attire—for men but primarily for women. Authors of *novelle* poked fun at these laws and congratulated the adroitness of women in evading them.[23] The issue was not exclusively one of extravagance and waste. Ostentation in dress was one means by which some women, otherwise muted, could make public statements. What those statements were is now a fascinating topic of research and discussion.[24]

Much more yielding than the public laws in information about women are private tracts on good manners and the management of the household. From the early fourteenth century there have survived *Avertimenti di Maritaggio*, instructions or rules supposedly given by mothers to their newly married daughters, on how to become good wives.[25] Francesco da Barberino, who died in the plague of 1348, wrote a long poem, "The Deportment and Customs of the Woman," in which he gave advice on all stages of the woman's life.[26] Similar works of admonition and instruction proliferate after the Black Death. The revival of classical studies in the humanist movement greatly enriched the fund of materials that could be exploited for the purposes of moral exhortation. Among the humanist tracts extolling marriage is *De re uxoria*, written in 1415–16 by the Venetian humanist Francesco Barbaro in celebration of a Florentine marriage. Less erudite tracts on household management remained popular, and women figure prominently, if sometimes passively, within them. In the first decade of the fifteenth century, the Florentine Dominican friar, Giovanni Dominici, wrote the *Rule of Government and the Care of the Family* specifically for a woman.[27] She was Bartolomea Alberti, who was rearing her four children alone during the exile of her husband. In part a devotional tract, the book gives many detailed instructions on the training of children. Probably the best known of these tracts on household management is Leon Battista Alberti's *Four Books on the Family*.[28] About one-half the work is devoted to the choice of a wife and the running of the household. The essay shows an extreme condescension toward the wife, but this is an accurate reflection of the prejudices that the young commonly encountered and had to overcome.

❡ Prescriptive literature primarily preserves the commands or recommendations of a legislator or counselor; in contrast, administrative records, often referred to as "documents of practice," record better than do the laws and counsels what actually was happening. These administrative documents may further be classified into surveys (inquests or censuses) that describe a situation at a given moment in time and serial records distributed over time (minutes of meetings, lists of court decisions, or lists of payments of rents or taxes). The information recorded may be primarily verbal, as in inquests or court decisions, or numerical, as in censuses or counts of deaths or baptisms.

Church archives yield the oldest deposits of administrative records; of special interest, though often concerned with rural monasteries and churches, are deposits of charters or collections of transcribed charters known as cartularies. The oldest charters date from about 750, and even before 1200 they are numbered in the tens of thousands. Italy, moreover, is distinguished by the wealth of its episcopal, which is to say urban, archives. The see of Lucca, for example, possesses the oldest and richest run of such charters antedating 1200 in all of Italy and probably all of Europe.[29] Those dating after the year 1000 are still not completely published. Deposits of charters have survived from many other urban institutions—cathedral chapters, collegiate churches, monastic orders, and, from the thirteenth century, mendicant houses. Some of the religious communities were female, though these were again few in relative numbers.

The charters typically record conveyances of land—donations, sales, exchanges, and leases. They often involve either urban property or urban residents. Copies of wills giving land to churches appear occasionally, as do marriage and dotal agreements that helped establish title to lands subsequently acquired by churches. In showing how the laws were followed (or ignored) in practice and in clarifying inheritance rules and marital conveyances, the charters cast invaluable light on the legal and social status of women. They also illuminate changes in kin organization. In about the year 1000, an association of heirs, holding property in common and known as the *consorteria*, appeared in Italy; historians track its appearance and development principally through the funds of charters. Still another novel form of kindred is the agnatic lineage, or patrilineage; it made its appearance at a slightly later date, the eleventh and twelfth centuries. Again, the charters provide the most detailed picture of its formation and functioning, and both new forms of kindred organization had profound repercussions on the status of women.

This voluminous charter material illuminates the experiences of women in other ways as well. It is possible to assess how often women appear as principals in land transactions. The charters also identify pieces of land by naming the contiguous owners, and this offers another way of investigating the relationships of women with property. In identifying the principals in a contract, the scribe usually uses a patronymic, but he sometimes uses a matronymic: "Peter, son of Mathilda," for example, instead of "Peter, son of Bernard." The use of matronymics, which again can be measured over time, offers an indirect but still useful index to the social visibility of women.[30] Until the surge of lay documentation from the middle thirteenth century, ecclesiastical charters and surveys are our principal sources for both legal and social history, including the history of women.

As government and private records grow in volume from about the middle thirteenth century, the ecclesiastical charters lose importance, but other types of serial records associated with the church retain interest. Since ancient times, churches and monastic houses had kept necrologies—lists of deceased members or benefactors for whom prayers were offered upon the anniversaries of their deaths.[31] Appearing later are baptismal registrations: registrations at Siena survive from 1381, at Pescia from the end of the fourteenth century, at Florence from 1450, and at Pistoia from 1471.[32]

In addition to the administrative records produced by the church are those produced by the town governments. Among the most illuminating records generated by town governments are fiscal surveys, variously called *libbre, estimi,* or *catasti.* The towns of San Gimignano and Prato in Tuscany, for example, possess surveys for both city and countryside from the late thirteenth century.[33] Over the course of the fourteenth century, these surveys become ever more detailed. An *estimo* of the population of Bologna, dated 1395, gives even the ages of the residents.[34] The city of Verona possesses eight surveys of its population between 1424 and 1502.[35]

The greatest of all these population surveys is beyond doubt the Florentine *catasto* of 1427–30. It describes nearly 60,000 households and gives the names and ages of 260,000 persons settled in both the Tuscan cities and the countryside.[36] It also describes the households' assets and liabilities. It is therefore possible to trace quite precisely the life cycle of Tuscan women (and men), establishing their ages of marriage and their changing status and fortunes as they aged. Though there are problems associated with these registrations and especially the registrations of women, this survey is unsurpassed in the information it supplies about the life cycles and the social and economic status of Tuscan women, including those of Florence. (A copy of the coded survey is available at nominal cost from the Data Program and Library Service at the University of Wisconsin, Madison.)

The fiscal needs of the communal governments also generated serial records, which primarily reflect the income and expenditures of various entities. One such serial record of particular interest for women's history is the *monte delle doti*, a special fund created in 1425 to aid Florentine families in accumulating dowries for their daughters. A father deposited a sum of money in the fund at the birth of a daughter (he could make the same provision for a son), and the sum would be returned to him with interest when the daughter married, entered the religious life, or died. Julius Kirshner and Anthony Molho are currently engaged in a systematic exploitation of the massive serial record associated with this fund.[37]

The courts of the communal government and its associated institutions, such as guilds, also preserved records both of criminal prosecution and of civil litigation of all kinds. The recorded testimony of witnesses provides one of the few occasions when women are directly quoted. (Gene Brucker's recent account of a Florentine marriage is based on the trial minutes of an ecclesiastical court, preserved in notarial cartulary.)[38]

The oldest administrative records generated out of and directly reflective of private life are notarial acts and the bundles of notarial acts known as cartularies. Between 1154, the date of the earliest surviving notarial acts, and around 1300, when other types of records begin to slowly replace them, they yield almost all that we know of citizens' transactions not directly involving church or government. The notarial act in Italy acquired, probably from the middle eleventh century, the special quality of public faith. This means that a document drawn up by a licensed public notary could prove in court the existence of a contractual obligation, even after the death or in the absence of the principals, witnesses, or the notary himself.[39] The notary received his commission from the universal heads of the Christian commonwealth, the emperor or pope, or from those (usually the communal governments) to whom they had delegated the authority. The act, in other words, was a valid means of proof accepted throughout Christendom. Given the solemn importance of the acts they witnessed and redacted, the notaries very early entered copies of the agreements into cartularies, and it is chiefly in cartularies that they have been preserved.

The great port city of Genoa possesses the oldest series of cartularies, which date from December 1154.[40] Many deal with commercial investments; these are the only extant quantitative sources in the whole of Europe that bear on business affairs before 1200. From the thirteenth century, particularly after 1250, cartulary deposits survive in numerous urban archives. They contain nearly every conceivable type of document: contracts for sales and exchanges of land or of animals, records of loans and business investments, letters and commissions, apprenticeship agreements, appointments of agents and procurators, marriage contracts, acts of emancipation, wills, and every other sort of binding agreement or contract. Their volume and variety tend to diminish after 1300 and particularly after 1350 (for reasons that I shall mention), but even in the late Middle Ages, Italians who wished to record a particularly solemn agreement went before a notary. Notaries also served both the ecclesiastical and the secular governments in recording, for example, the testimony of witnesses in litigation. Notarial acts, written in a formulaic Latin that only slowly gave way to Italian, rarely betray feeling or sentiment. Nonetheless, especially for the late thirteenth century, they are our principal window looking out upon the private life of the period and upon the role of women within it.

Notaries have a special and continuing importance in regard to marriage and dotal agreements. The parties anticipating marriage or their representatives appeared before a notary more commonly than before a priest. (Not until the Council of Trent were Catholics required to make their marital vows in the presence of a priest.) The notary was needed to record the *instrumentum sponsalitii*, or formal betrothal, and a *confessio dotis*, or dotal agreement. (The *ductio ad maritum*, or procession that took the bride to the groom's house, confirmed the marriage and led directly to its consummation.)

Women figure prominently in many kinds of notarial acts: contracts of apprenticeship or of household service, litigation of all sorts, betrothals and dotal agreements, and many last wills and testaments, both as testators and as beneficiaries. They were often litigants in trials and were just as often summoned as witnesses. The cartularies further illuminate women as property owners and business investors. To be sure, the factors mentioned above that limited the public role of Italian women reduced their visibility here as everywhere. But the researcher who sets out to explore the vast sea of the notarial archives can be sure that women will be encountered in impressive numbers.

❡ From about 1300, the apparently rising levels of literacy within the urban populations made the services of the notary dispensable. Moreover, the literate citizens, apparently pressed by mounting volumes of transactions, seem to have found it troublesome and expensive to have continuous recourse to notaries. They therefore recorded more and more of their transactions and agreements in other forms. One of the most common means of registering transactions was the private account book. The governments obliged by accepting entries in the private account books as proof of the existence of an obligation or of its satisfaction.

Women were only rarely direct and active participants in economic exchanges and are only occasionally noticed in account books. They are much more visible in a kind of source closely related to account books: family memoirs, or *ricordi*. In recording moneys received and given, many heads of household also recorded other events affecting their families, such as marriages, births, and deaths. By their wealth of observations, some writers made of their *ricordi* true domestic chronicles or family histories.[41] Many also often included advice and counsel for their expected readers, their own descendants. The most revealing *ricordi* thus combine characteristics of a statistical record, narrative account, and prescriptive literature.

The authors were, to be sure, all of them male. But many were also diligent observers, and they describe in detail all aspects of family life, from the physical structure of houses to domestic rituals. They often describe the experiences of or comment upon their female relatives. The memoirs rarely directly record feminine voices, but they brilliantly illuminate the milieu in which women lived and the attitudes with which their fathers, brothers, husbands, and sons viewed them. Christiane Klapisch-Zuber's studies of Italian women of the Renaissance and the various symbols and rituals that marked their existence are based in large measure on the *ricordi*.[42]

Also from the early fourteenth century, high levels of literacy within the urban communities, characteristic of women as well as men, enabled the urban dwellers to communicate by writing letters. In particular, Italy's far-flung merchants often wrote letters to and received letters from their wives, mothers, or other female relatives. The Datini archives

located at Prato, the largest of all the collections of private mercantile
records, include from 1381 exchanges of letters between Francesco di
Marco Datini, then at Pisa, and his wife, Margherita.[43] These letters
are an exceptional source in recapturing the spirit of a medieval Italian
marriage. Notable too are the letters written in the middle fifteenth century by a Florentine matron, Alessandra Macinghi-Strozzi, to her exiled
sons;[44] these letters, remarkable for their content and also for their rarity,
are unexcelled for the insight they offer into the social world and social
values of a middle-class woman in quattrocento Florence. Letters survive
from several noblewomen of the Renaissance, including Lucrezia Borgia,
whose correspondence with Pietro Bembo constituted, in the opinion of
its editor, "the prettiest love letters in the world."[45]

¶ The same limited public functions that women fulfilled won them limited notice in the narrative accounts—the many chronicles and histories
that tell the history of the free commune.[46] They are better represented in
another narrative form—biographies. In 1111–15, a priest named Donizo
composed a metrical biography of Matilda of Tuscany, patroness of Pope
Gregory VII.[47] It is a rare example of a medieval biography dedicated to a
woman who is not a saint. In the fourteenth and fifteenth centuries, the
new humanist scholars favored the genre, as the lives of virtuous persons would presumably inspire emulation among their readers. Giovanni
Boccaccio supplemented the available lives of famous men by publishing
a collection of the lives of famous women.[48] The women he remembers
are taken either from ancient literature or from folklore; he includes, for
example, the fabulous biography of a lady pontiff, Pope Joan. Vespasiano
da Bisticci, a book dealer turned author and perhaps the most famous
biographer of the Renaissance, included in his *Vite* the life of one woman,
Alessandra de' Bardi.[49] In 1483 the Bolognese writer Giovanni Sabadino
deli Arienti composed the biographies of thirty-three women, one of
them still living. Most were queens and duchesses, but he also wrote
about Joan of Arc and his recently deceased wife.

Even more numerous than these secular biographies are the lives of
women saints. An incomplete list of women saints would include Umi-
liana dei Cerchi of Florence, Clare of Pisa, Angela of Foligno, and Margaret of Cortona.[50] Many of these women saints were tertiaries, that
is, members of the "third orders" associated with the Dominicans or
Franciscans. In other words, they spent all or most of their lives outside of a cloister, and they interacted intensively and frequently with the
lay world. But as tertiaries, they also attracted male biographers, who

often also served as their confessors. Margaret of Cortona (d. 1297) was married and widowed young. Her father and stepmother would not take her back into the paternal home; for a while she supported herself as a prostitute.[51] Angela of Foligno (1248–1309) dictated her life to a Franciscan friar named Arnaldo or Adamo, who recorded her accounts in the first-person singular as direct quotations. Her life, rich in realistic details about her extraordinary career and written with passion, is one of the richest surviving testimonies we have, one that is ostensibly from the mouth of an urban woman of the Italian Middle Ages.[52] The biographer of Catherine of Siena, Raymond of Capua, was also her confessor and thus acquired an intimate knowledge of this extraordinary woman. [53]

For some women saints, such as Francesca Ponziani of Rome, the patron saint of the city, we possess not only contemporary lives but the minutes of their canonization processes, in which those who knew these "friends of God" testify as to their characters. [54]

Many of these holy women had been married and had adopted a religious life only after the deaths of their husbands. Their biographies thus give vivid information about the training of little girls, courtship and marriage, the tasks of running a household, relations (including even, as with Francesca, sexual relations, which nauseated her), and, of course, religious culture. These lives are yet to be fully mined for what they reveal about urban women in the late Middle Ages.

❡ In regard to the information it yields about women, the imaginative literature of late medieval urban Italy shows the same strengths and weaknesses found in the entire body of historical records. First in poetry and then in prose, literary output grew rapidly beginning in the late thirteenth century. On the one hand, in all the genres, depictions of women or allusions to them are plentiful, and they offer to the historian an inexhaustible mine of materials for social history. On the other hand, the number of women authors is exiguous, hardly more than a handful.[55] And the dominant interest of women authors was, as we have mentioned, religion.

Love is, of course, a constant theme in refined and learned poetry, though the poet's mistress is usually an unreal figure, an icon, in a genre dominated by stilted conventions. Often more revealing are oblique allusions to women. Even the exalted poetry of Dante Alighieri contains realistic and colorful vignettes of women: of girls married at too young an age; of the merchant's wife who sleeps alone while her husband is in France; of the old grandmother relating to her grandchildren as she spins tales of Troy, Rome, and Fiesole.[56] The traditions of popular poetry contain carnival songs, supposedly sung by masques during the carnival time.[57] Some of the masques are women—nuns, the unhappily married, peddlers, and the like—and many more songs are addressed to women. They are, of course, burlesques, but they have the truth of many things said in jest. Even the learned Latin and Italian poetry of the humanists is rich in social references. The whole tradition of elegiac poetry, represented by such masters as Angelo Poliziano (1454–94), flourished in these centuries when ancient forms of expression were assiduously imitated. Many elegies remember women. Of the Latin poets, the Neapolitan Giovanni Pontano (1426–1505) deserves special notice.[58] In his *De amore conjugali*, he celebrates conjugal love at every stage, from betrothal to the wedding to the giving of a daughter in marriage. He also composed lullabies (*naenia*) and nursery songs. His poems are among the most elegant expression of family sentiments that the age has bequeathed.

In regard to prose, the period's many collections of short stories (*novelle*) have a special interest for social history. The *Decameron* of Giovanni Boccaccio is the recognized masterpiece of the genre. Although the plots of these often ribald tales hardly represent common occurrences, their settings, both social and material, are certainly realistic. Even the commonly encountered triad of beautiful young wife, aged and ineffective husband, and eager and unattached young man set on seducing her reflects the prevalent pattern of urban marriages. One of Boccaccio's tales, that of the patient Griselda, offers a model of feminine submissiveness that would be cited for centuries.[59] Boccaccio also presented in his *Il Corbaccio* one of the most vicious portraits of a woman extant in medieval literature.[60] It seems hardly necessary to review other genres, such as drama, for the common pattern holds everywhere: abundant survivals, rich and often realistic in circumstances, if not always in plots, but scarcely a handful of works written by women.

❡ Perhaps we can summarize the reasons for the low visibility of women in medieval Italian urban documentation in the following fashion. Documents are born out of an effort to communicate. Certain circumstances made it necessary or likely that that communication be recorded in writing. The message conveyed might have been especially solemn or formal, such as a law or an administrative degree. It might have created a future obligation, as, for example, a notarized contract did. The originator of the message might have been seeking to reach someone at a distance;

thus, a traveling merchant sent a letter to his agent in another city or to his wife at home. Or the author of the message thought that its contents ought to be preserved; they might later prove instructive, whether for the author or for a successor or a descendant. Now, in generating these solemn, seemingly important, and usually written communications, men were much more active than women. They were the legislators, administrators, merchants, and diarists. The archives therefore overflow with documents written by male hands, out of male interests. But historians must recognize that the written documents preserve only a small part of the communications that actually occurred. The messages, requests, and conversations that were carried on informally and at close range, as among members of the same household, depended almost exclusively upon the spoken word. And women were active and often the leading participants in the conversations of private life or in those reflective of private, mundane, but continuing interests, such as the day-to-day supervision of households, instruction of children, or religious life within the home. Unfortunately, however, their words are largely lost to historians. The written documents, focusing on other matters, serving other functions, catch those conversations only rarely and echo them only distantly.

But historians cannot assume that the surviving written records are an exact projection of reality. Women's low visibility in the documentation does not indicate their low importance in shaping the culture of the day. On the contrary, they seem to have dominated major areas of cultural life, most notably mystical and charismatic religion. The historians of medieval Italian urban women are not well served by the surviving written records, though neither are they totally denied. But they must learn to be alert, patient, sensitive listeners.

NOTES

1. In the regions of Lombardy and Tuscany, persons living in the ten largest cities constituted between 19.1 percent of the entire population in Milanese territory, 23.4 percent in the Veneto, and 26 percent in Tuscany (Russell, *Medieval Cities*, p. 235, table 32).

2. For a general introduction to the historiography of women in the Middle Ages, see Stuard, *Women in Medieval History*, and especially the essay by Diane Owen Hughes, "Invisible Madonnas," pp. 25–50, with its bibliography on medieval Italian women on pp. 143–59.

3. For a guide to the collections of the Archivi di Stato, see *Guida generale*.

4. The number comes from Villani, *Cronica* 6:185. In 1427 in Tuscany, notaries constituted the largest profession at Florence and ranked second after the shoemakers at Pisa. They ranked third at both Pistoia and Arezzo, fifth at Prato, and fourth at Volterra and Cortona. The larger the city, the more numerous notaries were likely to be. See Herlihy and Klapisch-Zuber, *Tuscans and Their Families*, p. 128, table 4.7.

5. "Dimonstrava essere officio del mercatante e d'ogni mestiere, quale abbia a tramare con più persone, sempre scrivere ogni cosa . . . quasi sempere avere la penna in mano" (Alberti, *I libri della famiglia*, p. 205).

6. "O'inteso più volte da' savi e antichi mercatanti ch' egli sta così bene al mercatante avere sempre le mani tinte d'inchiostro, perchè dimostra essere officio di mercatante essere sollecito di scrivere ogni cosa, ogni compere, ogne vendite, ogni ricorde e contratto, ogni entrate et uscita, in bottega et fuori di botega sempre avere la penna in mano. E questo è necessario, perchè indugiando lo scrivere et fare credenza alla penna, le cose si domenticano et invecchiano" (Rucellai, *Il zibaldone quaresimale*, pp. 6–7).

7. Villani, *Cronica* 6:184.

8. Bellomo, *La condizione giuridica*, offers a survey of the juridic position of women in medieval Italy.

9. For example, the matriculation lists of the Florentine guild of Por Santa Maria, preserved in the Manoscritti deposit of the Archivi di Stato, record hundreds of matriculants from the early thirteenth century on. I have found not a single woman. The guild included the silk trades, in which women held a special importance. But they were not allowed representation in this organization of workers—or of masters.

10. Christine de Pisan, *City of Ladies*, p. 30. Christine died in about 1431.

11. *Acta sanctorum quotquot toto orbe coluntur* (hereafter cited as *ASS*), III Aprilis, p. 863.

12. On medieval sermons in general, see Dargan, *History of Preaching*, an informative if not especially profound survey. Recent works based on Italian sermons, though not particularly concerned with women, are Weinstein, *Savonarola and Florence*, and O'Malley, *Praise and Blame*.

13. On the rise of the Franciscan order, see Sessevalle, *L'Ordre de Saint François*.

14. See, for example, Giordano da Pisa, *Quaresimale fiorentino*, pp. 255–59, 430–34. See also Cherubino da Siena, *Vita matrimoniale*, for an especially frank treatment of sex in marriage.

15. On Bernardine's style, see Delcorno, "L'ars praedicandi."

16. See Bernardino da Siena, *Prediche volgari*; Bernardino da Siena, *Opera omnia*; and Origo, *World of San Bernardino*.

17. See Bernardino da Siena, *Opera omnia* 2:83, for the reference to the girls deposited into convents, and pp. 306–18, Sermo 48, "De honestate coniugatorum," for the descriptions of domestic life.

18. Vauchez, *La sainteté*, pp. 243–49.

19. Her life may be found in *ASS*, II Martii, pp. 35–89, and in Sabadino deli Arienti, *Gynevera*, pp. 204–45. For the most recent edition of her *Seven Spiritual Arms*, see Catherine of Bologna, *Le sette armi spirituali*.

20. See Catherine of Genoa, *Purgation and Purgatory*.

21. Bellomo, *La condizione giuridica*, includes much material from statutes bearing upon marriage and the dowry. For an old but still valuable bibliography of northern Italian statutes (including unpublished statutes), see Fontana, *Bibliografia degli statuti*.

22. "I coniugi che vissero dolcemente insieme nulla hanno lasciato alla storia e agli storici" (Tamassia, *La famiglia italiana*, p. 196).

23. "Come le donne fiorentine, senza studiare o apparare leggi, hanno vinto e confuso alcuno dottor di legge" (Sacchetti, *Il libro delle trecento novelle*, no. 136, p. 338).

24. See, for example, Hughes, "Sumptuary Law."

25. See Del Lungo, *La donna fiorentina*, pp. 93, 105–9, for an example of this popular genre.

26. Francesco da Barberino, *Del reggimento e costume di donne*.

27. Dominici, *Regola del governo di cura familiare*.

28. Alberti, *I libri della famiglia*.

29. See *Raccolta di documenti*.

30. See Herlihy, "Land, Family, and Women," pp. 92–101.

31. See, for example, "Nomi di uomini e di donne seppelliti," the great necrology of laypersons, including many women, buried in the Dominican convent of Santa Maria Novella.

32. See Herlihy and Klapisch-Zuber, *Les Toscans*, p. 351 n. 4.

33. See Fiumi, *Storia economica e sociale* (for San Gimignano), and Fiumi, *Demografia* (for Prato).

34. Montanari, *La popolazione di Bologna*.

35. Herlihy, "Population of Verona."

36. See Herlihy and Klapisch-Zuber, *Les Toscans* and *Tuscans and Their Families*.

37. Kirshner, "Pursuing Honor"; Morrison, Kirshner, and Molho, "Life-Cycle Events"; Kirshner and Molho, "Dowry Fund"; Kirshner and Molho, "Il Monte delle doti"; Molho, "Investimenti nel Monte delle doti"; Molho, "L'amministrazione del debito pubblico."

38. Brucker, *Giovanni and Lusanna*.

39. The standard introduction into the juridical character of the notarial instrument is Moresco and Bognetti, *Per l'edizione dei Notai liguri*.

40. On the Genovese sources, see Bach, *La Cité de Gênes*, pp. 11–29.

41. Pezzarossa, "Memorialistica," discusses Florentine *ricordi*. Florence offers by far the richest numbers of these domestic accounts, many of them still unpublished.

42. Klapisch-Zuber, *Women, Family, and Ritual.*

43. See the description of these letters in Origo, *Merchant of Prato,* pp. 165–87.

44. Macinghi-Strozzi, *Lettere.*

45. This is the title the editor gave to her edition of their correspondence; see Borgia, *Prettiest Love Letter.*

46. For recent comment on the chronicles of medieval Italy, see Zanella, *Storici e storiografia* (a collection of reprinted essays).

47. Donizo presbyter, "Vita Mathildis."

48. Boccaccio, *De mulieribus claris;* for an English translation, see Boccaccio, *Concerning Famous Women.*

49. Vespasiano da Bisticci, *Le Vite;* for an English translation, see Vespasiano da Bisticci, *Renaissance Princes, Popes, and Prelates.*

50. Bibliographies on all these women may be found in Stuard, *Women in Medieval History.*

51. The life of Margaret of Cortona is in *ASS,* III Februarii, pp. 302–63.

52. The life of Angela of Foligno is in *ASS,* I Januarii, pp. 186–234.

53. An English translation is found in Raymond of Capua, *Life of Saint Catherine of Siena.*

54. For the Latin lives of Francesca Ponziani, see *ASS,* II Martii, pp. 89–178; see also Lugeno, *Il processo inedito.*

55. See the critical remarks, bibliography, and selections compiled in Costa-Zalessow, *Scrittrici italiane.*

56. Dante, *Paradiso,* canto 16, lines 25ff.; these vignettes are taken from the celebration by Dante's ancestor Cacciaguido of the virtues of old Florence and the failings of contemporaries.

57. See *Canti carnascialeschi* and *Nuovi canti carnascialeschi.*

58. Representative selections of his large output can be found in Pontano, *Carmina.*

59. See the chapter entitled "The Griselda Complex" in Klapisch-Zuber, *Women, Family, and Ritual,* pp. 273–46.

60. For an English translation, see Boccaccio, *The Corbaccio.*

BIBLIOGRAPHY

Primary Sources

Acta sanctorum quotquot toto orbe coluntur. Paris, 1863–.

Alberti, Leon Battista. *I libri della famiglia.* In *Opere volgari,* ed. Cecil Grayson, 1:1–341. Scrittori d'Italia, no. 218. Bari, 1960.

Barbaro, Francesco. *De re uxoria.* Ed. A. Gnesotto. *Atti e Memorie della R. Accademia di Scienze Lettere ed Arti in Padova,* 2d ser., 32 (1915–16):6–105.

Bernardino da Siena. *Opera omnia.* Patres Collegii S., Bonaventurae. 9 vols. Florence, 1950–65.

———. *Prediche volgari.* Ed. L. Banchi. 3 vols. Siena, 1880–88.

Boccaccio, Giovanni. *Concerning Famous Women.* Trans. Guido A. Guarino. New Brunswick, N.J., 1963.

———. *The Corbaccio.* Trans. and ed. Anthony K. Cassell. Urbana, Ill., 1975.

———. *De mulieribus claris.* Ed. Vittorio Zaccaria. Tutte le opere, no. 5. Classici Mondadori. Milan, 1967.

———. *Il Corbaccio.* Ed. Mario Marti. Galatina, 1982.

Borgia, Lucrezia. *The Prettiest Love Letter in the World: Letters between Lucrezia Borgia and Pietro Bembo, 1503–1519.* Trans. Hugh Shankland. Boston, 1987.

Canti carnascialeschi del rinascimento. Ed. Charles S. Singleton. Scrittori d'Italia, no. 150. Bari, 1936.

Catherine of Bologna. *Le sette armi spirituali.* Ed. Cecilia Foletti. Medioevo e Umanesimo, no. 56. Padua, 1985.

Catherine of Genoa. *Purgation and Purgatory: The Spiritual Dialogue of Catherine of Genoa.* Trans. Serge Hughes. New York, 1979.

Cherubino da Siena. *Regola della vita matrimoniale.* Ed. F. Ambrini and C. Negroni. Scelta di Curiosità Letterarie Inedite o Rare dal Secolo XIII al XVII, no. 228. Bologna, 1888.

Christine de Pisan. *Book of the City of Ladies.* Trans. Earl Jeffrey Richards. New York, 1982.

Cicchetti, Angelo, and Raul Mordenti. *I Libri di Famiglia in Italia.* Vol. 1, *Filogia e storiografie letterarie.* Rome, 1985.

Costa-Zalessow, Natalia, ed. *Scrittrici italiane dal XIII al XX secolo: Testi e critica.* Ravenna, 1982.

Dante. *Le opere di Dante: Testo critico della Società dantesca italiana.* 2d ed. Florence, 1960.

Dominici, Giovanni. *Regola del governo di cura familiare.* Ed. Donato Salvi. Florence, 1860.

Donizo presbyter. "Vita Mathildis." Ed. Luigi Simeoni. In *Rerum Italicarum Scriptores,* nuova edizione, vol. 5, pt. 2, pp. 3–106, 118–27. Città di Castello, 1931–40.

Francesco da Barberino. *Del reggimento e costume di donne.* Ed. Giuseppe E. Sansone. Collezione di "Filologia Romanza," no. 2. Turin, 1957.

Giordano da Pisa. *Quaresimale fiorentino, 1305–1306.* Ed. Carlo Delcorno. Florence, 1974.

Giordano da Rivalto. *Prediche del beato fra Giovanni recitate in Firenze dal 1303 al 1309.* Ed. D. M. Manni. Milan, 1839.

Guida generale degli Archivi di Stato italiani. Directed by Piero d'Angiolini and Claudio Pavone; edited by Paola Carucci, Antonio Bentoni-Litta, and Vilma Piccioni Sparvoli. 3 vols. to date. Rome, 1981–.

Lugeno, Placido Tommaso, ed. *Il processo inedito per Francesca Bussa dei Ponziani (Santa Francesca Romana), 1440–1453.* Vatican City, 1945.

Macinghi-Strozzi, Alessandra. *Lettere di una gentildonna fiorentina ai figliuoli esuli.* Ed. Cesare Guasti. Florence, 1877.

"Nomi di uomini e di donne seppelliti in S. Maria Novella, tratti da un Libro di cartapecora esistente nelle mani de' Fratri di detta chiesa." In *Delizie degli eruditi toscani,* ed. Ildefonso di San Luigi, 9:123–203. Florence, 1777.

Nuovi canti carnascialeschi del rinascimento. Ed. Charles S. Singleton. Modena, 1940.

Paolo da Certaldo. *Il libro di buoni costumi, documento di vita trecentesca.* Ed. A. Schiaffini. Florence, 1945.

Pontano, Giovanni. *Carmina: Ecloghe—elegia—liriche.* Ed. Johannes Oeschger. Scrittori d'Italia, no. 198. Bari, 1948.

Raccolta di documenti per servire alla storia ecclesiastica di Lucca. Ed. Domenico Barsocchini. In *Memorie e documenti per servire all' istoria del Ducato di Lucca,* vol. 5, pts. 1–3. 1837–44. Reprint. Lucca, 1970.

Raymond of Capua. *The Life of Saint Catherine of Siena.* Trans. George Lamb. New York, 1960.

Rucellai, Giovanni. *Zibaldone.* Vol. 1, *Il zibaldone quaresimale: Pagine scelte.* Ed. Allesandro Perosa. Studies of the Warburg Institute, no. 24. London, 1960.

Sabadino de li Arienti, Giovanni. *Gynevera de le clare donne di Joanne Sabadino de li Arienti.* Ed. Corrado Ricci and A. Bacchi della Lega. Scelta di Curiosità Letterarie e Rare, no. 223. Bologna, 1888.

Sacchetti, Franco. *Il libro delle trecentonovelle.* Ed. Ettore Li Gotti. Milan, 1946.

Savonarola, Girolamo. "Libro della vita viduale." In *Oeuvres spirituelles choisies,* ed. E. C. Bayonne, 2:5–51. Paris, 1880.

Vespasiano da Bisticci. *Renaissance Princes, Popes, and Prelates: The Vespasiano Memoirs. Lives of Illustrious Men of the Fifteenth Century.* Trans. William Goerge and Emily Waters. New York, 1963.

———. *Le Vite.* Ed. Aulo Greco. 2 vols. Florence, 1970–76.

Villani, Giovanni. *Cronica.* 8 vols. Florence, 1823–25.

Secondary Sources

Bach, Erik. *La Cité de gênes au XIIe siècle.* Classica et mediaevalia, no. 5. Copenhagen, 1955.

Bellomo, Mario. *La condizione giuridica della donna in Italia.* Turin, 1970.

Benvenuti Papi, Anna. "Penitenza e santità femminile in ambiente cateriniano e bernardiniano." In *Atti del Simposio Internazionale Cateriniano-Bernardiniano,* ed. Domenico Maffei and Paolo Nardi, pp. 865–75. Siena, 1982.

Brucker, Gene A. *Giovanni and Lusanna: Love and Marriage in Renaissance Florence.* Berkeley, 1986.

Dargan, Edward Charles. *A History of Preaching from the Apostolic Fathers to the Great Reformers, 70–1572.* New York, 1968.

Delcorno, Carlo. *Giordano da Pisa e l'antica predicazione volgare.* Pisa, 1975.

————. "L'ars praedicandi' di Bernardino da Siena." In *Atti del Simposio Internazionale Cateriniano-Bernardiniano*, ed. Domenico Maffei and Paolo Nardi, pp. 419–49. Siena, 1982.

Del Lungo, Isidoro. *La donna fiorentina del buon tempo antico*. 2d ed. Florence, 1926.

De Matteis, Maria Consiglia, ed. *Idee sulla donna nel Medioevo: Fonti, aspetti giuridici, antropologici, religiosi e letterari della condizione femminile*. Il Mondo Medievale. Bologna, 1981.

Fiumi, Enrico. *Demografia, movimento urbanistico e classi sociali in Prato dall'età comunale ai tempi moderni*. Florence, 1968.

————. *Storia economica e sociale di San Gimignano*. Florence, 1961.

Fontana, Leone, ed. *Bibliografia degli statuti dei comuni dell' Italia superiore*. 3 vols. Milan, 1907.

Herlihy, David. "Land, Family, and Women in Continental Europe, 701–1200." *Traditio* 18 (1962): 89–120.

————. "The Population of Verona in the First Century of Venetian Rule." In *Renaissance Venice*, ed. J. R. Hale, pp. 91–120. London, 1973.

Herlihy, David, and Christiane Klapisch-Zuber. *Les Toscans et leurs familles*. Paris, 1978.

————. *Tuscans and Their Families: A Study of the Florentine Catasto of 1427*. New Haven, Conn., 1985.

Hughes, Diane Owen. "Invisible Madonnas: The Italian Historiographical Tradition and the Women of Medieval Italy." In *Women in Medieval History and Historiography*, ed. Susan Mosher Stuard, pp. 25–50, 143–59. Philadelphia, 1987.

————. "Sumptuary Law and Social Relations in Renaissance Italy." In *Disputes and Settlements: Law and Human Relations in the West*, ed. John Bossy, pp. 69–99. Cambridge, Eng., 1983.

Kirshner, Julius. "Pursuing Honor While Avoiding Sin: The *Monte delle Doti* of Florence." *Studi senesi* 87 (1977): 175–256.

Kirshner, Julius, and Anthony Molho. "The Dowry Fund and the Marriage Market in Early Quattrocento Florence." *Journal of Modern History* 50 (1978): 404–38.

————. "Il Monte delle doti a Firenze dalla sua fondazione nel 1425 alla metà del sedicesimo secolo." *Ricerche storiche* 10 (1980): 21–48.

Klapisch-Zuber, Christiane. *Women, Family, and Ritual in Renaissance Italy*. Trans. Lydia C. Cochrane. Chicago, 1985.

Longère, Jean. *La Prédication médiévale*. Paris, 1983.

Molho, Anthony. "Investimenti nel Monte delle doti di Firenze: Un'analisi sociale e geografica." *Quaderni storici* 61 (1986): 147–60.

————. "L'amministrazione del debito pubblico a Firenze nel quindicesimo secolo." In *I ceti dirigenti nella Toscana del Quattrocento*, pp. 191–207. Florence, 1987.

Montanari, Paolo. *Documenti su la popolazione di Bologna alla fine del Trecento.* Fonti per la storia di Bologna, no. 1. Bologna, 1966.

Moresco, H., and Gian Piero Bognetti. *Per l'edizione dei Notai liguri del sec. XII.* Genoa, 1938.

Morrison, Alan, Julius Kirshner, and Anthony Molho. "Life-Cycle Events in Fifteenth-Century Florence: Records of the *Monte delle doti.*" *American Journal of Epidemiology* 106 (1977): 487–92.

O'Malley, John. *Praise and Blame in Renaissance Rome.* Durham, N.C., 1979.

Origo, Iris. *The Merchant of Prato: Francesco di Marco Datini, 1335–1410.* 1957. Reprint. Boston, 1986.

———. *The World of San Bernardino.* New York, 1962.

Pereira, Michela, ed. *Né Eva né Maria: Condizione femminile e immagine della donna nel Medioevo.* Bologna, 1981.

Pezzarossa, Fulvio. "La tradizione fiorentina della memorialistica." In *La "Memoria" dei mercatores: Tendenze ideologiche, ricordanze, artiginato in versi nella Firenze del Quattrocento,* ed. Gian-Mario Anselmi, Fulvio Pezzarossa, and Luisa Avellini, pp. 39–149. Bologna, 1980.

Russell, Josiah Cox. *Medieval Cities and Their Regions.* Bloomington, Ind., 1972.

Sessevalle, François de. *Histoire générale de l'ordre de Saint François: Le Moyen Âge.* 2 vols. Le Puy-en-Velay, 1937.

Stuard, Susan Mosher, ed. *Women in Medieval History and Historiography.* Philadelphia, 1987.

Tamassia, Nino. *La famiglia italiana nei secoli decimoquinto e decimosesto.* L'Indagine moderna, no. 15. Milan, 1911.

Vauchez, André. *La Sainteté en Occident aux derniers siècles du moyen âge d'après les procès de canonisation et les documents hagiographiques.* Rome, 1981.

Weinstein, Donald. *Savonarola and Florence: Prophecy and Patriotism in the Renaissance.* Princeton, N.J., 1970.

Zanella, Gabriele, ed. *Storici e storiografia del medioevo italiano: Antologia di saggi.* Il Mondo Medievale, no. 14. Bologna, 1984.

OLD NORSE SOURCES ON WOMEN

Jenny Jochens

he Scandinavians were unique among the peoples of early medieval Europe in producing at an early stage of their development a large body of writings not in Latin, the language of the Roman Empire, but in their own vernacular. Although Scandinavia and northern Germany had remained outside the empire, these territories nonetheless attracted the attention of the Roman and, in due course, of the native writers who described in Latin the history, geography, and ethnography of the northern region and its inhabitants. Three authors who convey information about Germanic and Scandinavian women in this Latin tradition stand above the others: Tacitus, Adam of Bremen, and Saxo Grammaticus. Describing the Germans and their encounters with the Roman army toward the end of the first century, Tacitus includes valuable information about women's religious and prophetic roles, their position in marriage, and their importance for the economic life of the tribes.[1] The canon Adam arrived in Bremen in about 1066, and for the next fifteen years he worked on his important *History of the Archbishops of Hamburg-Bremen*.[2] Since all of Scandinavia belonged to the mission field of this see, he found occasion to include many observations about the marital and sexual behavior of Nordic kings. His description of a certain *terra feminarum* located on the Baltic coast and inhabited by *Amazonas* is of special interest.[3] In the monumental *Gesta Danorum*, Saxo Grammaticus provided contemporary Danish kings not only with a glorious history of their recent deeds but also with a rich mythic-heroic past that—in contrast to the contemporary section—contains a large number of prominent women.[4] Writing in the decades around 1200, he mentions Icelanders as his informers, but it is not clear whether he was tapping this Old Norse reservoir through oral or written channels. ❡ By 1200, however, writings in Old Norse were already abundant. These sources are of great interest to students of women's history not only because they illuminate women's lives in an important area of medieval Europe but particularly because they permit at least an oblique glance at women's conditions before the advent of Christianity.

One of the most controversial issues in women's history pertains to the influence exerted by Christianity on the female half of the human race. An influential point of view argues that from the beginning Christianity was deeply impregnated with Jewish and Roman patriarchy, which, over time, was intensified by the all-male clergy, resulting in misogyny as Christianity's most lasting and profound legacy for women. An opposite argument, heard distinctly in South America today, claims that the Christian message was a fundamentally liberating force that included women as well. Although the original radicalism of Jesus on this issue, as on so many others, became diluted with time, women's conditions were different during the Christian period and in Christian countries from what they had been before or elsewhere. Personal freedom in the choice of a marriage partner, for example, is one of the changes that have been interpreted—at least from a Western standpoint—as improvements for women.

Reasonable answers to this problem require care in formulating the problem. Few would deny the close association between misogyny and Christianity, and hardly a Christian church today can claim innocence. The most cogent comparison, however, is not between Christianity and modern secular society but between Christians and non-Christians in a contemporary setting or before and after the advent of Christianity in a historical context. The second proposition entails an analysis of Roman society before and after its acceptance of the new religion, but since Christianity became immediately and inextricably involved with the host society, it is often difficult to disentangle the original Christian influence from its adaptation to the existing Roman world.

In this context the Nordic sources offer advantages in approaching the problem. Accepting the new religion half a millennium after the rest of western Europe had, the Scandinavians retained a society less influenced by Christian ideas than the Roman was. Since Iceland and Norway have preserved the largest body of literary, historical, and legal sources written not in Latin, the language of the church as well as the empire, but in the Old Norse vernacular spoken by the people, and since much of this literature purports to describe the pagan period in the Scandinavian world, these sources are well suited for the examination of women's positions before and after the arrival of Christianity in the tenth and eleventh centuries.

Aside from runic inscriptions, writing was the gift of churchmen. Prior to their arrival, much Old Norse literature and the tradition behind it were kept alive orally during the several centuries from the formation of such works during pagan times to far into the early Christian era, when they were written down. The remaining sources are the direct product of Christian authors who describe an increasingly Christianized society. In the period during and immediately after the conversion to Christianity, the young Nordic church had urgent liturgical and instructional needs. As is evident from the oldest preserved manuscripts dating from the late twelfth century, parchment and writing were employed to serve those needs.[5] The recording of pagan myth and legend, the closest evidence of the old religion, had to wait for at least two generations, but even such early efforts have perished, leaving us with no existing manuscripts of pagan lore before the late thirteenth century. Some Christian mediation is obviously embedded even in this seemingly pagan literature. Poetic in form, the primary mythological and heroic sources are grouped together and set in pagan times, although some of the heroic figures may have belonged originally to the Christian period.

Equally pagan in setting are most of the sagas. In order to get an overview of the voluminous body of saga literature, historians are best served by following Sigurður Nordal's suggestion to classify the sagas according to the time span between the events they describe and the time when they were written down.[6] Distributed in this fashion, the sagas fall into three categories. The first is the contemporary sagas that treat the period after around 1100 and were composed by authors who either lived simultaneously with the events or had access to reliable contemporary sources. In this group belong the episcopal sagas dealing with esiastical issues in Iceland and Norway;[7] Sturlunga saga, a bulky composite work describing Icelandic politics and society in the twelfth and thirteenth centuries[8]; and the later kings' sagas, such as Hákon saga Hákonarsonar.[9] Known as the sagas of the past, the second group focuses on the period from 850 to 1100 and encompasses most of the (mainly Norwegian) kings' sagas and all of the sagas of the Icelanders, also known as the family sagas, the flower of Icelandic literature.[10] Although realistic and objective in tone, these accounts are separated by several centuries from the events they describe. Finally, the third group, designated as the sagas of ancient times, attempts to deal with the period before 850 on a larger Scandinavian or even European scale.[11] The last to be written, these stories are the furthest removed from the events they describe. Thus, the formal acceptance of Christianity in Iceland in the year 1000 and the tumultuous imposing of this new religion on the Norwegians

during the first half of the eleventh century are distant markings an-
chored far downstream in this long combination of narrative accounts.
In these writings, nonetheless, Christian ideas made their way back into
the pagan tradition.

All the Scandinavian peoples produced legal codes in their vernacular languages. Originating in pagan times but committed to writing
only during the Christian period, these laws also display a fusion of old
and new. Disseminated orally through yearly performances by the law-
speaker, the earliest secular laws were probably articulated before the
advent of Christianity.[12] However, churchmen quickly became instrumental in committing the laws to writing, and they formulated and had
accepted the special, so-called Christian-law sections, which precede all
existing law codes with the exception of the Danish provincial laws. The
influence of the church on the important issue of marriage can be gauged
by observing the changes, involving both content and placement, in the
marriage legislation as it moved from the pagan *festa-þáttr*, or engagement section, in the secular laws to the Christian preambles. Among all
medieval Germanic law codes, the "giant bird," in the words of Andreas
Heusler, is the Icelandic *Grágás* (Grey Goose), which is preserved in
several versions. [13]

In addition to serving as the language of legal documents, Old Norse
was also used to write charters in Iceland and Norway, but Latin was
preferred in Sweden and Denmark.[14] Such charters are the first mirrors
of the new marriage legislation proposed by the church.

Within this quick overview of Nordic sources, we shall focus our attention on three areas of myth, heroic images, and society, areas where the
Old Norse sources—when treated with care—can not only provide information about the perception of women and their role in pagan society
but also yield insight into the changes caused by Christianity. By looking
more closely at the three areas, we shall deal with the methodological
problems that have special importance for interpreting women's roles,
before we reach brief conclusions about women in the Old Norse world.

Mythology

A diachronic study of mythology and heroic literature
will expose not only life-sustaining perceptions and
realities concerning gender roles, and women's roles
in particular, in the societies that produced these stories but also insights into the subsequent cultures that utilized the myths and stories in
a historical and self-conscious manner, thereby creating new social and
literary myths.

Working with societies where oral traditions are still active, anthropologists have been more aware than historians have been of the importance of myths and the relationship between myth and society. There is as yet little agreement over the exact nature of this interaction, and a generation ago Claude Lévi-Strauss summarily dismissed sociological explanations of myths by remarking that evil grandmothers in myth do not imply evil grandmothers in society.[15] Although mythical occurrences and phenomena need not be direct or even indirect reflections of society, there must have been some original experience—a distorted memory or a dream of an experience—that enabled the first teller of a myth to conceive the story. It may also be inferred that gender divisions within the cosmos as well as roles and attributes ascribed to gods and goddesses who figure in myths must have had an impact on the generations of men and women who recounted and listened to these stories and who, through performances of the dramatic contents, may have strengthened their faith in the religious system behind the myths.[16] Through cross-cultural studies women anthropologists are beginning to unravel connections between gender roles in society and those in myth.[17] Societies with undifferentiated or egalitarian gender roles appear to allow female participation in creation symbolism and the divine hierarchy, whereas in male-dominated cultures, myths portray fear of women, especially of their sexuality.

While the problem of the relationship between myth and society is thus clearer today than it was a generation ago, another concern persists —the connections between myth and religion. Witnessing contemporary oral societies in which myths are reenacted through cultic ceremonies, anthropologists speak with confidence about the religious significance of these myths. In the case of Nordic mythology, however, the historian's materials are limited to the wreckage of previously unified and vital religious systems left behind for subsequent generations, whose attitudes ranged from hostility and indifference to sympathy, at best, but never included unquestioning acceptance and genuine faith. It must nonetheless be assumed that the body of Nordic myths formed at one time a religious system and was used for the purposes of worship, but taken as a whole or individually, the myths could degenerate at any point and be subjected to deforming interpretations or serve merely as entertainment.[18]

In Western society, where the study of myths and heroic legend has been an integral part of humanistic education since its inception, the impact of these stories has, of course, continued long after they ceased to convey a living religion and vital cultural context. Already in medieval

Iceland, Christian authors and copyists preserved and interpreted these pagan tales. After the discovery of Tacitus's *Germania* in the fifteenth century, German humanists in the sixteenth century began to develop a social myth of the Germanic tribes as free and democratic, a construct reinforced by the first publication of the Edda poetry a century later.[19] Accepting Jordanes' idea of Scandinavia as the *vagina gentium*, Montesquieu, in his *Esprit des lois*, envisioned the north as the cradle of political freedom. This idea was given full treatment in 1755 by Paul-Henri Mallet in his influential *Introduction à l'histoire de Dannemarc* and was substantiated the following year by his companion volume of translations, *Monumens de la mythologie et de la poésie des anciens Scandinaves.*[20] In the romantic era, such thinkers as Herder and the brothers Grimm used mythology to demonstrate differences between Germanic peoples and their Latin cousins. They perceived these differences not only as historical but also as continuing through time. Wagner, relying on *Vǫlsunga saga* and the newly discovered *Nibelungenlied*, used Nordic mythology and heroic tales to frame his titanic vision of divine and human history, and Freud and his followers have given new life to the interpretation of all myths. In the last half century, Scandinavian mythology has been exposed to structural analysis. Georges Dumézil, for example, finds here some of the best illustrations for his tripartite Indo-European model of myth and society.[21] Although Lévi-Strauss has not worked with Nordic myth, scholars have applied his ideas to individual episodes of the Scandinavian materials.[22] As a result of this generation's interest in women's studies, a few poems have been analyzed with specific focuses on female issues,[23] and certain goddesses have been singled out for special study,[24] but we still lack a comprehensive analysis of Nordic mythology from a feminist perspective.[25]

On a smaller scale, what are the possibilities of examining the female role in the mythological cosmos of the Germans? It is generally assumed that all Germanic tribes worshiped similar or identical divinities, but only the Old Norse sources provide relatively detailed information about pagan mythology and legend. While all evidence was penned during the Christian era and thus susceptible to Christian influence, one group of sources, the skaldic poetry, was almost impervious to change because of the stringent poetic rules governing its form and structure. We know the names of about 250 poets, or skalds, from the early ninth to the middle of the fourteenth centuries. Comprising more than a thousand pages in a modern edition, their works are impressive by any standard.[26] Besides being constrained by a conservative and resistant medium, some poets were themselves firmly rooted in the pagan past, while others, living during the period of transition, demonstrate the tension between heathen and Christian beliefs. This poetry at first appears, therefore, as a promising gathering ground for pagan myths, but it is nonetheless difficult to use. Heavily oriented toward a male world of kings and retainers, most poems do not refer to myths directly but describe, at best, scenes on shields or tapestries representing well-known mythological episodes.[27] Furthermore, the bulk of the material is hidden in the kennings, or metaphorical circumlocutions, the hallmark of skaldic poetry. Only the listener/reader already versed in pagan myth is able to decipher relevant information from these heavily ornamented lines.

The most important source for Nordic mythology is the collection of poems grouped under the name of the Edda, of which the majority is found in a single manuscript, the famous *Codex regius*, penned during the third quarter of the thirteenth century.[28] Outside of this manuscript, a few additional lays bring the total of mythological poems to fifteen. Created over a long period of time, the Edda poems must be examined individually.[29] The oldest lays are now usually ascribed to the late ninth century, the most recent to the thirteenth century. Divided almost evenly between poems treating the mythological cosmos of gods and goddesses and those describing the heroic realm of Germanic heroes and heroines, the Eddic corpus connects these two worlds through mythological females who consort with human heroes.

As pagan knowledge increasingly lost ground against the incoming tide of Christian instruction and, at the same time, the skaldic poets required detailed knowledge of myths to supply materials for their elaborate kennings, it is not surprising that the twelfth-century renaissance in Iceland stimulated, among many other accomplishments, a revival of mythology. To Snorri Sturluson, the greatest of all medieval Nordic intellectuals, we owe a textbook in poetics, the Prose Edda.[30] Composing numerous examples of skaldic versification, Snorri also provided basic mythological data by offering prose renditions of some lays found in the Poetic Edda. To these he added poetic and prose variations as well as his own prose versions of lost poems. Written about 1220, the Prose Edda captured pagan mythology as it had filtered through oral tradition during past generations and refracted it through still another powerful but unified mind. In *Ynglinga saga*, the first part of his great historical work, *Heimskringla*, Snorri also included mythological information by tracing the ancestry of the Swedish kings to Nordic gods.[31]

An analysis of this material reveals a starkly patriarchal cosmology

and mythology. The male gods, such as Odin, Thor, and Frey, appear
as doers and creators, whereas the goddesses are not clearly defined or,
at best, are permitted only subservient roles. Even the female specialty
of reproduction is at times performed by males or is simply taken for
granted. Since the most celebrated goddess, Freya, can be best characterized as a sex symbol created for male consumption, she may have meant
little for other goddesses or human women. Only in the area of magic,
seiðr, did Freya possess special knowledge that she was supposed to have
transmitted to gods and humans. We never see her perform magic, however—perhaps because the other gods considered the activity revolting
and suitable only for priestesses.

The male gods, however, are not almighty. Like humans, they reside in
the hands of fate, personified by three female figures, and both gods and
humans are headed toward final disaster, the inevitable *ragnarøk*. Knowledge of this fate, however, is accessible only to a woman—the old seeress,
or *vǫlva*. In the magnificent poem *Vǫluspá*, or vision of the sybil,[32] which
combines Old Norse creation and revelation myths, the *vǫlva* both re-
luctantly shares her knowledge of the future with Odin, the chief god,
and reveals her full cognizance of the past, reaching back to creation.
Although Loki, a male god, is directly responsible for the final disaster, this vision makes it clear that the original introduction of evil into
the gods' world was produced by the arrival from Giantland of women
knowledgeable in magic. The *vǫlva* also envisages a rebirth of the cosmos, the gods, and humans. While women are included in this future
among the humans, females are strangely absent from the new world of
the gods. This may be an oversight on the author's part, but it can be
argued that the new world is perceived as being better because of the
goddesses' absence.

Beyond this important evidence of association between femaleness and
evil, the mythological vocabulary includes for evil creatures or witches
words used only in the feminine form, which suggests covert misogyny.
In other words, the Nordic pantheon may be seen as the creation of a
society dominated by males who made room for important female figures
only when males—facing an unknown future—had to admit helpless-
ness or when they voiced fear of women, a fear induced, perhaps, by the
occasional success of women to predict the future.

The figure of the *vǫlva*, or wise woman, has ancient roots in the
Germanic past. Tacitus had already noticed that the Germans ascribed a
sacred and prophetic quality to women and that men relied on women's
advice and forecasts.[33] It is perhaps no coincidence that long hair—often

a sign of holiness—was a common attribute of women, priests, and kings among all Germanic and Scandinavian peoples. Why women were perceived in this way is open only to speculation.

The female divinities in the Old Norse pantheon are, however, echoes of older, more shadowy, but originally more powerful figures, some of whom were known as the *dísir*, who are referred to occasionally in the texts. They should probably be linked with the fertility goddesses of whom Tacitus gives a glimpse. Such female figures may have been drawn from the religion of the original inhabitants of the Germano-Scandinavian area, where, perhaps during some distant period, a full-fledged mother goddess reigned supreme. Reflecting a society that hailed maternity as the only life-giving principle, this female figure may also be at the root of the deference with which the Germanic tribes treated prophetesses. In due course the invading, patriarchal Indo-Europeans swept this religion away and absorbed only a few traces. A more simple solution would suggest that Scandinavian mythology arrived in its entirety with the Indo-Europeans. In this case, the elements of older female deities and cult practices can be seen as fragments of an ancient, more primitive Indo-European religion and society, or they are vestiges—embedded into the later tripartite division—from peoples absorbed by the Indo-Europeans during their march through Europe. [34]

Profoundly patriarchal in nature, Old Norse mythology does not simply subordinate female divinities to the more powerful male gods but requires associations among femaleness, evil, and wisdom, which suggests reactions of a predominant male society to an older belief in strong female deities.

Heroic Poetry   Originating in the Nordic world, the mythological poems presented in the seeress, or *vǫlva,* a single figure who possessed a counterpart among human women. Pagan women in Norway, Iceland, and Greenland exercised the profession of *vǫlva* (plural: *vǫlur*), who predicted the future for their fellow farmers and occasionally helped them by performing magic. In contrast, the most important Old Norse heroic lays most likely go back to lost originals arising in continental Europe, and they are almost exclusively peopled with human subjects inhabiting this region.

Perhaps the most remarkable feature of the heroic poetry is simply the presence of women who actively play a role in the unfolding of the drama. A comparison with skaldic poetry makes this phenomenon all the more striking, especially when it is recognized that the societies responsible for the two different genres of poetry must have been remarkably similar. The ancient Germanic society from which grew the first heroic lays was dominated by kings, retainers, and their war activities in ways similar to those operative at the medieval Norwegian court, home of the skaldic poetry. The professional skaldic poets, singing the praises of the martial deed of changing royal masters, included women only rarely and as occasional love objects at best.[35] On the other hand, the two heroines, Brynhild and Gudrun, were prominent in the original versions of the heroic lays, if not in the events behind them. Their behavior justified and explained men's actions and ultimately the fate of tribes and nations. Having caught the attention of medieval Icelandic authors, the roles of these female figures were elaborated, fleshed out, and multiplied in the existing Old Norse heroic lays, making it difficult to distinguish between original features and later additions, beyond the mere assertion that the female presence originated from the Continent. Using these poetic figures as models, later prose writers further amplified their roles, particularly that of the inciting and egging woman, to describe their own pagan foremothers.

We have already noted the importance of the *Codex regius* manuscript for Nordic mythology.[36] It played a comparable role for heroic literature, since its second half contains the largest single collection of Germano-Nordic heroic lays. In almost twenty lays, male and female figures form a personal and textual bridge from the mythological to the heroic world. In the Nordic tradition, these heroic figures were understood to have lived in the pagan period. The oldest versions of some of the existing poems may have been formulated by pagans, but, of course, the writers, compilers, and later authors were Christians. Exercising extreme care in arranging the poems sequentially, the compiler of the *Codex regius* grouped the stories of the two half brothers, Helgi and Sigurd, and their wives to follow the poems devoted to the gods, and he connected the male heroes in a genealogical lineage originating in Odin. The action moves from the mythological north of the gods, to the human, Nordic world of Helgi, and—after the death of Helgi's mother and his father's subsequent marriage to a southern princess—to the Continental world of Sigurd, the subject of the original German lays.

Because of the Continental origin and settings of most of the heroic lays, they, more than the mythological poems, have provoked an endless and often acrimonious scholarly debate that at times reveals more about the national origin of the scholars than about that of the songs. Two issues, however, seem beyond dispute, namely, that most of the events that furnished the raw material for the lays took place in Europe during the age of the Germanic migrations (from the third through the fifth centuries) and that only the efforts of Icelandic and possibly Norwegian compilers, scribes, and authors prevented the total loss of this common legacy of the Germanic world. Relying on heroic lays, some verifiable from the *Codex regius*, Snorri Sturluson also included heroic stories in the mythology of his Prose Edda, and he tapped the heroic-mythic sources in his *Ynglinga saga*.[37]

These stories now written down, as well as other heroic tales not yet committed to writing, nonetheless continued their oral life, especially since the energies of Icelandic and Norwegian authors during the rest of the thirteenth and the beginning of the fourteenth centuries were absorbed by writing and copying the sagas of the past, namely the kings' and the family sagas (or sagas of Icelanders).[38] By the end of the fourteenth century, however, when Icelandic authors had exhaustively covered their own contemporary age as well as the immediate past of Norway and Iceland, they turned their attention toward ancient times, focusing on the Nordic arena, the larger European and even global stage. Their purpose was to transcribe poems and stories that had been circulating for a long time and to create new tales about these subjects that continued to fascinate native writers and audiences far into the nineteenth century.[39] The results were the *fornaldarsögur*, or legendary sagas, which depict ancient Nordic history, and the *riddarasögur*, or chivalric sagas, which attempt to describe the remote ages of Europe but which often do so with a purely imaginary setting.[40] For our purposes the most important of these groupings is the legendary sagas, a corpus of some thirty pieces written during the fourteenth century and dealing with the Nordic heroic or mythic age.[41] At times they throw additional light on characters mentioned in the older poetic sources, such as Helgi and Brynhild, or bring to life heroes unknown elsewhere, such as Thorstein Vikingson and Princess Thornbjörg.

In this group also belongs the important *Vǫlsunga saga*, which provides the most extensive coverage of the Sigurd legend.[42] Going beyond the chronological scope of the older heroic poems as well as the *Nibelungenlied*, it places the Germanic heroes in a genealogical chain descending from Odin and continuing through Sigurd's daughter, Aslaug, and the Danish king Ragnar Lodbrok through a series of Danish heroic figures. *Vǫlsunga saga* is particularly significant for reconstructing the full story of the Sigurd legend as it originally existed in the *Codex regius*. The loss of eight leaves from this manuscript—the famous lacuna—is remedied to some extent by the *Vǫlsunga* author's possession of a complete copy of the available manuscript. This prose version makes it possible to reconstruct, with some degree of plausibility, the contents of the missing poems. [43]

It is obvious that fantasy and imagination have been influential at all stages of the formation of these sagas. The term *lygisögur*, or lying sagas, which was already employed by the Swedish king Sverrir in the twelfth century, is not totally incorrect, and it is impossible to determine the historicity of details about known people, let alone totally new figures. It cannot be denied, however, that these legendary sagas contain elements drawn from the same well of oral tradition that had irrigated the imagination of the authors of the older heroic lays. This is particularly true of the lays and *lausavísur*, or individual stanzas, which are embedded in but often far older than the sagas, although, admittedly, it is difficult to distinguish between authentic old poems and later imitations. In other words, when one reads these sagas, skepticism is permitted.

Skaldic poetry and contemporary prose accounts more recent than the original or preserved form of the heroic lays will occasionally include references to heroic figures known from the poetry and thereby reveal a contemporary consciousness of heroes, a finding all the more precious when it is datable. [44]

This heroic tradition was likewise tapped by the Danish author Saxo Grammaticus in his *Gesta Danorum*. [45] Saxo's frequent use of similar or different versions of the heroic or legendary sagas (*fornaldarsögur*) testifies to the fact that, although these stories were written as late as the fourteenth century, the subject matter had been known for a long time. [46]

Assembled and created over a long span of time, this heroic literature conveyed images of women in the areas of war, revenge, incitement, wisdom, and love—images that were imitated and sometimes amplified in various ways by contemporary and later prose writers who described pagan society. Among these, the three first areas were the most important. With little correspondence to existing society in either the distant Germanic past or the more recent Viking period, the figure of the fighting woman fascinated Nordic authors, who promoted her as the Scandinavian contribution to the gallery of literary female figures. In the heroic poetry she appeared as a winged Valkyrie hovering over the heroes in battle or as a shieldmaiden actively participating in the conflict. Also found in the legendary sagas, the latter figure developed into the maiden king, who ruled her country as well as any man could and at times even assumed a male name. [47]

Closely connected with warfare are personal violence and revenge. *Atlakviða,* one of the oldest of the heroic lays, contains a startling portrait of Gudrun, Sigurd's widow, who killed her children born of her second husband, Atli, leader of the Huns, and later stabbed her husband in bed to revenge his killing of her two brothers.[48] Again, this kind of behavior had little foundation in contemporary society. When the theme of female violence was occasionally used by later prose writers, the women were remarkably unsuccessful in their quest for physical revenge. [49]

Heroic poetry's most lasting contribution, however, was the image of the inciting and egging woman, who, by hurling insinuations and accusations at her relatives, accomplished the revenge she was unable to otherwise obtain because of her lack of physical strength. *Hamðismál,* likewise belonging among the oldest poems,[50] connects the legend of the death of Ermanaric with the *Vǫlsung* cycle and shows Gudrun egging her sons from her third marriage to take revenge for Ermanaric's ("Jǫrmunrekkr" in the Old Norse version) killing of Svanhild, her daughter by Sigurd. The egging woman par excellence, however, is Brynhild, who, in her pique of not having married Sigurd, whom she considers to be the best man, eggs her husband, Gunnar, to kill Sigurd and his young son, a cataclysmic event that eventually brings down the two houses of the Vǫlsungs and the Huns. [51]

Since the figure of the egging and revenging woman caught the imagination of Icelandic prose writers, this *Hetzerin,* or inciting or whetting woman, became the ubiquitous female figure in medieval Icelandic literature. Nagging her husband and other relatives to perform evil deeds of revenge, she achieved terrifying results.[52] Undoubtedly fueled by the church's misogyny that infected the authors through their clerical training, the whetting woman appeared first in the kings' sagas, such as *Saga Ólafs Tryggvasonar* by Oddr Snorrason.[53] In Snorri Sturluson's *Heimskringla,* inciting is the chief function exercised by pagan women.[54] From these accounts the figure spread to the family sagas, where not only are the leading characters constantly nagging, but such minor figures as servants and female beggars, exercising the same function, often appear only when the motif is needed. [55]

Literature and Society

The intrusion of the female inciter into the prose accounts has already introduced us to the largest, most important, and, for women's history, the most controversial body of Old Norse literature— the sagas of the past. During the twelfth and thirteenth centuries, when vernacular prose was making an appearance in Europe, the Icelanders had already created a vernacular narrative prose whose products we have examined in Snorri's mythology and in the legendary sagas. The finest prose, however, is found in the kings' and the family sagas. Mainly concerned with political history, the large body of kings' sagas, generally older than the family sagas, include women primarily as queens and consorts and are thus amenable for examining marriage and succession policies among Norwegian kings.[56] We have seen that the use of the female inciter is limited to the pagan period of these accounts and that the figure is mainly a product of literary borrowing and clerical misogyny. [57]

The family sagas, the pride of Icelandic literature, offer more opportunities for examining women but also present more problems.[58] Written during the thirteenth century and preserved in manuscripts, the best of which belong to the fourteenth century, the fifty-odd extant sagas and short stories (*þættir*) vary in length from a dozen to several hundred pages. In long, generational surges, they describe the origins of the immigrants in Norway and their travels abroad until their final settlement in Iceland, concentrating on the century following the establishment of the General Assembly (the *alþing*) in 930, which constitutes the so-called saga age. The tantalizing feature of these accounts is their apparent realism and verisimilitude. Without parallel in European literature until the nineteenth century, the family sagas describe the everyday lives and activities of farmers and their wives, including geographic details still verifiable in the Icelandic landscape today, as well as genealogical lists that can be confirmed from the older *Landnámabók,* generally considered by scholars as historically reliable. It would be difficult to find anywhere a more realistic and detailed picture of a farm woman and her work than that of Katla spinning wool, arranging her living room, giving orders to have a locked room opened, and playing with her favorite goat in *Eyrbyggja saga* (chap. 20). The problem consists of which society is covered in this vignette. Does it portray ancient history, the tenth century (when Katla lived), the thirteenth century (when the medieval author lived), the author's perception of Katla's age, or a synchronism of all of these? Since the acceptance of Christianity in the year 1000 falls in the intervening time span, this question is important, especially since Katla is also shown performing magic, an activity frowned upon by the church. The question of historical veracity is, however, intimately connected with the equally difficult problem of the sagas' origins and interpretations. [59]

As the only genre not to fall into total oblivion by the late Middle Ages, the kings' sagas continued to be accepted as reliable historical sources.

In due course this reputation for historical veracity was transferred to the legendary and the family sagas when they reemerged during the seventeenth century through the efforts of Scandinavian historians to collect them. However, because the heroes and mythic kings of the legendary sagas were far older than the protagonists of the kings' sagas, historians were forced to consider the question of the survival of this material in the period between the occurrence and the recording of the events. They usually solved the problem by postulating an oral tradition carrying a true picture of the events and keeping them alive for generations until they were finally committed to writing by a person acting more as a scribe than as an author. From the beginning of saga scholarship, the combination of historicity and oral transmission was attached to all genres of saga literature. In this context, the family sagas, or sagas of the Icelanders, were thus understood to provide accurate historical accounts of pagan Icelanders whose political, cultural, and religious activities could be pieced together by a comprehensive perusal of all the sagas to form a coherent picture of ancient society.

By the middle of the nineteenth century, however, a few voices began to suggest that the family sagas should be considered as literature rather than history. As a consequence, the role of the author increased, and faith in the fixed oral tradition diminished. In 1914 the Swiss scholar Andreas Heusler coined the terms "freeprose" for the older view, which emphasized the oral tradition, and "bookprose" for the newer perception, which stressed the role of the author.[60] Heusler's terminology resulted in the formation of two sharply opposed camps, each attacking the alleged opinions of the opponent without clearly defining its own turf. Although Heusler had not included historicity in defining the two terms, those in the bookprose camp came to attach faith in the oral tradition as part of the freeprose baggage, while they themselves came under the spell not so much of the author, who in most cases remained anonymous, as of his literary borrowings, which were being increasingly uncovered by scholars. Such borrowings further undermined faith in the accuracy of oral tradition.

Bookprose theories have flourished in the past fifty years, especially in the form practiced by the so-called Icelandic school, which does not deny but minimizes as unknowable the oral tradition behind the written saga. Instead, the practitioners of the school have performed meticulous work on individual sagas, in each case analyzing the literary style and borrowings, the author's milieu, and the possible influence of contemporary society on the events described, in an effort to accord to each saga its place in the development of Icelandic literature between 1100 and 1400. The result has been the penetrating introductions to the sagas in the splendid editions in the series *Íslenzk fornrit*, the foundation of all modern saga scholarship. [61]

In the last few decades, however, faith in the oral tradition has re-emerged. Structuralism has inspired scholars to search for general patterns in the macro- and microstructures of the sagas.[62] Anthropologists and social historians, looking for parallels with other tribal societies, have focused attention on functions with little concern for chronology.[63] Like the Icelandic school, these new trends draw attention away from the native soil of the island. Where the Icelandic school's studies point to the Christian culture of medieval Europe, formalist and anthropological studies seek connections with deep and universal structures that precede Christianity and persist beyond its imposition.[64] Other scholars are more concerned with the medieval society represented in Icelandic literature. Arguing that the problem of historicity for the ancient period is less important than the fact that issues in the sagas were meaningful for medieval Icelanders, they disregard the problems of saga origins and intertextual relationships. By distilling the texts' *mentalité*, they obtain, instead, insights into the generations that not only produced the sagas but also copied and consumed the texts as readers and listeners. While these results are more modest than those obtained by long diachronic studies, they are probably the only safe ones, given the nature of the sources.[65] For the twin problems of historicity and oral tradition, this approach implies that the stories and concepts are understood as having their origin in a historical context no longer retrievable. Modified according to societal needs and historical consciousness by succeeding generations, changes were incorporated to follow existing narrative patterns in ways observed by modern anthropologists among tribes at political and economic stages of development similar to those of the ancient and medieval Icelanders.

How do these changing views of the family sagas influence the study of women? Unlike the fallow fields plowed elsewhere by historians of women, the Old Norse sources had already yielded fruit of strong, independent women who centuries earlier had caught scholars' imaginations. The problem for historians has been to come to terms with these images. Although Mallet had been one of the first to voice skepticism about the use of the Icelandic sources for political history because of "the doubtful facts which are supposed to have happened among the Northern nations, during the dark ages of paganism," he was convinced that the same accounts gave "a just picture of the opinions, customs and even inclinations of a people."[66] As we saw, Mallet was the first to express fully for a wide European audience the idea of the north as the fountainhead of political freedom. Echoing Montesquieu, he credited harsh climate, difficult geography, and primitive societal structure with the achievement that "liberty [was] preserved among the inhabitants of Germany and the North, as it were in the bud, ready to blossom and expand through all Europe, there to flourish in their several colonies." Now challenging Rome, "all these people breaking forth as it were by agreement, overturned this unhappy empire, and formed out of its ruins limited monarchies."[67] The essence of this spirit of freedom Mallet found in Iceland.[68] Not surprisingly, Mallet shelters women within the cloak of liberty, arguing that "the northern nations . . . did not so much consider the other sex as made for their pleasure, as to be their equals and companions." Extolling the female roles of prophetesses and healers, he went so far as to credit northern men with the creation of the spirit of chivalry and gallantry, "at this day the distinguishing characteristic of European manners . . . which was so little known to the Greeks and Romans, how polite soever in other respects."[69]

Mallet's general perception of Nordic freedom was quickly abandoned, but in spite of a few cautioning remarks from Guizot, the perception of the liberty and equality of Germano-Scandinavian women continued to thrive among French intellectuals;[70] in the nineteenth century it became dogma for German, Dutch, and Scandinavian scholars.[71] Quarried for details, the saga corpus provided members for an impressive composite statue of a proud and dominant pagan woman. When a suitor approached her father about marriage, she was asked for her opinion, and she expected to have it taken seriously. Easily her husband's equal in the joint management of the family farm, she bore the keys to the all-important larder. At times she was even her husband's superior in upholding the family honor when she urged a reluctant mate to take revenge. She was stoic in the loss of children and relatives and could divorce her husband at will, and she could enter a new marriage as a widow or divorcée with an ease even greater than that of a young girl. Inheriting goods from her native family and receiving property from her husband, she ended her years as an older woman, greatly respected, wealthy, and powerful. One complete story, the famous *Laxdœla saga,* can be interpreted as a biography of such a woman—Gudrun Osvifsdaughter.[72] Features that were from the sagas and, in particular, the law codes and that did not fit this model, however, were quietly ignored.

The bookprose theories dealt a blow to these theories. In 1958 the

German scholar Rolf Heller argued that the saga heroine had no basis in society. The figure was not a real person but a composite image of literary motifs, created by the author from his contemporary society or inspired by his knowledge of heroic literature. Chief among the motifs were the forbidden love visit and the female inciter. Transferred from one saga to the next, the motifs were introduced when needed to unfold the drama of men's activities. The female carriers were thereafter quickly dropped. At best, Heller was willing to see in these motifs a few cultural features from the Sturlunga age, the period of writing.

Heller undoubtedly went too far and did not sufficiently investigate the reasons behind the creation of the saga heroine. His views have been accepted only in the sense that historians felt free to eliminate the strong saga woman from their pages, but she still lived in the popular imagination. Although new trends within recent saga scholarship do not allow conclusions about the pagan period, they do admit, as we have seen, the usefulness of the texts for social analysis of the thirteenth century and thus revalidate the heroine for this period, and some women's historians would like to reinstate the strong woman in the pagan period as well. [73]

With the few parallels that exist elsewhere, it is understandable that the image of the Icelandic heroine has been cherished by women in Scandinavia and most particularly in Iceland, where the sagas still abide in people's minds as emotional and intellectual realities. Nor is it to be denied that a certain socialization occurs whereby in each generation the reading of texts with strong images of women produces both a conviction of their past reality and a present desire to emulate them. The twice-elected president of Iceland, a woman, fits this tradition well, as do attempts by modern scholars, mainly women, to undergird the image.

The problem is not simply to accept or reject the saga image of the strong woman. Clarifications and nuances can be added from the laws and the charter material of Iceland and Norway, thus enabling the historian to distinguish multilayers of these images. As we have seen, Mallet's suggestion to read the sagas not as political but as cultural history has been followed by modern social historians, who have simply changed the chronological focus. When Mallet's perception of general freedom among the Germans remained attached to their women, it was undoubtedly because women, generally outside the mainstream of political events, were involved in unchanging activities.

Not all concerns and activities involving females remained constant, however; nor were their descriptions equally reliable. On one end of the spectrum stands women's work. The technology of an economy based on animal husbandry and gathering provided an unchanging frame-work for the activities of work in which women spent most of their time: childbirth, child rearing, milking of animals, and production of food and clothing.[74] Read for these subjects, all the sagas—regardless of their setting—can provide illustrations that will fit traditional societies. Transhumance, the custom of sending milk animals away from the farm during the summer months to distant pastures, where they were attended by shepherds and milkmaids, connects Iceland not only with Norway but with other mountainous regions where this system was an economic necessity. It must be admitted, however, that women's work was not high among the concerns of the saga writers. Women were traditionally responsible for indoor work pertaining to the running of the household (innan-stokks), while men were in charge of the outdoor activities (útan-stokks). Nonetheless, the sagas more often portray women working outdoors than indoors—raking hay, washing clothes, tending animals, or running errands. While such activities may fall under female purview, one suspects that the saga author placed women out of doors in order to integrate them into men's actions.

Another stable feature, one still in need of detailed investigation, is women's property rights. As portrayed in both past and contemporary accounts, women enjoyed almost equal inheritance rights with brothers, although, when sharing, men often preferred the real estate, leaving the movables to women. Similar conditions were also enjoyed by European women during the early Middle Ages but came to end with feudalism and resulting primogeniture. In other words, Nordic women's continued control of property need not be seen as a facet of the strong woman but can instead be seen simply as a sign of an archaic society.

At the opposite end are the semipolitical activities of inciting, where the family sagas would have us believe that ordinary farm women spent their time egging and abetting their male relatives to revenge.[75] Most often followed, such advice nonetheless is considered in bad light, and the statement "Cold are the counsels of women" (Kǫld eru kvenna ráð) runs like a refrain through much of the saga literature depicting the pagan period.[76] We have seen that only a few nagging women appear in the kings' sagas dealing with the past. In the contemporary society, however, the kings' sagas do not know this figure. Although four cases can be found in the dense Sturlunga saga, the women involved were remarkably unsuccessful in their aims. It seems that in Iceland and Norway the goading woman was far less prominent than the family sagas would have us believe.[77]

Between these two extremes remains the large area of marriage, sexuality, and divorce. Here it is possible to read from the allegedly pagan
sagas concerns (revealed by the contemporary narratives, laws, and ecclesiastical charters) that preoccupied Christian authors and audiences in the
twelfth and thirteenth centuries.[78] This was the period when the church
attempted to impose its marital legislation throughout Europe. Con-
sisting of monogamy, female consent, and indissolubility of the marital
bond, the program provoked resistance everywhere. By this time the
European royalty and aristocracy had acquiesced to the first two proposi-
tions but still needed encouragement in the third. In the north, however,
persisted older, pagan practices, including polygamy, serial marriages,
and numerous concubines, that were abhorrent to local churchmen and
compelled them to emphasize the counterprogram of monogamy and
female consent. Intimidated by the hostile reaction to this program,
however, bishops were inclined to grant divorces more easily. While not
absent from the family sagas, these features of free sexuality were nonetheless subdued. Instead, the pagan saga world teemed with stable married couples whose marriage arrangements had included female consent,
although it is clear from the oldest laws that this concept was not native.
In other words, the authors' contact with the church's training and
preaching induced them to describe the marriages of their forefathers and
foremothers according to current church doctrine, even though churchmen did not expect heathens to live according to Christian principles.
Undoubtedly hoping to create models to be emulated by their audiences,
the authors admitted the normative role of consent by creating disastrous
endings to the few marriages that did not allow it to operate. The fictional
literature of the legendary and the chivalric sagas makes it clear that later
authors associated consent with Christianity and southern Europe and
allowed it to appear only within the boundaries of this milieu.

❡ Containing numerous portraits of women, the Old Norse sources
paint unusually rich and nuanced pictures of women, from pagan goddesses and Viking queens to humble medieval maids and hermitesses.
Among these, greatest interest has been attached to figures from the
pagan sphere, but, given the nature of the sources, they cannot be taken
as unmediated images of the old religion and pagan society. Only the
mythological sources provide full and reliable evidence for Germanic
heathenism. In Snorri's prose version of the old myths we find the thirteenth century's view of this religion, by then repudiated. His source,
the Poetic Edda, contains the closest possible approach to the old pa-

ganism. Among these poems, the oldest take us back only to the ninth century, a period when several generations of Viking men had already come into direct contact with Christianity on their campaigns overseas and had brought home notions about the new religion, as is clear from the poetry. If we see pagan mythology as reflecting Scandinavian society before the Viking age or possibly, on a larger scale, Germanic society before the great migrations, we must conclude that these cultures were staunchly patriarchal. Like the goddesses, mortal women were kept in their place by men, who permitted them, when necessary, a small role as prophetesses but nonetheless clearly associated them with evil.

The Viking age and the acceptance of Christianity introduced changes into this patriarchal system. While in any traditional society women are responsible for the production of children, food, and clothing, the prolonged absence of men on expeditions abroad increased the role of women. They could not handle all farm work without male help when the husband left to go a-viking. He therefore asked other men to look after his work subject to the orders of his wife, who maintained final authority during her husband's absence. Given the isolation of Iceland, these conditions prevailed longer there than elsewhere in Scandinavia when Viking campaigns changed into trading journeys and general travel.

While women may have increased their social standing during the Viking age, men undoubtedly widened their geographic and intellectual horizons immensely. From their travels they brought home a mixed baggage of Germanic and Christian stories and ideas. Tales of strong and dominant women impressed them so vividly that they began to compose songs about similar women, perhaps imagining their own wives in these roles, which permitted such increase in authority that they could not escape notice. These dominant figures then reverberated in the later literature.

Christian ideas influenced the image and role of women in more complex ways. From a study of the oldest runic inscriptions in Germany from the sixth and seventh centuries, Reinhold Bruder has concluded that the respect for women, noticeable in these inscriptions and normally considered an original Germanic trait, was in fact fostered by the acceptance of Christianity.[79] More specifically, the Old Norse sources, even when depicting pagan settings, bear the imprint of the church's new marital legislation, in which monogamy and consent eventually produced far-reaching effects. On the other hand, the restrictions on male sexuality made necessary by this program often induced clergymen to blame women for the problems that arose.[80] In other words, Old Norse sources reveal both respect for women and traditional misogyny, fostered by Christianity.

Old Norse literature, therefore, composed of multilayered and super-imposed traditions, presents not flat, one-dimensional silhouettes of pagan women but richly variegated images that reveal their secrets only after prolonged beholding.

NOTES

Except in titles, all Old Norse proper names have been anglicized. References to works in Scandinavian languages have been kept to a minimum. Whenever possible, references are given to texts in translation. For readers of Scandinavian languages, the entries in *Kulturhistorisk Leksikon for Nordisk Middelalder* are essential.

1. Tacitus's *Germania* and *Histories* are both important. The classic edition of *Germania* is Much's. Most recent is Lund's, which has been used here. Both provide Latin texts and German translations. For English translations, see Mattingly (*Germania*) and Wellesley (vol. 1 contains *Germania* and vols. 2 and 3 contain *The Histories*). For Tacitus's and other classical authors' treatment of women, see Bruder, *Die germanische Frau*, pp. 121–84.

2. Adam of Bremen, *Gesta Hammaburgensis ecclesiae pontificum*. Schmeidler's edition provides the Latin text and a German translation. For English translation, see Adam of Bremen, *History*.

3. Adam of Bremen, *Gesta Hammaburgensis ecclesiae pontificum*, 4.19, pp. 246–48. The term may originate in "Kainulaiset," the native name for Finland that became known in Sweden as "Quänland," Womanland.

4. The standard edition of Saxo Grammaticus is *Saxonis Gesta Danorum*. The first nine books, the mythical part, are translated in *Saxo Grammaticus: History of the Danes*; the last seven books are translated in *Saxo Grammaticus: Books 10–16*. On Saxo's treatment of women, see Strand, *Kvinnor och män*; Damsholt, *Kvindebilledet i dansk højmiddelalder*, pp. 109–54; Holmqvist-Larsen, *Møer, skjoldmøer og krigere*.

5. Turville-Petre, *Origins of Icelandic Literature*, pp. 109–42; *Liturgica Islandica* 1:1–8.

6. Nordal, "Sagalitteraturen," esp. p. 181. For more recent accounts, see Hallberg, *The Icelandic Saga*; Boyer, *Les Sagas islandaises*; Schach, *Icelandic Sagas*.

7. The standard edition is *Biskupa sögur*; new editions are appearing in Iceland and Denmark. A few episcopal *vitae* have been translated to English, such as *The Life of Gudmund the Good, Bishop of Holar*. Since these sources illuminate

sexual behavior among the clergy and the population at large, they are important for a study of women; see Jochens, "Church and Sexuality."

8. The standard edition is *Sturlunga Saga;* an English translation is provided by Julia H. McGrew. This work permits an analysis of family and household in medieval Iceland; see Jochens, "En Islande médiévale."

9. Belonging in this group are also *Sverris saga* and *Bǫglunga sǫgur.* An English translation of *Hákonar saga Hákonarsonar* can be found in *Icelandic Sagas and Other Historical Documents.* These sources are useful for a study of marital and reproductive patterns among Norwegian royalty; see Jochens, "Consent in Marriage"; Jochens, "Politics of Reproduction."

10. For editions of these groups, see below, nn. 56, 58.

11. For editions of these, see below, nn. 40, 41.

12. The Icelandic law was revised and written down in 1117–18. The result, *Hafliðaskrá,* has been lost, but the oldest remaining fragment of the preserved law code is dated to around 1150.

13. The three main manuscripts are *Grágás* 1a–b, *Grágás* 2, and *Grágás* 3. Parts of the law have appeared in English translation in *Laws of Early Iceland: Grágás 1.* The medieval Norwegian laws are available in *Norges gamle love indtil 1387.* Some of the Norwegian laws have also been translated in *Earliest Norwegian Laws.* For Sweden, see *Corpus iuris sueo-gotorum antiqui.* For Denmark, see *Danmarks gamle landskabslove.*

14. For the editions of charters, see the article "Diplomatarium" in *Kulturhistorisk Leksikon for Nordisk Middelalder* 3:82–86.

15. Lévi-Strauss, "Structural Study of Myth," esp. p. 429.

16. On the difficult problem of the relationship between myth and religion in the Nordic context, see the perceptive remarks by Bibire in "Freyr and Gerðr," esp. pp. 25–32.

17. Sanday, *Female Power and Male Dominance,* pp. 15–51.

18. Lindow, "Mythology and Mythography," esp. pp. 21–23. See Phillpotts, *Elder Edda,* for a possible cultic and ritual use of the Edda poetry.

19. Greenway, *Golden Horns,* pp. 60–82. For a full treatment of the subject, see Mjöberg, *Drömmen om Sagatiden.* For the appearance of editions and translations of the Nordic sources, see Farley, *Scandinavian Influence,* pp. 1–28.

20. Both works by Mallet were translated by Bishop Percy as *Northern Antiquities,* the edition I use in what follows. In his introduction and footnotes, Percy corrected Mallet's "celtic error" of blending the Celtic and the Germanic peoples. It is curious that Mallet's work, stressing Nordic freedom, should have been written at the instigation of the new, absolutist Danish government to counteract the bad impression caused by Robert Molesworth's *Account of Denmark as It Was in the Year 1692* (see Beck, *Northern Antiquities in French Learning,* pp. 9–45).

21. Among Dumézil's many works on Nordic mythology, see his *Gods of the*

Ancient Northmen. For a detailed list of his works, see bibliography in Clover and Lindow, *Old Norse–Icelandic Literature,* pp. 57–58. Dumézil's last word on the subject was *Loki.*

22. Bauchatz, *The Well and the Tree;* Mitchell, "*Fǫr Scirnis* as Mythological Model"; Lönnroth, "Skírnismál."

23. This is especially true for *Fǫr Skírnis* or *Skírnismál.* See bibliography in Clover and Lindow, *Old Norse–Icelandic Literature,* p. 152.

24. This is the case with Gerðr and Freyja. See Motz, "Gerðr," and Motz, "Freyja, Anat, Ishtar, and Inanna."

25. The best recent overview of the literature is Lindow's "Mythology and Mythography."

26. The poems are in *Norsk-islandske skjaldedigtning;* for selected poems in a translation, see *The Skalds.* See also Turville-Petre, *Scaldic Poetry;* Frank, *Old Norse Court Poetry;* Hallberg, *Old Icelandic Poetry.* For the most recent overview and bibliography, see Frank, "Skaldic Poetry."

27. See the description in *Laxdœla saga* 5:80.

28. Text in *Edda: Die Lieder des Codex Regius nebst verwandten Denkmälern.* Of the several English translations, the most recent is *Poems of the Vikings.* A classic in its own right is Lee M. Hollander's translation. For the most recent survey, other translations, and bibliography, see Harris, "Eddic Poetry," pp. 68–156.

29. See de Vries, *Altnordische Literaturgeschichte.*

30. See Snorri Sturluson, *Edda Snorra Sturlusona.* For a recent treatment and bibliography, see John Lindow, "Mythology and Mythography," pp. 21–67. A complete recent translation is Snorri Sturluson, *Edda.*

31. Snorri Sturluson, *Ynglinga saga,* in *Heimskringla* 26:1–83. See also Hollander's English translation, *Heimskringla: History of the Kings of Norway.*

32. A bilingual edition is provided in *Vǫluspá: The Song of the Sybil.* There is a large literature on this poem; see the bibliography in Clover and Lindow, *Old Norse–Icelandic Literature,* pp. 154–56. An important study is Nordal, *Vǫluspá* (a translation of the author's Icelandic work from 1923). On the perception of women, see Jochens, "Vǫluspá."

33. Tacitus, *Germania,* chap. 8 (Lund, p. 76): "Inesse quin etiam sanctum aliquid et providum putant."

34. For the evidence of female fertility cult in the Balkan region, see Gimbutas, *Goddesses and Gods of Old Europe.* For a new, controversial view on the Indo-Europeans, see Renfrew, *Archaeology and Language.*

35. On the difficult question of the age and authenticity of the love poetry attributed to the skalds about whom full sagas were written, see Einarsson, *Skáldasögur;* Andersson, "Skalds and Troubadours"; Einarsson, "Lovesick Skald"; Sveinsson, "Kormakr the Poet."

36. For edition and translations, see above, n. 28.

37. For editions and translations, see above, nn. 30, 31.

38. For editions of these, see below, nn. 56, 58.

39. Schlauch, *Romance in Iceland*, pp. 31–36. This interest included both myth and heroic tales.

40. On the taxonomic problems of the legendary and the chivalric sagas, see Kalinke, "Norse Romance." See also Pálsson and Edwards, *Legendary Fiction*.

41. Because the legendary sagas were the last genre to attract scholarly attention, most of these narratives still lack critical editions. The most convenient collection is *Fornaldar sögur Norðurlanda*. Several have been translated to English; see, for example, Pálsson and Edwards's translation, *Seven Viking Romances*.

42. *Vǫlsunga saga: The Saga of the Volsungs* is a convenient bilingual edition.

43. There is a large literature on this subject. The classic treatment is Heusler, "Die Lieder der Lücke." The most recent work in English is Andersson, *Legend of Brynhild*, and his "Lays in the Lacuna."

44. An intriguing case is found in *Gísla saga*, chap. 19, where Gísli in verse compares his sister, who is torn between loyalty to husband and loyalty to brother (the latter had killed the former), to Gudrun, who in a similar situation in the heroic lays demonstrated steady attachment to her brothers. On this issue, see Turville-Petre, "Gísli Súrsson and His Poetry." Other heroic features in the saga are discussed in Sørensen, "Murder in Marital Bed."

45. For edition and translation, see above, n. 4.

46. As a case study, see Martinez-Pizarro, "An *Eiríks þáttr málspaka?*" See also Skovgaard-Petersen, *Da Tidernes Herre var nær*.

47. See, for example, Thornbjörg in *Hrólfs saga Gautrekssonar*, in *Hrolf Gautreksson: A Viking Romance*. On the figure of the woman warrior and maiden king, see Clover, "Maiden Warriors"; Kalinke, "Misogamous Maiden Kings"; Holmqvist-Larsen, *Møer, skjoldmøer og krigere*.

48. For an English translation of and commentary on this poem, see Ursula Dronke's translation in *The Poetic Edda*, pp. 3–74.

49. See, for example, the behavior of Thordis, who appears both in *Gísli saga* (chap. 37) and *Eyrbyggja saga* (chap. 13). From the contemporary *Sturlu saga* (part of *Sturlunga saga*) (chap. 31) there is the case of a woman who got so provoked by a man that she attacked him with a knife; aiming at his eye, she cut only his cheek (*Sturlunga saga* 1:109).

50. See Dronke's translation of *The Poetic Edda*, pp. 161–242.

51. The fullest expression of Brynhild's egging is found in the lost poem *Meiri*; see Andersson, "Beyond Epic and Romance." See also Andersson, *Legend of Brynhild*.

52. Heller, *Die literarische Darstellung der Frau*, pp. 98–123; Wolf, *Gestaltungskerne und Gestaltungswesen*, pp. 109–47; Bouman, *Pattern*.

53. *Saga Óláfs Tryggvasonar af Oddr Snorrason*.

54. Jochens, "Female Inciter."

55. Jochens, "The Medieval Icelandic Heroine," esp. p. 40.

56. The only overview in English of the difficult textual problems of the

kings' sagas is Andersson, "Kings' Sagas (*Konungasögur*)"; see his bibliography for editions of the texts. For the use of the kings' sagas in women's history, see Jochens, "Consent in Marriage" and "Politics of Reproduction."

57. Jochens, "Female Inciter."

58. Almost all texts have now been published in the series Íslenzk fornrit, of which twelve volumes contain family sagas and seven volumes contain kings' sagas. Practically all family sagas have been translated to English; for a comprehensive bibliography, see Fry, *Norse Sagas Translated into English*.

59. On the problem of the sagas' origins and interpretations, see Andersson, *Icelandic Saga Origins*; Sveinsson, *Dating the Icelandic Sagas*; Clover, "Icelandic Family Sagas." For an annotated selection of the most important documents pertaining to the debate, see Mundal, *Sagadebatt*.

60. Heusler, *Die Anfänge der isländischen Saga*, esp. pp. 27–33.

61. See above, n. 58.

62. Andersson, *Icelandic Family Saga*, suggests a general structure encompassing whole sagas, and Clover, "Scene in Saga Composition," identifies smaller narrative components.

63. See, for example, Miller, "Choosing the Avenger"; Miller, "Gift, Sale, Payment, Raid"; Miller, "Dreams, Prophesy, and Sorcery."

64. Clover, *Medieval Saga*.

65. See Byock, *Feud in the Icelandic Saga*; Byock, *Medieval Iceland*; Sørensen, *Saga og samfund*; Sørensen, *Unmanly Man*.

66. Mallet, *Northern Antiquities* 1:55.

67. Ibid., 1:164–65.

68. Ibid., 1:172–82.

69. Ibid., 1:314–15; see also pp. 313–36.

70. Beck, *Northern Antiquities in French Learning*, pp. 86–118, esp. p. 106.

71. The classic formulation was given by Grimm, *Deutsche Mythologie*. It has produced a large literature and was clearly expressed in the oldest work, Engelstoft, *Forsög til en skildring af Quindekjönnets . . . kaar*. Among more recent works, see Ritterhaus, *Altnordische Frauen*; Klose, *Die Familienverhältnisse auf Island*; Merschberger, *Die Stellung der Frau*.

72. This is pointed out by Kress, "Meget samstavet må det tykkes deg."

73. See Andersen, *Skjoldmøer*; Damsholt, "Icelandic Women in the Sagas." See also the balanced account in Foote and Wilson, *Viking Achievement*, pp. 108–17.

74. For an impressive record, in texts and pictures, of the work of Icelandic women through a millennium, see Sigurðardóttir, *Vinna kvenna á Íslandi*.

75. Almost half of the more than fifty cases of the *Hetzerin* motif identified by Heller in the family sagas occur in two of the latest ones, *Laxdœla saga* and *Njáls saga*. The motif appears also in *Eyrbyggja saga*, *Hávarðar saga Ísfirðings*, and *Grettis saga*. For a complete list, see Heller, *Die literarische Darstellung der Frau*, p. 154. Inspired by cross-cultural anthropological studies, scholars have

recently pointed to similarities between the role of whetting women in contemporary tribal societies and that in pagan Iceland found in the family sagas, and they conclude that a social reality may lie behind the whetting woman in Eddas and sagas. See Miller, "Choosing the Avenger"; Clover, "Hildigunnr's Lament."

76. See Clover, "Hildigunnr's Lament," esp. n. 8.
77. Jochens, "Female Inciter"; Jochens, "Medieval Icelandic Heroine."
78. Jochens, "Consent in Marriage"; Jochens, "Politics of Reproduction."
79. Bruder, *Die germanische Frau*, pp. 5–55, esp. pp. 12, 54.
80. Jochens, "Church and Sexuality."

BIBLIOGRAPHY

Primary Sources

Adam of Bremen. *Gesta Hammaburgensis ecclesiae pontificum.* Ed. Bernhard Schmeidler. 3d ed. Hannover, 1917.

———. *History of the Archbishops of Hamburg-Bremen.* Trans. Francis J. Tschan. Records of Civilization, no. 53. New York, 1959.

Atlakviða. See Edda.

Biskupa sögur. 2 vols. Copenhagen, 1858–78.

Bǫglunga sögur. Fornmanna sögur, vol. 9. Copenhagen, 1835.

Brennu-Njáls saga. Ed. Einar Ól. Sveinsson. Íslenzk fornrit, vol. 12. Reykjavík, 1954.

Codex regius. See Edda.

Corpus iuris sueo-gotorum antiqui: Samling af Sweriges gamla lagar. Ed. H. S. Collin and C. J. Schlyter. 13 vols. Stockholm, 1827–77.

Danmarks gamle landskabslove. Ed. Johannes Brøndum-Nielsen. 8 vols. Copenhagen, 1945–48.

The Earliest Norwegian Laws. Trans. Laurence M. Larson. Records of Civilization, no. 20. New York, 1935.

Edda: Die Lieder des Codex Regius nebst verwandten Denkmälern. Ed. Gustav Neckel. 4th rev. ed. Hans Kuhn. Heidelberg, 1962.

Eyrbyggja saga. Ed. Einar Ól. Sveinsson and Matthías Þórðarson. Íslenzk fornrit, vol. 4. Reykjavík, 1935.

Fornaldar sögur Norðurlanda. Ed. Gúðni Jónsson. 4 vols. N.p., n.d.

Fǫr Skírnis = Skírnismál. See Edda.

Gísla saga. In *Vestfirðinga sǫgur,* ed. Björn K. Þórólfsson and Gúðni Jónsson. Íslenzk fornrit, vol. 6. Reykjavík, 1943.

Grágás. Ed. Vilhjálmur Finsen. 1852–83. Reprint (3 vols.). Odense, 1974.

Grettis saga Ásmundarsonar. Ed. Gúðni Jónsson. Íslenzk fornrit, vol. 7. Reykjavík, 1936.

Hákonar Saga and a Fragment of Magnus Saga. Ed. Guðbrandur Vigfússon. Rerum Medii Aevi Scriptores, no. 88:2. London, 1887.

Hamðismál. See Edda.

Hávarðar saga Ísfirðings. In *Vestfirðinga sǫgur,* ed. Björn K. Þórólfsson and Gúðni Jónsson. Íslenzk fornrit, vol. 6. Reykjavík, 1943.

Heimskringla. See Snorri Sturluson.

Hrolf Gautreksson: A Viking Romance. Trans. Hermann Pálsson and Paul Edwards. Toronto, 1972.

Icelandic Sagas and Other Historical Documents Relating the Settlements and Descents of the Northmen on the British Isles. Trans. George Webb Dasent. Rolls Series 88. London, 1887–94.

Landnámabók. In *Íslendingabók: Landnámabók,* ed. Jakob Benediktsson. Íslenzk fornrit, vol. 1 (pts. 1 and 2). Reykjavík, 1968.

Laws of Early Iceland: Grágás 1. Trans. Andrew Dennis, Peter Foote, and Richard Perkins. Winnipeg, 1980.

Laxdœla saga. Ed. Einar Ól. Sveinsson. Íslenzk fornrit, vol. 5. Reykjavík, 1934.

The Life of Gudmund the Good, Bishop of Holar. Trans. E. O. G. Turville-Petre and E. S. Olzewska. Coventry, 1942.

Liturgica Islandica. Ed. Lilli Gjerløw. Bibliotheca Arnamagnæana, vols. 35–36. 2 vols. Copenhagen, 1980.

Das Nibelungenlied. Ed. Karl Bartsch. 9th ed. Leipzig, 1931.

The Nibelungenlied. Trans. A. T. Hatto. Harmondsworth, 1965.

Njáls saga. See Brennu-Njál.

Norges gamle love indtil 1387. Ed. R. Keyser and P. A. Munch. 5 vols. Oslo, 1846–95.

Norsk-islandske skjaldedigtning. See Skjaldedigtning, den norsk-islandske.

Oddr Snorrason munk. *Saga Óláfs Tryggvasonar af Oddr Snorrason.* Ed. Finnur Jónsson. Copenhagen, 1932.

Poems of the Vikings: The Elder Edda. Trans. Patricia Terry. Indianapolis, 1969.

The Poetic Edda. Trans. Henry Adams Bellows. New York, 1923.

The Poetic Edda. Vol. 1, *Heroic Poems.* Ed. and trans. Ursula Dronke. Oxford, 1969.

The Poetic Edda. Trans. Lee M. Hollander. 2d ed. 1962. Reprint. Austin, Tex., 1986.

The Prose Edda. See Snorri Sturluson.

Saxo Grammaticus. *Saxo Grammaticus: Books 10–16.* Trans. Eric Christiansen. 3 vols. BAR International Series, nos. 84, 118 (prts. 1, 2). Oxford, 1980–81.

———. *Saxo Grammaticus: History of the Danes, Books 1–9.* Trans. Peter Fisher and Hilda Ellis Davis. 2 vols. Cambridge, 1979–80.

———. *Saxonis Gesta Danorum.* Ed. Jørgen Olrik and Hans Ræder. 2 vols. Copenhagen, 1931–57.

Seven Viking Romances. Trans. Hermann Pálsson and Paul Edwards. Harmondsworth, 1985.

The Skalds: A Selection of Their Poems, with Introduction and Notes. Trans.

Lee M. Hollander. 2d ed. Ann Arbor, Mich., 1968.

Skírnismál. See Edda.

Skjaldedigtning, Den norsk-islandske. Ed. Finnur Jónsson. 4 vols. 1908–15. Reprint. Copenhagen, 1967–73.

Snorri Sturluson. *Edda.* Trans. Anthony Faulkes. London, 1987.

———. *Edda: Prologue and Gylfaginning.* Trans. Anthony Faulkes. Oxford, 1982.

———. *Edda Snorra Sturlusona.* Ed. Finnur Jónsson. Copenhagen, 1931.

———. *Heimskringla.* Ed. Bjarni Aðalbjarnarson. 3 vols. Íslenzk fornrit, vols. 26–28. Reykjavík, 1941–51.

———. *Heimskringla: History of the Kings of Norway.* Trans. Lee M. Hollander. Austin, Tex., 1964.

———. *The Prose Edda of Snorri Sturluson.* Trans. Jean I. Young. Berkeley, 1954.

———. *Ynglinga saga.* In Snorri Sturluson, *Heimskringla,* Íslenzk fornrit, vol. 26.

Sturlunga saga. Ed. Jón Jóhannesson, Magnús Finnbogason, and Kristján Eldjárn. 2 vols. Reykjavík, 1946.

Sturlunga saga. Trans. Julia H. McGrew and R. George Thomas. 2 vols. New York, 1970–74.

Sturlu saga. In *Sturlunga saga.*

Sverris saga. Ed. Gustav Indrebø. Oslo, 1920.

Tacitus. *Agricola and the Germania.* Trans. Hugh Mattingly. 1948. Reprint. Harmondsworth, 1971.

———. *Die Germania des Tacitus.* Ed. Rudolf Much. Heidelberg, 1937.

———. *Germania.* Ed. Allan A. Lund. Heidelberg, 1988.

———. *The Histories.* Trans. Kenneth Wellesley. Harmondsworth, 1964.

———. *Works.* 5 vols. Cambridge, 1968–80.

Vǫlsunga saga ok Ragnars saga loðbrókar. Ed. Magnus Olsen. Samfund til Udgivelse af Gammel Nordisk Litteratur, no. 36. Copenhagen, 1906–08.

Vǫlsunga saga: The Saga of the Volsungs. Ed. and trans. R. G. Finch. London, 1965.

Vǫluspá: The Song of the Sybil. Trans. and ed. Paul B. Taylor, W. H. Auden, and Peter H. Salus. Iowa City, Iowa, 1968.

Ynglinga saga. See Snorri Sturluson.

Secondary Sources

Andersen, Lise Præstgaard. *Skjoldmøer: En kvindemyte.* Copenhagen, 1982.

Andersson, Theodore M. "Beyond Epic and Romance: *Sigurðarkviða in meiri.*" In *Sagnaskemmtun: Studies in Honour of Hermann Pálsson,* ed. Rudolf Simek et al., pp. 1–11. Vienna, 1986.

———. *The Icelandic Family Saga: An Analytic Reading.* Cambridge, Mass., 1967.

———. "Kings' Sagas (*Konungasögur*)." In Clover and Lindow, *Old Norse–Icelandic Literature*, pp. 197–238.

———. "The Lays in the Lacuna of *Codex Regius*." In *Speculum Norroenum: Norse Studies in Memory of Gabriel Turville-Petre*, ed. Ursula Dronke et al., pp. 6–26. Odense, 1981.

———. *The Legend of Brynhild*. Islandica, no. 43. Ithaca, N.Y., 1980.

———. *The Problem of Icelandic Saga Origins*. New Haven, Conn., 1964.

———. "Skalds and Troubadours." *Mediaeval Scandinavia* 2 (1971): 7–41.

Anna Sigurðardóttir. *See* Sigurðardóttir, Anna.

Bauchatz, Paul C. *The Well and the Tree: World and Time in Early Germanic Culture*. Amherst, Mass., 1982.

Beck, Thor J. *Northern Antiquities in French Learning and Literature*. New York, 1934.

Bibire, Paul. 1986. "Freyr and Gerðr: The Story and Its Myth." In *Sagnaskemmtun: Studies in Honour of Hermann Pálsson*, ed. Rudolf Simek et al., pp. 19–40. Vienna, 1986.

Bjarni Einarsson. *See* Einarsson, Bjarni.

Bouman, A. C. *Pattern in Old English and Old Icelandic Literature*. Leiden, 1962.

Boyer, Régis. *Les Sagas islandaises*. Paris, 1978.

Bruder, Reinhold. *Die germanische Frau im Lichte der Runeninschriften und der antiken Historiographie*. Quellen und Forschungen zur Sprach- und Kulturgeschichte der germanischen Völker, n.s. 57 (181). Berlin, 1974.

Byock, Jesse L. *Feud in the Icelandic Saga*. Berkeley, 1982.

———. *Medieval Iceland: Society, Sagas, and Power*. Berkeley, 1988.

Clover, Carol J. "Hildigunnr's Lament." In *Structure and Meaning in Old Norse Literature*, ed. John Lindow et al., pp. 141–83. Odense, 1986.

———. "Icelandic Family Sagas." In Clover and Lindow, *Old Norse–Icelandic Literature*, pp. 239–315.

———. "Maiden Warriors and Other Sons." *Journal of English and Germanic Philology* 85 (1985): 35–49.

———. *The Medieval Saga*. Ithaca, N.Y., 1982.

———. "The Politics of Scarcity: Notes on the Sex Ratio in Early Scandinavia." *Scandinavian Studies* 60 (1988): 147–88.

———. "Scene in Saga Composition." *Arkiv för Nordisk Filologi* 89 (1974): 57–83.

Clover, Carol J., and John Lindow, eds. *Old Norse–Icelandic Literature: A Critical Guide*. Ithaca, N.Y., 1985.

Damsholt, Nanna. *Kvindebilledet i dansk højmiddelalder*. Copenhagen, 1985.

———. "The Role of Icelandic Women in the Sagas and in the Production of Homespun Cloth." *Scandinavian Journal of History* 9 (1984): 75–90.

de Vries, Jan. *Altnordische Literaturgeschichte*. 2 vols. 2d ed. Berlin, 1964–67.

Dumézil, Georges. *Gods of the Ancient Northmen*. Ed. Einar Haugen. Publications of the UCLA Center for the Study of Comparative Folklore and Mythology, no. 3. Berkeley, 1973.

————. *Loki.* New rev. ed. Paris, 1986.

Einar Ól Sveinsson. *See* Sveinsson, Einar Ól.

Einarsson, Bjarni. "The Lovesick Skald: A Reply to Theodore M. Andersson." *Mediaeval Scandinavia* 4 (1971): 21–41.

————. *Skaldasögur: Um uppruna og eðli ástaskáldasagnanna fornu.* Reykjavík, 1961.

————. *To skjaldesagaer: En analyse af Kormáks saga og Hallfreðar saga.* Bergen, 1976.

Engelstoft, Laurits. *Forsög til en skildring af Quindekjönnets huslige og borgerlige kaar hos Skandinaverne för Kristendommens Indförelse.* Copenhagen, 1799.

Farley, F. E. *Scandinavian Influence in the English Romantic Movement.* Studies and Notes in Philology and Literature, no. 9. Boston, 1903.

Foote, P. G., and D. M. Wilson. *The Viking Achievement.* London, 1970.

Frank, Roberta. *Old Norse Court Poetry: The Dróttkvætt Stanza.* Islandica, no. 42. Ithaca, N.Y., 1978.

————. "Skaldic Poetry." In Clover and Lindow, *Old Norse–Icelandic Literature,* pp. 157–96.

————. "Why Skalds Address Women." Paper presented at the Seventh International Saga Conference, Spoleto, September 1988.

Fry, Donald. *Norse Sagas Translated into English: A Bibliography.* New York, 1980.

Gimbutas, Marija. *The Goddesses and Gods of Old Europe, 6500–3500 B.C.: Myth and Cult Images.* Berkeley, 1982.

Greenway, John L. *The Golden Horns: Mythic Imagination and the Nordic Past.* Athens, Ga., 1977.

Grimm, Jacob. *Deutsche Mythologie.* 3 vols. 4th ed. Berlin, 1875–78.

Hallberg, Peter. *The Icelandic Saga.* Trans. Paul Schach. Lincoln, Nebr., 1962.

————. *Old Icelandic Poetry: Eddic Lay and Skaldic Verse.* Trans. Paul Schach and Sonja Lindgrenson. Lincoln, Nebr., 1975.

Harris, Joseph. "Eddic Poetry." In Clover and Lindow, *Old Norse–Icelandic Literature,* pp. 68–156.

Heller, Rolf. *Die literarische Darstellung der Frau in den Isländersagas.* Halle, 1958.

Heusler, Andreas. *Die Anfänge der isländischen Saga.* Berlin, 1914.

————. "Die Lieder der Lücke im Codex Regius der Edda." In *Germanistische Abhandlungen Hermann Paul dargebracht,* pp. 1–98. Strasbourg, 1902. Reprinted in Heusler, *Kleine Schriften,* ed. Helga Reuschel, 1:26–64. Berlin, 1969.

Holmqvist-Larsen, H. N. *Møer, skjoldmøer og krigere.* Studier fra Sprog- og Oldtidsforskning, no. 304. Copenhagen, 1983.

Jochens, Jenny M. "The Church and Sexuality in Medieval Iceland." *Journal of Medieval History* 6 (1980): 377–92.

————. "Consent in Marriage: Old Norse Law, Life, and Literature." *Scandinavian Studies* 58 (1986): 142–76.

———. "En Islande médiévale: À la recherche de la famille nucléaire." *Annales ESC* 40 (1985): 95–112.

———. "The Female Inciter in the Kings' Sagas." *Arkiv för Nordisk Filologi* 102 (1987): 100–119.

———. "The Medieval Icelandic Heroine: Fact or Fiction?" *Viator* 17 (1986): 35–50.

———. "The Politics of Reproduction: Medieval Norwegian Kingship." *American Historical Review* 92 (1987): 327–49.

———. "Vǫluspá: Matrix of Norse Womanhood." *Journal of English and Germanic Philology* 89 (1989). In press.

Kalinke, Marianne. *In Want of a Wife: The Bridal Quest in Icelandic Romance.* Ithaca, N.Y.: in press.

———. "The Misogamous Maiden Kings of Icelandic Romance." *Scripta Islandica* 37 (1986): 47–71.

———. "Norse Romance." In Clover and Lindow, *Old Norse–Icelandic Literature,* pp. 316–63.

Klose, Olaf. *Die Familienverhältnisse auf Island vor der Bekehrung zum Christentum auf Grund der Islendingasǫgur.* Nordische Studien, no. 10. Brunswick, 1929.

Kress, Helga. "Meget samstavet må det tykkes dig: Om kvinneopprör og genretvang i Sagaen om Laksdölene." (Norsk) *Historisk Tidsskrift* 59 (1980): 266–80.

Kreutzer, Gert. *Kindheit und Jugend in der Altnordischen Literatur. Teil I. Schwangerschaft, Geburt und früheste Kindheit.* Münster, 1982.

Kulturhistorisk Leksikon for Nordisk Middelalder. 22 vols. Copenhagen, 1956–78.

Lévi-Strauss, Claude. "The Structural Study of Myth." *Journal of American Folklore* 68 (1955): 428–44.

Lindow, John. "Mythology and Mythography." In Clover and Lindow, *Old Norse–Icelandic Literature,* pp. 21–67.

———. *Scandinavian Mythology: An Annotated Bibliography.* New York, 1988.

Lönnroth, Lars. 1977. "Skírnismál och den fornisländiska äktenskapsnormen." *Bibliotheca Arnamagnæana* 25.2. *Opuscula* 2.2., pp. 154–78.

Mallet, Paul-Henri. *Northern Antiquities.* Trans. Bishop Percy. 2 vols. London, 1770.

Martinez-Pizarro, Joaquín. "An *Eiríks þáttr málspaka?*: Some Conjectures on the Source of Saxo's Ericus Disertus." In *Saxo Grammaticus: A Medieval Author between Norse and Latin Culture,* ed. K. Friis-Jensen, pp. 105–19. Copenhagen, 1981.

Merschberger, Gerda. *Die Stellung der Frau im Eherecht und Erbrecht nach den deutschen Volksrechten unter Berücksichtigung der nordischen Quellen.* Leipzig, 1937.

Miller, William Ian. "Choosing the Avenger: Some Aspects of the Bloodfeud in Medieval Iceland and England." *Law and History Review* 1 (1984): 159–83.

————. "Dreams, Prophesy, and Sorcery: Blaming the Secret Offender in Medieval Iceland." *Scandinavian Studies* 58 (1986): 102–23.

————. "Gift, Sale, Payment, Raid: Case Studies in the Negotiation and Classification of Exchange in Medieval Iceland." *Speculum* 91 (1986): 18–50.

Mitchell, Stephen A. "*Fǫr Scirnis* as Mythological Model: *Frið at kaupa.*" *Arkiv för Nordisk Filologi* 98 (1983): 108–22.

Mjöberg, Jöran. *Drömmen om Sagatiden.* 2 vols. Stockholm, 1967–68.

Motz, Lotte. "Freyja, Anat, Ishtar, and Inanna: Some Cross-Cultural Comparisons." *Mankind Quarterly* 23 (1982): 195–212.

————. "Gerðr: A New Interpretation of the Lay of Skírnir." *Maal og Minne* (1981): 121–36.

Mundal, Else. *Sagadebatt.* Oslo, 1977.

Nordal, Sigurður. "Sagalitteraturen." In *Litteraturhistorie B: Norge og Island,* ed. Sigurður Nordal, pp. 180–288. Nordisk Kultur, no. 8B. Stockholm, 1953.

————. *Vǫluspá.* Trans. B. S. Benedikz and John McKinnell. Durham and Saint Andrews Medieval Texts, no. 1. Durham, 1978.

Pálsson, Hermann, and Paul Edwards. *Legendary Fiction in Iceland.* Studia Islandica, no. 30. Reykjavík, 1971.

Phillpotts, Bertha. *The Elder Edda and Ancient Scandinavian Drama.* Cambridge, 1920.

Renfrew, Colin. *Archaeology and Language: The Puzzle of Indo-European Origins.* London, 1987.

Ritterhaus, Adeline. *Altnordische Frauen.* Frauenfeld, 1917.

Sanday, Peggy Reeves. *Female Power and Male Dominance: On the Origins of Sexual Inequality.* Cambridge, 1981.

Schach, Paul. *Icelandic Sagas.* Boston, 1984.

Schlauch, Margaret. *Romance in Iceland.* Princeton, N.J., 1935.

Sigurðardóttir, Anna. *Vinna kvenna á Íslandi í 1100 ár.* Reykjavík, 1985.

Skovgaard-Petersen, Inge. *Da Tidernes Herre var nær: Studier i Saxos historiesyn.* Copenhagen, 1987.

Sørensen, Preben Meulengracht. "Murder in Marital Bed: An Attempt at Understanding a Crucial Scene in *Gísla saga.*" In *Structure and Meaning in Old Norse Literature: New Approaches to Textual Analysis and Literary Criticism,* ed. John Lindow et al., pp. 235–63. Odense, 1986.

————. *Saga og samfund: En indføring i oldislandsk litteratur.* Copenhagen, 1977.

————. *The Unmanly Man: Concepts of Sexual Defamation in Early Northern Society.* Trans. Joan Turville-Petre. Viking Collection, no. 1. Odense, 1983.

Strand, Birgit. *Kvinnor och män i Gesta Danorum.* Kvinnohistorisk arkiv, 18. Göteborg, 1980.

Sveinsson, Einar Ól. *Dating the Icelandic Sagas.* London, 1958.

————. "Kormakr the Poet and His Verses." *Saga-Book of the Viking Society* 17 (1966): 18–60.

Turville-Petre, Gabriel. "Gísli Súrsson and His Poetry: Traditions and Influence." *Modern Language Review* 39 (1944): 373–91.

———. *Origins of Icelandic Literature.* Oxford, 1953.

———. *Scaldic Poetry.* Oxford, 1978.

Wolf, Alois. *Gestaltungskerne und Gestaltungswesen in der altgermanischen Heldendichtung.* Munich, 1965.

WOMEN AND THE LITERATURE OF
OBSTETRICS AND GYNECOLOGY

Helen Lemay

he early history of obstetrics and gynecology is traditionally regarded as two different tales: the story of doctors
and the story of midwives. The first of these is more
prominent: there has existed since ancient times a medical
profession whose ideas about the woman's reproductive
system have had a tremendous influence on European culture. Doctors
preached that females needed regular sexual intercourse to prevent their
wombs from wandering in search of sperm or becoming poisoned by
inactivity, and churchmen were quick to persecute women as witches because they were hungry for sexual intercourse with the Devil. Physicians
maintained as well that the female sex was biologically inferior, and society was shaped to reflect woman's perceived physiological limitations.
The history of doctors, then, is presented as the record of a dominant
male professional group with a monopoly over theoretical notions that
were used to buttress the persecution of women. ❡ The tale of midwives
is told somewhat differently. Wise women, the story goes, have existed
since time immemorial. Unlearned in booklore but skilled in the ways
of the world, they used magic and folk wisdom to heal and to harm.
Patiently wiping the brow of the woman in labor or providing her with
herbal teas to speed contractions and ease the pain, they also frightened
her with innumerable superstitions and infected her with dirty hands.[1]
While doctors pontificated and prescribed, midwives touched and cast
spells, until the development of technology like the short straight forceps
and the birth of modern surgical methods made them either dangerous or irrelevant. ❡ This latter story especially is based on scanty source
materials; it is always difficult to uncover the practices and beliefs of a
largely illiterate group in the remote past. We see traces of this female
culture in accounts of childbirth customs, in vernacular translations of
gynecological treatises made for women, in statutes regulating urban

midwives, in requirements that a wise woman be involved in the process of annulment of a marriage.[2] Inquisitorial accusations of the evil wrought by midwives dominate accounts of the witchcraft trials, and records of folk beliefs are to be found in some of the most prestigious medical writings.

This last category of source material is by far the most abundant; the history of medieval medicine is written largely from learned medical treatises, and it is this genre that will be explored here.[3] I will address the question of what we can learn about medieval women from these writings, and I will reexamine the validity of these two different tales. I will concentrate my remarks mainly on two groups of fifteenth-century sources: the first, two Latin medical manuscripts of French provenance, and the second, the *Tractatus de matricibus* (*Treatise on the Womb*) by Anthonius Guainerius, professor of medicine at the University of Pavia. [4]

Latin treatises represent, of course, the male medical world, and the historian must be careful in searching for traces of women's culture in these biased records. Indeed, much of the information presented in these works does not even reflect the contemporary scene: the authors quote at length, sometimes without acknowledgment, ancient and earlier medieval medical authorities, and the material is often theoretical in nature. Yet if we read these manuscripts carefully, we can glean from them information about the practice of medicine by doctors and midwives alike.

Let us turn first to the doctors and see what types of evidence lead us to discover their actual medical experience. First of all, we have general comments about local practice; doctors will often survey a number of different treatments and say what happens "in our regions" (*in nostris regionibus*).[5] More specifically, however, these treatises contain anecdotes about how a certain patient's experience reflects the efficacy of a remedy or the truth of a maxim. Lille MS. 334, a fifteenth-century book on the diseases of women whose author is identified simply as Nicholaus, provides us with a couple of examples of this. The author informs us that one cause of difficult birth is premature rupture of the amniotic membranes and comments that he observed this in many cases, especially in Lady Bartholomea, the wife of Salto of Permis.[6] Similarly, we learn in a marginal note that Nicholaus or a reader of his treatise saw the daughter of Goulian follow Avicenna's precepts of taking two hours' rest followed by sudden motion and crying out in an attempt to get the fetus to descend and the womb to open. [7]

Not only do we discover that medical authorities are proven true, but the manuscripts furnish us with considerable information on medieval

pharmacological practice. Authors characteristically state their prefer-
ences for certain ingredients when presenting recipes,[8] and they sometimes boast about their personal formulas. In a fifteenth-century treatise
on impregnation of the female ascribed to Jordanus de Turre and preserved in Paris, Bibliothèque nationale, MS. lat. 7066, the author sets
down a recipe for a fertility drug. He gives us two case histories: one,
a noblewoman who had been unable to conceive during thirteen years
with her husband but was successful after seven months' treatment and
subsequently bore a healthy male child, and another, the wife of the
companion and administrator of the viscounty of Lomagne, who also
conceived a son after nine months of taking the electuary and other
treatments. [9]

Finally, we occasionally discover something of doctors' emotional reactions to their patients' situations. Anthonius Guainerius, for example,
the fifteenth-century university professor of Pavia, exposes to us his
genuine feeling for the suffering of parturient women. Toward the end
of the section on childbirth in his *Treatise on the Womb*, Guainerius comments that he has such great compassion for these poor women that he
cannot bring the chapter to an end without adding some information
from Avicenna. He then goes on to say, "And when she feels sharp pains
and great weight in her lower abdomen which cruelly, ceaselessly and
powerfully molest her the poor woman cries out, emitting mournful
noises to the heavens and often compresses the spirit that is retained
below." After providing additional instructions on facilitating birth, he
states, "You will lead back the good woman with her fetus to a safe
haven by the gift of God." [10] The emotional character of these remarks is
not found in his source, Avicenna's *Canon of Medicine*; [11] Guainerius is
allowing us here a rare glimpse of a medieval physician's emotional involvement with his patients. We have similar evidence in Lille MS. 334:
at the point where the author has set down directions for using forceps,
a reader made a marginal notation of "helas, helas," obviously affected
by the horror of such a procedure. [12]

We are able, therefore, to obtain certain information about male medical practice from medical treatises written by males, but what about the
midwives? Can we learn anything about lay female medicine during the
Middle Ages from these learned tracts?

Certainly the first kind of material we can find relates to the point
at which doctors and midwives interact. For the most part, doctors did
not perform physical examinations and procedures involving women's
genitals; they relied on female assistants when any intimate physical

contact was necessary. A typical example can be found in the Petrus de Nadillis treatise: in the case of dislocation of the womb, it is up to the midwife to diagnose and treat this disorder.[13] This tradition goes back to ancient medicine: the privacy of women's reproductive parts was violated in Western culture only with the rise of the male midwife in the seventeenth century.[14] Midwives were given, along with access to women's physical mysteries, authority in pronouncing on the condition of patients. Thus, when discussing the birthing stool, the Lille manuscript points out that the thirteenth-century medical writer Gilbertus Anglicus[15] states that the size of the fetus is known by the degree of abdominal swelling and by the judgment of the midwife; he tells us further that Galen and Rhazes both set down in their medical books that midwives hold that the parturient woman should not sit on the stool until after the mouth of the uterus is touched and found to be open.[16] We read in Petrus de Nadillis's treatise in the Paris manuscript that the midwife also determines whether a woman has conceived by feeling if the mouth of the womb is closed.[17] This judgment may be made by touch, according to modern gynecologists, four weeks after conception, and at this point other signs, such as a missed menstrual period or breast changes, are also evident.[18] We may wonder, therefore, how well founded was the confidence that doctors placed in their assistants if they pronounced on this subject earlier in the pregnancy. A similar situation arises in midwives' determination of patients' virginity, of which we have evidence in some earlier medical texts.[19] It is impossible in almost all cases to tell if a hymen has been penetrated,[20] and here, too, we may question the accuracy of their pronouncements. Perhaps the power of the wise woman was exaggerated by the doctors, to whom women's mysteries were hidden, and this fed into the fear in which midwives came to be held.

No matter what was the validity of their conclusions, we know that midwives were relied on by doctors to make diagnoses and to carry out procedures. The Lille manuscript indicates that female practitioners did indeed have some awareness of the configuration of the internal organs: a woman who will bear sons is one whose *os* is directly opposite the vagina[21] and not in a twisted position, for then the power of the sperm is not lost in the journey. Petrus de Nadillis provides us with many references to *obstetrices* carrying out standard gynecological treatments: massage of the genitals for suffocation of the womb, replacement of the uterus after prolapse, suffumigation for counteracting disease.[22] In accounts of childbirth, the midwives are in complete control; the texts, for the most part, simply recount their obstetrical procedures. Thus, we see midwives working extensively as doctors' assistants, and, in this case, the story of doctors and the story of midwives turn out to be one and the same.

Women's medicine consists of much more than helping doctors, however; there is a long tradition of folk medicine, which is cast by historians as the complete opposite of learned, or school, medicine. Folk medicine, the standard interpretation goes, relies on a mythology, an attempt to explain the mysteries of life, while learned medicine begins with a theory about the cause of disease and builds from there a system.[23] Folk medicine, or women's medicine, would therefore consist largely in magic,[24] whereas school medicine would be based on the theory of the four humors.

It is a central thesis of my argument that, in medieval obstetrics and gynecology, the distinctions between these two types of medicine become blurred and that the notion that there are in fact two clearly different approaches to dealing with childbirth and women's medical problems is erroneous. Perhaps because of the mystery surrounding women's bodies, midwives and doctors alike were heavily influenced by the folkloric or magical tradition, although doctors did make an effort to disguise the degree to which they bought into it. Not only did physicians rely on midwives to diagnose and treat their patients, but they also absorbed many of their magical remedies and, on occasion, feared their diabolical powers. This fear was connected with sex and with women's association with sex and their perceived control over it.

Although I intend to present evidence that magic and folklore worked their way into school medicine, I do not mean to give the impression that academic writings on the female reproductive system contain mostly information on incantations and magical amulets. These treatises are based, rather, on the ancient idea that the body contains four humors, each with a different set of qualities, and that when the balance of these humors and qualities is upset, disease results. Thus, typical of this genre would be Petrus de Nadillis's treatise *On the Impregnation of the Woman*, which deals with female sterility caused by defects of the womb. These problems, the author tells us, come from illness in the complexion of the womb (excess cold and density, excess lubricity and humidity, or excess heat and dryness) or from compositional defects (hemorrhoids, obesity, disproportion in the passages, or dislocation).[25] Remedies include bloodletting, dietary management, digestives and purgatives, and baths and suffumigations. Similarly, Avicenna's *Canon of Medicine*, an important source for late medieval medical writers, treats disorders of the womb as it deals with other organs of the body, both male and female—entirely without reference to the supernatural. [26]

The search for magical elements in these writings is complicated by the ambiguity of the material: it is often difficult to tell whether a particular remedy or treatment is based on a humoral or supernatural rationale. One example is the herb artemesia, or wormwood. If we turn to a study by Lucille Pinto of Bern codex 803, a rotulus dating from the late eleventh or early twelfth century and containing a record of folk medicine, we learn that the herb was named after the goddess Artemis or Diana, a protectress of women, because of its efficacy in certain female ailments, and in a circular way it was then considered to be effective because it bore her name.[27] Yet artemesia is often found in scientific writings: *De impregnatione mulieris*, the treatise ascribed to Jordanus de Turre, for example, prescribes artemesia as a digestive: it is included in one recipe to digest cold matter in the womb and in another to dry up humidity that renders the womb incapable of retaining the seed.[28] It seems to me quite likely that Jordanus is furnishing here a scientific rationale for a substance that had been used for women's problems since time immemorial.[29] As a physician, he must place the herb in a humoral context.

Similar situations appear in medical discussions of missed menses, of difficult childbirth, and of extracting a dead fetus. The Bern codex states that to bring on the menstrual period a woman should consume the urine of a she-goat, and Pinto comments that here we have at work the sympathetic principle—urine seemingly flows from the same place as menstrual blood. Similarly, human milk is prescribed for expelling a dead fetus, the sympathetic notion here being that a woman who has already given birth can have a positive influence. In a slightly different vein, the rotulus instructs that, in cases of difficult childbirth, an herb normally used against epilepsy be placed on the genitals, and Pinto sees in this an effort to exorcise a demon, because epilepsy was considered to be caused by demons and because the medicine was not taken internally.[30] Sympathetic magic and exorcism, then, are the bases of gynecological folk medicine.

If we look at some scientific works, however, we find echoes of these magical practices set in a humoral context. As noted earlier, Avicenna did not believe in magic, and yet the *Canon of Medicine* states that for difficult childbirth a woman should be rubbed with the ashes of a donkey's hoof, since it comes last in the body. This reminds us of sympathetic reasoning: something that is found at the terminus of the body will draw the fetus to its natural place. This also appears to have little to do with rational medicine: to affect the body's humoral balance, the ashes would presumably have to be taken internally. Yet Avicenna makes it clear that no hocus-pocus is involved when he entitles the chapter "Medicines which [aid in difficult childbirth] because of their property." He perceives these substances as having properties that work externally, not internally, and he lists others, such as a magnet to be held in the parturient woman's left hand.[31] Similarly, Nicholaus of the Lille manuscript and Anthonius Guainerius also present us with lists of substances to tie to the hip, which, as Guainerius puts it, "are effective in their properties both extrinsic as well as intrinsic . . . and have the property of accelerating birth or greatly mitigating its pain."[32] Included in the remedies in Nicholaus's treatise are Gilbertus Anglicus's prescriptions to hang artemesia on the woman's left hip and to administer a woman's milk mixed with oil to bring forth a dead fetus, in exactly the same way as described in the Bern codex. But if we look at the context once again, we see that Nicholaus's outlook is basically humoral. He emphasizes recipes from Avicenna and Rhazes to lubricate and fumigate the birth canal and to provoke vomiting to restore the body's balance. Whatever magical remedies may have crept in are presented as part of a rational medical approach.[33]

Another problematic area for the medical historian is the discipline of astrology. Today astrology is classified with the occult; in many newspapers, astrological predictions are found on the same pages as the comics, and revelations of astrological consultations proved to be a source of considerable embarrassment for a recent American president. Similarly, many medieval astrological statements might seem at first glance to derive immediately from the folk tradition. We read in the Lille manuscript, for example, about a story told by Porphyry in which an eclipse of the sun in Sicily caused women to bear children with two heads and to suffer an emission of menstrual blood through their mouths.[34] Another example of the belief in supercelestial influences on human events is the statement found in these texts that children born in the eighth month of pregnancy do not live or are born lame, blind, hunchbacked, or leprous because of the influence of the planet Saturn.[35] Yet we have here another instance of popular beliefs that have been absorbed into the learned tradition. Astrology was a science in the Middle Ages; it was taught at the universities and was therefore connected with academic medicine.[36] The astrological statements in these texts often have the backing of ancient authority. Porphyry was a respected third-century philosopher who wrote a commentary on Ptolemy's *Quadripartitum*, the bible of ancient astrological learning, and raised the science to a high philosophical level. Nicholaus of the Lille manuscript quotes Aristotle in connection with the influence of the supercelestial bodies on such matters as the moment of birth.[37] If astrology was part of the folk tradition, then, it was also part of school medicine.

We get closer to popular practice when we deal with the subject of the menstrual period, although here we have a topic where beliefs run counter to the woman's tradition and reflect the fear it engendered. Scientific medicine came to bolster the popular notion that menstrual blood is harmful: the substance was believed to cause grass to die, iron to rust, dogs to become rabid, and people to become ill. We see here the concept that the female organism produces poison, which leads to illness or even death,[38] and that academic physicians must provide remedies against this evil substance. Thus, Anthonius Guainerius tells us that an individual who takes menstrual blood is made either leprous, lunatic, malefic, or forgetful, and the antidote is composed not only of herbs but also of serpents whose tails and heads have been cut off.[39] Surely here we have something other than simple humoral medicine.

Similarly, when we deal with some human and animal substances and with certain beliefs about sexual intercourse, it is hard to put this material in a scientific context. The Lille author cites Gilbertus Anglicus to the effect that a sterile woman should be fumigated with the tooth of a dead man and that a birth girdle should be made of deerhide because it has the occult power of helping birth.[40] These materials seem to have at least a quasi-magical character. In the same vein, we find the organs of the hare prescribed for a postcoital suppository to aid conception in the Petrus de Nadillis treatise and in pills taken before sexual intercourse in the Jordanus de Turre text,[41] and Lucille Pinto provides a lengthy discussion of their significance. The hare, Pinto explains, was associated both by the Greeks and by Germanic tribes with fertility gods and was proscribed in the Old Testament. By 755 its use as an aphrodisiac was so widespread that it was forbidden by the pope, and it was also used to ensure the conception of a son and as a contraceptive.[42] With so heavy a mythological and historical tradition, it is difficult to see the use of these animal parts as having an entirely humoral rationale.

Although this magic may have been associated with woman's culture, it is not necessarily gender-bound. It is the power of the witch that is most clearly identified with the female, and this also makes a mark on male, or "public," medicine. Scientific writers in many cases accept without comment the reality and efficacy of occult practitioners; in their study of sexuality in medieval medical writings, Danielle Jacquart and Claude Thomasset point out that even a philosopher-scientist like Albertus Magnus lists in his book *On Vegetables and Plants* the substances traditionally used by soothsayers and magicians to induce abortions. Similarly, the treatise on male and female infertility ascribed to Jordanus de Turre begins by enumerating the causes of male sterility. Excess of humidity, or *gomorrea*, is most prominent, and other possible factors are exceeding heat or cold of the members, poorly proportioned genitals, or problems with the kidneys.[43] Although the emphasis here is on physiology and the treatise clearly derives from the humoral tradition, the supernatural also plays a part. "If the heat fails," the author tells us, "*approximeron* [failure of the generative members to produce erection or ejaculation] results." The text continues, "This can come from malefice or a curse, and the cure is to be left to God and to those who perform the malefice, although certain books of medicine set down empirical cures such as carrying silver wine at the neck in the shell of a filbert nut and hanging artemesia over the threshold of the house where the man and woman lie together."[44] We see here a clear acceptance of the potency of the witch and a resignation in the face of her power, as well as an instance of magical use of the herb artemesia.

Anthonius Guainerius, professor of medicine at the University of Pavia, also records his feelings about witches and leaves no doubt about their female gender. We see him struggle with his own ambivalence about their dark powers, and he provides as well a glimpse of how a medieval doctor interacted with his parturient patients.

Guainerius begins his chapter on childbirth by stating that women, especially delicate ones, often call doctors to their side in difficult births. The physician should have solicitude for these patients, he instructs his reader, and should comfort the poor parturient woman with prayerful words.

At the time of birth, it is good that the legend of blessed Margaret be read, that she have relics of the saints on her, and that you carry out briefly some familiar ceremonies in order to please your patient and the old women. Act this way so that if there be suspicion of a certain soothsaying old woman she will be expelled outside. For in birth, as you know, many amazing things happen. For did not Ovid, if I recall correctly, tell in the ninth book of the *Metamorphoses* about Alkimena, Hercules' mother, that when she went into labor, Lucina [the goddess of childbirth] appeared, and with her fingers bound together placed her hands on Alkimena's knees and recited incantations, lest she be prevented from being able to give birth. Although this is a fable, nevertheless, believe me, it has some truth in it; however if you believe the opposite you will not be excommunicated since it is not one of the articles of faith. [45]

Guainerius is doing more here than reciting a fable; he is providing a rationale for the doctor to engage in behavior that medieval schoolmen would hardly consider professional. The physician should participate in a quasi-religious ritual not only to please his clientele but also to fortify himself and his patient against the power of a witch who might cast a spell and prevent the child from being born. Having gone this far, however, the Pavian professor retreats to skepticism as he continues his account:

Some do not doubt that this can be done, and even believe strongly in it, as we can see in Pliny's book *On Natural History*. For he tells us that if parturient women eat wolf meat they will give birth more easily, and along with this, noxious incantations will not be powerful against the woman giving birth if there is someone present who has eaten this meat. You know yourself how much the old philosophers investigated numerous *maleficia*, demons, incantations and amulets, but such things are magic for ribald monks and old women who pass these things on amongst themselves. But all of this is to be dismissed. [46]

Guainerius then continues the chapter by listing substances to be tied to the woman's hip which are effective, as noted before, because of their extrinsic and intrinsic properties. Although Guainerius is fearful of the witch, then, and lets us glimpse this fear for a moment as he instructs the physician to recite prayers, he believes it necessary eventually to censure the belief in supernatural powers and to take materials like a feather from the left wing of an eagle or ashes from a donkey's hoof and place them in a scientific context.

It is important to note here that Guainerius was not a particularly credulous individual and that he did not typically include mythology and stories about old women in his medical book. It is only when he is treating women's mysteries—childbirth and female disorders—that he takes at all seriously the notion that occult powers could somehow affect the physiological process. More typical of his general approach is his discussion of demons, found in chapter 1 of the section of his medical work entitled "Treatise on Pain in the Head." "It often happens," Guainerius tells us, "that the passages through which the spirits pass from the heart to the cerebrum and from the cerebrum to other members are blocked." He explains that this blockage prevents the members from their normal motions—the chest cannot be dilated as usual; the diaphragm is constricted; the lung and the heart are affected. It seems to the patient that a weight or a phantasm is preventing proper dilation and depriving the members of spirits, and because a common person will conclude in this case that a demon is suffocating him, this disorder is named "incubus," the word for demon. Guainerius goes on to add that some people believe that old woman soothsayers who claim to be able to take on various shapes can cause this suffocation, and he identifies these as witches or *zobianae*, who, people say, often take the form of cats. He explains that the origin of this belief derives from the fact that nursing babies are often afflicted and eventually killed by this illness, and common people think that the old women are responsible for their deaths. [47]

We have in this passage a completely rational explanation for a physiological disorder as well as an implicit rejection of some of the charges of infanticide levied against witches. Guainerius is dealing here with the respiratory system, which is common to men and women, and consequently feels none of the intimidation we detected in his section on human reproduction. His explanation for headache is based entirely on human physiology, and indeed his cure involves the usual sequence of vomiting, digestives, dietary management, and medication.[48] In this context, it is easy for him to dismiss the notion that midwives kill newborn babies, even though earlier we saw him worried about the power of soothsayers to stop a labor that is already in progress. When dealing with pain in the head, he is on familiar ground; when treating women's mysteries, on the other hand, he is treading on dangerous paths.

I have discussed so far mostly the "professionals"—doctors and midwives—and their dealings with women's bodies. But professionals, as we know, are part of a larger society and, in the Middle Ages, reflected rather than created the prevailing values. Thus it is important to learn what we can about popular beliefs—not only from the point of view of whether doctors recognized their validity but also from the perspective of how they touched people's lives. In this examination, we find that doctors and midwives were not the only practitioners accorded "professional" status in this society; indeed, just as today we consult nurses or Aunt Millie, the Middle Ages, too, had its alternate authorities on sex and pregnancy. Therefore, we must look beyond the circle of wise women who assisted doctors and carried out private practice; we must discover what we can about various magicians, empirics, and ordinary people who passed on folkloric beliefs and practices.

Our French manuscripts, especially the Lille codex, are permeated with popular beliefs that, as pointed out earlier, are often difficult to distinguish from scientific tenets about the female reproductive system. The Lille manuscript tells us, for example, that male sterility is caused by sex without love, by a man jumping backward from the woman after sexual intercourse, by unnatural intercourse, especially when a man sees the female organs, or by shamelessly engaging in anal intercourse.[49] We see here a collection of popular notions, and we must write these into our story of medieval obstetrics and gynecology, just as today we must acknowledge as part of today's culture our relatives' and friends' judgments that a pregnant woman is carrying a girl or a boy by the shape of her abdomen.

Further on in this text, the author, Nicholaus, relates some information drawn from the thirteenth-century physician Gilbertus Anglicus about a practice concerning fertility. Gilbertus tells us that a young man of twenty years or more will not fail to generate if on the eve of Saint John the Baptist (i.e., on 23 June) he digs up first a large comfrey plant and afterward a smaller one, with its root, before the third hour. He must then say the Lord's Prayer three times, and, pacing back and forth, he must extract the juice from the plant and write the words of the prayer with this juice on a card or cards. If the card were worn around the neck by the man during sexual intercourse, the offspring would be male; if the woman were to wear it, the offspring would be female.[50] Once again, it seems to me that here we are very close to the private world of medieval folkloric beliefs.

One focus of superstitious belief in both medieval and modern times is the child born with a caul—a piece of the amniotic membrane covering the head—which signified that the child would be lucky or able to foretell the future.[51] Medieval doctors were certainly aware of this phenomenon, and the Lille manuscript records the description by the ninth-century Arabic physician Rhazes which states simply that the fetus is sometimes covered with the secundine and in this case is called a "clothed newborn" and that the covering should be removed immediately after birth.[52] Anthonius Guainerius also describes this condition, but the Italian physician presents a case history that sheds light on how it could be perceived by the woman's culture. Guainerius tells of a jealous husband whose wife often visited the Franciscan church and who became suspicious when she bore him a child with a caul, even though he was told how fortunate the child would be. Since the resemblance between the "clothed newborn" and the friar in his cowl was striking, the husband was immediately convinced that the friar had fathered the child. He became so enraged that he would have killed the child and the mother if others had not prevented him, and indeed he managed to beat his wife to the point where she could hardly be revived. Another mother, Guainerius relates, dedicated her son to the harsh rule of the Franciscan order because he appeared to be born dressed in the habit and she believed that he had miraculously assumed the habit in the womb. The Italian physician cautions doctors to "disregard the corrupt fantasy of such common people,"[53] but we must acknowledge this fantasy as an important part of medieval women's private world.

We see, then, that medieval obstetrics and gynecology are not a simple story of learned doctors versus ignorant midwives, the one passing on Galenic and Aristotelian notions from above, the other monopolizing supernatural forces; rather, magic had a wide-ranging influence in medieval women's medicine. Respected medical authorities unconsciously adopted folkloric remedies in their prescriptions, setting them within a humoral context and thereby providing them with a scientific justification. In the manuscripts composed by less exalted medieval physicians, we find more overt examples of superstitious cures, which are drawn from the woman's culture and juxtaposed with citations from Galen and Avicenna. Our French and Italian sources both provide us with real examples of doctors' respect for and fear of female practitioners, who are privy to occult secrets and who wield dark powers. And, finally, midwives' beliefs and practices became part of the everyday world of simple folk for whom pregnancy and childbirth are central life episodes, as they continue to be today.

NOTES

1. On this point see Shorter, "A History of the Birth Experience," pt. 2 of his *History of Women's Bodies.*

2. See Eccles, *Obstetrics and Gynecology,* pp. 119–21; Rowland, *Medieval Woman's Guide to Health;* O'Neill, "Giovanni Michele Savonarola"; Benedek, "Midwives and Physicians"; Benton, "Trotula, Women's Problems, and Medicine"; Jacquart and Thomasset, *Sexualité et savoir medical,* p. 158.

3. Some recent investigations into archival material have been very fruitful. See, for example, Park, *Doctors and Medicine.*

4. We find similar characteristics in medieval gynecological manuscripts from all over the Continent. See Thorndike and Kibre, *Mediaeval Scientific Writings in Latin.*

5. "Dicunt hoc in nostris regionibus non multum verificatur . . ." (Nicholaus, *De passionibus mulierum,* fol. 48v).

6. "Dixit Rasis nono continentis propter subtilitatem secundine scinditur ante partum et egreditur humiditas per spatium longe temporis ante et est causa difficultatis partus et hoc ego vidi in multis et maxime in domina Bartholomea uxore Saltonis de Permis" (Ibid., fol. 74r).

7. "Et oportet ut sedeat dixit Avicenna mulier hora una et extendat pedes suos deinde resupinetur supra dorsum suum hora una postea surgat subito et ascendat in gradus et descendat et clamet. Debet enim ambulare per loca decliniva ascendendo et descendendo ut fetus descendat ut [MS: et] sua gravitate os matricis aperiat [*Note:* 'Ego vidi in Goulian filia in montibus baronum']" (Ibid., fol. 81v).

8. Ibid., fols. 54r–55r.

9. "Hec autem sunt que ego probavi sex vel septem annis circa. Primo in quadam nobili domicella que moratur in vicecomitatu leomanie que fuerat xiii annis cum viro suo quod nunquam concepit, quam feci uti propter inopportunitatem temporis hyemalis in quo eramus ellectuariis spectantibus ad conceptum, videlicet dyacodon abbatis cum bethonica ut superius dictum est de mane et post prandium, de nocte stomaticho confortivo quibus utendo infra septem menses concepit et habuit masculinum qui vivit. Et de quadam domina que habuit virum militem qui est socius et dispensator vicecomitatus leomanie que cum viro fuerat ix annis neque umquam signa conceptus habuerat; data purgatione et alia, infra duos mensis concepit filium" (*Jordanus de Turre, Tractatus de impregnatione mulieris,* fol. 11r).

10. "In hoc tamen casu tantum his pauperculis mulieribus compacior ut huic capitulo finem imponere nesciam quin aliqua paucula a nostro bono Avicenna descripta ad hunc subiungam et ibi erit finis . . . Cumque dolores immites et magno cum pondere in pectinem partura senserit que eam crudeliter et sine intermissione molestent potenter paupercula clamet et ad celum usque lamentabiles voces [*ed.:* vocet] emittat retentem spiritum sepe inferius comprimat. Et in isto casu cum pipere et oleo tu sternutationem provoca et isto modo hec et que scripta ordinate faciendo partum facilitabis et bonam cum fetu suo dei dono ad salutis portum reduces" (Anthonius Guainerius, *Tractatus de matricibus,* fol. 2.4rb [Series 2 follows quire z in this book]).

11. Cf. Avicenna, *Liber canonis* (1964), fols. 569v–570r.

12. "Et Avicenna dixit si partus difficilis fiat propter magnitudinem fetus oportet ut inveniat obstetrix possibilitatem huius fetus in extractione eius paulatim . . . quod si illud non confert administretur forcipes scilicet non incidentes dicte canes ut sunt tenacule et extrahatur cum eis" (Nicholas, *De passionibus*

mulierum, fol. 92v). Marginal note of "helas, helas," refers specifically to this section and not to the following sentence, which instructs the operator to follow the procedure for removal of a dead fetus if forceps are not successful. The reader's sympathy is directed toward the mother, therefore, and not toward the infant.

13. "Signum autem principii precipitationis matricis est quod obstetrix videat utrum orificium extrinsecum sit directum intrinsece. Si vero non sed sit tortuosum, signum est quod precipitatio et dislocatio est versus latus quod tendit . . . Debet etiam iuvari dirimatione manuali per obstetricem ut ad suum locum naturalem reddeat" (Petrus de Nadillis, *De impregnatione mulieris,* fol. 19r). On the use of female assistants, see H. R. Lemay, "Anthonius Guainerius and Medieval Gynecology," pp. 323–24, and Jacquart and Thomasset, *Sexualité et savoir medical,* p. 241.

14. See Jacquart and Thomasset, *Sexualité et savoir medical,* p. 241; Donnison, "The Office of Midwife," chap. 1 of *Midwives and Medical Men.*

15. On Gilbertus Anglicus, author of the *Compendium medicinae,* see Wickersheimer, *Dictionnaire biographique,* pp. 191–92, and Jacquart, *Supplement,* pp. 88–89.

16. "Signa causarum dixit Gilibertus magnitudo fetus cognoscitur per nimiam inflationem ventris et per obstetricis iudicium"; "Dixit enim Galienus tertio de virtutibus naturalibus et ponitur nono continentis dixerunt obstetrices quod paritura non debet super scampnum sedere nec comprimi debet quando parturit nisi si tactum fuerit os matricis et inveniatur quod fuerit apertum tendens in augmento in apertione ipsius paulatim" (Nicholaus, *De passionibus mulierum,* fols. 75v, 82v).

17. "Signum autem quod concepit est clausio orificii matricis quod scitur per obstetricem" (Petrus de Nadillis, *De impregnatione mulieris,* fol. 20v).

18. Six weeks from the last menstrual period, Hegar's sign, a softening of the cervix, may be detected by manual examination. At this point Chadwick's sign, a purple color of the vagina and cervix, may also be noted. See Hellman and Pritchard, *William's Obstetrics,* pp. 245, 281. I am grateful for this information to Dr. Douglas Lee of Suffolk Obstetrical and Gynecological Associates, Port Jefferson, N.Y.

19. E.g., "Trotula," William of Saliceto. See H. R. Lemay, "William of Saliceto," pp. 175–76.

20. Personal communication of Dr. Douglas Lee, Suffolk Obstetrical and Gynecological Associates, Port Jefferson, N.Y. See also Warner, *Joan of Arc,* pp. 20–21.

21. "Et illa cuius os matricis est directe oppositum vulve orificio est masculinans quia tunc non perditur de virtute spermatis ex mare que contrahat in introeundo per os tortuosum non directe oppositum" (Nicholaus, *De passionibus mulierum,* fol. 47r; Avicenna is cited as the authority for this statement). I have

translated *orificium vulve* as "vagina"; the term "vagina" is not normally used in these texts. For a discussion of medical vocabulary, see Jacquart and Thomasset, "L'Anatomie et la quete des mots," chap. 1 of *Sexualité et savoir medical.*

22. Petrus de Nadillis, *De impregnatione mulieris*, fols. 18rff.

23. See Pinto, "Folk Practice," p. 513.

24. For further discussion of the distinction between science and magic, see Rydberg, *Magic of the Middle Ages*, p. 52.

25. "Unde sterilitas ex parte matricis est triplex. Aut enim provenit ex parte morbi complexionalis aut compositionalis aut communis . . . Impedimentum ergo conceptionis ex parte matricis est triplex, quedam ex parte frigiditatis et dempsitatis, secundum ex parte lubricitatis et humiditatis, tertium ex parte caliditatis et siccitatis . . . Visis de morbis complexionalibus, videndum est de morbis compositionalibus ipsius matricis. Unde ibi possunt contingere veruce pinguedo superflua emorroydes. Potest etiam ibi contingere amplitudo strictura simiiliter de aliis. Unde vie aliquando sunt ita ample quod non possunt semen retinere . . . Potest etiam venire morbus officialis ex dislocatione matricis" (Petrus de Nadillis, *De impregnatione mulieris*, fols. 13r, 13v, 17r).

26. Avicenna, *Liber canonis*, Liber III, fen xxi, fols. 362vff.

27. Pinto, "Folk Practice," p. 520.

28. "Si autem sterilitas sit propter causam frigidam et humidam quod contingit et accidit frequentius digeratur materia cum isto sirupo. Recipe radices rubee ma. arthemesie savine" (Jordanus de Turre, *Tractatus de impregnatione mulieris*, fol. 8v). John Riddle has informed me that artemesia is being effectively used today to treat malaria, especially in Third World countries.

29. John Riddle has pointed out that our knowledge of most Hippocratic drugs comes predominantly from the treatises on gynecology and women's diseases. He speculates that Hippocratic physicians tried to distinguish themselves from lay medical practitioners, who emphasized drug and magic therapy, by denying these practices as much as possible, but in the case of women's diseases and gynecological practices, they were unable to do so because they were helplessly dependent on the Greek equivalent to a midwife (see Riddle, "Folk Tradition and Folk Medicine").

30. Pinto, "Folk Practice," pp. 523, 516, 519, 517.

31. "Medicine facientes illud cum proprietate. Dicitur oportet ut difficultatem patiens teneat in manu sua sinistra magnetem, aut limatur cum cinere ungule asini quoniam est ultimum [*ed.*: 'quomiam est ulumum']" (Avicenna, *Liber canonis*, fol. 370va; the reading "quoniam est ultimum" has been corrected on the basis of BN lat. 14301, fol. 237ra, and BN lat. 14392, fol. 325va).

32. "In hoc casu a proprietate valere tam extrinsecis quam intrinsecis applicanda reperi multa de quorum proprietate est partum accelerare ac dolores mitigare multum" (Anthonius Guainerius, *Tractatus de matricibus*, Cap. 35, fol. 2.3vb).

33. Nicholaus, *De passionibus mulierum*, fols. 89v–90r.

34. "Dixit Porphirius supra terras Cicilie accidit eclipsis solis magna et illo anno mulieres terrarum regionibus illis filios deformes et habentes duo capita generarunt. Et accidit quibusdam mulieribus emissio menstrui per os suum" (Ibid., fol. 78r).

35. "Assignatur autem ab astrologiis alia causa quare natus in octavo non vivit quam ipsi sumunt ex ordine planetarum quem habent in eductione fetus a matrice . . . Et ut octavo menso Saturnus influat iterum super eo qui sua frigiditate calorem eius debilitat naturalem vias matricis constringat ipsum fetum immobilitat . . . verum etiam quadam maliciosa et occulta impressione vita [MS: vite] animantium immutatur quapropter non vivet octavo exiens mense et dato quod tunc vivat vel vivus exeat non durat communiter vita eius ultra septem vel octo dies vel parum post. Et si durat in vita non evadet infortunum scilicet vel claudus vel cecus vel gibbosus vel leprosus vel aliam notam habens malicie erit" (Ibid., fols. 67r, 69r).

36. See R. Lemay, "Astronomy in Medieval Universities."

37. "Et Aristoteles quidem quarto de generatione animalium dixit causam partus in determinatis mensibus dictis procedere ex aspectu et ordine superiorum corporum" (Nicholaus, De passionibus mulierum, fol. 64v).

38. Jacquart and Thomasset, Sexualité et savoir medical, pp. 101–6.

39. "De sanguineo menstruo rubrica. Qui sanguinem menstruum sumpserit aut leprosus lunaticus maleficus et obliviosus efficitur. Et horum bezear est trociscus unus de tiro aut de serpentibus a quibus cauda et caput per palmum fuerint abscissa manducare" (Anthonius Guainerius, Tractatus de matricibus, fol. nn3v; note that this comes from his section on poisons ["Capitulum septimum omnium venenorum quocumque et qualitercumque a proximatorum curam ponit generalem"]).

40. "Dixit Guil[bertus] fumigetur mulier cum dente hominis morti"; "dixit Gilibertus cinctorium parientis sit corrigia cervina quia habet occultam virtutem iuvandi partum" (Nicholaus, De passionibus mulierum, fols. 54r, 83r).

41. "Et post coitum, truncatur istud pessarium. Recipe: coaguli leporis olei violacei ana drachmas ii" (Petrus de Nadillis, De impregnatione mulieris, fol. 20r); "Et fine quattuor vel quinque dierum post menstrua deglutinat mulier per modum pillule drachmam semissem vel drachmam unam coaguli leporis" (Jordanus de Turre, Tractatus de impregnatione mulieris, fol. 10r).

42. Pinto, "Folk Practice," p. 520.

43. "Si vero in hoc impedimentum non superveniat et mulier a conceptione impediatur, hoc est certum signum esse ex deffectu vivi . . . Ita ex deffectu causatur sterilitas quia si habundat humiditas et alia sunt ablata causatur gomorrea que est humoris spermatis continuus fluxus . . . Si autem accidit sterilitas ex causa exteriori hoc contingit ex una de quinque causis aut quia homo utitur eis que corrumpunt complexionem eius aut propter membra genitalia que sunt improportionata aut propter nimiam caliditatem aut frigiditatem membrorum aut propter renes et alia membra genitalia aut propter aliquas exterius

quod est factum viro quod est causa sterilitatis" (Jordanus de Turre, *Tractatus de impregnatione mulieris*, fols. 6r–7r).

44. "Si vero deffecerit calor causatur approximeron que est inoperatio generativorum membrorum quando nec virga ter.ditur nec sperma emittitur. Quod fit ex aliqua trium causarum, vel ex malicia vel ex oxifimate sicut in maleficiis quorum cura deo dimittitur et hiis qui fecerunt maleficium licet aliqui libri medicine ponant aliqua remedia videlicet empirica sicut est portatio argenti vini ad collum in testa avellane et suspensio artemesie insuper liminari domus ubi iacent vir et mulier" (Ibid., fol. 6v).

45. "Et in summa difficultatis [*ed.*: difficultas] partis cause iste sunt quamobrem mulieres et delicate maxime in suis partibus medicos ad se vocant sepe . . . Verbis etiam oratoriis pauperculam partentem comforta . . . et in presentis bonum est ut legenda beate margarite legatur sanctorum reliquias super se habeat et breviter quas sciveris cerimonias ut infirme tue ac vetulis applaudas facito tamen quo si sortilegicam mulierem aliquam ibidem esse suspicio sit ea pellenda foris erit. Nam his in partibus ut scias et [*ed.*: in] consimilibus stupenda sunt plurima miraris forsan nonne ovidius si bene recolo in novo methamorposeos et alkimena herculis matre recitat quod dum eam accidentia partus infestarent superveniens lucina cum concathcnatis digitis ad gcnua positis suis cum incantationibus ne parere posset prohibeat. Et esto hec fabula sit veritatis tamen aliquid mihi crede habuit cuius oppositum nihilominus si crederis cum de articulis fidei hec non sit anthomizandus non eris" (Anthonius Guainerius, *Tractatus de matricibus*, fols. 2.3r–2.3v).

46. "Aliqui tamen talia fieri non dubitant immo posse fieri forte credebant ut a plinio in de naturali historia elici posse videtur. Recitat enim quod si lupinas carnes paritura manducaverit pariet facilius cum quo si quis presens sit qui carnes illas ediderit adversus eam incantationes noxie non valebunt. Quanta de malificio et demonio et de incantatione et colli suspensione veteres philosophi pertractaverint tu ipse scis sed talia ribaldis fratribus ac vetulis sortilegicis qui sibi talia revelent omnia dimittenda sunt" (Ibid., fol. 2.3v).

47. "Sepe accidit ut vie per quas spiritus a corde ac cerebrum deferuntur et a cerebro ad membra cetera grossis ab humiditatibus opilantur et pupis quam maxime, quo fit ut membra debitis suis motibus careant, quare tunc cum pectus ad necessarias diversiones dillatari nequeat diafragma constringitur et ab ipso plurimo, a pulmone vero cor, qua ex causa cor ipsum debite dillatari non potest et tunc infirmo super se ut pondus vel fantasma talem habeat prohibens dilatationem apparet, et cum extrema propter illam opilationem citius spiritibus quam membra cetera depauperantur fantasma hoc a pedibus initium facit et paulative secundum quod membra ipsius spiritibus privantur sursum repit quod vulgares demonem homines suffocantem putant. Ob hoc ergo passio hec incubus appellatur, quod est nomen demonis. Alii vetulas quasdam incantantes que se in formas varias ut inquiunt mutare possunt hoc facere putant et eas strias seu zobianas nostri vulgares appellant que ut dicunt gatorum formam

sepius accipiunt. Hec credulitas ob hoc ortum habuit quare passio hec lactantes sepe deprehendit quos tunc suffocat cuius causas vulgares ignorantes vetulas illas zobianas illud fecisse putant. Ex dictis itaque quod sit incubus apparet" (Ibid., fols. c3v–c4r).

48. Ibid., fol. b3r.

49. "Et sunt qui addunt predictis causis coytum factum sine desiderio et amore sed potius odio et saltum factum a muliere post coytum subito ad posteriora et coytum factum cum muliere modo inepto et maxime cum vir videt muliebria et coytus in propaculo et sine verecundia steriles facit viros honestos" (Nicholaus, *De passionibus mulierum*, fol. 13v).

50. "Empiricum de quo dixit Guilbertus quod numquam fallit masculo XX annorum vel ultra in vigilia beati Iohannis Baptiste consolidam maiorem primo et dum consolidam minorem cum radice de terra ante horam terciam dicendo ter orationem dominicam effodiat et accipiat nenum in eundo et redeundo respondendo et loquendo aliquid dicat et sic tacendo succum extrahat et cum illo succo scribat in tot quartis quot indiguerit ista verba, dixit dominus crescite + uthiboth + et multiplicamini + thabethav + et replete terram + almach + si talem cartam cum zucco impressam et verbis scriptam masculus circa collum habeat dum feminam cognoscit marem generabit et si femina eam habuerit feminam generabit" (Ibid., fols. 30r–30v).

51. See Forbes, *The Midwife and the Witch*, pp. 94ff.

52. "Et fetus quidam aliquando exit involutus secundina et vocatur natus vestitus. Oportet autem ut cito secundina frangatur et extrahatur ab eo" (Nicholaus, *De passionibus mulierum*, fol. 77v).

53. "Est et item panniculus tertius ab ea nomine membrane subtilissime similis qui immediate fetum attingens ipsum totum circumdat et in se humiditates sudorales fetus recondit omnes. Sed si deus te adiuvet de ipso panniculo ab eo trupham audi queso his proximis diebus zelotipi in quendam fratrem minorem de uxore suspicio erat sic ut ipsa ad beati francisci ecclesiam ire auderet et nequaquam pregnans, facta ab eo [*ed.:* ea], panniculo fetum involutum ut plerumque accidit peperit mulier vero quedam puerum [*ed.:* puberum] natum tristi zelotipo nuntiatum it, et devoto parvulo gaudium sperans adiungere, bene fortunatus inquit erit cum minorum more ad lucem indutus deveniret. Mulieres plurime ut sic scias ab ea vestitum infantem nasci ad bonum omne putant. Infelix zelotipus ille sic ab ea vestitum infantem cum audivit statim [*ed.:* statum] a minore fratre genitum pensavit, paciencia tamen omni extincta puerum rapiens de eo, terra protinus allibere volebat ni astantibus prohibitum fuisset. Is tristis rabiem inducentem edomere non valens puerpera[m] misera[m] invadit et tantum eam pugnis ac calcibus mulctavit ut vocatus ad vitam pene reducere eam potuerit. Alia cum filium habuisset nunquam me consulit et oportunis remediis adhibitis pregnans facta vestitum ab ea infantulum peperit quod in ventre minorum habitum assumpsisse miraculose cum crederet habito illo eum induit et innocentem tandem asperam minorum obedientiam religavit. Tu igitur ubi opus esset pau-

perculas mulieres excusato et talium vulgarium fantasiam remove" (Anthonius Guainerius, *Tractatus de matricibus*, fol. 2.4v).

BIBLIOGRAPHY

Primary Sources

Anthonius Guainerius. *Tractatus de matricibus.* in *Opera omnia.* Pavia, 1481.
Avicenna. *Liber canonis.* Paris, Bibliothèque nationale, MS. lat. 14301.
———. *Liber canonis.* Paris, Bibliothèque nationale, MS. lat. 14392.
———. *Liber canonis.* 1507. Reprint. Hildesheim, 1964.
Jordanus de Turre. *Tractatus de impregnatione mulieris.* Paris, Bibliothèque nationale, MS. lat. 7066.
Nicholaus. *De passionibus mulierum.* Lille MS. lat. 334.
Petrus de Nadillis. *De impregnatione mulieris.* Paris, Bibliothèque nationale, MS. lat. 7066.

Secondary Sources

Benedek, Thomas G. "The Changing Relationship between Midwives and Physicians during the Renaissance." *Bulletin of the History of Medicine* 51 (1977): 550–64.
Benton, John F. "Trotula, Women's Problems, and the Professionalization of Medicine in the Middle Ages." *Bulletin of the History of Medicine* 59 (1985): 30–53.
Donnison, Jean. *Midwives and Medical Men: A History of Interprofessional Rivalries and Women's Rights.* New York, 1977.
Eccles, Audrey. *Obstetrics and Gynecology in Tudor and Stuart England.* Kent, Ohio, 1982.
Forbes, Thomas Rogers. *The Midwife and the Witch.* New Haven, Conn., 1966.
Hellman, Louis, and Jack A. Pritchard. *William's Obstetrics.* 14th ed. New York, 1970.
Jacquart, Danielle. *Dictionnaire biographique des médecins en France au moyen âge: Supplément.* Geneva, 1979.
Jacquart, Danielle, and Claude Thomasset. *Sexualité et savoir medical au moyen âge.* Paris, 1985.
Lemay, Helen Rodnite. "Anthonius Guainerius and Medieval Gynecology." In *Women of the Medieval World,* ed. Julius Kirshner and Suzanne Wemple, pp. 317–36. New York, 1985.
———. "William of Saliceto on Human Sexuality." *Viator* 12 (1981): 165–81.
Lemay, Richard. "The Teaching of Astronomy in Medieval Universities, Principally in Paris, in the Fourteenth Century." *Manuscripta* 20 (1976): 197–217.

O'Neill, Ynez Viole. "Giovanni Michele Savonarola: An Atypical Renaissance Practitioner." *Clio Medica* 10 (1975): 77–93.

Park, Katharine. *Doctors and Medicine in Early Renaissance Florence.* Princeton, N.J., 1985.

Pinto, Lucille. "The Folk Practice of Obstetrics and Gynecology in the Middle Ages." *Bulletin of the History of Medicine* 47 (1973): 513–23.

Riddle, John. "Folk Tradition and Folk Medicine: Recognition of Drugs in Classical Antiquity." In *Folklore and Folk Medicines,* ed. John Scarborough, pp. 33–61. Madison, Wis., 1987.

Rowland, Beryl. *Medieval Woman's Guide to Health.* Kent, Ohio, 1981.

Rydberg, Viktor. *The Magic of the Middle Ages.* New York, 1879.

Shorter, Edward. *A History of Women's Bodies.* New York, 1982.

Thorndike, Lynn, and Pearl Kibre. *Catalog of Incipits of Mediaeval Scientific Writings in Latin.* Cambridge, Mass., 1963.

Warner, Marina. *Joan of Arc: The Image of Female Heroism.* New York, 1981.

Wickersheimer, Ernest. *Dictionnaire biographique des medecins en France au moyen âge.* Geneva, 1979.

"LEGAL HISTORY AND THE MEDIEVAL ENGLISHWOMAN" REVISITED

Some New Directions

Janet Senderowitz Loengard

inety-seven years ago, the English legal historian Frederic William Maitland gave a lecture called "Why the History of English Law Is Not Written."[1] This essay has something of a similar theme, on a much more modest scale: why a recent, scholarly, relatively comprehensive history of medieval English law as it applied to women has not been written. Its purpose is both to examine factors that may have deterred historians from undertaking such a project and to attempt an overview of the kind of work that has been and is being done in women's legal history.

⁋ The nineteenth and early twentieth centuries saw some interest in the history of women's legal rights and liabilities, and in both Britain and the United States there were attempts at summarizing, in relatively slender volumes, hundreds of years of Englishwomen's experience. Sometimes there were also efforts to discuss comparative legal systems; the result was often a scope too broad to permit depth, as in Edward D. Mansfield's *Legal Rights, Liabilities, and Duties of Women, with an Introductory History of Their Legal Conditions in the Hebrew, Roman, and Feudal Systems,* published in 1845. Even when authors limited themselves as to place, their work still had a rather wide focus: some examples are *Women under the English Law from the Time of the Saxons to the Present Time,* the present time being 1896 and the author Arthur Rackman Cleveland; *The Status of Women under the English Law,* by Annie Beatrice Wallis Chapman and Mary Wallis Chapman, published in 1909; and *British Freewomen: Their Historical Privileges in Common Law and Equity,* an 1894 volume by that remarkable woman, Charlotte Carmichael Stopes. And then there were some studies that did define their limits more sharply; Courtney Stanhope Kenny's *History of the Law of England as to the Effects of Marriage on Property and on the Wife's Legal Capacity*, published in 1879, is a good example.

But all these works reflect scholarship as it stood 80 or 100 or 140 years ago. This is not to belittle the men and women who wrote these volumes. Annie Beatrice Wallis Chapman was a fine scholar who edited the *Black Book* of Southampton. Charlotte Stopes published her book because she could not get a hearing any other way; she proposed a paper on what she called "a Woman's Subject" to be read before the British Association in 1885 and was turned down with the explanation that "although they formed valuable contributions to Constitutional History, the Committee felt they would certainly lead to political discussion, which must not be risked."[2] Her book and those by the Chapmans and others were pioneer works. But these older books obviously cannot reflect and incorporate work done in our lifetimes; often, almost a century of scholarship lies between them and us. Moreover, at least some were written by authors who used history to explain and even to justify the legal status of women as they knew it.[3] And, most important, none is based on a wide study of cases because none is based on in-depth work in the plea rolls, and few make extensive use of unprinted archival sources. Most offer only a handful of cases, often those transcribed into chronicles and genealogies. Instead, the studies look to statutes, treatises, and commentaries for authority—reputable sources, of course, but all going to the same point: they give information about what the law should be or what it is in theory, but they do not speak to practice. Work based on them lacks an evidentiary base sufficiently wide to permit conclusions about how medieval law or laws affected heiresses or doweresses or executrices —or murderesses, for that matter. One cannot know from *Glanvil's* or *Bracton's* pronouncements about dower rights how often those rights were thwarted by intimidation or harassment of the widow, any more than one can know how much de facto control over her land an heiress with an ineffective (or loving) husband might in fact retain. And, quite apart from provisions designed to apply only or especially to women, one cannot know how general law affected the female half of the population. A widow was free to bring an action in debt, but how was she received in court? Was she as likely as a man was to recover the amount claimed? Conversely, women were no more free to commit a felony than men were, but when accused, were they convicted as often and punished as severely?[4] Only a quantitative study of cases would allow even a guess. But the nineteenth- and earlier twentieth-century historians of law were not interested in making such a guess. They—and many later legal historians—were studying institutional history or the history of legal principles, for both of which their sources were admirably suited. Questions of how doctrine and the rules of law affected the lives of actual women would never have to be answered, because they were not asked.

In any event, the studies were attempts at a definitive treatment of "the law of women." In more recent years, so far as I am aware, no one has seriously attempted such an overview, and no one has written a scholarly, comprehensive history of medieval English law in its application to women. One reason may be that until within the past fifteen or possibly twenty years, anyone who wanted to do a synthetic piece, an overview (which is what a comprehensive history must be), would have started with very little help available by way of published books or articles dealing with specific topics and based on extensive research in primary sources.[5] One can point to Frédéric Joüon des Longrais's 1962 piece, "Le Statut de la femme en Angleterre," to S. J. Bailey's excellent "The Countess Gundred's Lands," published in 1948, and to Michael M. Sheehan's equally excellent "The Influence of Canon Law on the Property Rights of Married Women in England," published in 1963. And there are others. But it is not easy to list a dozen more pieces of the same caliber from the 1940s or the 1950s or even the early 1960s. A historian would have been pretty much a pioneer in using many of his or her primary sources.

That is in itself a formidable challenge. In her essay "Women under the Law in Medieval England, 1066–1485," Ruth Kittel points out that legal records may be one of the best sources for studying medieval women and that much remains to be done, with whole classes of documents virtually untouched. But there follows an ominous postscript, a cautionary note to the unprepared enthusiast: "Because of the nature of the available legal documents, research on the history of medieval English women based on these sources must be done by people trained in medieval studies."[6] Most documents are in Latin, while others are in Anglo-Norman French. Nor are they printed, for the most part; the historian must therefore be trained in paleography. And the amount of unpublished material is staggering: "For example, only two percent of the common law records for the thirteenth century are printed. In the other ninety-eight percent, there are at least 27,500 membranes in one class, the rolls of the justices itinerant." The conclusion seems inevitable: "Any new work on medieval English women will probably come from people trained in both languages and paleography, who can work with what are often quite difficult sources."[7]

She is right, of course. The amount of material is incredible. The legal records are not as voluminous for the thirteenth century—which I think helps to explain why Pollock and Maitland's *History of English Law* stops at 1272—but they grow steadily until, by the end of the medieval period, just for each of the central courts for each of the four terms of the legal year there is a heavy bundle of parchment with foxing-leather covers and tied up with knotted ropes, each one with hundreds of membranes sewed together at the top, each membrane nearly three feet long and almost a foot wide, written often front and back, in Latin, in highly stylized court hand. Moreover, the central courts are not the only courts, and plea rolls are not the only important legal records. One can safely guess why a comprehensive study based on these primary sources has not been written for the four-hundred-odd years between the Norman Conquest and the first Tudor.

But difficulty of sources is not the only reason. The fact seems to be that few have been discouraged by the difficulty because few wanted to write a legal history of medieval Englishwomen in the first place. Some have worked with one aspect or another of "women's law," but it is perfectly possible to write on a legal topic that necessarily concerns women, or even to write about a woman, without writing women's legal history. An example might be the absorbing article by Ralph A. Griffiths, "The Trial of Eleanor Cobham: An Episode in the Fall of Duke Humphrey of Gloucester," which appeared in 1969. Even the title proclaims Griffiths's real interest: he is concerned with Duke Humphrey's loss of power, and the attack on Humphrey's duchess was an attack on that power, just as an attack on his tenants or his horses might have been. The trial does, in fact, have some importance for women, but Griffiths takes that up only on the very last page of his article: as a result of a Commons petition growing out of the case, it became law that peeresses accused of treason should be judged by the judges and peers of the realm, as peers accused of treason were judged. "So stands the trial of Eleanor Cobham. It has a timeless importance in the history of English law and the definition of the legal status of peeresses, if not women generally."[8] The article then returns to a consideration of the effects of the trial on Duke Humphrey, the theme of the preceding seventeen pages. This is not to fault Griffiths; he did not claim in his article to be writing women's legal history, and he did what he had set out to do. But it illustrates the point made earlier: most modern historians who have worked with law have begun with an interest in a legal idea or event or institution, not with a concern for how it affected women. Very few have started with an interest in women's history that they might have elected to pursue through various areas of law. And the result of all this is that the view of law and the medieval Englishwoman is fragmented.

❡ But it does exist today, even if in fragments. A great deal has been written on relatively narrowly defined topics, much of it within the last fifteen years and certainly within the last twenty, much but by no means all of it written by women. Most of it has not been published in law reviews or journals of legal history. D. Kelly Weisberg, who did some counting, has reported that over the past sixty years an average of only one historical work on women per year has appeared in legal periodicals.[9] The new history has appeared, instead, in journals dealing with childhood, economics, social history, and interdisciplinary studies. At least in part, it is tied in with the newly expanded interest in the family and family law. Some of this material should be noted, because it is important to see what concerns the authors of the new work in medieval Englishwomen's legal history.

Kelly Weisberg, in the introduction to *Women and the Law: The Social Historical Perspective,* a collection of essays published in 1982, comments that women have been of legal historical interest primarily in a few areas. In criminal law, they have figured as witches and/or murderers and/or prostitutes. In civil law, they have been of interest particularly in relation to their property rights following marriage.[10] Her comments on criminal law are not limited to work on the Middle Ages and may pertain less to that period. In the context of medieval England, the work that first comes to mind is Barbara A. Hanawalt's, whose studies on peasant families and crime and on female felons and victims do not focus on women as either witches or murderers; her work tends to show, in fact, that women committed proportionately fewer crimes of violence than men and that their criminal acts tended to involve property.[11] And she discusses not only crimes frequently committed by women but also those frequently committed against them, the obvious example of the latter being rape. Perhaps because it was an offense in which women were virtually always the victims and never the perpetrators, rape has received attention from a number of historians interested in medieval women and law.[12] Moreover, recent work shows the influence of social history; one example is John M. Carter's 1982 article, "Rape and Medieval English Society: The Evidence of Yorkshire, Wiltshire, and London, 1218–1276." Carter uses eyre rolls, but his real interest is in neither procedure nor the substantive law of rape. He is concerned with women's history, with the changing status of women in the thirteenth century, and he uses a perceived laxity in punishment of the crime as evidence that that status suffered.[13]

One form of murder that does seem to have usually involved women perpetrators was infanticide, and considerable work has been done on it for all periods of English history. As far as the medieval period in England is concerned, Barbara A. Kellum's "Infanticide in England in the Later Middle Ages" appeared in 1974 and was followed the next year by Richard Helmholz's "Infanticide in the Province of Canterbury during the Fifteenth Century." The Kellum article in particular attempts to assess some of the many factors that went into making infanticide increasingly appear to be a woman's offense, an interesting line of thought, although her speculation on the mentality of the "murdering mother" (the term is not mine but Peter C. Hoffer and N. E. H. Hull's)[14] cannot be substantiated from legal records.

There is no question about the fascination that women's property rights have had for historians. It is not surprising. A great deal of legal history has been written about property rights in general because property—the right to obtain it by inheritance or purchase or gift, the right to hold it, the right to sell or pledge or give or will it, the right to seize or protect it—looms very large in medieval law. Nor is it surprising that married women have been singled out for study. By the time that legal records begin to exist in quantity, in the first half of the thirteenth century, some adult women without husbands enjoyed a capacity similar to that of men to hold and deal with property, although women were, of course, at a disadvantage for inheritance purposes. In many instances, the real distinction was not between men and women but between men and single women on the one hand and married women on the other.[15]

Property-related research involves a wide range of subjects: dower, maritagium, writs of entry *cui in vita*, inheritance by coheiresses, and so on. Perhaps the grandmother of all is Florence Griswold Buckstaff's 1894 article, "Married Woman's Property in Anglo-Norman Law and Origins of the Common Law Dower." It is subject to all the criticisms made of nineteenth-century scholarship, but it was a pioneering work when it appeared and apparently the only one in the field until Frédéric Joüon des Longrais's 1924 study, *La Conception anglaise de la saisine du XIIe au XIVe siècle*, which, despite its lack of case material and some brilliant surmises that have turned out to be untenable, is still essential for anyone looking for an overview of the institution of dower. A good example of a new approach to questions of married women's property is Charles Donahue's probe of the circumstances underlying some accepted medieval concepts in his 1980 article, "What Causes Fundamental Legal Ideas?: Marital Property in England and France in the Thirteenth Century." Donahue, in an interweaving of legal and nonlegal materials, offers what he calls a political explanation (the power of the English king) and social and anthropological explanations (based on the strength of the French family and familial communities) to account for the divergence in practice between the two countries. [16]

Inheritance—patterns of inheritance, changing customs in inheritance —is a growth industry in history writing, and much of what has been written is concerned with the effects of a rule or a custom on women. One example is Cicely Howell's "Peasant Inheritance Customs in the Midlands, 1200–1700," published in 1976.[17] Ten years earlier, Rosamund Faith published a widely-cited article, "Peasant Families and Inheritance Customs in Medieval England," and, more recently, R. M. Smith's "Some Thoughts on 'Hereditary' and 'Proprietary' Rights in Land under Customary Law in Thirteenth- and Early-Fourteenth-Century England" offered information about women in several different situations (and, incidentally, references to numerous works in the field). This is an area where virtually every recent work devotes at least some space to women.

The same is true, of course, in another, even bigger growth area: the law of marriage and the family and the multitude of rights and liabilities connected with it. It is in fact impossible to separate the study of marriage in medieval England from the study of women's property rights or, indeed, of any of women's rights or liabilities in medieval England. Because almost all women who had not entered the religious life were married at one point or another in their lives, married women's rights or liabilities are effectively the norm that must be studied. Marriage touched most aspects of the medieval woman's life: questions relating to it could subject her to the jurisdiction of two separate legal systems, since church courts alone were competent to make many decisions relating to the marriage's very existence; moreover, an ecclesiastical court's decision on an issue affecting the validity of a marriage often had repercussions in the common law courts, which had to consider the effects of the invalidity of a marriage on inheritance by offspring, on dower rights, or on maritagium. Other questions are also involved. What was the effect of a canonically valid but socially or tenurially unacceptable marriage on a woman's property rights: did the need for consent, insisted on by the church, involve freedom of choice—and on whose part, under what circumstances, and, realistically, at what cost? In a valid marriage that had had the approval of lord and family, the death of a husband meant that a widow could experience significant alteration in her relationship to her children, most especially her minor children. How likely was she, in practice, to play a role in determining their future, especially in the crucial matter of arranging or at least vetoing their marriages? What happened, in practice, to her right of dower, suddenly no longer inchoate? What about property she had brought to a marriage but had never controlled?

Given this complex interrelationship of marriage, family, property, and law, it is not surprising that legal historians as well as social historians have been interested in the institution of marriage. Sir Frederick Pollock and Frederick W. Maitland devoted a considerable number of pages to it in their *History of English Law*.[18] Modern work, again, has tended to be on more narrowly defined topics; only a few can be mentioned here. Canon law issues have been commented on in a series of articles and monographs. In 1971 Michael M. Sheehan published "The Formation and Stability of Marriage in Fourteenth-Century England: The Evidence of an Ely Register," and James Brundage published "Concubinage and Marriage in Medieval Canon Law." On the question of consent, John T. Noonan's "Marriage in the Middle Ages: The Power to Choose" appeared in 1973. Issues related to the church courts' enforcement of marriage contracts and impediments to those contracts, which could result in divorce or annulment, are discussed by Richard H. Helmholz in his highly regarded 1974 volume, *Marriage Litigation in Medieval England*.

Even more has been written about the common law and common law courts' handling of issues arising from matrimony. On the related issues of choice and consent, there is Sue Sheridan Walker's study of widows' remarriage, "Feudal Constraint and Free Consent in the Making of Marriages in Medieval England: Widows in the King's Gift," and, at least tangentially, her "Marrying of Feudal Wards in Medieval England." In less strictly technical terms, Lady Stenton treats the same subject in her 1957 book, *The Englishwoman in History*; it has, of course, been touched on by a number of historians interested in feudal society.[19] The freedom to marry as one chose could also involve manorial jurisdiction. One thinks of the ongoing debate between Eleanor Searle and Jean Scammell on the meaning of merchet, the payment required of a peasant who wished to marry off his daughter: was merchet an attempt to control the marriage of women tenants, or was it a tax reflecting assets lost to the lord by reason of the marriage? Scammell's original article, "Freedom and Marriage in Medieval England," and a second article, "Wife Rents and Merchet," both appeared in the *Economic History Review*, as did Searle's "Freedom and Marriage in Medieval England: An Alternative Hypothesis." Searle went on to write "Seigneurial Control of Women's Marriage:

Antecedents and Functions of Merchet in England," and it is perhaps significant that a revised version of that paper has appeared as "Merchet and Women's Property Rights in Medieval England." Marriage and property, property and marriage.

Marriage inevitably meant widowhood for a number of women, and widowhood in medieval England had important legal consequences. Sue Sheridan Walker has written on the question of the widow's relationship to and control over her children, specifically over her husband's heir, in her 1976 article, "Widow and Ward: The Feudal Law of Child Custody in Medieval England." Barbara A. Hanawalt's paper, "Widowhood in Medieval English Villages," given originally at the Fifth Berkshire Conference on the History of Women in 1981 and now a chapter in her book on the English peasant family (discussed below), mentions a number of the rights and liabilities of the widow at a lower level of society. She has used manorial court rolls as her source, and what she has found often reflects customary law and practice. There is, again, an instructive distinction to be drawn between work such as hers and articles such as George Haskins's "Development of Common Law Dower." Haskins wanted to present an overview of dower for an extended period; he chose to write institutional history. One would not know from it that widows were faced with legal, social, and familial limitations that affected their suits and, indeed, the action itself or that the adjudication of dower rights could affect an entire family's future. Haskins was not interested in widows as women any more than he was interested in heirs as children. He was not writing women's legal history; he did not try to.

❡ Even this brief outline makes evident that much work has been done. More is being done. But the result still provides a very spotty picture. Women's property rights, their legal limitations vis-à-vis their husbands or guardians, their rights of guardianship, and other relationships with their children's persons and property are being discussed. But if we learn a great deal about women as wards, criminals, heiresses, victims, guardians, tenants in chief, doweresses, and the like, there are still aspects of their life that we have not seen.

We know very little, for example, about women's commercial activities, although apparently not only single women but both the widows and the wives of urban tradesmen and artisans frequently carried on economic enterprises, and there is evidence that other women sometimes did also, if only within defined limits. Until recently, little has been written about them, apart from the important work of Sylvia Thrupp and a few commentaries on guilds controlled by women in various European cities, most notably the narrowly focused but impressively researched 1932 article by Marian K. Dale on fifteenth-century London "silkwomen and throwsters."[20] Is it because, in the eyes of the law, these women's legal status was no different from men's? Or is it because their commercial activities had no effect on their legal status or rights? The custom of London was not alone in making provision for married women who carried on their trade activities; what did that mean in practice? Where women were not acting alone, how often were suits by husband and wife really based on the wife's economic activities? And in a related area, what of the many women who were named executrices in their husbands' wills, who were charged with the settlement and often the long-term management of their husbands' estates? They appear in the records, and, what is more, they appear in their own persons; it would be useful to know more about them and their transactions and how they used the legal system to protect their assets and to facilitate their activities.

Nor are these the only blank spots in the legal history of women; what about the whole area of what we would call tort law, much of it handled by the actions of trespass and trespass on the case? There are women plaintiffs in the plea rolls: who were they in terms of both economic and legal status? Were they always single or widowed, given the rule that a married woman could not sue or be sued without her husband's being joined in the action? What were their causes of action—what kinds of suit were they most likely to bring? Against what kind of defendant? How likely were they to be successful? How important, in economic terms, were suits by women?

There are many such blank spots, many gaps; some may never be filled in because records are missing or uninformative or simply so massive and difficult to use that it is not worthwhile to ask the questions necessary for a meaningful answer. But in some instances the material is there and relatively manageable: it is just that no one has asked questions designed to elicit more information about women rather than about an action or an institution. Ideally, then, people interested in women's legal history would ransack legal records for information about every aspect of women's lives and how they were touched by law and would then write articles setting out what they had found. The articles themselves would be worth having, but each would be useful beyond its own limits because it would be a piece in the mosaic that must be reconstructed, the jigsaw puzzle that must be put together. There are now enough scholars primarily interested in the legal history of women. But only when there are enough pieces will someone be able to write the comprehensive, scholarly, synthetic history that does not now exist. And only then will the view in the kaleidoscope be resolved into a coherent picture of the relationship between English medieval women and law, as it existed for the better part of half a millennium.

Postscript   Because this essay, an earlier version of which appeared in *Law and History Review* in 1986, is based on a paper read at the Sixth Berkshire Conference on the History of Women in 1984, most of the research for it was done at that time. But even a cursory investigation indicates the increased rate at which articles and books concerned with medieval women have reached print since then; a field that hardly existed twenty years ago appears to be one of the most rapidly burgeoning of all areas of history. The specialized subfield, the legal history of the medieval Englishwoman, has shared somewhat unevenly in that growth. The admittedly less than extensive research I have done in an attempt to make the article's bibliography more current suggests that there are topics in which increased interest has resulted in a flow of monographs and articles but that there are still significant lacunae.

Two points in particular stand out, and they may well be interrelated. First, some of the most interesting work now being done is actually concerned with a group of which women form only a part: the legal history of women appears to be increasingly subsumed in the history of the family, of women and children, of parent and child. Barbara A. Hanawalt's 1986 *The Ties That Bound*, which deals with peasant families in medieval England, is one example. Another is the set of papers presented at a session on the use of legal records for the history of the family at the Conference on British Legal Manuscripts at the Newberry Library in 1986 and published in the January 1988 issue of the *Journal of Medieval History*. The essays—Michael M. Sheehan's work on wills at both canon and common law, Barbara A. Hanawalt's on manorial families, Maryanne Kowaleski's on town families, and Sue Sheridan Walker's on the feudal family and common law records—all contain much valuable information about women within the family context.

The related point is that more historians have become expert at using legal sources to write what is essentially social history, or at least history that is not legally oriented. If asked, most of these historians would deny any intention to do otherwise; they would insist that they are not, or are not primarily, legal historians. The results are often excellent.

Hanawalt's *The Ties That Bound* is a good example; others are Judith M. Bennett's work on alewives in fourteenth-century Brigstock in "The Village Ale-Wife: Women and Brewing in Fourteenth-Century England" and her recently published *Women in the Medieval English Countryside*, of which her discussion of the alewives forms a part. Her examination of the formation of peasant marriage also comes to mind,[21] as does Joel T. Rosenthal's "Aristocratic Widows in Fifteenth-Century England," touching women at the other end of both the social scale and the marital relationship.

A legal historian will find much of interest in these works. Despite their disclaimers, social historians using legal sources are necessarily writing legal history of a sort, often a commentary on how an institution or action affected the lives of the women (and men) it touched. But a social historian asks questions different from those that a legal historian might ask and gets a different set of answers. Not wrong: different. Questions the legal historian might have posed are often answered obliquely or not at all.

The interests of social historians have also dictated the topics explored, but the interests of people who would characterize themselves as historians of law have run along remarkably similar lines. As noted earlier, there has been a great deal written about marriage from the point of view of both common and canon law, much of it very important. Paul Brand and Paul Hyams's "Seigneurial Control of Women's Marriage," Rosamund Faith's additional comments, and Eleanor Searle's rejoinder carry on a long-standing debate about the extent of such control. Charles Donahue's "Canon Law on the Formation of Marriage and Social Practice in the Later Middle Ages," Charles Duggan's "Equity and Compassion in Papal Marriage Decretals to England," Ralph Houlbrooke's "Making of Marriage in Mid-Tudor England: Evidence from the Records of Matrimonial Contract Litigation," and Robert C. Palmer's "Contexts of Marriage in Medieval England: Evidence from the King's Court circa 1300" all explore the vexing question of what makes a marriage and how it is proved or disproved. It is perhaps significant that, although many of these men and women rank among leading legal historians, none of their articles was published in a legal journal or law review. (Another was O. F. Robinson's "Canon Law and Marriage," based on a thirteenth-century Exeter case, appeared in the *Juridical Review*.)

Writing of marriage, of course, does not necessarily involve writing about the legal history of women; Donahue's and Robinson's articles speak, respectively, of national trends and of canon law procedure. Duggan's interest in equity and compassion in papal marriage decretals to England is just that—his article is an examination of decretals and how they responded to complex marital situations. Duggan is defending the decretals against charges of papal lack of feeling; he wishes to show that popes from Alexander III to Celestine III desired to protect women (and children) whenever it was possible to do so without controverting the moral law: "There are limits to which any pope can go, in adapting his judgments to human situations, and such limits stop short of distorting the moral law as he receives it. At the same time, where vital moral principles were not at stake, it is noteworthy that many papal verdicts worked to the advantage or protection of the women involved."[22] Houlbrooke's lively article is quite different in feeling. It shows many more men and women acting to pledge themselves or to deny such a contract, so that one gets a feeling for attitudes of—and toward—young women with respect to matrimony as well as an understanding of how valid marriages were made. Palmer's article, dealing with a similar subject but for a period more than two hundred years earlier, is a model of its kind: written by a legal historian, it uses examples from the plea rolls of the king's courts, often entertaining and always informative in themselves, as background for drawing theoretical conclusions. Palmer explains that his purpose is to supply the social context often lacking in the records of the ecclesiastical courts, which tended "to treat marriage litigation as a self-contained unit, whereas such cases were often part of a more complicated social reality."[23] In the process, we learn not only of the circumstances of individual women but also of what a series of decisions meant for the social practices that grew up around marriage, most particularly how they affected grants made in contemplation of marriage and how that, in turn, affected the interests of women. This is women's legal history at its best.

Other issues related to marriage have also excited interest. Rowena Archer, in "Rich Old Ladies: The Problem of Late Medieval Dowagers," treats a social problem created by the existence of a legal right but does so chiefly by use of administrative documents. Sue Sheridan Walker's "Common Law Juries and Feudal Marriage Customs in Medieval England," on the other hand, uses legal records to get behind textbook or treatise rules and to ascertain how the wellborn young, male and female, actually chose marriage partners.

Widowhood, dower, wardship, choice of a partner: the emphasis in all is on law based on family relationships. Crime is, of course, not necessarily so based, and crime has continued to interest those working in women's history. Kathleen E. Garay has recently investigated the rolls of gaol delivery—that is, the records of a traveling court that, acting under royal commission, determined the cases of those held on suspicion of felony—for the period 1388–1409 and has attempted to ascertain both how often women came before the court and the sorts of crime of which they tended to be accused. Peter Rushton's "Women, Witchcraft, and Slander in Early Modern England, 1560–1675," although mostly concerned with postmedieval England, again uses legal evidence to speculate about the position of women in society; defamation cases overwhelmingly involved women and were often based on defendant's calling plaintiff a witch. The suggestion, says Rushton, is that women felt a greater need to defend their reputations in a world where they competed "to prove themselves in the face of a generally misogynist double standard applied by a male legal system."[24] John Marshall Carter's *Rape in Medieval England* attempts to deal with a single issue at criminal law, although the attempt is marred by murky syntax and some failure of understanding of medieval court procedure.

In 1984, I suggested that more work was needed in areas of the law that have not been as thoroughly considered as have crime, domestic relations, and rights in real property. Women's commercial activities, which could involve both contract and tort law, came to mind. There are still great gaps in these areas, although a beginning has been made; it is interesting that almost every writer on the topic cites Eileen Power's "Position of Women," which appeared in 1926, and many mention also Sylvia Thrupp's *Merchant Class of Medieval London* and Annie Abrams's even more venerable "Women Traders in Medieval London."[25] Again, much of the work has been carried on by men and women who do not think of themselves as legal historians, and here, I think, the differing focus does matter. The emphasis has been on work done by women for payment, over and above the usual household chores and to some extent outside the home—although in the nature of things more work was done from home by both men and women than would today be the case, and one cannot make nice distinctions among home, office, shop, and factory. The questions asked, for the most part, have concerned the trades and crafts women could or could not enter, in theory and/or in practice, and how entry altered or did not alter the status of women in a given location.

Rodney H. Hilton, in "Women Traders in Medieval England," uses evidence drawn largely from the fourteenth century in order "to give some impression of the scale both of retail trading and of the female role in it."[26] There is no discussion of what that role entailed in terms of legal rights and liabilities. When Judith M. Bennett studies Brigstock ale-wives of the same century in an attempt to understand how brewing for profit, that is, for other than household consumption, affected women's lives, she concludes that it changed them very little. Her work shows the continued exclusion of alewives from positions of responsibility in the peasant community, while men who followed a similar trade used it for their public advancement. It is the very lack of references to women in manorial court records as pledges or members of a tithing or as village officers that confirms her in her opinion; alewives rarely appeared except in connection with payment of ale fines, and even then they were "almost inevitably accompanied or assisted by their husbands."[27]

But Bennett does not discuss a legal factor that might explain the situation: Brigstock possibly had no provision for a woman to trade as a femme sole. Diane Hutton, on the other hand, speculates on the lack of just such a provision in fourteenth-century Shrewsbury, where court rolls rarely show a married woman's appearance in court without her husband. "Women in Fourteenth-Century Shrewsbury" uses lay subsidy returns and the records of various courts to discuss the kinds of work women engaged in; the focus is on economic, not legal, history, but simply watching women's court appearances—as plaintiff or defendant, in varying kinds of cases—presents some interesting questions for which the same records might be mined for answers. Hutton is aware of the possibilities, but, as she points out, the Shrewsbury records make it extremely difficult to learn about both the economic and the legal activities of married women, since even a married woman's commercial dealings apart from her husband would result in his appearance in court.[28]

Appearing in the same volume as Hutton's work but far more ambitious in scope is Kay E. Lacey's "Women and Work in Fourteenth- and Fifteenth-Century London." The first half of the essay deals with law, or laws: common law, canon law, and borough custom on testaments and contracts, particularly as they affected women. The second section, "Women and Work in London," discusses women's entry into various occupations, obstacles to advancement, and so on. The essay is bifurcated: the first section's extended discussion of testament and contract does not seem closely related to the second section. Moreover, the discussion of law, which attempts to provide a kind of overview, is, given the length of the article, necessarily overgeneralized and as a result could sometimes be misleading. There is also perhaps too much reliance on tract and treatise. Nonetheless, Lacey is to be congratulated. She is doing much-needed work in an area that has too long been neglected and where, as a result, there is little guidance. And she has attempted to synthesize the various laws bearing on the problems she examines, an effort as difficult as it is important.

Maryanne Kowaleski's "Women's Work in a Market Town: Exeter in the Late Fourteenth Century" is more limited in scope. Kowaleski has examined, among other things, 4,526 debt cases over a ten-year period and various other legal and administrative records over a twenty-year period, "to obtain 435 documented cases of Exeter women who worked for wage or profit."[29] From her data, she is able to draw conclusions about the trades in which women worked, the size of their debts, and the courts' attitudes toward them when they appeared as both plaintiffs and defendants. Her work sharpens the appetite for more answers on these important issues.

One final point. There is something of a contrast between research on law as it affected the medieval Englishwoman and that on law touching medieval women from other parts of the British Isles. Law in its application to Irishwomen was examined as long ago as 1936, with the publication of *Studies in Early Irish Law,* edited by Daniel A. Binchy. More recently, *The Welsh Law of Women,* edited by Dafydd Jenkins and Morfydd E. Owen, carried on the tradition for Wales. Both collections include essays on women in various capacities (Binchy's "The Legal Capacity of Irish Women in Regard to Contracts," Kathleen Mulchrone's "The Rights and Duties of Women with Regard to the Education of Their Children," and Morfydd E. Owen's "Shame and Reparation: Women's Place in the Kin") as well as several fine essays (noted in the bibliography that follows) in the more familiar fields of marriage, matrimonial property, and inheritance.

What, then, is the conclusion to be drawn? There is none, of course: this is an interim report. But two tentative suggestions can be made. First, the tendency to associate women's legal history with the history of the family as a whole may not be entirely productive because it may discourage research in areas of law that do not necessarily involve women in a domestic grouping: women as creditors, as executrices, as tortfeasors. Second, if the legal history of women continues to be written in large part by people who consider themselves as primarily social historians and to be published outside law reviews and journals, these two factors must shape and even change the nature of the field. This is not intended as a warning: the result may be all to the good. But the reshaping and the changes should be made deliberately, or at least not inadvertently or through default. The medieval Englishwoman deserves as much.

NOTES

The original version of this essay was presented at the Sixth Berkshire Conference on the History of Women at Smith College in June 1984. I am grateful for all the comments made by the audience, and special thanks go to Marylynn Salmon, the session's moderator, and to Sue Sheridan Walker, who saw a later draft of the paper and offered both good advice and bibliographic suggestions. A later version of the paper was published as "Legal History and the Medieval Englishwoman: A Fragmented View" in *Law and History Review* 4 (1986): 161–78; it is used here by permission of *Law and History Review,* for which I am grateful. I am also indebted to David B. Walters of the Department of Civil Law, University of Edinburgh, and to Elena C. Thomas-Hall of Ryan Library, Iona College, for their help in securing material that I could not otherwise have readily obtained.

1. Maitland's "Why the History of English Law Is Not Written," delivered as an inaugural lecture in the Arts School at Cambridge University on 13 October 1888, was published in his *Collected Papers.*

2. Stopes, *British Freewomen,* p. vii.

3. Edward Mansfield's *Legal Rights, Liabilities, and Duties of Women* provides a good example. Virtually his sole source for English legal history is Blackstone, but his "introductory history" is not really the point of the book: he is writing to explain "to intelligent women a mass of legal information concerning their persons, property, and happiness" (p. 6), and he firmly believes that history proves "that women have, in Christian countries, made such vast progress, especially in our republican government" (p. 102). They cannot be sold in marriage; their husbands cannot practice polygamy; and, concerning existing inequalities as to the property rights of married women, "an apologist for the existing state of things may very reasonably say that it is an inequality depending on the free will of women themselves. If they do not choose to avoid marriage, the laws still allow them to make a settlement on trustees for their separate use" (p. 104).

4. Recently, historians have offered suggestions on both points: on crime, see Hanawalt, "Female Felon," and her other works listed in the bibliography following; on debt litigation, see Kowaleski, "Women's Work."

5. Maitland found the same situation frustrating: "Then think of the tons of unprinted plea rolls . . . There is so much to be done that one hardly knows where to begin. He who would write a general history thinks perhaps his path should be smoothed by monographs; he who would write a monograph has not

the leisure to win his raw material from manuscripts; but then only by efforts at writing a general history will men be persuaded that monographs are wanted, or be brought to spend their time in working at the rolls" ("Why the History of English Law Is Not Written," 1:484).

6. Kittel, "Women under the Law in Medieval England," pp. 132–33.

7. Ibid., p. 133.

8. Griffiths, "Trial of Eleanor Cobham," p. 399.

9. Weisberg, *Women and the Law* 1:xi n. 1.

10. Ibid.

11. See, for example, Hanawalt's comments in "Women before the Law"; she points out that women, who were ordinarily charged with providing their families' clothing, food, and household items, usually stole goods related to that function when they committed criminal acts. "The modern ascriptions of the roles of chief perpetrators of infanticide and stealthy deaths through poisoning of spouses are not borne out by the records. Rather, women were more likely to be the victims" (p. 179).

12. See the useful article by Kittel, "Rape in Thirteenth-Century England."

13. Carter, "Rape and Medieval English Society," pp. 60–61. It is possible to question the author's interpretation of several points of procedure without rejecting his conclusions.

14. Hoffer and Hull, *Murdering Mothers.*

15. For an analysis of an earlier period, when women's right to inherit land was not settled, see Milsom's "Inheritance by Women."

16. Donahue, "What Causes Fundamental Legal Ideas?"

17. Jack Goody's essay "Inheritance, Property, and Women," which appears with Howell's essay in the same collection, touches on medieval England, although it has a wider focus.

18. Pollock and Maitland, *History of English Law* 2:364–436; see also the subsection entitled "Women" (1:482–85), which immediately follows subsections on excommunicates, lepers, lunatics, and idiots, the point being that medieval women were not "normal persons . . . free and lawful men" (p. 482), and which ends by cautioning that everything there said applies only to spinsters and widows (p. 485). For a comparative study, contemporary with the *History of English Law,* of the law of marriage, see Bryce's "Marriage and Divorce under Roman and English Law."

19. As an example, see Painter, "Family and the Feudal System."

20. Sylvia Thrupp's classic study *The Merchant Class of Medieval London, 1300–1500* does not focus on women, but in addition to comments on girls and women in various capacities, there is the useful section "The Woman's Role" (pp. 169–74). Marian K. Dale's article, "The London Silkwomen of the Fifteenth Century," uses chancery proceedings, wills, deeds, the *Rotuli Parliamentorum,* the plea and memoranda rolls, and other original sources and would be immeasurably useful to anyone interested in women artisans and traders. Very

recently, there has been some new work begun in this area; for examples, see above, n. 4.

21. See Bennett's "Medieval Peasant Marriages" and her "Ties That Bind."
22. Duggan, "Equity and Compassion in Papal Decretals," p. 87.
23. Palmer, "Contexts of Marriage," pp. 42–43.
24. Rushton, "Women, Witchcraft, and Slander," p. 131.
25. See above, n. 20. See also Power, *Medieval Women.*
26. Hilton, "Women Traders in Medieval England," p. 153.
27. Bennett, "Village Ale-Wife," p. 28.
28. Hutton, "Women in Fourteenth-Century Shrewsbury," pp. 85–87.
29. Kowaleski, "Women's Work," p. 147.

BIBLIOGRAPHY

The following is a working bibliography—it doubtless omits through oversight works that it should include, and it probably omits by choice materials that another compiler would have included. Only a few entries deal with the period after 1500; the exceptions are surveys that include the Middle Ages, studies centered in a later period but reflecting or referring to medieval practices or problems, and articles that are the only treatment of a topic relevant to medieval women's legal history. A number of bibliographies dealing with women or with legal history exist; some especially useful ones are listed below.

Abrams, Annie. "Women Traders in Medieval London." *Economic Journal* 26 (1916): 276–85.

Archer, Rowena. "Rich Old Ladies: The Problem of Late Medieval Dowagers." In *Property and Politics: Essays in Later Medieval History,* ed. A. J. Pollard, pp. 15–35. New York, 1984.

Arnold, Morris S., Thomas A. Green, Sally A. Scully, and Stephen D. White, eds. *On the Laws and Customs of England: Essays in Honor of Samuel E. Thorne.* Chapel Hill, N.C., 1981.

Bailey, S. J. "The Countess Gundred's Lands." *Cambridge Law Journal* 10 (1948): 84–103.

Baron and Feme: A Treatise of Law and Equity, concerning Husbands and Wives. London, 1700.

Bennett, Judith M. "Medieval Peasant Marriages: An Examination of Marriage License Fines in the *Liber Gersumarum*," In *Pathways to Medieval Peasants,* ed. J. A. Raftis, pp. 193–246. Toronto, 1981.

————. "The Tie That Binds: Peasant Marriage and Families in Late Medieval England." *Journal of Interdisciplinary History* 15 (1984): 111–29.

————. "The Village Ale-Wife: Women and Brewing in Fourteenth-Century England." In *Women and Work in Preindustrial Europe,* ed. Barbara A. Hanawalt, pp. 20–36. Bloomington, Ind., 1986.

————. *Women in the Medieval English Countryside: Gender and Household in Brigstock before the Plague.* New York, 1987.

Binchy, Daniel A. "The Legal Capacity of Irish Women in Regard to Contracts." In Binchy, *Studies in Early Irish Law,* pp. 207–34.

————, ed. *Studies in Early Irish Law.* Dublin, 1936.

Brand, Paul A., and Paul R. Hyams. "Seigneurial Control of Women's Marriage." *Past and Present* 99 (1983): 123–33.

Brook, Christopher N. L. "Aspects of Marriage Law in the Eleventh and Twelfth Centuries." In *Proceedings of the Fifth International Congress of Medieval Canon Law,* ed. Stephan Kuttner and Kenneth Pennington, pp. 333–44. Vatican City, 1980.

Brundage, James. "Concubinage and Marriage in Medieval Canon Law." *Journal of Medieval History* 1 (1975): 1–17.

Bryce, James. "Marriage and Divorce under Roman and English Law." In *Studies in History and Jurisprudence,* 2:782–859. New York, 1901.

Buckstaff, Florence Griswold. "Married Woman's Property in Anglo-Norman Law and Origins of the Common Law Dower." *Annals of the American Academy of Political and Social Science* 4 (1894): 233–64.

Carter, John M. "Rape and Medieval English Society: The Evidence of Yorkshire, Wiltshire, and London, 1218–1276." *Comitatus* 13 (1982): 33–63.

————. *Rape in Medieval England: An Historical and Sociological Study.* Lanham, Md., 1985.

Chapman, Annie Beatrice Wallis, and Mary Wallis Chapman. *The Status of Women under the English Law.* New York, 1909.

Charles, Lindsay, and Lorna Duffin, eds. *Women and Work in Preindustrial England.* London, 1985.

Cioni, Maria. "The Elizabethan Chancery and Women's Rights." In *Tudor Rule and Revolution: Essays for G. R. Elton from His American Friends,* ed. DeLloyd J. Guth and John W. McKenna, pp. 159–82. Cambridge, 1982.

Clark, Elaine. "Some Aspects of Social Security in Medieval England." *Journal of Family History* 7 (1982): 307–20.

Cleveland, Arthur Rackman. *Women under the English Law from the Time of the Saxons to the Present Time.* London, 1896.

Cooper, J. P. "Patterns of Inheritance and Settlement by Great Landowners from the Fifteenth to the Eighteenth Centuries." In Goody, Thirsk, and Thompson, *Family and Inheritance,* pp. 192–237.

Crofts, Maud Isabel, ed. *Women under English Law.* London, 1928.

Crump, C. G., and E. F. Jacob, eds. *The Legacy of the Middle Ages.* Oxford, 1926.

Dale, Marian K. "London Silkwomen of the Fifteenth Century." *Economic History Review,* 1st ser. 4 (1933): 324–35.

Davies, R. R. "The Status of Women and the Practice of Marriage in Late Medieval Wales." In Jenkins and Owen, *The Welsh Law of Women,* pp. 93–114.

Diefendorf, Barbara. "Widowhood and Remarriage in Sixteenth-Century Paris."

Journal of Family History 7 (1982): 379–95. This article is included because it is a model of the kind of examination useful for England at an earlier period.

Dillon, Myles. "The Relationship of Mother and Son, of Father and Daughter, and the Law of Inheritance with Regard to Women." In Binchy, *Studies in Early Irish Law*, pp. 129–79.

Donahue, Charles, Jr. "The Canon Law on the Formation of Marriage and Social Practice in the Later Middle Ages." *Journal of Family History* 8 (1983): 144–58.

———. "Lyndwood's Gloss *propriarum uxorum:* Marital Property and the Ius Commune in Fifteenth-Century England." In *Europäisches Rechtsdenken in Geschichte und Gegenwart,* ed. N. Horn, pp. 19–37. Munich, 1982.

———. "What Causes Fundamental Legal Ideas?: Marital Property in England and France in the Thirteenth Century." *Michigan Law Review* 78 (1979): 59–88.

Duggan, Charles. "Equity and Compassion in Papal Marriage Decretals to England." In *Love and Marriage in the Twelfth Century,* ed. Willy van Hoecke and Andries Welenhuysen, pp. 59–87. Louvain, 1981.

Engdahl, David. "English Marriage Conflicts before the Time of Bracton." *American Journal of Comparative Law* 15 (1966–67): 109–35.

Faith, Rosamond Jane. "Peasant Families and Inheritance Customs in Medieval England." *Agricultural History Review* 14 (1966): 77–95.

Fell, Christine, with Cecily Clark and Elizabeth Williams. *Women in Anglo-Saxon England and the Impact of 1066.* Bloomington, Ind., 1984.

Fox, Vivian C., and Martin H. Quitt. *Loving, Parenting, and Dying: The Family Cycle in England and America, Past and Present.* New York, 1980.

Frey, Linda, Marsha Frey, and Joanne Schneider, eds. *Women in Western European History: A Select Chronological, Geographical, and Topographical Bibliography from Antiquity to the French Revolution.* Westport, Conn., 1982.

Garay, Kathleen E. "Women and Crime in Later Medieval England: An Examination of the Evidence of the Courts of Gaol Delivery, 1388 to 1409." *Florilegium* 1 (1979): 87–109.

Goody, Jack. "Inheritance, Property, and Women: Some Comparative Considerations." In Goody, Thirsk, and Thompson, *Family and Inheritance,* pp. 10–36.

———. "Marriage Prestations, Inheritance, and Descent in Preindustrial Societies." *Journal of Comparative Family Studies* 1 (1970): 37–54.

Goody, Jack, Joan Thirsk, and E. P. Thompson, eds. *Family and Inheritance: Rural Society in Western Europe, 1200–1800.* Cambridge, 1976.

Griffiths, Ralph A. "The Trial of Eleanor Cobham: An Episode in the Fall of Duke Humphrey of Gloucester." *Bulletin of the John Rylands Library* 51 (1969): 381–99.

Hanawalt, Barbara A. "The Female Felon in Fourteenth-Century England." In

Women in Medieval Society, ed. Susan Mosher Stuard, pp. 125–40. Philadelphia, 1976.

───. "Seeking the Flesh and Blood of Manorial Families." *Journal of Medieval
History* 14 (1988): 33–45.

───. *The Ties That Bound: Peasant Families in Medieval England.* New York,
1986.

───. "Widowhood in Medieval English Villages." Paper presented at the
Fifth Berkshire Conference on the History of Women, 1981.

───. "Women before the Law: Females as Felon and Prey in Fourteenth-
Century England." In Weisberg, *Women and the Law* 1:165–95.

───, ed. *Women and Work in Preindustrial Europe.* Bloomington, Ind., 1986.

Haskins, George. "The Development of Common Law Dower." *Harvard Law
Review* 62 (1948): 42–55.

Helmholz, Richard H. "Bastardy Litigation in Medieval England." *American
Journal of Legal History* 13 (1969): 360–83.

───. "Infanticide in the Province of Canterbury during the Fifteenth Century." *History of Childhood Quarterly* 2 (1975): 379–90.

───. *Marriage Litigation in Medieval England.* Cambridge, 1974.

Hilton, Rodney H. "Women Traders in Medieval England." *Women's Studies* 6
(1984): 139–55.

Hines, William. "Bibliography on British and Irish Legal History." *Cambrian
Law Review* 14 (1983): 98–106.

───. "Bibliography on British and Irish Legal History." *Cambrian Law Review* 17 (1986): 94–100.

Hoffer, Peter C., and N. E. H. Hull. *Murdering Mothers: Infanticide in England
and New England, 1558–1803.* New York, 1981.

Hogrefe, Pearl. "Legal Rights of Tudor Women and Their Circumvention."
Sixteenth-Century Journal 3 (1972): 97–105.

Houlbrooke, Ralph. "The Making of Marriage in Mid-Tudor England: Evidence
from the Records of Matrimonial Contract Litigation." *Journal of Family
History* 10 (1985): 339–52.

Howell, Cicely. "Peasant Inheritance Customs in the Midlands, 1280–1700." In
Goody, Thirsk, and Thompson, *Family and Inheritance,* pp. 112–55.

Howell, Margaret. "The Resources of Eleanor of Provence as Queen Consort."
English Historical Review 102 (1987): 372–93.

Hutton, Diane. "Women in Fourteenth-Century Shrewsbury." In *Women and
Work in Preindustrial England,* ed. Lindsay Charles and Lorna Duffin, pp.
83–99. London, 1985.

Ingram, Martin. "Spousals Litigation in the English Ecclesiastical Courts
c. 1350–c. 1640." In *Marriage and Society: Studies in the Social History of
Marriage,* ed. R. B. Outhwaite, pp. 35–57. New York, 1982.

Ives, E. W. " 'Agaynst the Taking Away of Women': The Inception and Operation of the Abduction Act of 1487." In *Wealth and Power in Tudor England: Essays Presented to S. T. Bindoff,* ed. Eric Ives, R. J. Knecht, and J. J. Scarisbrick, pp. 21–44. London, 1978.

Jenkins, Dafydd. "Property Interests in the Classical Welsh Law of Women." In Jenkins and Owen, *The Welsh Law of Women,* pp. 69–92.

Jenkins, Dafydd, and Morfydd E. Owen, eds. *The Welsh Law of Women.* Cardiff, 1980.

Joüon des Longrais, Frédéric. *La Conception anglaise de la saisine du XIIe au XIVe siècle.* 1924. Reprint. Ann Arbor, Mich., 1963 (microfilm).

———. "Le Statut de la femme en Angleterre." In *La Femme: Receuils de la Société Jean Bodin* 12 (1962): 135–241.

Kanner, Barbara. *The Women of England from Anglo-Saxon Times to the Present.* Hamden, Conn., 1979.

Kellum, Barbara A. "Infanticide in England in the Later Middle Ages." *History of Childhood Quarterly* 1 (1974): 367–88.

Kenny, Courtney Stanhope. *The History of the Law of England as to the Effects of Marriage on Property and on the Wife's Legal Capacity.* London, 1879.

Kittel, Margaret Ruth. "Married Women in Thirteenth-Century England: A Study in Common Law." Ph.D. diss., University of California, Berkeley, 1973. This dissertation is not available from University Microfilms, and I have not seen it.

Kittel, Ruth. "Rape in Thirteenth-Century England: A Study of the Common-Law Courts." In Weisberg, *Women and the Law* 2:101–15.

———. "Women under the Law in Medieval England, 1066–1485." In *The Women of England from Anglo-Saxon Times to the Present,* ed. Barbara Kanner, pp. 124–37. Hamden, Conn., 1979.

Klinck, Anne Lingard. "Anglo-Saxon Women and the Law." *Journal of Medieval History* 7 (1982): 107–21.

Kowaleski, Maryanne. "The History of Urban Families in Medieval England." *Journal of Medieval History* 14 (1988): 47–63.

———. "Women's Work in a Market Town: Exeter in the Late Fourteenth Century." In *Women and Work in Preindustrial Europe,* ed. Barbara A. Hanawalt, pp. 145–64. Bloomington, Ind., 1986.

Lacey, Kay E. "Women and Work in Fourteenth- and Fifteenth-Century London." In *Women and Work in Preindustrial England,* ed. Lindsay Charles and Lorna Duffin, pp. 24–82. London, 1985.

The Lawes Resolutions of Women's Rights; or, The Lawes Provision for Women. London, 1632.

Leedom, Joe W. "Lady Matilda Holland, Henry of Lancaster, and the Manor of Melbourne." *American Journal of Legal History* 31 (1987): 118–25.

Loengard, Janet S. "'Of the Gift of Her Husband': English Dower in the Year 1200." In *Women of the Medieval World,* ed. Julius Kirshner and Suzanne Wemple, pp. 215–55. Oxford, 1985.

Maitland, Frederic William. "Why the History of English Law Is Not Written." In *The Collected Papers of Frederic William Maitland*, ed. H. A. L. Fisher, 1:480–97. 1911. Reprint. Buffalo, N.Y., 1981.

Mansfield, Edward D. *The Legal Rights, Liabilities, and Duties of Women, with an Introductory History of Their Legal Conditions in the Hebrew, Roman, and Feudal Systems*. Salem, Ohio, 1845.

Mason, Emma. "Maritagium and the Changing Law." *Bulletin of the Institute of Historical Research* 49 (1976): 286–89.

Meyer, Marc Anthony. "Land Charters and the Legal Position of Anglo-Saxon Women." In *The Women of England from Anglo-Saxon Times to the Present*, ed. Barbara Kanner, pp. 57–82. Hamden, Conn., 1979.

Milsom, S. F. C. "Inheritance by Women in the Twelfth and Early Thirteenth Centuries." In *On the Laws and Customs of England: Essays in Honor of Samuel E. Thorne*, ed. Morris S. Arnold, Thomas A. Green, Sally A. Scully, and Stephen D. White, pp. 60–89. Chapel Hill, N.C., 1981.

Mulchrone, Kathleen. "The Rights and Duties of Women with Regard to the Education of Their Children." In Binchy, *Studies in Early Irish Law*, pp. 187–206.

Noonan, John T. "Marriage in the Middle Ages: Power to Choose." *Viator* 4 (1973): 419–34.

Ostrogorskii, Moisei Iakovlevich. *The Rights of Women: A Comparative Study in History and Legislation*. New York, 1893.

Owen, Morfydd E. "Shame and Reparation: Women's Place in the Kin." In Jenkins and Owen, *The Welsh Law of Women*, pp. 40–68.

Painter, Sidney. "The Family and the Feudal System in Twelfth-Century England." *Speculum* 35 (1960): 1–16.

Palmer, Robert C. "Contexts of Marriage in Medieval England: Evidence from the King's Court circa 1300." *Speculum* 59 (1984): 42–67.

Pollock, Sir Frederick, and Frederic W. Maitland. *The History of English Law before the Time of Edward I*. 2 vols. 2d ed. 1898. Reprint. Cambridge, Engl., 1968.

Post, J. B. "Ravishment of Women and the Statutes of Westminster." In *Legal Records and the Historian*, ed. John Baker, pp. 150–64. London, 1978.

Power, Eileen. *Medieval Women*. Ed. M. M. Postan. Cambridge, 1975.

———. "The Position of Women." In *The Legacy of the Middle Ages*, ed. C. G. Crump and E. F. Jacob, pp. 401–33. Oxford, 1926.

Rivers, Theodore John. "Widows' Rights in Anglo-Saxon Law." *American Journal of Legal History* 19 (1975): 208–15. (Reprinted in Weisberg, *Women and the Law* 2:35–43.)

Robinson, O. F. "Canon Law and Marriage." *Juridical Review* (1984): 22–40.

Rosenthal, Joel T. "Aristocratic Widows in Fifteenth-Century England." In *Women and the Structure of Society*, ed. Barbara J. Harris and Jo Ann K. McNamara, pp. 36–47. Durham, N.C., 1984.

Rushton, Peter. "Women, Witchcraft, and Slander in Early Modern England, 1560–1675." *Northern History* 18 (1982): 116–32.

Scammell, Jean. "Freedom and Marriage in Medieval England." *Economic History Review,* 2d ser., 27 (1974): 523–37.

———. "Wife Rents and Merchet." *Economic History Review,* 2d ser., 29 (1976): 487–90.

Searle, Eleanor. "Freedom and Marriage in Medieval England: An Alternative Hypothesis." *Economic History Review,* 2d ser., 29 (1976): 482–86.

———. "Merchet and Women's Property Rights in Medieval England." In Weisberg, *Women and the Law* 2:45–68.

———. "Women and the Legitimization of Succession at the Norman Conquest." In *Proceedings of the Battle Conference on Anglo-Norman Studies 3, 1980,* ed. R. Allen Brown, pp. 159–70. Woodbridge, Engl., 1981.

Shahar, Shulamith. *The Fourth Estate: A History of Women in the Middle Ages.* London, 1983.

Sharpe, J. A. "Domestic Homicide in Early Modern England." *Historical Journal* 24 (1981): 29–48.

Sheehan, Michael M. "English Wills and the Records of the Ecclesiastical and Civil Jurisdictions." *Journal of Medieval History* 14 (1988): 3–12.

———. "The Formation and Stability of Marriage in Fourteenth-Century England: The Evidence of an Ely Register." *Mediaeval Studies* 32 (1971): 228–63.

———. "The Influence of Canon Law on the Property Rights of Married Women in England." *Mediaeval Studies* 25 (1963): 109–24.

———. "The Wife of Bath and Her Four Sisters: Reflections on a Woman's Life in the Age of Chaucer." *Medievalia et Humanistica,* n.s., 13 (1985): 23–42.

Sheehan, Michael M., ed., with Kathy D. Scardellato. *Family and Marriage in Medieval Europe: A Working Bibliography.* Vancouver, 1976.

Sheringham, J. G. T. "Bullocks with Horns As Long As Their Ears." *Bulletin of the Board of Celtic Studies* 29 (1982): 697–708.

Simms, Katherine. "The Legal Position of Irishwomen in the Later Middle Ages." *Irish Jurist,* n.s., 10 (1975): 96–111.

Smith, J. Beverley. "Dower in Thirteenth-Century Wales: A Grant of the Commote of Anhuniog, 1273." *Bulletin of the Board of Celtic Studies* 30 (1983): 348–55.

Smith, R. M. "Kin and Neighbors in a Thirteenth-Century Suffolk Community." *Journal of Family History* 4 (1979): 219–56.

———. "Some Thoughts on 'Hereditary' and 'Proprietary' Rights in Land under Customary Law in Thirteenth- and Early-Fourteenth-Century England." *Law and History Review* 1 (1983): 95–128.

Spring, Eileen. "Law and the Theory of the Affective Family." *Albion* 16 (1984): 1–20.

Stenton, Lady Doris Mary. *The Englishwoman in History*. 1957. Reprint (with new introduction by Louise A. Tilly). New York, 1977.

Stopes, Charlotte Carmichael. *British Freewomen: Their Historical Privileges in Common Law and Equity*. London, 1894.

Stuard, Susan Mosher, ed. *Women in Medieval Society*. Philadelphia, 1976.

Thompson, E. P. "The Grid of Inheritance: A Comment." In Goody, Thirsk, and Thompson, *Family and Inheritance*, pp. 328–60.

Thrupp, Sylvia. *The Merchant Class of Medieval London, 1300–1500*. Chicago, 1948.

Thurneysen, Rudolf. "Heirat." In Binchy, *Studies in Early Irish Law*, pp. 109–28.

Todd, Barbara. "The Remarrying Widow: A Stereotype Reconsidered." In *Women in English Society, 1500–1800*, ed. Mary Prior, pp. 54–92. New York, 1985.

Walker, Sue Sheridan. "Common Law Juries and Feudal Marriage Customs in Medieval England: The Pleas of Ravishment." *University of Illinois Law Review* 3 (1984): 601–14.

———. "Feudal Constraint and Free Consent in the Making of Marriages in Medieval England: Widows in the King's Gift." In *Historical Papers: A Selection from the Papers Presented at the Annual Meeting [of the Canadian Historical Association] Held at Saskatoon, 1979*, ed. Terry Cook and Claudette Laceke, pp. 97–109.

———. "The Feudal Family and the Common Law Courts: The Pleas Protecting Rights of Wardship and Marriage, c. 1225–1375." *Journal of Medieval History* 14 (1988): 13–31.

———. "Free Consent and Marriage of Feudal Wards in Medieval England." *Journal of Medieval History* 8 (1982): 123–34.

———. "The Marrying of Feudal Wards in Medieval England." *Studies in Medieval Culture* 4 (1974): 209–24.

———. "Punishing Convicted Ravishers: Statutory Strictures and Actual Practice in Thirteenth- and Fourteenth-Century England." *Journal of Medieval History* 13 (1987): 237–50.

———. "Widow and Ward: The Feudal Law of Child Custody in Medieval England." In *Women in Medieval Society*, ed. Susan Mosher Stuard, pp. 159–72. Philadelphia, 1976. (Also published in *Feminist Studies* 3 [1976]: 104–16.)

Walters, D. B. "The European Legal Context of the Welsh Law of Matrimonial Property." In Jenkins and Owen, *The Welsh Law of Women*, pp. 115–31.

Waugh, Scott L. "Marriage, Class, and Royal Lordship in England under Henry III." *Viator* 16 (1985): 181–207.

Weisberg, D. Kelly, ed. *Women and the Law: The Social Historical Perspective*. 2 vols. Cambridge, Mass., 1982.

Westman, Barbara H[anawalt]. "The Peasant Family and Crime in Fourteenth-

Century England." *Journal of British Studies* 13 (1974): 1–18.

Wright, Thomas. *A Contemporary Narrative of the Proceedings against Dame Alice Kyteler, Prosecuted for Sorcery in 1324, by Richard Ledrede, Bishop of Ossory.* London, 1843.

Wrightson, Keith. "Infanticide in European History." *Criminal Justice History: An International Annual* 3 (1982): 1–20.

Young, Ernest. "Anglo-Saxon Family Law." In *Essays in Anglo-Saxon Law,* ed. Henry Adams, pp. 121–82. 1876. Reprint. South Hackensack, N.J., 1972.

DE QUIBUSDAM MULIERIBUS

Reading Women's History from Hostile Sources

Jo Ann McNamara

n the thirteenth century, the articulated structures of the medieval church became increasingly inaccessible to religious women. Convents were overcrowded and expensive to enter. They frequently lacked the protection of the privileged orders, whose directors found the *cura monialium* to be a thankless burden. Orders for women were rare and greatly handicapped by their dependence upon male agents for both secular and spiritual services. Monastic women were burdened with the disadvantages of autonomy in an ever more efficiently organized world. Religious women outside of convents were exposed to the distrust and persecution of the isolated in an ever more orthodox world. In northern Europe, many of them found shelter among the beguines, a group with sufficient cohesion and prestige to merit being called "a woman's movement" by modern historians.[1] Under the protection of philogynous clergymen, monks, and friars, their reformist sentiments and enthusiasm for liturgical innovation were delicately steered into orthodox channels to avoid the shoals of anticlericalism and heresy that always threatened the spiritual creativity of women. Their ideas and achievements are retained for us in a body of friendly sources that preserve their individual contributions to a complex spiritual fabric.[2] Assuredly, this was a woman's movement, but its success depended upon the imprimatur of male orthodoxy. ❡ In southern France and northern Italy, the arc between Avignon and Rome, misogyny was easily reinforced by fear of heresy. Avoidance of women was practically a measure of sanctity. Saint Francis himself became increasingly unwilling to associate with women and even with Saint Clare, despite her lonely battle to adhere to his teachings. Saint Louis of Anjou, bishop of Toulouse, shunned even the saintly women of his own family.[3] In the Dominican provinces of Rome and Provence, repeated statutes warned against the dangers of hearing the confessions of women, particularly nuns and beguines. Women anxious to carry out an orthodox and carefully directed religious life were therefore apt to find that clerical fear of women was fueled even by their desire for frequent sacraments. [4]

Nor could there be any question of symmetrical segregation. Women inclined to flee from men found no ready refuge within the bounds of orthodoxy. The beguines and other pious women of the south enjoyed little official approval or supervision. Their foundress, Douceline de Digne, began with a dream vision of three women, dressed in the beguine habits of the north, who offered her a veil like their own. [5] In addition, she adopted the Franciscan cord, as though she were a tertiary. Her biographer and associate, Philippine de Porcelet, suggested that she invented their life-style as she went along and that she was guided in visions by the example of the Virgin Mary, whom she called the first beguine. She told her followers, "You are gathered here together for love of Christ and are bound together in his love. All other holy orders are strictly bound by their rules, but you are bound by love alone." [6] She imposed vows of poverty and chastity on a pair of small communities and acted as their prioress with no apparent outside intervention. Her public preaching included discussions of the Trinity as well as praise of poverty. Philippine claimed that the "masters of Paris" declared that they could command no better understanding of those mysteries than the one she displayed. [7]

When Douceline de Digne died in 1274, her burial was conducted amid scenes of hysterical popular devotion. Her cult was promoted by such prominent people as Charles of Anjou, whose wife she had cured during a difficult pregnancy. [8] But her followers were not an order and found few friends within the clerical hierarchy to shape and interpret their religious activities within an orthodox context. In the year of her death, the Council of Lyons prohibited the founding of new orders without papal authorization, signaling a sterner view of unauthorized groups committed to the ideal of strict poverty and the prophetic anticlerical sentiments of Joachim of Flora. Nevertheless, for the next two decades, the beguine movement spread and flourished in the south as in the north. It clearly answered a need among women for an independent expression of their own religious creativity.

The "woman's movement" of the south, if we can call it that, did not find its friends among bishops or even among monks of settled orthodoxy. It found its place among the enthusiasts drawn to evangelical poverty and the ideal of a new age when the church of Christ would be superseded by the church of the Holy Spirit. In the last decade of the thirteenth century, their hopes centered on Peter of Murrone, a wonder-working hermit from the Abruzzi. In 1294, he was elected to the papacy as Celestine V by a reduced college of cardinals caught up in an unprecedented surge of emotional religiosity.[9] Six months later, he resigned, and the spiritual climate changed drastically. The skeptical men who ruled the church became justifiably distrustful of the otherworldly commitments of his devotees.

Because of this shift, certain women were subjected to the shocks of changing male standards of orthodoxy. Behavior that was saintly or at least devout in the friendly sources of the thirteenth century became heretical or at least anticlerical in the hostile sources of the fourteenth century. Admittedly, the strife over evangelical poverty, which developed between the papacy and the Franciscan order in the aftermath of Celestine V's brief pontificate, was a quarrel among men. Nevertheless, women were attracted to the ideal, and as early as 1297, Boniface VIII condemned the preaching of women who adopted habits of their own design and deceived simple souls with errors as intolerable as their sexual immorality.[10] At the Council of Vienne in 1311, Clement V condemned "certain women commonly called beguines who, although they promise no one obedience and neither renounce property nor live in accordance with an approved rule . . . wear a so-called beguine habit and cling to certain religious to whom they are drawn by special preference." The pope claimed that "as if possessed with madness, they dispute and preach about the Highest Trinity and divine essence and spread opinions in respect to articles of faith and the sacraments of the church contradictory to the Catholic faith, deceiving many simple folk and leading them into various errors."[11]

Who were these "certain women"? Did they constitute a woman's movement of the south? Can we write a history for which there were no historians, from records that resist the project? There were women there who attempted to be the center of their own lives and even to draw others around them. But our sources reveal them only on the fringes of religious movements dominated by others. Their histories are fractured by hostile sources. This is the history we were all trained not to write: a history in confrontation with our sources rather than in conformity with them. In this paper, I want to experiment with the matching of two rather disparate voices whose experiences frame the years when the women's movement of the south may have tried and failed to enter the mainstream of religious experience. The northern beguines became sanctified by their sources and accordingly centered and unified as well.

The southern women were split apart and isolated. Two of them, at least, speak in their own voices. One was Catania, wife of Johannes Riczardi of Sulmona in the Abruzzi, who testified in support of the canonization of Celestine V in 1306. The other was Na Prous Boneta of Montpellier in Provence, who testified about her own belief and her devotion to Peter John Olivi before the Inquisition of Carcassonne in 1325.[12] Their textual worlds are far apart. Yet, I am persuaded, they lived in the same world, spoke the same spiritual language, and may help to illuminate one another and the female religious milieu of their age by a cross-textual comparison aimed at dissolving the structural patterns that separated them.

Catania and Prous lived on opposite sides of the Alps, and both came from respectable and reasonably prosperous urban milieus whose inhabitants claimed the courtesy of calling one another "lady." Their homelands were linked by the political interests of the Angevin family. They were part of a spiritual network devoted to evangelical poverty and a dream that an age of renewal was about to begin. We have much evidence concerning the transalpine connections of the men who spoke of the movement in books, preaching, and institutions. We know how they were shaken by the traumatic experience of Celestine V's brief pontificate. Since the men had little regard for the adherence of women, the sources effectively obliterate any of the women's connections that may have reached across the Alps. We can only suppose that they had their ears and eyes open and were at least aware of what was happening among the men.

Catania was forty years old in 1306, when she came to testify to the apostolic inquisitors appointed by Clement V to gather evidence on Peter's claims to canonization.[13] The investigators were working unwillingly. Clement V had appointed them only under unrelenting pressure from the king of France, who made no secret of the fact that he linked Celestine's canonization with charges that Boniface VIII was a heretic who had criminally usurped the papacy and perhaps even murdered his predecessor. Catania's tale of her miraculous cure in 1291 and her long career as a promoter of Peter's cult therefore spanned many years and potentially touched on many dangerous sentiments.

Catania spoke in dialect, the Italian of the Abruzzi. Rendered into Latin and rudely sculpted to the formal methods of the process, her tale nevertheless still bears the stamp of an energetic and enterprising religious personality proudly acting as the self-appointed apostle of a man whom many theologians and prelates had associated with the coming age of the Holy Spirit. She was determined to memorialize the devotion and marvels of her life. The investigators humored her by recording some of the things she did. They stopped her whenever she might have told them what she believed. They were suspicious even of the publicly witnessed miracle she claimed to have experienced. They were reluctant to explore the nature of the popular piety that had attached itself to Brother Peter, and perhaps they feared that their inquiry would take a dangerous turn. The record is full of deletions, and the margins contain caustic remarks that reflect the scorn of the inquisitors for their witnesses. In fact, the corroborating testimony of her uncle was partially torn out of the manuscript along with that of another witness who may have been involved in the same incident. The bull proclaiming the canonization of Celestine V states only that a nameless blind woman had been cured.

Prous also focused her religious life on the cult of a local holy man, Peter John Olivi, a French Franciscan whose writing on poverty and on the Apocalypse came under attack in 1285. His prudent superior sent him to Italy, where he may have been instrumental in the development of a spiritual Franciscan movement.[14] The suspicions about his orthodoxy came to nothing in his lifetime, and Olivi, like Celestine, remained a strong candidate for sainthood for some years after his death in 1298. His tomb became the center of a local cult promoted particularly by the same beguines who attracted the enmity of Clement V a dozen years later.[15] Even as late as 1325, when Prous Boneta maintained that she had wondrously conceived the Holy Spirit while standing on his grave, she may have believed that association with Olivi could be of some protection to her.

The notary who recorded her confession states that she was not tortured. Nevertheless, some violence was done to her testimony to make it suitable for the needs of her inquisitors. It is written in Latin, with an occasional phrase in the French dialect that Prous actually spoke.[16] The inquisitors interrupted her with questions and probably suggestions of various sorts intended to point up the heretical nature of her thought. She confessed that she was the bearer of the Holy Spirit and was destined to suffer persecution and death to redeem humanity anew because the grace of Christ had been lost through the sins of John XXII, as Adam lost the original grace of paradise. Prous refused to retract any of her ideas and was finally handed over to the secular arm and presumably executed.[17]

Though both Catania and Prous focused their faith on charismatic men, neither received guidance or support from her mentor. Both men were decisively unattainable. Peter spoke to Catania only in her dreams. She could listen to his sermons because he was unable to keep her away. She could make of them what she wanted and fill in the rest from her imagination. In real life, the testimony seems to indicate, Peter was more inclined to guide her husband than to guide Catania. Though the saint was widely known to have a strong aversion to women, even resisting their attendance at his sermons, numerous women testified to having gained health through his intercession, and they made up a good proportion of the following we glimpse in the process.[18] Catania told the examiners that she had seen Peter living in many places around the small villages of Santo Spiritus and Orfento and implied that she was often present with the people of Sulmona who "happened upon him at his devotions." In his autobiography, Peter described his vain efforts to flee from their attentions to more inaccessible sites in the mountains.[19] Yet one witness said that thousands of people, many of them decrepit, aged, and diseased, climbed the mountains daily in search of him.[20] From the saint's point of view, therefore, the devout Catania must have been one of those persistent pests who always managed to spy out his presence and lead unwelcome crowds to his hiding place.

Olivi and the French friars grouped around him were somewhat more receptive to teaching and encouraging the devotion of women. But he died many years before Prous had her revelations concerning his apocalyptic mission. She read his writings, provided by a friar, Raymond Johm, who later got in trouble with the inquisition and mentioned his association with her in his testimony.[21] When she was twenty-five years old, she went as a pilgrim to stand on Olivi's grave, where she was enveloped with warmth and peace, as though a cloak had been wrapped around her. Nine months later a vision informed her that by their combined spirits, the Holy Spirit had been incarnated. Prous would be his avatar until her passion and death should redeem the world anew.

It may have been their very inaccessibility that made these men attractive instruments to our heroines. Though their histories are profoundly different in this respect, there is an element of troubled sexuality in both cases, which may have been soothed by devotion to unattainable spiritual guides. By the time she was twenty-five years old, Catania had been married for some years to the notary Johannes Riczardi, and the marriage appears to have been a suitable one socially, for her husband was of the same social class and group as her father. In all probability, if one assumes that they conformed to the Mediterranean marriage pattern discerned in the fifteenth century, he was some years older than she.[22] But Catania was unhappy. She claimed that her husband was an impious and dissolute man. Master Benedict, her father, confirmed it.

It is not clear whether or not her husband was still alive in 1306 or what their marital relations were like. Her father said offhandedly that her life had become more honest and healthy since her cure in 1291 but did not elaborate.[23] Neither she nor any other witness indicated that she had children. Her sister-in-law, Lady Gemma, testified that when Johannes brought her son to Peter to be cured, he thought the boy was the notary's son. This suggests that he thought they did have children, though he had never seen them, or that Catania and Johannes had never been associated with any other child. One is tempted to speculate that she may have been one of those women, such as Angela da Foligno (d. 1309), who regarded the normal life of marriage as a hindrance to her spiritual development. Catania spoke about her husband as though he had died after his conversion to a devout life, but her father spoke as though he were still alive.[24] It is possible that her illness and subsequent cure resulted in a life of mutual continence.

An unhappy marriage, possibly compounded by childlessness, brought Catania to a crisis when she was twenty-five years old. One day, when she was sewing with some of the neighboring women, she was overcome with dizziness and fainted. She heard their voices, as if from a great distance, asking her what was wrong and then realized that she was blind. One of the maids helped her home and told her that her left eye seemed larger than the right. According to the testimony of her father, a physician, she remained in this condition for nearly two weeks and responded to none of his efforts to cure her.[25] Fearing for her sanity, unable to take up any occupation, she dreamed that she saw Peter of Murrone in a church near Sulmona and that he promised to guide her in the right way, and she began to hope that he could cure her and introduce her to a new life.

Her husband was hostile to her repeated requests to be taken to the hermit. "He was unwilling to do it," she said, "for he scorned my devotion, being a man of dissolute life." Her persistence was finally rewarded, and her husband, with four of his friends, tied her to a horse and led her to Peter's retreat at Orfento. The meeting began badly. Master Johannes was offended by the hermit's refusal to see a woman and threatened to turn back on the instant rather than answer questions about his own life. Undaunted, the holy man began to preach, and at length he moved the notary's heart to such repentance that from that moment, Catania said, he abandoned his evil ways and lived a life of abstinence, fasting, and incessant devotion until the day of his death.

While Peter was thus occupied with her husband, Catania fell asleep and dreamed that Peter came to her through the crowd of men who surrounded him. He made the sign of the cross over her. It seemed to her then that she could see if only she could dispose of a weight she sensed on her eyes. But when she asked the visionary Peter for advice, he told her to resign herself and rest. The vision ended, and she woke to see her husband with a little cross that Brother Peter had sent out to her. She took it "with great devotion," signed herself with it from head to toe, and placed it on her eyes. Immediately she could see, and, when the hermit refused to see her to receive her thanks, she sent her husband back to him with expressions of lifelong devotion, begging that Peter give her instructions for the future pursuit of her life. Needless to say, Peter refused—as she must have known he would—and instructed her to return to Sulmona and to say nothing except that God had cured her. This last instruction was beyond Catania's power to obey. At the foot of the mountain she found ten or more boys to whom she made witness of her cure and return on foot from the mountain that she had scaled on horseback, unable to see her way. She added that the miracle was well known in Sulmona, and a procession of later witnesses bore her out. [26]

Like Catania, Prous was about twenty-five years old when the pressures of her life caused a spiritual crisis in around 1320. [27] Some years earlier, she and her sister had taken a vow of virginity and thereafter had lived in a common household with some other celibate women. There is no indication that any of them had the formal approval or backing of the local clergy, though the friars whom the Inquisition later questioned might then have been considered perfectly adequate advisors for them. In the late thirteenth century, anticlericalism was widespread in southern France and was not systematically punished by church officials. Carcassonne had been placed under interdict in 1298 for its resistance to inquisitorial authority. But outbreaks recurred in 1300 and 1303–4 under the leadership of Bernard Délicieux, who received a sympathetic hearing at the royal court for his complaints.

Prous was about sixteen years old in 1312, when the Council of Vienne met and published the bull canonizing Celestine V. *De quibusdam mulieribus* appeared at the same time. Though it was not fully promulgated until 1316, when John XXII determined to prosecute Celestine's faithful devotees, it cast a shadow of disapproval over the very groups who might have hoped to gain support after Celestine's canonization. The inquisitor, Bernard Gui, claimed that the heretical beguines practiced chastity in preparation for the apocalypse Olivi had predicted. The council, meanwhile, had renewed the attacks on Olivi's apocalyptic writings.[28] As part of his general attack on the anticlerical practitioners of evangelical poverty, John XXII forbade women to live under self-imposed vows of chastity as well as poverty. Thus Prous took her vows in an atmosphere that was already threatening serious danger for her and her friends. In 1317, the pope singled out the beguines of Maguelonne and Béziers. They were first interrogated by the inquisitors, and some of them were burned in Marseille. [29]

In 1325, Prous said that Jesus revealed to her that all her sins had been forgiven and her soul made immaculate when she took her vows of chastity. She passionately denied that the pope had the power to dispense anyone from such vows, let alone command that they be broken. She said that all women who had not taken vows of chastity would be condemned in the coming apocalyptic crisis and that the pope who had forced consecrated virgins to marry was the Antichrist. [30]

In 1320, Prous was worshipping in the Franciscan church in Montpellier when she had her first vision of Jesus, who opened his heart to her in a stream of golden light that seemed to enter into her and suffuse itself through her opened body.[31] In the days that followed, he revealed to her that he had entered into her as he had entered into the Virgin Mary, that she was chosen to become the bearer of the Holy Spirit as Mary had been chosen to bear the Son of God. Her miraculous conception of the divinity had occurred nine months earlier on Olivi's feast day, when Prous and other devotees had undertaken a pilgrimage to the site of his burial in Narbonne. While she stood on his tomb, she had been seized with an ecstasy so intense that she believed that ever since she and Olivi had been mystically joined together. She believed that she had spiritually given birth to the Holy Spirit on Good Friday 1321, though her "child" never separated itself from her but spoke from within her.

Prous was not always clear as to whether she herself was the Holy Spirit or, more likely, its mother. Neither claim, however, was as exotic as it appears when her testimony is isolated from the milieu in which she lived. The notion of the Holy Ghost as a female manifestation of God was not an entirely new idea, and it may have appealed to apocalyptic visionaries as the ultimate symbol of spiritual renewal against a church whose leaders were universally male.[32] The widely studied works of Joachim of Flora prophesied that the second age of world history, represented by the

Son of God and his church, was drawing to a close, soon to give way to the age of the Holy Spirit. In 1285, Olivi and his followers were accused of maintaining that in the age of the Holy Spirit the church, the clergy, and their sacraments would be rendered superfluous. Admirers of Celestine V called him the prophesied "angel pope" who would usher in the age of the Holy Ghost, when the world would no longer have need of the clergy or their sacraments.[33] Even the cardinals who elected him claimed that they had been spontaneously possessed by the Holy Spirit.[34] Joachitism came to be associated with Franciscans, but Joachim himself was a Cistercian abbot, and his order may have nurtured his ideas more discreetly than the highly publicized friars did. The Cistercians of Chiaravalle were promoting the sainthood of a Lombard woman, Guglielma, establishing a feast for her death in 1279 and translating her body to their cemetery with great ceremony in 1281.[35] Her claims appear to have been recognized as very strong at that time, though Guglielma has subsequently been claimed by hostile sources and is now known only from the testimony of her followers to the Inquisition in 1300 that she was the incarnation of the Holy Spirit.[36]

The Dominican chronicler of Colmar, where there was an important center of female adherents to the order, noted that in 1301 an English virgin arrived in the city saying that she was the Holy Spirit, incarnated for the salvation of women. He said that she baptized many in the names of the Father, Son, and herself.[37] He adds that after her death she was burned at the stake, which suggests that, like Guglielma, she escaped persecution during her lifetime. Both cases suggest that either the original preaching of the prophetesses was less clearly heretical than investigators and believers thought after 1300 or the atmosphere changed dramatically in the first decade of the fourteenth century.

This testimony may throw a new light on Bernard Gui's insensitive treatment of Margarita d'Arco, one of the leaders of a sect that the inquisitor dubbed the False Apostles. Margarita heard a friar, Dolcino, preach on a life of perfect liberty admitting of no constraint by priests or pope. Converted to his doctrine, she fled from her family against her father's will.[38] They gathered a following, accepting any applicant unconditionally, including, according to Gui, married men who did not have the consent of their wives.[39] The inquisitor tells us that the couple pretended to live together in complete chastity and honesty as a sister and brother in Christ until she became pregnant and declared that the Holy Spirit was responsible.[40] It is possible that Margarita was not really pregnant at all but maintained, as Prous did a few years later, that another spirit (Dolcino's or God's) had joined with hers when she became the avatar of the Holy Spirit. Bernard Gui said they claimed that all contemporary popes, with the single exception of Celestine V, were destined to be damned for deserting the true Christian path.[41] In 1306, while his investigators were in Sulmona taking Catania's testimony, Clement V ordered the inquisitors of Lombardy to preach a crusade against them, and the group withdrew into the mountains of Novara, where many perished from cold and hunger. About forty of the faithful remained at the end to see Margarita and then Dolcino cut into pieces.

Catania's reaction to all this, if any, was not recorded by her auditors, whose brief did not include the discovery of heresy among their witnesses. She did not make or was not allowed to make extravagant claims for herself, but she seems to have believed that her connection with the holy man entitled her to a quasi-priestly career of her own. Her apostolate occupied her from 1291 until 1306 and presumably continued until her death, whenever that occurred. She said that she had saved the cross blessed by the hermit and had cured many other blind people by placing it on their eyes. She also claimed that it had proved efficacious for a number of other afflictions. Presumably, she was prepared to go on at some length discussing these feats of her own, but the inquisitors silenced her and inserted in the manuscript a recommendation that they let the pope himself decide what to do with her deposition. Unabashed, Catania went on talking. She said that Brother Peter was accustomed to offering refreshments to his visitors and consequently had given her and her companions two loaves of bread, one round and the other long, and bade them eat. She said that although they had all eaten as much as they liked, they finished the meal with more bread than they had at the beginning. She had kept the wonderful bread, and after fifteen years it had not decayed. Again the commission discouraged her from continuing, and she was prevented from touching upon material that might have been construed as critical of the established sacramental system. The man she admired so much had spent too much of his life on the margin between sainthood and heresy to be a very safe subject for her devotion. According to his own autobiography, he never attended mass in his years as a hermit and resisted ordination until God himself commanded him to take the sacrament. When, after a chaotic six months in office, he renounced the papacy, he stated publicly that the office was incompatible with salvation.[42]

In the aftermath, in 1297, Olivi proclaimed the advent of the age of the Holy Spirit and called the new pope a "pseudopope."[43] This doubt cast

on the election of Boniface VIII was the probable cause of the crisis that
overshadowed certain women after 1300. Boniface himself connected the
preaching of women with immorality and heresy.[44] The Guglielmites
challenged the sacramental power of the archbishop of Milan (the same
prelate who promulgated the Crusade against Margarita and Dolcino)
because he had been appointed by the hated Boniface VIII.[45] Their leader,
a woman named Mayfreda, celebrated mass on Guglielma's grave and
proclaimed herself the first pope of the Holy Spirit. [46]

Despite her apparent attachment to the cult of the burned beguines,
Prous had not deserted the regular Catholic observances before 1320.
Jesus first came to her when she was at mass. But the shock of Olivi's
condemnation in 1312 must have been germinating in her soul for many
years. The inquisitors assumed that she knew and condemned the burning of 1318. The condemnation of Olivi's work in 1319, followed by the
destruction of his grave in 1320, closely precede her revelations and explain her ecstasy on that very site.[47] She later claimed that Jesus himself
prevented her from seeking an indulgence being offered at Maguelonne
and then rebuked her for consulting with a confessor and sharing her
confidences with mortal men. In 1325, she claimed that Jesus had revealed to her that the sacraments had lost their virtue when Olivi's
writings had been condemned. The pope himself, she said, had lost grace
through his condemnation of Olivi, just as Adam had lost grace when he
had blamed Eve for his sin.[48] She blamed the pope for the spiritual death
of all Christendom, just as she blamed Adam for the corporal death of
all mankind. In the new age, she maintained, people would be saved by
their own devotion in hearing mass, making confession, and taking the
Eucharist without the intervention of the clergy.

When she could no longer attend him in person, after his elevation to
the papacy or after his death, Catania had formed the habit of making
the rounds of the eremitical foundations that still practiced Peter's rule.
She said that she visited at least nine such places on a regular basis. But
there is no indication that the brothers responded to her efforts to promote their founder's cult. None of them appeared in Sulmona to support
her testimony, while a number of her friends and neighbors did come.
Collectively, their stories reveal a network that might almost have become a sect if Peter had not been canonized and safely transformed into
a suitable object for orthodox devotion.

Catania clearly put herself at the heart of this little group, and they did
not deny that she had been serving as a sort of consultant to her neighbors. When the son of Panfili Riczardi and his wife, Gemma, was found

to be suffering a malady similar to leprosy and no doctor could cure him, she came to the rescue by bringing the boy to Peter, who cured him permanently, and she produced both the boy and Lady Gemma in court.[49] She was also eager to testify to other miracles that she had witnessed in Sulmona and elsewhere. The examiners apparently stopped her there, for the other miracles she claimed to know about are not included in her testimony. From the later witnesses, however, it becomes clear that there was a network of devotees of about the same age and social condition in Sulmona who were promoting the story of Catania's cure and gathering other evidence of Peter's miracles. Lady Maria de Gualterio testified that she cured her son of paralysis by laying him in a fountain near Brother Peter's cell after hearing about Gemma's son.[50] Catania's example inspired Lady Granata, the wife of Judge Leonardus, to get some bread, herbs, and two hosts from Brother Peter through the intermediary services of her husband's relative and thus cure herself of a paralysis of the arm.[51] Many other witnesses testified that they had been witnesses to Catania's cure or knew about it from public fame. Several other women had been the recipients of artifacts through which they were cured when Brother Peter refused to see them himself. Catania, however, remains unique in being the only witness to testify that she kept her cross and her bread and used them to perform further miraculous cures.

The commission showed no real interest in Catania's efforts to organize Brother Peter's cult or to multiply his miracles with her own activities. Nevertheless, Catania's contribution to the successful completion of her mission was substantial, and her own satisfaction in her accomplishments was evident. By 1306, it was almost certain that the loyalty of the women and men who had maintained Celestine's cult in the Abruzzi for twenty years would be vindicated by his canonization. But for many years before, there had been a real and immediate danger that his following would be condemned in the reaction that followed his abdication and death. Only the determination of the king of France to obtain vengeance against his successor saved his memory and his followers from sharing the fate that would so soon overwhelm the devotees of Dolcino in Italy and Olivi in France. Let us hope that Catania thereafter lived a long and fruitful life as an intermediary between her neighbors and her saint and continued to exercise her thaumaturgic powers through the medium of her cross and her two loaves of unstaled bread.

It is probable that when Prous first attached herself to his cult, Olivi was still considered an orthodox, if radical, thinker. It may even have seemed to Prous that his part in her own religious vision might lend her some protective coloration. However, no fortuitous political interests intervened to provide Olivi with the respectable cover of canonization. From the beginning of his papacy, John XXII showed himself determined to suppress the zealots whose devotion to evangelical poverty cast doubt on the spiritual value of the hierarchy and its sacraments.

In turn, they accused the pope himself of heresy and made a cult of the beguines burned in 1317.[52] The household shared by Prous and Alisette was clearly one of the "houses of poverty" in which, according to Gui, the beguines gathered other devotees who lived only for prayer and discussion. They honored the burned beguines for their defense of evangelical poverty and compared them to the crucified Christ, celebrating a martyr's feast in their honor.[53] Prous was already a familiar figure among them and probably well versed in the teachings of Olivi. She could read at least in the vernacular and knew Olivi's texts. Her claim to learning was probably as strong as Douceline's, whose revelations concerning the Trinity had impressed the "masters of Paris" as being more correct than any insights of theologians.[54] She defiantly told her Dominican judges that, while Olivi was the teacher of truth, their own Thomas Aquinas was the teacher of lies.[55] In her home, she may have been actively promoting his cult before she began to put herself forward as the avatar of the godhead of the new age, though her following was probably not very large.[56] Her own testimony implicated only people who had listened to her preaching but rejected her claims to their devotion. Her sister, Alisette, believed strongly enough in her teachings to hold out against the pressures of the inquisitors for three years before she abjured her faith in her sister's revelations in October 1328.[57] She was mentioned in a couple of later confessions, but even the renegade friar Raymond John, who had apparently provided her with the texts of Olivi's writings, denied his faith in Prous's teachings, though he confessed to some heretical ideas of his own.[58]

Through her direct communion with God, Prous felt herself to be driven more and more from human society, especially from the church. As we have seen, her voice was not unique in prophesying the coming of a new age. She shared her vision of the Holy Spirit's coming with many persons, and her vision of herself as its mother, or even its persona, with at least several other women. As was common to most of them, in an age when the crusading power of the old church was fading away, she believed that in the new age the Jews and the Saracens would not refuse salvation. Douceline de Digne had envisioned the victories of Saint Louis under the oriflamme. The Guglielmites maintained that the failure of the

Jews and Saracens to convert was linked to the corruption of the present church. Guglielma's "pope," Mayfreda de Pirovano, celebrated mass on her grave as the inauguration of a new age when she would secure the conversion of the Jews and Saracens.[59] The sect of the Free Spirit, which was spreading from the Rhineland to the Abruzzi, was accused of repudiating Christ's Passion, disputing that hell and purgatory exist, and saying that even Jews and Saracens inevitably return to unity with the godhead. If Prous was questioned about this, she held to her own point of view.

She believed that the spirit that had entered her had made her one with God and that the same spirit would harrow hell and save all humanity once a new redemption had been accomplished. The message that Prous derived from these encounters was one of love and mercy. The Lord revealed to her that he would include Jews and Saracens and all the people of the world in his forgiveness. Prous even urged that clergy and laity overcome their differences and love one another with the spiritual friendship (*amicitia spiritualia*) that distinguished Christ and the apostles, maintaining that God would forgive even Satan (whom she called Lucibel) if he would recognize his fault. Finally, she saw herself as the woman of the Apocalypse who had trodden the serpent underfoot, saying that Christ had promised that, as the church had formerly been ruled by him and his mother, so the coming age would be ruled by Olivi and Prous, who shared the spirit he had transmitted to them. Olivi's writings and Prous's preaching were the two necessary pillars of the new doctrine, without which no one could be saved.

The age of the Holy Spirit never came. These two women survive, almost by accident, to speak for those who dared hope for it. The nature of the processes in which they were questioned obscure the similarities that bound them across the space between Sulmona and Montpellier. Catania, we hope, lived a life of some honor; Prous met a grimmer fate. If they testify to a woman's movement of the south, it was a movement that never found cohesion in the sources. But even our hostile sources illuminate the ingenuity with which women of the thirteenth and later centuries might hope to give creative shape and cosmic meaning to the restricted places they occupied. These women were actively pursuing goals of their own. Their voices, speaking to us directly or indirectly, indicate that they placed themselves at the center of their own lives, though they may have been very marginal to the concerns of a male-oriented society. When we do hear their voices directly, these voices have been sculpted and shaped to serve the purposes of their male recorders. Thus women who were once whole and complex appear to us only as broken images.

To John XXII, they were "superstitious, pernicious, pestiferous, apostate, and heretical."[60] To Clement V, they were fit only to be silenced and banished from history: "Therefore after hearing frequently from these and others about their perverted principles on account of which suspicion has rightfully fallen on them, we believe that we must, with the approval of the holy council, prohibit forever their status and abolish them completely from the church of God. We must forbid these and all other women on pain of excommunication which we wish to impose forthwith on the recalcitrants to retain in any way in future this status which they have long assumed or to be allowed to accept it again in any form."[61]

NOTES

1. This is the happy thought of Herbert Grundmann in *Religiöse Bewegungen im Mittelalter*, p. 170. Similarly, Ernest W. McDonnell, in *Beguines and Beghards*, bases his concept of a coherent movement on the Belgian scene with little reference to the beguines of the south.

2. See Roisin, *L'Hagiographie cistercienne*, for the peculiar styling contributed by the Cistercians. Bynum, "Women Mystics and Eucharistic Devotion," has refined the question of the dialectic between the hagiographer and his subject to show the careful modeling of female saints as critics of corrupt clergy and, at the same time, models of devout laity.

3. Manselli, "Divergences," p. 379.

4. Carozzi indicates that this trend began almost with the foundation of the order outlined by the bull *Utriusque sexus* (1221) ("Le Ministère de la confession," p. 342).

5. *La Vie de Sainte Douceline*, testifying to her flourishing, if unauthorized, cult, was written by one of her community, Philippine de Porcelet. Popes Clement V and John XXII in the early fourteenth century tended to refer to them as false or so-called beguines.

6. Philippine de Porcelet, *La Vie de Sainte Douceline*, p. 23.

7. Ibid., bk. 11. Bernard Gui, in *Manuel de l'inquisiteur*, written in about 1326, devoted a whole chapter to the beguines. He accused them of teaching that, after Christ and his mother, Francis was the teacher of the doctrine of poverty. This idea, in an orthodox context, was revealed by Margarita of Cortona to her friendly Franciscan confessor, Juncta Bevegnatis, in 1297, and he accepted it as a direct revelation from Christ (*De B. Margarita*, p. 67).

8. Angevin interests may have protected the beguines, for the patronage of

Charles's son as king of Sicily protected many Italian evangelicals until his death in 1308, when he was buried in a Dominican convent that he had endowed for a hundred nuns at Aix. Charles may also have procured the exception made for the small community attached to Peter of Murrone, who made a personal plea at the Council of Lyons. Twenty years later, his son was instrumental in procuring Peter's election to the papacy. Clement V wrote to the Bishop of Cremona on 1 April 1311 and complained that in the area of Spoleto he heard rumors of the heresy of the Free Spirit attracting men and women to the teachers from the Rhineland who had fled to the relatively beneficent climate of Charles II's kingdom. (McDonnell, *Beguines and Beghards*, p. 523).

9. Stefaneschi, "*Opus metricum*," 2.2.

10. *Nuper ad audientiam*, in *Archiv für Literatur- und Kirchengeschichte* 2:156–58.

11. *Constitutiones Clementinae* 3.11, *De religiosis domibus* 1, both in Hefele and Leclercq, *Histoire des conciles* 6.2.681.

12. See May, "Confession of Prous Boneta."

13. *Akten des Kanonisationsprozesses*, pp. 209–331.

14. Douie, *Heresy of the Fraticelli*, p. 89. Olivi's return to Provence in 1290 was marked by fresh demonstrations from his followers, though he was able to maintain his own orthodoxy until his death in 1298. In the ten years that followed, nearly three hundred friars were disciplined because of their attachment to his doctrines. By 1312, his tomb had become a center of popular pilgrimage and attracted pious donations even from some cardinals. It was only after the election of John XXII in 1317 that the tide turned decisively against the Olivites, and his followers began to find themselves in peril of their lives from the inquisitors of southern France.

15. Bernard Gui charged the beguines with the heresy of describing Olivi's work as the scripture of a new age (*Manuel de l'inquisiteur* 1:120).

16. The inquisitor notes at the end of the document that it was read to her several times in the vernacular before she signed it, so she presumably had some difficulties in making the official formulation conform to her own ideas.

17. See Lea, *History of the Inquisition* 3:653–54, for her sentence.

18. Thirty-five women figured among the hundred-odd witnesses whose testimony has been preserved. Trocta Benedict of Castro Sangri testified that she had made pilgrimages to all of the local places where Peter had established communities after he had cured her blindness; another witness testified that she had indeed been cured, but from a distance, because Peter refused to allow a woman near him even in prayer. (*Akten des Kanonisationsprozesses*, nos. 13, 16).

19. Petrus de Murrone, *Tractatus*, p. 6.

20. *Akten des Kanonisationsprozesses*, no. 8.

21. May, "Confession of Prous Boneta," p. 6. Durieux speculates on the common language of the Languedoc into which Olivi was translated ("L'Histoire franciscaine," p. 94).

22. Herlihy and Klapisch-Zuber, _Tuscans and Their Families,_ p. 202.

23. _Akten des Kanonisationsprozesses,_ no. 20.

24. Catania's statement seems to imply that her husband died some time before she testified, but her father's testimony suggests that he was still alive in 1306 (Ibid., no. 18). The witness whose testimony followed that of her father, if I read the implication of her uncle's testimony correctly, was probably her husband, but his remarks were torn out of the manuscript.

25. Unfortunately, the remainder of this portion of Dr. Benedict's testimony has been deleted from the manuscript, but it presumably detailed the medical methods tried by him and his fellow physicians in Sulmona.

26. Her uncle, the doctor Raynaldus Gentili, was one of the party. At age eighty he also appeared to testify and said that Catania had proclaimed the news of her miracle to all the people of Sulmona, beginning with a group of women who came out to meet them on their return (_Akten des Kanonisationsprozesses,_ no. 23).

27. Prous said that her family had taken up residence in Montpellier when she was about seven years old. Her sister Alisette testified that they had lived there for about twenty-two years. That would make Prous about thirty years old when she made her confession in 1325.

28. A commission was set up in Avignon in 1319 to examine his _Postilla on the Apocalypse,_ which was ultimately condemned after Gui had completed his book on 8 February 1326 (Douie, _Heresy of the Fraticelli,_ p. 113).

29. Douie says that the problem was intensified by their connection with the spiritual Franciscans and their belief that John himself was the Antichrist and had lost his sacramental power, ideas found in Prous's testimony (Ibid., p. 251). In 1317–18, spiritual Franciscans fled south from Tuscany to escape persecution into the kingdom of Sicily (which included the Abruzzi at its northern end). According to John XXII's bull _Sancta romana,_ they had previously been sheltered by privileges gained from Celestine V (_Bullarium franciscanum,_ 297, 134).

30. She was not simply being hysterical. A chronicler in Strasbourg complained that local German prelates had compelled devout women to resume lay clothing instead of their accustomed habits and had even persuaded continent women who had taken vows of chastity to marry (McDonnell, _Beguines and Beghards,_ p. 529, citing "Chronica provincia argentinensis," pp. 682–83). John of Saint Victor protected the beguines of Paris from similar persecution, and John of Winterthur wrote a lengthy description of their persecution in Switzerland (Ibid., p. 530, citing Georg von Wyss, _Archiv für Schweizerische Geschichte_ 11 [1856]: 66–67). John XXII was eventually prevailed upon to exempt the beguines of the north and even to befriend them (Ibid., p. 528).

31. Agathange Bocquet estimates that there were about eighty houses of Clares in the south under all four rules. One foundation had been established at Montpellier in 1250 ("Les Clarisses méridionale," p. 218).

32. Elaine Pagels has noted this idea in some of the Gnostic texts of the early church (*Gnostic Gospels*, pp. 51–53).

33. This idea is elaborated at length in Friedrich Baethgen's *Der Engelpapst*.

34. Stefaneschi, "*Opus Metricum*," p. 2.

35. Stephen Wessley suggests that the Cistercians were unaware of the heretical ideas circulating among the pilgrims who visited her tomb and participated in their services honoring her ("Thirteenth-Century Guglielmites," p. 301). It seems more likely, however, that her image was reshaped out of a general dialectic between radical but orthodox reformers and increasingly conservative defenders of the established hierarchy.

36. This enables at least one modern historian to claim that her "heresies" were invented by her followers after her death (Tocco, "Il Processo dei Guglielmiti"). Wessley, who is inclined to believe that Guglielma preached what her followers believed, connects the Guglielmites with the Joachite hope for the coming of *ecclesia spiritualia* ("Thirteenth-Century Guglielmites," p. 289). By the late fourteenth century, remnants of the Guglielmites apparently were still in existence and drawing the attentions of hostile writers, who accused them of being orgiasts who burned their illegitimate babies and drank the ashes in their wine (Russell, *Witchcraft*, pp. 88–93).

37. *Annales colmarienses maiores*, Anno 1301, MGHS, 17, 226.

38. Muratori, *Rerum italicarum scriptores* 9.5.31–32, who also notes that Margarita's brother, the notary Boninsegna, praised Dolcino's preaching.

39. Gui, *Manuel de l'inquisiteur*, p. 103; Gui might, of course, have included this information as a tool for discouraging women from succumbing to the attraction of Dolcino's teaching. Gui does not say whether women wishing to flee their husbands might have been welcomed, but Douceline's biographer states that the beguines of France did shelter married women who wished to take a vow of chastity.

40. Ibid., p. 105.

41. Gui quotes a letter of Dolcino, written in December 1303, stating that he expounded a doctrine of good and evil popes, with Celestine as the first of the good popes and Boniface VIII the first of the evil ones, whose careers would usher in the age of the Holy Ghost; after that, Dolcino predicted widespread destruction of those who did not follow him (Ibid., 1:79).

42. Petrus de Murrone, *Tractatus*, p. 7.

43. Olivi to Conrad of Offida, 14 September 1295 (on the legitimacy of Celestine's abdication and the poverty question): see Olivi, "Epistola ad Conradum de Offida."

44. *Nuper ad audientiam*, in *Archiv für Literatur- und Kirchengeschichte* 2:156.

45. Wessley asks what conditions led Guglielma and her followers into heresy. He attributes the disillusion of the Milanese to a long interdict which may have caused them to worry about the legitimacy of the sacraments ("Thirteenth-

Century Guglielmites," pp. 297–98). In 1298, Carcassonne, where Prous was later to be interrogated, also suffered a lengthy interdict because of local opposition to the Inquisition.

46. Ibid., p. 301.

47. *Archiv für Literatur- und Kirchengeschichte* 2:293.

48. "Littera magistrorum," 2:259.

49. Gemma called Catania her cognate in her own testimony. Indeed, she added that Johannes, Catania's husband, had become well known to Peter and had personally brought her son to his attention, which suggests some competition between wife and husband for command of the services of the hermit (*Akten des Kanonisationsprozesses*, no. 20).

50. Ibid., no. 21. Eight years after Peter's death, another Sulmonese woman of the same age attempted to duplicate this feat and failed (no. 79). Her son could be cured only by the use of a chain Peter had left behind in one of his monasteries.

51. Ibid., no. 41.

52. Gui mentions that they were found in Narbonne, Toulouse, and Catalonia in 1317 (*Manuel de l'inquisiteur* 1:109). Their principal errors are drawn from the writings of Peter John Olivi, which they have translated into the vulgar tongue.

53. Ibid., p. 115.

54. Philippine de Porcelet, *La Vie de Sainte Douceline*, p. 75.

55. Probably a reference to Olivi's refutation of Thomas's ideas on poverty (*Postilla in Matthaeum*, cited by Douie, *Heresy of the Fraticelli*, p. 98).

56. Lea says that the local Spiritual Franciscans reverenced her as a prophetess (*History of the Inquisition* 3:82). May, however, thinks that her following did not extend much beyond her sister and another woman, who shared her house and who were arrested with her ("Confession of Prous Boneta").

57. May, "Confession of Prous Boneta," p. 4.

58. Ibid., p. 6.

59. Wessley, "Thirteenth-Century Guglielmites," p. 294.

60. *Contra beguinos*, in Baluze and Mansi, *Miscellanea* 2:272.

61. *De quibusdam mulieribus*, in Hefele and Leclerq, *Histoire des conciles* 6.2.

BIBLIOGRAPHY

Primary Sources

Akten des Kanonisationsprozesses in der Handschrift des Kapitelsarchivs zu Sulmona. In *Monumenta coelestiniana*, ed. F.-X. Seppelt, pp. 209–331. Quellen und Forschungen aus den Gebiete der Geschichte, no. 19. Paderborn, 1921.

Annales colmarienses maiores. MGHS, 17.226.

Archiv für Literatur- und Kirchengeschichte. Ed. F. Ehrle. 2 vols. Berlin, 1886.

Baluze, S., and J. Mansi. *Miscellanea.* Lucca, 1761–64.

Bullarium franciscanum. 1759. Reprint. Quaracchi, 1898–1904.

"Chronica provincia argentinensis." *Archivum franciscanum historicum* 4 (1911): 682–83.

Gui, Bernard. *Manuel de l'inquisiteur.* Ed. G. Mollat. Paris, 1964.

Juncta Bevegnatis. *De B. Margarita Poenit: Tertii Ord. S. Francisci, Cortonae in Etruria. Acta Sanctorum,* III February, February 22, 302–62.

"Littera magistrorum." In *Miscellanea,* ed. S. Baluze and J. Mansi, 2:259. Lucca, 1761–64.

May, William H., ed. "The Confession of Prous Boneta, Heretic and Heresiarch." In *Essays in Medieval Life and Thought Presented in Honor of Austin Patterson Evans,* ed. John H. Mundy, Richard W. Emery, and Benjamin N. Nelson, pp. 3–30. New York, 1955.

Muratori, L. *Rerum italicarum scriptores.* Milan, 1736.

Olivi, Petrus Johannes. "Epistola ad Conradum de Offida." Ed. P. Lirarius Oliger. *Archivum franciscanum historicum* 11 (1918): 366–73.

Petrus de Murrone (Celestine V). *Tractatus de vita sua quam ipse propria manu scripsit et in cella sua reliquid.* In *Celestiniana,* ed. A. Frugoni, pp. 25–68. Rome, 1954.

Philippine de Porcelet. *La Vie de Sainte Douceline, fondatrice des beguines de Marseille.* Ed. J. H. Albanes. Marseille, 1879.

Stefaneschi, Jacobus. "*Opus metricum* das Kardinals Jacobus Gaietani Stephaneschi." In *Monumenta coelestiniana,* ed. F.-X. Seppelt, pp. 1–146. Quellen und Forschungen aus den Gebiete der Geschichte, no. 19. Paderborn, 1921.

Secondary Sources

Baethgen, Friedrich. *Der Engelpapst: Idee und Erscheinung.* Leipzig, 1943.

Bocquet, Agathange. "Les Clarisses méridionale." *Cahiers de Fanjeaux* 8 (1973): 217–24. (Summarized from a larger study, "L'Origines et la fondation des monastères de Clarisses en Aquitaine au XIIIe siècle," *Collectanea franciscana* 25 [1955]: 5–52).

Bynum, Carolyn W. "Women Mystics and Eucharistic Devotion of the Thirteenth Century." *Women's Studies* 11, nos. 1–2 (1984): 179–214.

Carozzi, Claude. "Le Ministère de la confession chez les Prêcheurs de la province de Provence." *Cahiers de Fanjeaux* 8, 342.

Douie, Decima. *The Nature and Effect of the Heresy of the Fraticelli.* Manchester, 1932.

Durieux, Francois-Régis. "Approches de l'histoire franciscaine du Languedoc au XIIIe siècle." *Cahiers de Fanjeaux* 8 (1973): 94.

Grundmann, Herbert. *Religiöse Bewegungen im Mittelalter.* Berlin, 1935.

Hefele, K. J., and H. Leclerq. *Histoire des conciles.* Paris, 1915.

Herlihy, David, and Klapisch-Zuber, Christiane. *Tuscans and Their Families.* New Haven, Conn., 1985.

Lea, H. C. *History of the Inquisition in the Middle Ages.* 3 vols. New York, 1955.

McDonnell, Ernest W. *The Beguines and Beghards in Medieval Culture.* New York, 1969.

Manselli, Raoul. "Divergences parmi les mineurs d'Italie et de France méridionale." *Cahiers de Fanjeaux* 8 (1973): 379.

Pagels, Elaine. *The Gnostic Gospels.* New York, 1979.

Roisin, Simone. *L'Hagiographie cistercienne dans le diocèse de Liège au XIIIe siècle.* Louvain, 1947.

Russell, Jeffrey Burton. *Witchcraft in the Middle Ages.* Ithaca, N.Y., 1972.

Tocco, F. "Il Processo dei Guglielmiti." *Reale Accademia dei Lincei memorie della classe di scienze morali . . . Rendiconti,* 8th ser., 5 (1899): 309–42, 351–84, 407–32, 437–69.

Wessley, Stephen. "The Thirteenth-Century Guglielmites: Salvation through Women." In *Medieval Women,* ed. Derek Baker, pp. 289–304. Oxford, 1978.

ANGLO-SAXON ATTITUDES

Men's Sources, Women's History

Joel T. Rosenthal

 would like to think that it is through the blessed intercession of Saint Hilda of Whitby that scholars have begun to
take a serious and systematic look at the women of Anglo-
Saxon England. However, agnostic realism forces me to
suspect that the high tides of social history, alongside our
current political consciousness, play an equal role in this welcome process; Marc Bloch and Simone de Beauvoir, among others, bless us from
their treasury of merit. ❡ However, we will not worry unduly in this
paper about our historiographic roots.[1] Though the primary purpose of
this essay is to cover the role of women in Anglo-Saxon society, the
nature of the topic forces me to talk to a number of purposes along the
way. Some comments about the current state of the question are unavoidable, though I am not primarily working to survey the existing
scholarly literature. In addition, I will offer a few comments about the
society itself and its outlook or worldview; that larger issue must lie
at the far end of any specific set of problems or any discussion of the
nature and preservation of sources. There is at least a passing correlation
between the importance or centrality of a particular source (or genre of
sources) and the question of its preservation and survival.

❡ The legal, social, and economic status of the Anglo-Saxon woman,
both up and down the social scale, is not particularly mysterious. For
some years historians have been able to speak with confidence about her
position on the ladder. As Dorothy Whitelock summed up the matter,
"She was, in short, very much more independent than were women after
the Norman Conquest."[2] We have considerable information about her
protection under law; her rights as a maiden, wife, mother, and widow;
and even the degree to which she could distance herself from an errant
(or dead) husband when she was but his unwilling or unwitting part-

ner. We can look at the laws of Wihtread of Kent or of Ine of Wessex to see how, under such circumstances, they were willing to distinguish between him and her: "If a husband sacrifices to devils without his wife's knowledge he is to be liable to pay all his goods and *healsfang;* if they both sacrifice to devils, they are to be liable to pay *healsfang* and all their goods."[3] And we can likewise turn to a later recognition of her possible separate or independent role: "If anyone steals without his wife and children knowing, he is to pay 60 shillings as a fine. If however, he steals with the knowledge of all his household, they are all to go into slavery."[4]

Naturally, there are some dark patches in the sunny sky. The main sources for detailed information about her status and treatment are the collections of Anglo-Saxon law codes. Unfortunately, as a window into society and social intercourse, the whole panoply of early medieval law codes—from the Continent as well as from insular society—has one peculiar deficiency: they are normative documents. We know a good deal about what Anglo-Saxon society thought *should* happen to one who slapped, mutilated, raped, or eloped with a servant girl. We have such information for a goodly number of chronological points along a line stretching from the time the missionaries codified the usages of Ethelbert of Kent in the early seventh century through such eleventh-century documents as Cnut's laws, the compilations of status, and the law of the Northumbrian priests. But what we cannot obtain from this kind of quick assessment is any real idea of how often these crimes or torts took place, how the girls' masters and mistresses reacted, how the girls (women) themselves responded, let alone what compensation really was paid, or to whom, or how quickly and how fully. Ethelbert decreed that "if anyone lies with the woman of a servant while her husband is alive, he is to pay two-fold compensation." Did he? And how fully, how quickly, and to whom?[5]

When we offer a quantitative assessment or a content analysis of law codes, we discover reasonable, if not startling, returns. Most of the codes have numerous chapters that talk explicitly about women, mainly in terms of compensations for injuries they received and of their need for and right to protection against attacks, especially for women who were in positions of unusual vulnerability, such as widows, women in a monastery (nunnery), or other women who lacked the sort of male protection that society expected. Beyond these categories, the codes carry their share of references to and condemnations of improper heterosexual activity by clerics and their partners, odd bits of misogyny, and an occasional reference to the wife and children as the family or domestic unit. In a similar vein, the penitentials worry a good deal about her sexual (mis)conduct and a good deal less about her peaceful and conventional passage through life.[6] Women as such are only named in five of the twenty-eight chapters of the laws of Wihtraed of Kent (ca. 695): three chapters that cover "illicit unions," one on the obligation of foreigners to regularize their marriages, and the passage about devil worship, which we have already seen.[7] In the laws of Hlother and Eadric of Kent (673–85), women are named in but one of nineteen sections. There is no reference to them in Edgar's code at Andover (955–63), nor do they appear in the code he issued at Wehtbordeston (962–63).[8] Society evidently kept on even keel without too much special consideration.

But the quality of our material is much better than this simple quantitative tally of some codes would indicate. The protection of women was at a high premium, even if the reasons for this were more likely to have been their value as sex and breeding objects than any concern for their independence of action or of identity. Protection there was, or at least there was meant to be, whatever the motives and whatever the interests served. We can see this from early in the period, in its midst, and toward the end of Anglo-Saxon times, just as we see how much of the protection was posited on the idea that women were an especially prized form of property: "If a freeman lies with the wife of a freeman, he is to atone with her wergild, and to obtain another wife with his own money, and bring her to the other's home."[9] Beyond her status as a wife, her role as a mother might accord her a degree of independent or autonomous status: "If a husband and wife have a child together and the husband dies, the mother is to have the child and rear it. She is to be given six shillings for its maintenance, a cow in summer, an ox in winter."[10] Her body, in some instances, may have been her own property: "If anyone ravishes a widow, he is to compensate for it with the wergild."[11] In addition to these general prescriptions, we also find odd passages that perhaps represent the codification of an older wisdom regarding the resolution of disputes: "If anyone in lewd fashion seizes a nun either by her clothes or her breast without her leave, the compensation is to be double that we have established for a lay person." These passages seem aflood with ambiguity. Nor does the law of Cnut necessarily indicate a high opinion of women's constancy: "A widow is never to be consecrated as a nun too hastily."[12]

But most of the protection she received was not incorporated in the explicit statements of the codes. Rather, it was contained within the much larger circle of protection offered to her because she shared or partook equally of her man's status, though in the course of life he would probably change from father to husband and her own status would also rise or fall with the ebb and flow of his fortunes and behavior. This was what we know as the *femme covert*. When the code of Alfred talks of a man of a six hundred-wergild and of a sixty-shilling compensation, it presumably recognized (and intended) that behind the man, also embraced within the arms of his role and social position, stood his equally protected and esteemed wife and children.[13] This all sounds very prosy and domestic, but no one knows how much litigious or violent reality is covered by this simple assertion. Nevertheless, it was a basic part of the way in which the sexes (as partners of a marriage or of a male kinsman–dependent relationship) were linked and of the way she was dealt with and given shelter: "As the lawyers said, the male embraced the female."[14] As long as women and children lined up in their proper order, that is, immediately behind their men so as not to be readily seen or identified as individuals, they were covered by the shadow he cast. They shared in his privileges, status, and wergild value. And on a descending scale, what was true for the wife of the six-hundred-wergild man doubtlessly applied to her less privileged sister. The highway robbery that King Ethelbert considered a three-shilling crime was presumably the same offense, with the same compensation, whether committed upon a man or a woman by a man or a woman.[15]

The other large body of sources we use on questions of status, equality, and independence of action is the corpus of charters. They run—usually in later copies of varying degrees of authenticity or adulteration—from the seventh century through the conquest. From them we learn about women as givers, exchangers, and receivers of property; as patrons of religious institutions; as favored governors of regular houses; as partners in transactions with husbands; and as people generally seen to be of worth, dignity, and status. Again, from a quantitative perspective, women were hardly involved in anything near half of the transactions we have. From the beginning of chancery or secretarial usage in the seventh century through the death of Athelstan in 939, Peter Sawyer's list of Anglo-Saxon charters gives us 458 documents.[16] Of these, 4 were joint grants by husbands and wives, 2 were grants by Aethelflaed, lady of the Mercians, and in another 20 instances a woman, usually an abbess, was named as the recipient in the transfer of land being recorded or confirmed. Nor was this male domination of diplomatics simply a characteristic of the early and middle periods. Sawyer lists 164 charters for the reign of Edward the Confessor (1042–66). Of these only a handful involve women in any significant fashion. Four times the king confirmed a grant made by a husband and wife to an ecclesiastical institution; once he regranted to Westminster Abbey land previously granted by the nun Aelfwyn; and once he gave land to Rutland with the proviso that the queen was to hold it for life. [17]

If we look at the documents in Margaret Gelling's handlist for the Thames valley, we see comparable quantitative returns. She presents 143 documents for Berkshire and Bedfordshire, and only about 17 involve a woman in any significant way.[18] However, in the miscellaneous collection of charters assembled by Agnes J. Robertson, there is a much higher incidence of material by and about women, precisely because the collection was assembled for the inherent interest of the materials rather than on a regional or chronological basis.[19] Of Robertson's 120 preconquest documents, women figure, in some role, in no less than 40. As we have been saying, the push and pull between quantity and quality offers some insights about when and why women make an appearance in the sources and about the interest and even the importance of the business under consideration.

Despite the laconic style of the charters, their precision sometimes makes them keys to the bustling and shifting world of power politics, of lordship and dominion, and of the growth of ecclesiastical institutions and power. Their formulaic phrases sometimes put flesh on the bones of the political vicissitudes that we know from narrative sources, and their formulaic approach can tell even about the aspirations, ambitions, and hierarchies of rulers. [20]

In a patchwork fashion we get many glimpses of women through the charters, cryptic though they often appear. High-quality finds, even if infrequent, help smooth the rough edges of quantitative deficiencies and give hints of a give-and-take dynamic in decision making by men and women of status rarely revealed through explicit phraseology. We can see a husband and wife making a co-grant, with the stipulation that "whichever of them lives the longer shall succeed to the estate"; such joint or shared activity is what we like to picture as characteristic of a successful marriage and partnership.[21] Sometimes the wife, as the survivor of such a couple, might now be covering the spiritual obligations for both souls.[22] There might be a record of the land going from the husband to their two children and then—if the children predeceased the mother—back to her for life. Then, "after her death, she shall bequeath it to whichever two of her brothers she pleases," and only when they died did it come, ultimately, to Worcester Cathedral—a long chain in which the woman was a key link. [23]

The charters (and the wills) show that both men and women worried about how their deaths would affect the future welfare of their female dependents.[24] Alfred's daughter entered Shaftesbury Abbey as a nun. When "she took the veil on account of her bad health," she came bringing one-hundred hides of land.[25] Wulfrid Spot was concerned with the future of "my poor daughter," and he left bequests accordingly.[26] Bishop Oswald of Worcester remembered "a certain woman whose name is Aelfhild, for the love of God and the relationship between us."[27] If the incidence of clauses that speak of care and obligation seems low, at least there is nothing in those that have been preserved to suggest that they were in any way regarded as unusual. Beyond that lies speculation.

The narrative sources of the Anglo-Saxons speak a different language. The sexism of the society becomes more marked and easier to discern; the focus on political and ecclesiastical events, on the upper classes and the elite, and on public roles largely serves to move women farther from the center. Most of them pass unnamed, unknown, unnoticed. Cultural conspiracies of silence and of definition (regarding rank and identity in the Christian world order) pushed most of them irremediably toward the margins, the periphery of history.

Our major secular narrative source is *The Anglo-Saxon Chronicle.* Of course, most women escaped the chroniclers' notice; they were rarely up to the standard of importance or centrality that virtually everyone named in its entries had to meet.[28] Accordingly, most of those named in the *Chronicle* were kings, bishops, thegns, and ealdormen; few men from lower strata made the grade either. We may argue that the men's womenfolk, their female counterparts, were often standing just behind them, perhaps pushing them forward. But even if this were so, the women were likely to be standing unmentioned, obscured by the men's shadow. Let us look at the *Chronicle's* entries, concentrating on the A text (the Parker version: CCCC, MS. 173), for a quantitative evaluation of the material.

Between the prototypical Germanic invasion of 449, when "they came in three ships to Britain at the place Ebbsfleet," and the death of Ethelred II in 1016, after "he had held his kingdom with great toil and difficulties," we have a span of 567 years.[29] These years are represented or reported by 257 entries, about one for every two years (though there are many blanks for the first four centuries and something for almost every year from 850 onward). In the overwhelming number of the 257 entries—early or late, long or short—there are no references of any sort to our "other" half of the population; royal, aristocratic, and common women, holy virgins, saints, simple wives, slave girls, and harlots are primarily noteworthy for their total absence, their absolute silence. Fair enough, we might argue, for early medieval chronicles are not synthetic, systematic, or catholic in their principles of inclusion or exclusion. The *Chronicle*'s entries were recorded to mark the cycles of life and time, the obituaries of the great white fathers, and political cataclysms, royal murders, and the fall of hailstones in July and August. Annalists were concerned with neither the social fabric nor the vast ranks of the many, regardless of gender.

But are the 40 entries that do mention women in some way, shape, or function really that different? In scope the entries are usually pretty jejune. Since anything about the kings' women and women's public and political lives is grist for our mill, we gladly take whatever comes our way. Furthermore, sympathetic interpretation allows many of the brief and uncommunicative entries to be read as touchstones leading us toward whole realms and circles of activity—public and private, perhaps ordinary or perhaps extremely eccentric—that went on below the surface, a surface that was a mixed compound of male indifference or hostility and of narrative brevity.

The poor quantitative returns make it unlikely that even the relevant entries in the *Chronicle* will give us any systematic picture of women at the top of society; nor are any hidden treasures apt to emerge. For the most part, women in politics have to be guessed at or inferred rather than illustrated.[30] But what we do get are some vignettes that, we like to argue, may well be indicative (and typical) of a much greater volume of activity. Of course, this is conjectural; perhaps each striking reference to a woman has been entered because it refers to anomalous behavior. Some entries reveal women at their most anonymous. When Ethelbert of Kent's son came to the throne, "He had his father's widow as his wife." Though we learn in some detail about the problems this caused with Archbishop Laurence, we never learn her name.[31] Some entries note women only at their moment of farewell; in 697 the Southumbrians slew Osthryth, queen to Ethelred and sister to Ecgfrith, king of Northumbria. This enigmatic entry is her only appearance in the written record. Werburg, Ceolred's queen, went more quietly, and her death is simply bracketed with the death of Cynewulf of Lindisfarne and the Synod of Aclea, *the* events of 782.

At times a fleeting glimpse of her larger role does flicker across the screen. Some women played active political roles, it would seem, even if only the briefest mention makes the recalcitrant source. It is often noted that there is but a single entry (for A.D. 672) for the one-year reign of Seaxburh of Wessex, coming on the heels of her husband Cenwealh's thirty-one years on the throne. What do we puzzle from the entry for 722, wherein we learn that Queen Aethalburh "demolished Taunton, which Ine had built"? What stories we might have if only the *Chronicle* would talk a bit more.

Marriage, usually for political and diplomatic reasons, was her accustomed secular destiny. A full exposition of the brief entries on this theme would lead us into the domain of international relations, and one of the entries on her refusal to marry would lead us to the role of upper-class women and the church.[32] The kingdoms of the heptarchy preserved their uneasy stasis in part by sexual diplomacy: "Burgred, king of the Mercians, married the daughter of Aethelwulf, king of the West Saxons" (853). This seems straightforward. Clearly, more was involved—for better or for worse—when Aethelwulf of Wessex married the daughter of Charles the Bald (855); he had been long away, and "afterward he came home to his people, and they were glad of it," or at least they were for a while. Women's hands across the sea: in 924 Athelstan of Wessex "gave his sister in marriage over the sea to the son of the king of the old Saxons." But before we become too sentimental about such unions, we should remember the skeptical words of the young Beowulf:

> She and that ripening soldier will be married,
> The Dane's great lord and protector has declared,
> Hoping that his quarrel with the Hathobards can be settled
> By a woman. He's wrong: how many wars
> Have been put to rest in a prince's bed?
> Few. A bride can bring a little
> Peace, make spears silent for a time,
> But not long. [33]

Despite such expressions of pragmatism and misogyny, there was also the possibility that a good woman was worth a moment of praise, even if it came only at the end.[34] Women who earned applause were more likely to have come up the steps of an ecclesiastical rather than a secular *cursus honorum*, and we wonder why the *Chronicle* even bothered to take note of them: perhaps Bede's gentle legacy was seen here. Nevertheless, we do have a few heroines among the short annual summations. There was Eormengeota, daughter of Eorcenberht of Kent and Saexburh of East Anglia, "a holy virgin and a wonderful person" (640). Wihtburh, sister of Saint Aethelthryth of Ely, was mentioned in 798. She had died in 743, but it was in the later year that her body was found to be "all sound and undecayed in Dereham, 55 years after she had departed from this life."[35] And not least among our women is the royal mistress with whom Cynewulf spent his last night, in the bower at Mereton, as described in the long entry for 755. She exemplifies a number of our themes: anonymity, the woman as sex object, and her sudden bravery in the face of an emergency and her man's death. It was her cry that alerted the thegns to unsheath their swords of loyalty and revenge. We hope she survived these harrowing events and lived to tell her dramatic tale to her grandchildren, gathered before the roaring oak logs.[36]

Toward the end of the Anglo-Saxon period, we begin to get a better quantitative return in the *Chronicle*, though the quality of the material is much the same. Between 1016 and 1066, short-lived dynasties and political uncertainty made the fertility, leadership, and trustworthiness of queens and princesses factors of some importance. Cnut's women and Godwin's women—to sum them up with a derogatory if common term—became figures of prominence, and in those years women of the royal family appear in eighteen of the fifty entries, a proportion far beyond their earlier presence (they now appear in 36 percent of the entries, as against an earlier rate of about 12 percent). But by the eleventh century, our source has also become relatively garrulous. As individuals, the women do not take much of a step forward, and even the elusive and possibly powerful Queen Emma, wife successively of Ethelred the Unready and of Cnut, remains a cipher (though named in the entries for twelve different years).

Some high moments of women's involvement in the politics of Anglo-Saxon life can be woven by intertwining the *Chronicle*, Bede, and whatever lesser sources prove pertinent. A number of recent studies have sought—with some success—to pursue this synthetic or eclectic course, and we are much in debt to some of our colleagues.[37] But for the most part we remain all too aware of the hidden-iceberg factor, floating beyond our powers of recovery.

If the information we derive from narrative history is low in quantity and uneven in quality, can we extract more from a biographical approach? In terms of learning about the lives of a few women, a qualified yes is permissible. Alfred's daughter, Aethelflaed, lady of the Mercians, is clearly a great figure, heroic if not quite Churchillian in her father's footsteps. She is our outstanding secular figure, at least before the eleventh century. And in her case the veil of darkness is due in some considerable part to the hostility in Wessex toward Mercia, not just to hostility toward her sex. At least between the extant ninth-century material and sympathetic modern reconstructions, we have a reasonable picture of her activities and her magnetism, patchy though the tale must remain.[38] However, neither Queen Emma, despite the existence of the *Encomium Emmae,* nor Queen Edith, daughter of Earl Godwin and wife of Edward, despite the valuable text of *The Life of King Edward Who Rests at Westminster,* comes across with much impact.[39] Other women generally pass more quietly, with decorum and meekness, across our pages; the odds are always against them receiving any notice at all. In the index of Bertram Colgrave's text of *Two Lives of St. Cuthbert,* only fourteen Anglo-Saxon women are even named.[40] Aethelweard's *Chronicle* is a traditional men's club, fighting equal rights and the currents of time.[41] This parochialism is particularly striking since he dedicates his volume to his kinswoman Matild, abbess of Essen. In the text he refers to her as "revered cousin," "sweet cousin," "most beloved," and he says that he writes for her edification because he is "spurred by family affection." She presumably had not asked for a tale of famous ladies and was going to be content with the deeds of famous men.

Can we shed a different (or a brighter) light by following the bits-and-pieces approach? What do the various sources tell us about women's views of self, of their relations to their men in a personal sense, or of their place in the world? Here we mostly get the broad brush of male chauvinism, with definitions about society and gender so rooted in men's interpretation of the norm that women's views are, at best, external or alternative ones. Women were apt to be delineated so as to emphasize, from the beginning, their lesser position. But now and then a source enables us to spot a patch of brighter color and to argue for identity; occasionally we find a bold splash of assertion, aggression, and strong ego or individuality.

The desire or the need to denigrate women bespeaks some deep male fear of the other. However, we must not posit an endless shooting war between the sexes. If men wanted to socialize women to be meek and deferential, the chances are that most women—even those of prominence and great ability—conformed to the norm. Individuality was predominantly a male preserve. For a rare burst of egoism in this culture we have King Alfred's prose, though it is nicely dressed in the language of tradition and the rituals of consultation: "Now I, King Alfred, have collected these laws and have given orders for copies to be made of those which our predecessors observed and which I myself approved of. But many of those I did not approve of I have annulled, by the advice of my councillors."[42] Compare this use of first-person pronouns with the muted tones of influential and powerful women when they spoke through the medium of personal correspondence: "The strength of my love increases the more I perceive for certain that through the support of your prayers I have come into a haven of security and peace. And so again I humbly beg you: deign to offer your earnest intercession to God for my unworthy self so that through your protection His grace may keep me safe from harm."[43] A woman's private letter turns out to be less assertive than the preface to a law code, though we know that Boniface thought enough of Abbess Bugga to ask her to look for books for him and to give her advice about a proposed pilgrimage.[44] Her language of deference indicates respect for the holy man, of course, but it also bespeaks her acceptance of accustomed role modeling with which neither party had any quarrel. Men stood to women, in such relationships, as fathers stood to daughters, elderly husbands to young wives. Leoba wrote to Boniface, her exalted and elderly kinsman, "I am my parent's only child, and, though I am not worthy of so great a privilege, I would like to regard you as my brother, for there is no other man in my family to whom I can put my trust as I can in you."[45]

But against such entries, with their flashes of real, if conventional, women, we can set a stock of folk wisdom that was always willing to warn us against the wiles and lusts of treacherous and "uppity" women. Unhappy was the realm that was called upon to suffer a tyrannous queen, and both the pages of *Beowulf* and the sober (if prejudiced) historical sources worry, at undue length, about the incidence and the power of such figures. A few case studies certainly sufficed for the construction of vast moral and political fortifications, and any Anglo-Saxon knowledge of the Merovingian history that came through Gregory of Tours would only reinforce the case for political misogyny.[46]

Women, we are generally told, were seen by medieval authorities, which mostly means men with theological credentials, as being more libidinous than men. Their sexuality, in need of the bridle best applied by fathers, husbands, and confessors, was a threat to us all: to them, and, because of example and contagion, to innocent men, children, and clerics. In our midst stood these vessels of impurity: menstruation, childbed, and evil thoughts and incantations that could spread their diabolic contamination and perhaps neutralize the sacraments. Some sources reveal

a desire to punish them, to drive home the idea that their inherent and irremediable feminine differences (and deficiencies) made them deserving
of their second-class citizenship in Christ's nation. The penitentials are
eager to proclaim these hierarchical distinctions. Some feminine wiles
seem less than threatening, even if they offended a male (and clerical)
sense of decorum: "A husband ought not to see his wife nude." [47] But
other tricks could be part of a compact with the great enemy himself:
"A wife who tastes her husband's blood as a remedy shall do penance for
forty days, more or less." [48] Danger lurked, though we could take steps
to neutralize it: "If a woman performs diabolical incantations or divina-
tions, she shall do penance." [49] And the church could offer purification
through penance: "If a woman works witchcraft and enchantment and
uses magical philters, she shall fast for twelve months." [50]

We can once more turn to Bede for a more hospitable and egalitarian
view of the territory. His account of the correspondence that passed between Augustine of Canterbury and Pope Gregory shows a decent reluctance to seize upon every possible excuse for the denigration of women.
Gregory tells us, in his answer to a question about purity and purification, that "a woman must not be prohibited from entering a church
during her usual periods, for this natural overflowing cannot be reckoned
a crime: and so it is not fair that she should be deprived from entering
the church for that which she suffers unwillingly." [51] In the context of
early ecclesiastical expression, this passes as a sympathetic response.

From the biological to the psychological is a rough path in the early
medieval countryside, and we pick our way with some care. A number of
the riddles preserved in the Exeter book allow us to look upon a different
face in the relations between the sexes. The wit of the "bawdy riddles" re-
volves around their ambiguity and their allusions to the mutual pleasure
of sexual activity: women could alternatively be passive or active, givers
or receivers, coquettes or bold, full partners. We have trouble keeping
a straight face when we tell students that surely every young man and
woman knew that bread dough was the proper answer to riddle 43:

> I hear of something rising in a corner,
> Swelling and standing up, lifting its cover.
> The proud-hearted bride grabbed at that boneless
> Wonder with her hands; the prince's daughter
> Covered that swelling thing with a swirl of cloth. [52]

The penitentials—with their obsessive vision of lurking (sexual) dangers—warned against lesbian activity and were also explicit about the

threat of female-initiated incest, as they were about more regular irregularities. Such passages bespeak a clerical recognition of that fearsome phenomenon, that "sexual pleasures clearly lay within the province of women."[53] Nor should we assume that she was immune to the pain of unrequited or separated love, that her only amorous or erotic concern was in leading men away from paradise. The stoical and chaste role that Tacitus's *Germania* has projected for women's behavior has perhaps fabricated a norm that may hide a softer and more romantic side. Possibly two of the short poems preserved in the corpus of Anglo-Saxon verse speak with the female voice. Admittedly, this is very little, but no other secular sources from barbarian Europe go this far, and part of the scholarly arguments about "The Wife's Lament" and "Wulf and Eadwacer" centers around the reluctance of modern readers to accept love as part of the literary agenda of early medieval Europe.[54] That, however, seems to be our problem, not theirs.

Of literary or private expressions of the joys of male-female companionship—beyond passion, sin, or procreation—we have but few. However, such links and ordinary sharings are the sort of relations least likely to be recorded.[55] We have seen that charters and wills can spring from joint activity, and behind such public assertions there must have been a good deal of bipartisan decision making, perhaps some of it in the nature of pillow talk as well as the boardroom discussions about *his* property and *her* property.[56]

Historical anecdotes and an occasional scrap of rough wisdom literature can be read to argue for low regard and for little empathy when men were inspired to generalize about women. While such comments are softened by some joking elements, much of their patriarchal condescension really represents the dominant social voice. Proverbs are a traditional way of covering derogatory and even outrageous generalizations: "If your wife accuses anyone to you, don't believe it too quickly because she often makes many a one her enemy because they are more faithful to her lord than [to] her; . . . she often hates what her lord loves."[57] Sometimes her foibles were seen as merely puerile: "Against a woman's chatter: eat a radish at night, while fasting; that day the chatter cannot harm you."[58] If hardly profeminist, it is not as bleak as some of the Viking wisdom we have: "Never trust what a maiden tells you / nor count any woman constant; their hearts are turned on a potter's wheel, their minds are made to change."[59]

But it was a warrior society, for men and women alike, and the turns of fortune were apt to be harsh, to be accepted and transmitted with resignation. For the laconic acceptance of the fate that befell a deviant, there is a businesslike charter from the 960s or 970s. An estate at Ailsworth, the point of focus in the document, had come on the market because the woman who had held it was no longer concerned with matters of property: "The estate . . . had been forfeited by a widow and her son because they drove an iron pin into Wulfstan's father, Ælfsige; and it was discovered, and they took the deadly thing from her closet. Then they seized the woman and drowned her at London Bridge; and her son got away and became an outlaw. And the estate went into the hands of the king, and the king then granted it to Ælfsige." [60]

❡ But we should not end on such a chilling note. If women's lives were so frequently buried by the avalanches of hostility and/or indifference that cover those without their own history—be they medieval or modern, Western or "third world"—we can also pick some smooth and inviting paths into sheltered valleys of peace and understanding. Nor is the end of our recent scholarly odyssey anywhere in sight. If it is unlikely that new (written) sources are awaiting us, there are still new directions, just as there are further journeys in some old directions. Where should we go? Whither future scholarly courses? Some suggestions seem fairly obvious and straightforward, though still worth listing as we move to conclude. We can certainly call for more efforts to integrate the political and ecclesiastical roles of leading women with the politics of their men. We can do more content analysis linking the role of women and the varieties of material contained in the corpus of extant charters, wills, and manumissions. We can correlate the changes through time (and in different kingdoms) as reflected in the law codes with what we know about status from charters and narrative sources; some recent efforts in this direction have been intriguing, if not wholly convincing. [61]

We can write a good deal more concerning the nature of the family and kinship. While occasional references in the law codes to maternal kin should not lead us to fantasize about a lost day of matriarchy or of pre-Christian mother cults and priestesses, they should help us to better our sensitivity regarding the networks of affiliation, affection, and action that were constructed by and around women. Was the bilateral social network a step toward the egalitarian one? [62] We know from the law codes that at her marriage she did not pass wholly and irrevocably from the penumbra of her natal family; the drama we see in the Finn fragment may have had innumerable, if more pedestrian, counterparts at many levels of society. How many of these to-and-fro—some in peace, some in blood

—can be traced in charters and manumissions and the pre-Domesday administrative records now being collected and analyzed?[63]

Comparative history today is easy to endorse and enjoin. How far can we use the voluminous literary materials of the Scandinavian world, recorded in the post-Viking period, as a guide to the women of the Danelaw—an obscure group even by the exiguous standards of tenth- and eleventh-century documentation?[64] How far can Continental ma- terials—primarily from the Carolingian empire—about village organi- zation and peasant economic and domestic life be correlated with the pre-Domesday materials already referred to? The other social sciences continue to offer us both insights and methods: "thick descriptions" may unravel familiar tangles of many sorts, and social psychology and the sociology of literature and the insights derived from participant obser- vation may add depth to the extant hagiographical materials, especially concerning the role of women in popular and lay religion. Cults, relics, pilgrimages, feasts, and festivals are more complicated, to our eyes, as well as more interesting than we once suspected. Such manifestations of personal and religious expression are neither as readily defined nor as easily governed from the top down as a structural and narrative ap- proach to the history of religion seemed to indicate. I have not tried here to open doors to the new rooms that archaeology and the study of material culture are constantly building onto the old literary edifice. Graveyards, rural sites, urban rescue work, numismatics, potshards and economic vectors, domestic space and the sexual division of labor, labo- ratory analysis of pollens and grains, urban and rural waste heaps, and a long list of related matters await exploration for our topic. Archaeology is just beginning to deal with questions of gender. Given the current rate of digs and finds, we may soon have a whole new agenda of suggestions and hypotheses from this direction.

Let me close with a couple of attempts at revisionism, at least of per- spective and interpretation if not of larger definitions of social structure. One of the familiar anecdotes about Alfred, from Asser's biography, con- cerns his literacy. His mother said the coveted book of poetry would go to the son who could first learn to read it. Alfred then "went to his teacher and learnt it," and he claimed his prize.[65] From this we are wont to see the earliest seeds of his interest in education; it is the foreshadow- ing anecdote for the great intellectual revival. It is also a nice story, with an edifying and useful moral.

We can also look at this episode in a different fashion and come up with a more intriguing interpretation. What we have here is a naked ex-

ample of a parent deliberately fostering sibling rivalry. Asser has already
told us that Alfred was "greatly loved, more than all his brothers, by
his father and mother—indeed, by everybody." [66] What we see in the
tale about the book is a mother determined to play Rachel to Alfred's
Jacob, with Athelstan, Aethelbald, Aethelberht, and Ethelred all available
for the role of Essau. After such a beginning, the fraternal cooperation
of Alfred's early years may be a surprise, but the rivalry may help to
explain his difficult relations with his nephews, Aethelwold and Aethel-
helm, after his own accession. It may also shed light on the peevish tone
we find in his will when he reflected on the problems encountered when
he had sought to claim his birthright: "I asked him in the presence of all
our councillors that we might divide the inheritance and he should give
me my share. He then told me that he could not divide it at all easily." [67]
All ended well, as we know; the Danes became civilized, Wessex became England. However, during some perilous years a mother's thumb
rested heavily upon the political as well as the personal pulse of the royal
family. Perhaps she sensed that kingdoms were too important to be left
wholly to accidents of birth. In any event—as Asser tells the story—she
spotted a likely winner, and her willingness to back him to the hilt was
of inestimable value to his people in their dark hour.

For our second example we turn to the hagiographic materials about
the great fathers. We have few insights into domestic or family life, and
much of what we have centers on the perilous and peculiar circumstances
of royal families. Given these lacunae in the sources, anything we can
learn about mother-child relations and the role of women in the family
is as welcome as it is rare. We would like to think that the eight-year-
old Cuthbert, "who surpassed all of his age in agility and high spirits,"
had a happy home life, one that supported him when he heeded his calling and "submitted his neck from early youth to the yoke of monastic
discipline." [68] We do know that he maintained excellent relations with
his foster mother, Kenswith, and that he eventually performed a miracle
to save her house from fire. [69] By way of contrast, young Wilfrid of York
had mixed experiences with women, and both the positive and the negative interactions were critical. As an unhappy young man, he "meditated
in his heart leaving his father's fields to seek the kingdom of Heaven.
For his step-mother (his own mother being dead) was harsh and cruel." [70]
Perhaps Wilfrid's difficult childhood helped to fix his personality; he
certainly lacked the inner calm and confidence that we see in Cuthbert.
Nor is there reason to think that Wilfrid's tale was the typical one, for
Guthlac, like Cuthbert, came of a seemly domestic life, suitably matched

parents, and an obedient boyhood before he heeded his calling (to which they do not seem to have objected). [71]

Admittedly, these are but a few scraps, hardly likely to lead us to an early medieval version of Aries's *Centuries of Childhood* or of Erikson's *Young Man Luther*. But these holy men were important teachers as well as soldiers, and not the least part of their message was what they had to say about the role and status of women—in words and in their inter-actions with friends, relatives, those in need of healing, and the women of the church. We saw that Wilfrid's early and perhaps formative con-tact with a woman had not been happy. But misogyny was not (yet?) ingrained, and better fortune in such relations awaited him. Despite his problems with his stepmother, when presented at court to Oswiu and Queen Eanfled, he "at once, by the help of God, found grace in her sight. For he was comely in appearance and exceedingly sharp of wit; so that his request, that he might be allowed to serve God under her counsel and protection, was granted." [72] He was on his way, and an important chapter in northern Christianity was about to be written. But how different the history of the Anglo-Saxon church might have been had Queen Eanfled chosen Potiphar's wife or Hippolytus's stepmother as her role model in her dealings with this attractive young man. But now—for neither the first nor the last time—we can look at Anglo-Saxon history and discover that we have the right woman in the right place at the right time.

NOTES

A shorter version of this paper was read at the Sixth Berkshire Conference on the History of Women, Wellesley College, 1987. I wish to thank Kathleen Bid-dick for her comments at the session and Michael Sheehan for his suggestions concerning the comparative value of Celtic sources.

1. For our roots, see F. M. Stenton, "Place-Name Studies"; D. M. Sten-ton, *English Woman in History*, chap. 1–3. For some recent work touching both the growth of the field and bibliography, see Fell, *Women in Anglo-Saxon En-gland;* Dietrick, "Women in Anglo-Saxon Society"; Judd, "Women before the Conquest." For a survey of women in literary sources and records, see Chance, *Woman as Hero.*

2. Whitelock, *Beginnings of English Society,* p. 94. This is the accepted inter-pretation; the condition of women was perhaps best in the early period, mediocre in the later Anglo-Saxon years, and in real decline by the eleventh century (nor did it improve in Anglo-Norman times). "The evidence which has survived from Anglo-Saxon England indicates that women were then more nearly the equal

counterpart of their husbands and brothers than at any other period before the modern age. In the higher ranges of society the rough and ready partnership was ended by the Norman Conquest, which introduced into England a military society relegating women in general to a position honourable but essentially unimportant" (D. M. Stenton, *English Woman in History*, p. 348; see also pp. 28–31). For an excellent discussion of women's status, both within and beyond marriage, see Ross, "Concubinage in Anglo-Saxon England."

3. Whitelock, *English Historical Documents*, p. 363 (hereafter cited as *EHD*).

4. *EHD*, p. 365; see also chap. 7 and sec. 7.1. "If a husband steals a beast and carries it into his house, and it is seized therein, he shall forfeit his share of the household property—his wife only being exempt since she must obey her lord. If she dare declare with an oath that she has not tasted the stolen meat, she shall retain her third of the household property" (Attenborough, *Laws of the Earliest English Kings*, p. 55, from the laws of Ine). In practice such an oath—if the woman actually swore to it—would certainly have been likely to terminate the marriage.

5. *EHD*, p. 359. See also Colman, "Abduction of Women." For a recent study that emphasizes the late medieval distinction between legislation about sexual behavior and misconduct and the enforcement of such legislation, see Nicholas, *Domestic Life of a Medieval City*, pp. 53–70.

6. See McNeill and Gamer, *Medieval Handbooks of Penance*. On the world constructed and reflected by the penitentials, see Oakley, "Penitentials as Sources for Medieval History." The major recent treatment is Frantzen, *Literature of Penance*.

7. Swanton, *Anglo-Saxon Prose*, pp. 1–4. An instructive discussion on the sexing of Old English words, especially pronouns, and on the modern translators' tradition of making people without specified gender into males is in Fell, *Women in Anglo-Saxon England*, pp. 15–21.

8. *EHD*, pp. 360–61, 394–97, 397–401.

9. Ibid., p. 358.

10. Ibid., p. 368.

11. Ibid., p. 426. But in the next chapter the decree is that "if anyone ravishes a maiden he is to compensate for it with the wergild," and it seems unlikely that it was the maiden who received the compensation (ibid., p. 426, 52.1).

12. Ibid., pp. 376, 429, though, in fairness, this passage is set amidst a group of decrees intended to protect widows in their right to resist pressures for remarriage and in their efforts to claim their fair share of the marital property. Anglo-Saxon law was generally supportive of widows: see Rivers, "Widows' Rights in Anglo-Saxon Law."

13. *EHD*, p. 377.

14. This quote is from neither Littleton nor Coke nor Bacon nor Blackstone, but rather a recent mystery novel: Aird, *Harm's Way*, p. 174.

15. *EHD*, p. 359.

16. Sawyer, *Anglo-Saxon Charters*, pp. 69–181. See also Meyer, "Land Charters."

17. Sawyer, *Anglo-Saxon Charters*, charters 998–1162; the relevant documents are nos. 1098, 1106, 1107, 1117, 1119, and 1123. One confirmation (1106) was of a grant made by his own mother, Queen Aelfgifu, and his half brother, Harthacnut, to Ramsey Abbey, and another (1098) was in confirmation of a grant made by the earl Leofric and Godgifu (Godiva) to Coventry.

18. Gelling, *Early Charters*, pp. 17–71.

19. Robertson, *Anglo-Saxon Charters*.

20. See *EHD*, p. 491: this passage, in a charter of 875, indicates how a man referred to in a narrative source as "a foolish king's thegn" was clearly—as shown in a grant of privilege to Worcester diocese—able to exercise the traditional powers of a local ruler and subking. See also *EHD*, p. 524: Whitelock says that this document has been included in the volume "to illustrate the type of evidence for social conditions that can be gathered from the will of a woman of no historical importance."

21. Robertson, *Anglo-Saxon Charters*, p. 5.

22. Ibid., pp. 31–32: the gifts were for fifteen hides. Of these, her brother's son was to hold one hide, for life and "rent free."

23. Ibid., p. 97.

24. See Whitelock, *Anglo-Saxon Wills*. About one-third of the documents in this collection involve women in some critical function.

25. Robertson, *Anglo-Saxon Charters*, p. 25.

26. Sawyer, *Charters of Burton Abbey*, p. xviii. The scholarly consensus is that the daughter's financial standing was not the operative factor in this description.

27. Robertson, *Anglo-Saxon Charters*, p. 87. Though the wording is ambiguous, it would seem unlikely—even in the pre-Gregorian church—that a scandalous relationship would have been acknowledged so boldly in a formal document.

28. See D. M. Stenton, *English Woman in History*, pp. 2–5, and Fell, *Women in Anglo-Saxon England*, pp. 25–38, for interesting reflections on how, why, and when women were apt to "become visible" in the eyes of those recording the sources.

29. Quotations in the text are from the edition of Whitelock, Douglas, and Tucker, *Anglo-Saxon Chronicle*.

30. The issue of women as witnesses to charters has not been treated here, and it might be one of the topics worth a systematic study: see Meyer, "Land Charters." For some instances of women witnessing, see *EHD*, pp. 452, 464, 465, 478, 480, 481, 488.

31. Perhaps the oversight or fault should be attributed to Bede, the original source of the information. He is content to concentrate on the apostate son

(Eadbald) and to liken him to the customary dog returning to its vomit, in keeping with the popular rhetorical trope that goes back to 2 Pet. 2:22; see Bede, *Ecclesiastical History*, p. 150.

32. Nicholson, *"Feminae gloriosae"*; Stafford, *Queens, Concubines, and Dowagers*, pp. 32–92.

33. *Beowulf*, lines 2025–32.

34. Robertson, *Anglo-Saxon Charters*, p. 101.

35. From *Anglo-Saxon Chronicle*, A.D. 798. However, she is mentioned only in the F text (p. xvii).

36. The considerable literature on the entry for A.D. 755 has recently been summarized by Ferro, "King in the Doorway." A royal mistress might be a figure of mixed approbation, but for an example of the popular interest in praising the memory of the heroines of the early church, see Swanton, *Anglo-Saxon Prose*, pp. 18–19.

37. See, for example, Stafford, "King's Wife in Wessex"; Stafford, *Queens, Concubines, and Dowagers*, pp. 93–174; Nelson, "Inauguration Rituals," pp. 67–71.

38. Wainwright, "Aethelflaed, Lady of the Mercians." For Aethelflaed as a case study of the way in which Anglo-Norman (monastic) historiography deliberately cut down the repute and importance of women, see Bandel, "English Chroniclers' Attitude towards Women."

39. For Emma, see Campbell, *Encomium Emmae reginae*, pp. x1–1 (on her life), pp. 55–65 (on her status and queenly title). For Edith, see Barlow, *Life of King Edward*. For a summary of work on royal women, see Rosenthal, "Historiographical Survey," which covers publications from World War II to 1983.

40. The women include four abbesses, two queens, two wives, a saint, a nun-princess, and Cuthbert's foster mother. But—lest Cuthbert be considered a misogynist—Bertram Colgrave talks of his friendly and sympathetic relations with the women of his world, in contrast to the behavior of some of his contemporaries and role models (Colgrave, *Two Lives of St. Cuthbert*, pp. 318–19).

41. Campbell, *Chronicle of Aethelweard*, pp. 42–43. For a saint's life, written (by a male author) at the behest of a woman, see Talbot, *Anglo-Saxon Missionaries in Germany*, pp. 181–202 ("The Life of St. Sturm," by Eigil, abbot of Fulda). For one of those horror stories so beloved because they legitimated the need to keep women under tight male control, see Adamson, *Illiterate Anglo-Saxon*, pp. 27–28.

42. Attenborough, *Laws of the Earliest English Kings*, p. 63.

43. Talbot, *Anglo-Saxon Missionaries in Germany*, p. 69.

44. See ibid., pp. 83–84, regarding her plans for a pilgrimage, and pp. 88, 91, for Boniface's use of his network of female friends in his book-hunting endeavors (a search that turned up a copy of Peter's epistles, with letters of gold).

45. Ibid., p. 87; Fell, *Women in Anglo-Saxon England*, pp. 111–17.

46. On bad queens—the phantom creatures about whom so many loved to

discourse—see Fell, pp. 90–91; on queens in general, see Stafford, *Queens, Concubines, and Dowagers*, pp. 15–21, 115–34. There was little theory or reflection on queenship, but rather some fairly obvious and casual moralizing: Wallace-Hadrill, *Early Germanic Kingship*, pp. 92–93; Sedulius Scottus, *On Christian Rulers*, pp. 59–61. For analysis of the strategy of queens, see Nelson, "Queens as Jezebels"; Jochens, "Politics of reproduction."

47. McNeill and Gamer, *Medieval Handbooks of Penance*, p. 211, chap. 31.

48. Ibid., p. 197, chap. 16; "so also shall she do penance who makes an unclean mixture of food for the increase of love" (p. 195, chap. 15). Compacts with the Devil were hardly the exclusive province of women, and the penitentials also contain many chapters about male practices: Attenborough, *Laws of the Earliest English Kings*, pp. 109, 131. See Swanton, *Anglo-Saxon Prose*, p. 29, on the odious female custom of eating while in the latrine.

49. McNeill and Gamer, *Medieval Handbooks of Penance*, p. 184, chap. 4; "if any woman puts her daughter upon a roof or into an oven for the cure of a fever she shall do penance for seven years" (p. 198, chap. 2).

50. Ibid., p. 246, chap. 29.

51. Bede, *Ecclesiastical History*, p. 91. But against the more sympathetic view, we can offer some harsh injunctions: see McNeill and Gamer, *Medieval Handbooks of Penance*, p. 197, chaps. 17, 18, and p. 208, chaps. 12.2, 3, for penances imposed on women, not for willful sin but rather for inherent impurities and inferiority. On the positive side, which is obviously thinner, there were a few injunctions designed for the edification of women in religious life: see Swanton, *Anglo-Saxon Prose*, pp. 135–36; McNeill and Gamer, *Medieval Handbooks of Penance*, pp. 201, 205. For examples of how women were incorporated into the structure of the church—another topic hardly touched in this paper—see *EHD*, pp. 447, 454–55, 464, 469, 474.

52. Williamson, *Feast of Creatures*, riddle 43. See also riddles 23, 40, 42, 52. Even Bede (*Ecclesiastical History*, p. 93) was at pains to distinguish between reproduction and sexual pleasure, and he quotes Gregory on the question of women reentering churches after childbirth: "It is the pleasure of the flesh, not its pain, which is at fault . . . It is in the intercourse of the flesh that the pleasure lies."

53. Williams, "What's New about the Sexual Revolution?" p. 74; see also Chance, *Woman as Hero*, pp. 81–94, 103–4, for this material and a similar viewpoint. See McNeill and Gamer, *Medieval Handbooks of Penance*, p. 185, chap. 12, for a woman's "vice with a woman"; p. 185, chap. 13, regarding the "solitary vice"; p. 186, chaps. 16 and 17, on mother-son and brother-sister incest; p. 186, chap. 20, "if a mother initiates acts of fornication with her little son"; p. 197, chaps. 5–7, for penances for abortion and infanticide. On women with women, see Brown, *Immodest Acts*, pp. 6–20.

54. See Davidson, "Erotic 'Women's Songs.'" Davidson quotes, in order to refute, the old view of C. L. Wrenn: "As a poetic theme love is practically alien

to the Germanic and Anglo-Saxon genius" (pp. 453–54). See also Greenfield, "*Wulf and Edwacer*": "Would we dream that an Anglo-Saxon audience had a mind set for a double entendre were it not for the few 'obscene' riddles?" (p. 8).

55. See Fell, *Women in Anglo-Saxon England*, pp. 66–69, 84–88, for the occasional reference to the pleasure derived from male-female companionship and to friendship and companionship between kin of both sexes; see also *EHD*, pp. 494, 496, 524. Both Anglo-Saxon literature and the narrative sources are much richer concerning the joy of male bonding.

56. While a woman's rights and dignity may have been protected when her family entered into marriage negotiations on her behalf, the sources hardly indicate that she had much say in the matter. Wulfric, for example, made an arrangement with Archbishop Wulfstan to marry the latter's sister, and she was to receive her own block of lands for the duration of three lives; Godwine made a compact with Brihtric "when he wooed his daughter," and the land was to go to the survivor of the marriage, an agreement that would surely be upheld because "every trustworthy man in Kent and Sussex, whether thegn or commoner, is cognisant of these terms" (Robertson, *Anglo-Saxon Charters*, pp. 149, 151). See also *EHD*, pp. 547–48.

57. Swanton, *Anglo-Saxon Prose*, p. 174.

58. Ibid., p. 185. The quote is from Bald's *Leechbook*, and it calls to mind the lost topic of women in medicine, healing, and curative magic. I learned of Deegan and Scraggs, *Medicine in Early Medieval England*, too late to consult it for this paper. For a literary reference to the popular view about women's special curative prowess, see Swanton, *Three Lives*, p. 13, from "The Life of Harold Godwinson."

59. From "Songs of the High One," in Terry, *Poems of the Vikings*, p. 25.

60. Swanton, *Anglo-Saxon Prose*, pp. 28–29. The royal legislation against witches and witchcraft, with strong biblical roots, was repeated from time to time; see *EHD*, p. 373, and Attenborough, *Laws of the Earliest English Kings*, pp. 109, 131.

61. See Klinch, "Anglo-Saxon Women and the Law," and Fell, *Women in Anglo-Saxon England*, pp. 20–21, for some disagreement with Klinch. Still of value is Buckstaff, "Married Women's Property."

62. For maternal kin, see *EHD*, p. 383. On the reemergence of her kin after the husband's death, on an assymetrical division of marital property, and on how maternal relatives could be expected to pay the wergild of a man if he had no paternal kin, see Attenborough, *Laws of the Earliest English Kings*, pp. 15 (quoting Aethelbert, chap. 81), 69 (in Alfred's code, chap. 8), 79 (Alfred, chap. 30). On the extent to which women were seen as part of their natal families and men as part of their mothers' families, see Lancaster, "Kinship in Anglo-Saxon Society"; Loyn, "Kinship in Anglo-Saxon England." For other aspects of the issue, see Woolf, "Naming of Women"; Clark, "English Personal Names," with a bibliography of relevant onomastic scholarship.

63. Pelteret, "Two Old English Lists of Serfs"; Percival, "Precursors of Domesday."

64. See Fell, *Women in Anglo-Saxon England*, pp. 129–47, on Viking women in Britain. Even more recent is Jochens, "Medieval Icelandic Heroine"; Jochens asks, "What of the search for the indelible image of strong, wilful, domineering women?" (p. 35). Alas: they must "be consigned to the realm of male fiction" (p. 50).

65. Keynes and Lapidge, *Alfred the Great*, p. 57.

66. Ibid., p. 74.

67. Ibid., p. 174.

68. Colgrave, *Two Lives of St. Cuthbert*, pp. 65, 155.

69. Ibid., pp. 89–91; "he entered the house of a certain faithful handmaid of God, whom he was careful to visit very frequently, because he knew that she was given to good deeds, and also because she had brought him up from his boyhood's earliest years and was therefore called mother by him" (p. 201).

70. Eddius Stephanus, *Life of Bishop Wilfrid*, p. 7.

71. Felix, *Life of Guthlac*, pp. 167–219; see pp. 170–76 for the saint's boyhood and early calling.

72. Eddius Stephanus, *Life of Bishop Wilfrid*, p. 7.

BIBLIOGRAPHY

Primary Sources

Aird, Catherine. *Harm's Way*. Toronto, 1984.

Attenborough, Frederick L., ed. and trans. *The Laws of the Earliest English Kings*. 1922. Reprint. New York, 1963.

Barlow, Frank, ed. and trans. *The Life of King Edward Who Rests at Westminster*. London, 1967.

Bede. *The Ecclesiastical History of the English People*. Ed. and trans. Bertram Colgrave and R. A. B. Mynors. Oxford, 1969.

Beowulf. Trans. Burton Raffel. New York, 1963.

Campbell, Alistair, ed. and trans. *The Chronicle of Aethelweard*. London, 1962.

———, ed. and trans. *Encomium Emmae reginae*. Camden Society, 3d ser., no. 72. London, 1949.

Colgrave, Bertram, ed. and trans. *Two Lives of St. Cuthbert*. 1940. Reprint. Cambridge, 1985.

Eddius Stephanus. *The Life of Bishop Wilfrid*. Ed. and trans. Bertram Colgrave. 1927. Reprint. Cambridge, 1985.

Felix. *The Life of Guthlac*. In *Anglo-Saxon Saints and Heroes*, trans. Clinton Albertson, pp. 167–219. New York, 1967.

Gelling, Margaret, ed. and trans. *The Early Charters of the Thames Valley.* Leicester, 1979.

Keynes, Simon, and Michael Lapidge, trans. *Alfred the Great.* Harmondsworth, 1983.

McNeill, John T., and Helena Gamer, eds. and trans. *Medieval Handbooks of Penance.* 1938. Reprint. New York, 1965.

Robertson, Agnes J., ed. and trans. *Anglo-Saxon Charters.* 2d ed. Cambridge, 1956.

Sawyer, Peter H., ed. *The Charters of Burton Abbey.* London, 1979.

Sedulius Scottus. *On Christian Rulers and the Poems.* Trans. E. G. Doyle. Binghamton, N.Y., 1983.

Swanton, Michael, ed. and trans. *Anglo-Saxon Prose.* London, 1975.

———, ed. and trans. *Three Lives of the Last Englishmen.* New York, 1984.

Talbot, Charles, trans. *The Anglo-Saxon Missionaries in Germany.* New York, 1954.

Terry, Patricia, trans. *Poems of the Vikings: The Elder Edda.* Indianapolis, 1963.

Whitelock, Dorothy, ed. and trans. *Anglo-Saxon Wills.* Cambridge, 1930.

———, ed. and trans. *English Historical Documents, c. 500–1042.* London, 1955.

Whitelock, Dorothy, David C. Douglas, and Susie I. Tucker, trans. *The Anglo-Saxon Chronicle.* London, 1961.

Williamson, Craig, trans. *A Feast of Creatures: Anglo-Saxon Riddle Songs.* Philadelphia, 1982.

Secondary Sources

Adamson, John W. *The Illiterate Anglo-Saxon.* Cambridge, 1946.

Bandel, Betty. "The English Chroniclers' Attitude towards Women." *Journal of the History of Ideas* 16 (1955): 113–18.

Brown, Judith. *Immodest Acts: The Life of a Lesbian Nun in the Italian Renaissance.* Oxford, 1986.

Buckstaff, Florence. "Married Women's Property in Anglo-Saxon and Anglo-Norman Law and the Origin of the Common Law Dower." *Annals of the American Academy of Political and Social Science* 4 (1894): 233–64.

Chance, Jane. *Woman as Hero in Old English Literature.* Syracuse, N.Y., 1986.

Clark, Cecily. "English Personal Names ca. 650–1300: Some Prosopographical Bearings." *Medieval Prosopography* 8 (1987): 31–60.

Colman, Rebecca V. "The Abduction of Women in Barbarian Law." *Florilegium* 5 (1983): 62–75.

Davidson, Clifford. "Erotic 'Women's Songs' in Anglo-Saxon England." *Neophilologus* 59 (1975): 451–62.

Deegan, Marilyn, and D. G. Scraggs. *Medicine in Early Medieval England.* Manchester, 1987.

Dietrick, Sheila C. "An Introduction to Women in Anglo-Saxon Society (c. 600–

1060)." In *The Women of England from Anglo-Saxon Times to the Present: Interpretive Bibliographical Essays,* ed. Barbara Kanner, pp. 32–50. Hamden, Conn., 1979.

Fell, Christine. *Women in Anglo-Saxon England and the Impact of 1066.* London, 1984.

Ferro, Karen. "The King in the Doorway: *The Anglo-Saxon Chronicle,* A.D. 755." In *Medieval Kings and Kingship,* ed. Joel T. Rosenthal, pp. 17–30. ACTA, no. 11. Binghamton, N.Y., 1986.

Frantzen, Allen J. *The Literature of Penance in Anglo-Saxon England.* New Brunswick, 1983.

Greenfield, Stanley B. "*Wulf and Edwacer:* All Passion Spent." *Anglo-Saxon England* 15 (1986): 5–14.

Jochens, Jenny M. "The Medieval Icelandic Heroine: Fact or Fiction?" *Viator* 17 (1986): 35–50.

———. "The Politics of Reproduction and Medieval Norwegian Kingship." *American Historical Review* 92 (1987): 327–49.

Judd, Elizabeth. "Women before the Conquest: A Study of Women in Anglo-Saxon England." *University of Michigan Papers in Women's Studies* 1 (1974): 127–44.

Klinch, Anne L. "Anglo-Saxon Women and the Law." *Journal of Medieval History* 8 (1982): 107–21.

Lancaster, Lorraine. "Kinship in Anglo-Saxon Society." *British Journal of Sociology* 9 (1958): 234–48, 359–77.

Loyn, Henry R. "Kinship in Anglo-Saxon England." *Anglo-Saxon England* 3 (1974): 197–209.

Meyer, Marc A. "Land Charters and the Legal Position of Anglo-Saxon Women." In *The Women of England from Anglo-Saxon Times to the Present: Interpretive Bibliographical Essays,* ed. Barbara Kanner, pp. 37–82. Hamden, Conn., 1979.

Nelson, Janet L. "Inauguration Rituals." In *Early Medieval Kingship,* ed. Peter H. Sawyer and I. N. Wood, pp. 50–71. Leicester, 1977.

———. "Queens as Jezebels: The Careers of Brunhild and Balthild in Merovingian History." In *Medieval Women: Studies in Church History, Subsidia 1,* ed. Derek Baker, pp. 31–78. Oxford, 1978.

Nicholas, David. *The Domestic Life of a Medieval City: Women, Children, and the Family in Fourteenth-Century Ghent.* Lincoln, Nebr., 1985.

Nicholson, Joan, "*Feminae gloriosae:* Women in the Age of Bede." In *Medieval Women: Studies in Church History, Subsidia 1,* ed. Derek Baker, pp. 15–29. Oxford, 1978.

Oakley, Thomas P. "The Penitentials as Sources for Medieval History." *Speculum* 15 (1940): 210–23.

Pelteret, David A. E. "Two Old English Lists of Serfs." *Medieval Studies* 48 (1986): 470–513.

Percival, John. "The Precursors of Domesday: Roman and Carolingian Land Registers." In *Domesday Book: A Reassessment*, ed. Peter H. Sawyer, pp. 5–27. London, 1985.

Rivers, Theodore J. "Widows' Rights in Anglo-Saxon Law." *American Journal of Legal History* 19 (1975): 208–15.

Rosenthal, Joel T. "A Historiographical Survey: Anglo-Saxon Kings and Kingship since World War II." *Journal of British Studies* 24 (1985): 72–93.

Ross, Margaret C. "Concubinage in Anglo-Saxon England." *Past and Present* 108 (1985): 3–35.

Sawyer, Peter H. *Anglo-Saxon Charters: An Annotated List and Bibliography.* London, 1969.

Stafford, Pauline. "The King's Wife in Wessex, 800–1066." *Past and Present* 91 (1981): 3–27.

———. *Queens, Concubines, and Dowagers.* Athens, Ga., 1983.

Stenton, Doris M. *The English Woman in History.* London, 1957.

Stenton, Frank M. "The Historical Bearing of Place-Name Studies: The Place of Women in Anglo-Saxon History." *Transactions of the Royal Historical Society*, 4th ser., 25 (1943): 1–13.

Wainwright, Frederick T. "Aethelflaed, Lady of the Mercians." In *Scandinavian England*, ed. H. R. P. Finberg, pp. 305–24. Chichester, 1974.

Wallace-Hadrill, John M. *Early Germanic Kingship in England and on the Continent.* Oxford, 1971.

Whitelock, Dorothy. *The Beginnings of English Society.* Harmondsworth, 1952.

Williams, Edith M. "What's New about the Sexual Revolution?: Some Comments on Anglo-Saxon Attitudes towards Sexuality Based on Four Exeter Book Riddles." *Texas Quarterly* 18, no. 2 (1975): 46–55.

Woolf, Henry B. "The Naming of Women in Old English Times." *Modern Philology* 36 (1938): 113–20.

SAINTS' LIVES AS A SOURCE FOR
THE HISTORY OF WOMEN, 500–1100

Jane Tibbetts Schulenburg

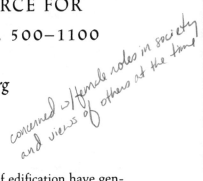

concerned w/female roles in society and views of others at the time

 edieval saints' lives or biographies of edification have generally not fared well among historians. Until the recent resurgence of interest in hagiography, or the study of sainthood and the cult of saints,[1] the historical value of these works had been discredited: historians had summarily dismissed the *vitae* of the holy dead as worthy of neither trust nor the expenditure of scholarly effort. Although Delehaye, in his classic study *Les Légendes hagiographiques*, argued that the lives of saints deserved the attention of scholars, he also underscored the unreliable character of these sources and the nearly insurmountable difficulties encountered in attempting to utilize them as historical documents. He warned scholars that "the important thing to be emphasized at the outset is the distinction between hagiography and history. The work of the hagiographer may be historical, but it is not necessarily so. It may take any literary form suited to honoring the saints, from an official record adapted to the needs of the faithful to a highly exuberant poem that is completely removed from factual reality."[2] Delehaye also cautioned scholars not to put excessive trust in the authors of saints' lives, whom he contended were neither historians nor biographers, but poets.[3] ❡ In general, the past's often hypercritical approach to the *vitae* of saints, based on its obsession with ascertainable "facts" and authenticity, has had the unfortunate result of discouraging historians from discovering the incredible richness and untapped wealth of information found in these early sources. Despite the negative evaluations of the past, this genre holds a remarkable potential for social historians and especially historians of medieval women, for, unlike many other sources of the Middle Ages, saints' lives focus a great deal of attention on women: the *vitae* are directly concerned with female roles in the church and society as well as contemporary perceptions, ideals, and valuations of women. The hun-

dreds of female and male *vitae* also afford us the unique opportunity to
observe broad patterns of change across the centuries and to compare the
expectations and descriptions of women's roles and images with those
of men's. They provide an excellent condensing lens to view shifts in
medieval women's worlds.

The *Vita*: Purpose and Audience

In *Sociologie et canonisations*, Pierre Delooz emphasizes the fact that one is only a
saint "for others" as well as "by others."
That is, the value of sanctity is first of all situated in the collective memory of the community; it is the saintly reputation recognized by one's
peers that is of primary importance. Secondly, one becomes a saint only
through the energetic expression of this opinion, through a pressure
group that formulates a public cult.[4] Therefore, in the process of the
"making of a saint," it was of primary importance to procure a worthy
propagandist or biographer to redact a *vita* of the candidate for sainthood,
for it was this dossier of the holy dead that became the main official vehi-
cle by which the saintly reputation was transformed into a public cult.
Over time, the *vita* also served the very important historical function of
keeping alive the memory of the saint and her cult.

The alleged purpose or express end of all saints' lives was didactic: to
edify the faithful, to teach Christian virtue, and to strengthen Christian
resolve. According to Delehaye, "To be strictly hagiographical the document must be of a religious character and aim at edification. The term
then must be confined to writings inspired by religious devotion to the
saints and intended to increase that devotion."[5] The church hoped that
through the use of *exempla*, or models of saintly behavior, the faithful
might modify their behavior or bring about "conversions" in their own
spiritually deficient lives.[6] The prologues to many of the saints' lives
therefore specifically mention edification as their primary purpose. The
prologue to the life of Saint Balthild, for example, stressed that, rather
than being addressed primarily to scholars, the *vita* was to be accessible
for the edification of the many.[7] The author of the life of Saint Leoba
also noted the instructive purpose of his work: this *vita* was dedicated to
Hadamout in order that she "may have something to read with pleasure
and imitate with profit."[8]

Although the encouragement of moral or spiritual improvement was
the express purpose of hagiographic literature, *vitae* were in fact often
written with more pragmatic, self-serving political and economic ends
in mind. Some were inspired or commissioned by the great families

of the period and served to legitimize and to exalt their noble lineage, reputations, or influence. (These *vitae* glorified a very prominent type of early medieval saint called the *Adelsheilige* by the German historians.)[9] However, in general, the *vitae* served as propaganda for the expansion or promotion of the cult of the saint and the exaltation of a religious center. Thus, through the *fama*, or celebrity, of the saint and her miracles (as advertised by the *vita*), churchmen and churchwomen hoped to attract crowds of pilgrims, material donations, as well as special privileges to the monastery or sanctuary that "owned" and displayed the precious remains of the holy dead.[10]

As a genre of didactic literature, the *vita* aimed at universal appeal: it addressed a very broad medieval audience composed of all Christians and especially "sinners." In their attempt to appeal to all social classes, the authors of the lives often portrayed their protagonists, who at this time were invariably recruited from the nobility, as classless, "socially amphibious" individuals.[11] Through a certain noblesse oblige, the saints accommodated themselves to the social diversity of the faithful. During their lifetimes they came into contact with the local serfs, peasants, townspeople, as well as the nobility and royalty. And after their deaths —now as citizens of both worlds—they remained faithful to their same earthly constituency. With their enhanced spiritual *potentia*, the saints continued to assist their supporters through the working of miracles; they served as protectors of their monasteries, or heavenly intercessors for their souls.

Despite ideological attempts at universal appeal, many of the cults of the holy dead remained rather localized, reflecting local roots and regional interests. This seems to have been especially true for female saints, who frequently had limited posthumous cults.[12] The Belgian *Vita Berlendis*, for example, appears to have been written for the parishioners of Meerbeke, the burial place of Saint Berlind. The hagiographer specifically notes that "the saints must be particularly honored where they are buried."[13] In this context, the favors or miracles of the holy dead remained rather specific and localized. They used their special intercessory powers, for example, to quiet local storms, extinguish fires, free the area of drought, famine, or pestilence; or they promoted bountiful crops and healthy livestock. Thus the audience of the saint's life was often geographically limited to a provincial or even microregional level. Many of the *vitae* seem to have been tied to the zone of influence of the monastery in which they were written; others were directed to the inhabitants of the specific locale or parish where the saint was buried.

Further distinctions were sometimes made in regard to the audience of the saint's life. It appears that the material of some of the *vitae* was recognized as much too subtle for the masses: it incorporated formal theology and dogma that supposed a level of sophistication, a capacity of abstraction too complex for the general faithful. Therefore, some of the saints' lives seem to have been especially directed to the more restricted interests and needs of religious specialists and the educated elite, namely, churchmen and churchwomen.[14] Since the majority of female saints for this early period acceded to sanctity by means of the cloister—specifically as founders and abbesses of monasteries—it appears that through validating certain monastic virtues and religious behavior, these *vitae* had particular appeal and relevance to audiences of female religious as well as to noblewomen who followed a life of monastic virtue within the confines of their home (as nuns manqué). In praising monastic spirituality, with its requirements of alienation from the world, harsh asceticism, the passion of Christ, a fascination with martyrdom, the cultivation of mystical experiences, and so forth, these *vitae* lent authority to their lives within the cloister.[15] These lives were often directed to the abbess or sisterhood of a particular saint's community, who, in turn, were responsible for promoting her cult. In some cases a number of *vitae* of female saints were condensed, collected, and then incorporated as *exempla* in a larger didactic work. This was the case, for example, of Aldhelm's famous prose treatise, *De virginitate* (ca. 680). This work, which capsulizes the lives of twenty-two virginal women saints, was addressed to Abbess Hildelith and a number of her nuns at Barking Abbey. [16]

Many of the lives of the *mulieres sanctae*, then, served as guides for female religious, and in this capacity they formed an integral part of women's monastic experience. These biographies of edification, for example, were recited in their monastic choirs; they were read to the nuns in chapter and in the refectory during their meals, as well as in their workrooms while they occupied themselves with various manual tasks such as weaving, sewing, and embroidery. The lives of saints were also available for private reading by the nuns. Female religious transcribed and illuminated the *vitae* in their monastic *scriptoria*. The especially dramatic events of the saints' lives or the saints with their special symbols were visually captured in the iconography of the monastery, which included sculptural programs, stained glass windows, frescoes, wall hangings, liturgical vestments, altarcloths, and reliquaries.

The *vitae* were incorporated into the monastic liturgy; prayers and hymns extolled the saints' virtues. Sermons focused on the lives of popular saints. The holy dead were cataloged in church calendars, legendaries, and martyrologies. The *vita* assumed special importance on the anniversary of the saint or her *dies natalis* (that is, on the day of her death), when the extraordinary acts of her life as well as posthumous miracles provided the focal points of the celebration.

Hagiographers and Their Craft

Despite severe scholarly criticism of the hagiographers of the early medieval period, many were in fact rather well-informed biographers. It appears that a good number of the *vitae* were actually compiled by contemporaries or near contemporaries of the candidate for sainthood. As eyewitnesses to many of the events ("iuxta id quod vidimus" or "iuxta id quod vidimus vel per idoneos testes audivimus"), they have left us numerous careful works describing female saints and their milieu.[17] While many of the *vitae* are the work of contemporaries, others are of uncertain date. Nevertheless, in their consistency with other sources of the period, some of these lives appear to have been redacted only a few generations after the death of the saint. Other lives seem to have been further removed from the lifetime of the saint and can be dated a century or more after the saint's death. Some of these *vitae* are total fabrications based on an amalgamation of popular hagiographic topos. However, among these later versions one frequently finds revisions or sometimes amplified editions of older *vitae*. In many cases these works appear to remain rather faithful to the original texts. During the Carolingian period and the time of the English revivals of the tenth and eleventh centuries, copies of saints' lives proliferated in monastic *scriptoria*. In regard to the tradition of revised *vitae* produced by Carolingian scribes, Jo Ann McNamara has argued, "In most cases, their contributions chiefly consist of repairing barbarities of literary style and embellishing the original with pious reflections and scriptural citations designed to heighten the didactic value of the story."[18]

The process involved in the selection of the hagiographer, the collection of information, and the actual redaction of the *vita* is of special interest to the historian. It appears that few authors of *vitae* began their holy biographies without having their "hand forced," or without receiving a formal commission to undertake the work.[19] The process usually originated with those involved in the promotion of the saint and the development of her cult center (i.e., the abbess or abbot of a monastery, the whole community, or the local bishop) approaching a monk, cleric, or nun to write the *vita* of their candidate for sanctity. We learn, for example, that the *vitae* of Saints Radegund, Gertrude, Rictrude, Aldegonde, Adelheide, and a number of others were written at the request of the abbess or monastic community of the saint. The life of Saint Gertrude, for example, was commissioned by Abbess Dominica, the third abbess of Nivelles. The *vita* was then written by one of the Irish priests of the double community of Nivelles. As a contemporary of the saint, he was a well-informed eyewitness to the events that he described, "iuxta id quod vidimus."[20] The first of six lives of Saint Aldegonde, abbess of Maubeuge (d. 684), was also written shortly after the saint's death. Again, the author appears to have been a contemporary of the saint and was present at many of the events he describes, including assisting at her funeral. It has been suggested that the author was perhaps a monk at Nivelles and was commissioned to write the *vita* by his community.[21] (This life is also of special interest because it incorporates Aldegonde's visions, which the saint had related to Abbot Sobinus of Nivelles and to another brother, whose name we do not know, who transcribed the visions as well as her *vita*.)[22]

The abbess or community then usually approached someone of their own monastery who was preferably both a writer and an acquaintance of the candidate for sainthood to compose the *vita*. However, if for some reason there was no one believed to be competent enough within one's own community, it was necessary to solicit a writer from another house.[23] Therefore, in some cases, professional hagiographers were sought out and commissioned to write the prescribed life. The primary *vita* of Saint Rictrude and the fourth life of Saint Aldegonde, for example, were commissioned by their communities to be written by Hucbald, a monk of Saint Amand. At this time he was apparently the "l'hagiographe à la monde" of their region.[24] It is also interesting to note that in some cases the *vitae* commissioned of "strangers" from outside of the community did not prove to be entirely successful in the long run. Such was the situation, for example, at Liessies, where the canons solicited a monk of Waulsort to redact a life of Saint Hiltrude. The chroniclers of Liessies later came to regret this choice for the saint's biographer, for, although he had been adept in hagiographic literature, he was ignorant of the abbey's unique history.[25]

Delehaye has noted that hagiography from its beginnings was an impersonal literature—the product of anonymous authors.[26] Although the majority of authors remain in the anonymous tradition, a good number of hagiographers of this period can be identified. From a collective study of some 1,130 saints' lives cataloged in the *Bibliotheca hagiographica latina* for the years 500–1100, we know the names of the redactors of approximately 41 percent of the male *vitae* and 39 percent of the female *vitae*. It is indeed significant to note that with the exception of two *vitae*, all of the lives of women saints with identifiable authors (found in the *Bibliotheca hagiographica latina*) were written by men. Also, as cataloged by this collection, only two of the lives of male saints have been officially attributed to female authors. [27]

Thus, despite the high level of educational and literary competency of female religious during this early period, it seems that nuns were relegated to function as copyists, and only infrequently were they designated as authors of *vitae*. [28] It would seem reasonable that the authorship of female saints' lives (as was the case for male *vitae*) would have been assigned to those closest to the holy candidate and most knowledgeable in regard to her attributes and activities, namely, female members of the saint's community. Nevertheless, it was apparently traditional for churchmen to assume the redaction of the "official" *vitae* of the female candidates for sainthood. It appears that this practice can already be found among the early church fathers. The letters of Saint Jerome, *The Lausiac History* by Palladius, and *The Dialogues* of Pope Gregory the Great all contain early "hagiographic" collections of female saints.[29] It is of interest to note that in Saint Odilo of Cluny's contemporary *vita* of the empress-saint Adelaide (d. 992), he comments on this tradition of learned men assuming the responsibility of recording the lives of holy women. He specifically refers to the role of Saint Jerome and his descriptions of the holy acts of Paula, Eustochium, Marcella, Melania, Fabiola, and others. [30]

Therefore, in general, the authors of female saints' lives from about 500 to 1100 appear to have been recruited from among educated churchmen. While the majority of the *vitae* were products of monastic hagiography, a few of the lives were written by popes, bishops, priests, and chaplains. It seems quite possible that the preference for churchmen as effective propagandists of female saints might have been perceived as politically and pragmatically expedient for communities wishing to promote their candidate's cult; that is, the close association of churchmen (sometimes prominent figures in the church hierarchy) with the *mulieres sanctae* and their *vitae* no doubt provided a greater authoritativeness or lent additional credence as well as enhanced visibility to the new saints' cults. It served perhaps as a type of validation of female sanctity by the church and its male hierarchy. Thus, often faced with the skepticism and contempt of *detractores* toward the holy dead (and this seems to have been especially problematic in regard to the *mulieres sanctae* and their cults), hagiographers had to rigorously defend the extraordinary acts and miracles of their saints.[31] The refutation of perceived objections or defense of saintly credentials was perhaps believed to be strengthened by a male-authored defense of the holy dead over and against the testimony, for example, of a "simple nun."

Although it appears from our survey of *vitae* with identifiable authors that it was traditional for churchmen to compose the lives of women saints, a closer study of internal clues of the *vitae* might in fact reveal an increased possibility of female authorship. A fascinating example of this concerns the authorship of the lives of Saints Willibald and Wynebald. The identification of this "anonymous" hagiographer was discovered by B. Bischoff. Through the interpretation of a cryptogram that had been placed between these two *vitae* in an early manuscript, Bischoff was able to identify Huneberc, an Anglo-Saxon nun of Heidenheim, as the author.[32] Although in the past scholars have assumed that anonymous authors of saints' lives were male ecclesiastics and have therefore searched for textual indicators that might help to identify them with certain monasteries or positions within the church, these sources need to be reexamined with the underlying assumption that "anonymous" could in fact be a woman, especially a female religious. Cases in which there are a series of several *vitae* commissioned over time for the same saint could prove to be especially important in the discovery of female authorship. It is in this context that Janet Nelson, for example, has come to the conclusion that the early A *vita* of Saint Balthild, originally attributed to a monk, was in fact redacted by a nun of Balthild's monastery of Chelles and commissioned by a community of monks—perhaps those of Corbie.[33]

Dossiers of the Holy Dead: Patterns and Content

While many of the *vitae* conform to a general pattern or schema, there still remains some variety in these spiritual biographies.

In general, the early hagiographers wrote in Latin and in prose. However, many vernacular saints' lives date to the ninth through eleventh centuries. One of the especially popular works of this genre was Aelfric's *Lives of Saints*, written in Anglo-Saxon in around 996. Despite the widespread existence of these early lives in the vernacular, the use of vernacular in the writing of *vitae* became especially popular in the twelfth century. In a few cases, a second life, based on the first, would be written in meter: *vita metrica* or *rhythmica*. It has been suggested that the metrical form of the *vita* was perhaps used in a less official or more popular context. It appears to have served pedagogical purposes, specifically as exercises for young students. [34]

Many of the saints' lives of this early period begin with a prologue that is especially valuable for historians. Although incorporating formulas and stereotypic language, the prologue nevertheless places the *vita* in the political and religious context of the age. It sometimes reveals the identity of the author, the commissioner(s) of the *vita*, and to whom the work was dedicated. In the prologue the biographer also attempts to bolster the *vita*'s credibility by carefully identifying the various sources of information. The alleged purpose of the *vita* and protestations of incompetence on the part of the author are also found in the prologue. [35]

In their attempts to scrupulously identify their sources of information, the prologues of some of the perhaps more reliable saints' lives are of special interest to historians. As noted, in naming their sources the authors intended to provide unassailable proof to the skeptics of the validity of the characteristics and supernatural acts of their protagonists.[36] It appears from the prologues that the hagiographers generally relied on a combination of written and oral sources in redacting their *vitae*. The monk Rudolf, in his *Life of St. Leoba* (ca. 836), for example, describes in some detail the procedure of collecting material for his *vita* as well as his specific sources of information.

> I have been unable to discover all the facts of her life. I shall therefore recount the few that I have learned from the writings of others, venerable men who heard them from four of her disciples, Agatha, Thecla, Nana and Eoloba. Each one copied them down according to his ability and left them as a memorial to posterity.
>
> One of these, a holy priest and monk named Mago, who died about five years ago, was on friendly terms with these women and during his frequent visits to them used to speak with them about things profitable to the soul. In this way he was able to learn a great deal about her life. He was careful to make short notes of everything he heard, but, unfortunately, what he left was almost unintelligible, because, whilst he was trying to be brief and succinct, he expressed things in such a way as to leave the facts open to misunderstanding and provide no basis for certainty. This happened, in my opinion, because in his eagerness to take down every detail before it escaped his memory he wrote the facts down in a kind of shorthand and hoped that during his leisure he could put them in order and make the book more easy for readers to understand. The reason why he left everything in such disorder, jotted

down on odd pieces of parchment, was that he died quite suddenly and had no time to carry out his purpose.

. . . I have tried to collect together all the scattered notes and papers left by the men I have mentioned. The sequence of events . . . is based on information found in their notes and on the evidence I have gathered from others by word of mouth. For there are several religious men still living who can vouch for the facts mentioned in the documents, since they heard them from their predecessors, and who can add some others worthy of remembrance. These latter appeared to me suitable for inclusion in the book and therefore I have combined them with material from the written notes.

Rudolf then concludes his fascinating discussion of sources and the justification for their use with the following argument: "For it seems to me that there should be no doubt in the minds of the faithful about the veracity of the statements made in this book, since they are shown to be true both by the blameless character of those who relate them and by the miracles which are frequently performed at the shrine of the saint." [37]

The *Life of St. Rictrude* (d. ca. 688) also provides some fascinating details on the process of gathering information and the problems of hagiographic production. Apparently during the Norman invasions (ca. 879), the old *vitae* or acts of the saint had been destroyed along with Rictrude's monastery of Marchiennes. At the beginning of the tenth century (ca. 907), Stephen, the bishop of Liege, and the community then approached Hucbald, a monk of the neighboring monastery of Saint Amand and a "professional hagiographer," to write a new biography of their patron saint. However, they were able to provide him only with fragmentary written information about the saint which corroborated facts found in the oral tradition. Thus, in the preface to the *vita*, Hucbald carefully relates that some individuals worthy of trust provided guarantees, that is, affirmed to him under sworn oath, that the facts that they recounted to him conformed to those of the ancient sources that had disappeared with the Norman pillaging of the monastery. [38]

The *vita* of Saint Adelheide, first abbess of Willich (d. ca. 1015), is also of interest in regard to the hagiographer's sources. This life is one of the very few that has the name of a female author attached to it. It was written by Bertha, a noblewoman and nun of the Abbey of Willich, in around 1056. In the prologue to the *vita*, the author notes her reliance on the oral tradition: she received her source material from the nuns who knew the saint and especially from an old woman, Engilrada, who was the faithful chambermaid of Adelheide (*cubiculariae fidelis*). [39]

The situation surrounding the writing of the contemporary *vita* of the empress-saint Adelaide (d. 992) appears to have been rather unusual. The life was written by the empress's friend, Abbot Odilo of Cluny. According to the author, it was based on a narrative of facts that the candidate for sainthood, Adelaide herself, had related to Odilo about the events of her own life. [40]

In addition to providing information on the source material used by the hagiographers in redacting their *vitae*, the prologues also contain the authors' protestations of humility and incompetence. Because of their perceived unfitness for the task, some hagiographers requested that their work be corrected or amended as necessary. Although these protestations of incompetence were essentially formulaic and part of hagiographic convention, one of the *vitae* attributed to female authorship (i.e., that of the nun Huneberc) notes the author's awareness of her own scholarly "disabilities" as well as her special vulnerability based on her sex. Perhaps recognizing that the writing of saints' lives was essentially a masculine prerogative, she was aware of the gender-specific criticism that her work might arouse simply because it was written by a woman. Yet her admission of "weakness" or female frailty could perhaps be read as a pretended or feigned diffidence, for beneath it all there appears to have been a great self-assurance and conviction of purpose.[41] She felt, after all, "compelled" as a relative of Saints Willibald and Wynebald to use her talent to keep alive their saintly memory. In the preface to her biography of the saint, the nun Huneberc writes, in a self-deprecating, submissive *topos*:

> I, an unworthy sister of Saxon origin, last and least in life and manners, venture to write for the sake of posterity and present to you who are religious and preachers of the Gospel a brief account of the early life of the venerable Willibald. Although I lack the necessary experience and knowledge *because I am but a weak woman*, yet I would like as far as lies in my power, to gather together a kind of nosegay of his virtues and give you something by which you may remember them. And here I repeat that I am not urged on through presumption to attempt a task for which I am so ill fitted . . . I know that it may seem very bold on my part to write this book when there are so many holy priests capable of doing better, but as a humble relative I would like to record something of their deeds and travels for future ages. [42]

The prologue of the *vita* is then followed by the saint's dossier per se. It is a type of spiritual itinerary, a biographic "ladder of perfection" that documents the saint's pursuit of the *vita perfecta*. Here the hagiographer consciously shapes the life of the saintly hero into a coherent whole with the purpose to sway the readers to the saint's cause. And while many of the *vitae* are arranged in a chronological and progressive order, others follow a less regular form and provide disconnected fragments and sporadic episodes of the saint's life. The organization of the sacred biography was aimed at providing a biographic image and emphasizing the virtues and attainments of the saint. [43]

The typical life contains a combination of the following biographical information: the saint's origins, parents and social status, birth, infancy, and adolescence (often accompanied by a life crisis); the adoption of a religious vocation within the cloister or the decision to pursue a holy life "in the world"; and the advancement and recognition of the candidate for sanctity within her chosen career. The *vita* also provides a catalog of the saint's virtues, miracles, visions, and prophecies. While many of the saintly dossiers furnish rather limited descriptions of the saint's early life and activities, they concentrate in some detail on the final illness of the *mulier sancta*, with the climax of the *vita* recounting the premonition, death, and burial of the saint. (Since the cult of the saint focused on the tomb and the saint's "invisible living presence" within this sacrosanct place, the events surrounding the actual death and burial of the holy dead played an extremely significant role for the propagandist as well as the faithful.)

The dossier of the holy dead is frequently followed by an appendix called the *miracula*, or the *gloria posthuma* (according to the Bollandists). It is in this section of the *vita* that the posthumous miracles of the saint are recorded. The collection of miracles formed one of the most important elements—the raison d'être—in the propagation of the saint's life and cult. Miracles were especially used to provoke the veneration of the faithful and to attract crowds and material advantages to the saint's tomb. Against the skepticism and contempt voiced by the *detractores* toward the holy dead, evidence of miracles provided irrefutable evidence of one's sanctity. [44]

In addition to the *miracula*, a final section called the *translatio* or *elevatio* was frequently appended to the *vita*. This appendix describes how the relics of the saint were acquired or recounts the process, events, and miracles surrounding the official elevation or translation of the saint's body to a new, more worthy place of burial. During this early period, it was this act of translation that publicly recognized the sanctity of the individual and the establishment of her cult: it was equated with an informal canonization for these popular saints. The saint's translation frequently provided the occasion for the actual redaction of the *vita*, with the purpose of providing a coordinated promotional effort of advertising or "selling" the saint and her cult. In some cases the building of a new church with a more magnificent setting for the saint's tomb provided the impetus for the translation of the saint's body and the writing of the *vita*.[45]

While many of the *vitae* followed a predictable pattern or schema, their actual content and orientation varied considerably. In the creation, elaboration, and reconstitution of hagiographic material, a number of forces were involved. As we have noted, the *vita* was shaped by its general purpose, patronage, and audience as well as by the information available to the author. In addition, the interests, values, perspectives, and "space" in which the author worked played a decidedly influential role in molding the *vita*.

To underscore the significant discrepancies that could occur in the content, ideals, and values of saints' lives, we are especially fortunate to have two contemporary *vitae* that were commissioned for the same sixth-century female saint, the Frankish queen Radegund. The original "official" *vita* was written in about 587 by Fortunatus, poet, friend, and spiritual advisor to Saint Radegund and later the bishop of Poitiers.[46] The "second *vita*," as it was called, was written some twenty years later by the nun Baudonivia, confidante, companion, and witness to the events of Radegund's life.[47] It is interesting that Baudonivia's redaction was written at the insistence of Deidimia, abbess of Radegund's monastery of Sainte Croix, to fill the many lacunae that Fortunatus had left in his *vita*. Her charge was to specifically broaden or enlarge upon that which he had passed over. She therefore notes that she does not wish to repeat those things that Fortunatus had written about in his *vita*.[48]

In the past, scholars in general have failed to take seriously the *liber secundus* by Baudonivia. They have frequently dismissed this *vita* as an invalid or unauthoritative source or have viewed it as merely a complementary text, a simple appendix or addition to the primary *vita* by Fortunatus.[49] The general disdain and lack of trust in Baudonivia's life seem to have been based on the author's rusticity of language (as she herself notes, "non polito sed rustico"), the digressions and lack of rigorous ordering in her presentation of facts, as well as discrepancies between some of her perceptions and "facts" with those of Gregory of Tours.[50] However, the lack of interest in Baudonivia as an early hagiographer and the devaluation of her *vita* as an authoritative text seem also to have been predicated, at least in part, on Baudonivia's position as female author—simple nun (who describes herself as "less learned but more devoted") in contrast to the prestige of the renowned author and bishop, Fortunatus. [51]

In the "avant-propos" of his biography of Radegund, René Aigrain noted the differences between the contemporary *vitae* of Fortunatus and Baudonivia. While commenting on Baudonivia's weakness in expressing herself, Aigrain nevertheless wrote that she deserves recognition. "Without her we would know nothing or nearly nothing of that which gives the life of Radegund its individual character, its particular charm: neither the resistance to the attempts of Clothair, nor the cult of relics, nor the apparitions, nor the last moments . . . Not that that of Fortunatus does not have its value, but it falls more in the common framework of hagiography, expanding on the virtues and series of miracles." [52] Later, in his classic work *L'Hagiographie,* Aigrain commented upon the "strange lacunae of Fortunatus' *vita* that the nuns of Ste-Croix requested that one of their own make good on it and complete it." He noted that Baudonivia undertook the task of completing this insufficient narration by recording her precious memories of the saint's intimate life, which had been revealed to her, as confidante, by the queen. [53]

In his fascinating study, "Sainte Radegonde, son type de sainteté et la chretienté de son temps," Etienne Delaruelle has argued that the two *vitae* of Saint Radegund reflect the age's opposing conceptions of sanctity. In his view, a sharp dichotomy existed between these two works: "Fortunatus saw in Radegund only the nun whose human horizon was voluntarily limited. Baudonivia, on the contrary, portrays for us a figure with the dimension of the world of her time, caring about all that happens and continuing to use her royal power to intervene." [54]

It was this pioneering study by Delaruelle that sparked a lively debate among scholars on the interpretation of the basic variations found in these *vitae.* Delaruelle's hypotheses of the strong opposition in the conceptualization of Radegund and the epic tradition underlying the political action of the queen have been criticized by Frantisek Graus. In stressing a general continuity of the *vitae,* Graus minimized the differences between Fortunatus's portrayal of Radegund as "ascetic" and Baudonivia's depiction of the saint as "nun and patron of a royal monastery." [55]

Jacques Fontaine, in his excellent study "Hagiographie et politique," has traced this scholarly controversy. Very briefly, while recognizing the merits of Delaruelle's arguments, Fontaine stresses the continuity of the literary and spiritual influence of the popular model *Vita Martini* on Radegund's sanctity as well as on the style and content of the biographies written by Baudonivia and Fortunatus. He argues that this Martinian archetype—at the same time spiritual and literary—allowed Fortunatus and Baudonivia to portray the Frankish queen as the type of complex reincarnation of most of the *virtutes Martini*. While Fortunatus emphasized Radegund's imitation of the ascetic and thaumaturgical roles of Saint Martin (in praising her heroic exercise of self-abnegation, penitence, and miracles), Baudonivia accentuated the active aspects of a "militant sanctity"—also present among the *virtutes* of Martin. Thus Baudonivia introduced a number of major episodes of the queen's active intervention in political affairs outside of the cloister of Sainte Croix, events absent from Fortunatus's account of the saint.[56] In praising Radegund's active, public role, for example, as peacemaker, proselytizer, and acquirer of relics, Baudonivia introduces a new concept, that of the queen-saint's service to her country.[57] It is, then, in this active political role as "militant saint" that Baudonivia depicts Radegund as sharing in the impressive historic legacy of other great female saints. Thus, in light of her protagonist's successful procurement of the relics of the Holy Cross and in an attempt to further strengthen her royal/saintly credentials, Baudonivia places Radegund in the great imperial tradition of the first Christian empress, Saint Helena (founder of the "true cross"). Baudonivia then argues that what Saint Helena did for the East, Blessed Radegund accomplished for Gaul.[58] And it was through the acquisition of the piece of the "true cross" that Radegund hoped to promote her monastery of Sainte Croix as the center of a dynastic cult that would serve as "an agency of intercession on behalf of kings."[59] According to Baudonivia, Radegund envisioned the relic of the "true cross" "as an instrument through which the salvation of the kingdom could be secured and the welfare of the country assured."[60]

In addition to describing the active, public aspects of Radegund's sanctity, the *liber secundus* also focuses in some detail on the saint's private virtues. Here Baudonivia utilized personal information that she had learned as a confidante of the saint. Fontaine argues that the choice of episodes found in Baudonivia's *vita* "is at the same time more interior and more exterior than in the first life. More interior in the sense of confidences on the interior life of the queen, on her vision and mystical grace, but also more exterior, in the sense of an exercise of an 'active sanctity' in the world."[61] Fontaine then suggests that the biographers' distinct choices in selecting different Martinian archetypes with which to present the virtues of Radegund were based on changes in the functional orientation required of each life. Fortunatus's *vita*, written shortly after the queen's death in 587 and the establishment of her cult, had the purpose of preserving the memory of the founder of the monastery. In contrast, Baudonivia's life, written some twenty years later, reflects a rather different milieu with different needs. The monastery of Sainte Croix had suffered a serious revolt of its nuns in 589 and was experiencing problems with the episcopacy and local powers. Faced with these critical threats, a new image of the saintly founder–protector was required. Fontaine argues that the second *vita* by Baudonivia might be seen as a type of "hagiographic reconstruction," which, in light of the difficulties at Sainte Croix, insisted on the active, political aspects of Radegund's "militant sanctity"—namely, her forceful intervention outside of the cloister. [62]

Suzanne Wemple has also observed the differing conceptions of sanctity found in the two lives of Radegund. She, however, argues convincingly that the preference for certain styles of sanctity—the diversity in ideals and values—was at least in part gender based. "Female authors writing about women introduced feminine values and ideals into hagiography. They replaced the ideal of the asexual female saint, the 'virago,' whose greatest accomplishment was the imitation of male virtues, with a heroine who relied on female attributes to achieve sanctity." [63] Wemple notes that Baudonivia was the first to emphasize typically female attributes. Her characterization of Radegund as mother figure, peacemaker, and promoter of a dynastic cult was an unusual theme in hagiography. Wemple argues that Baudonivia's presentation of the Frankish queen as a prototype of the ideal nun was not "a self-effacing and sexless abstraction. In contrast to Fortunatus' portrayal of Radegund as the withdrawn wife and reluctant queen whose main objective was to transcend her femininity and escape from her husband, Baudonivia described Radegund as an outgoing and emotional woman, who was as concerned about the affairs of the convent as about the developments in the kingdom." [64]

Both *vitae*, the *liber primus* by Fortunatus and the *liber secundus* by Baudonivia, are extremely useful in reconstructing the life and society of this fascinating Merovingian saint. They provide complementary information, which, as Baudonivia notes, was the reason her second life was commissioned. The *vitae* also reflect the special interests, orientations, ideals, and values of the authors. They are especially invaluable for historians, for they allow us to compare these two contemporary visions of sanctity. Clearly, the *vita* by the nun Baudonivia should not be dismissed as an unauthoritative source (as it has been in the past), nor

should it be considered as *merely* an appendix or supplement to Fortunatus's "official" *vita*. Rather, this life should be recognized and studied
on its own merits, for it is especially through Baudonivia's candid, "non-
professional" *vita*, with its personal details, observations, and strength of
characterization, that we are able to transcend Fortunatus's more learned
and abstract portrayal of the saint and to understand the unique aspects
of Radegund's personality, strategies, and experiences. Also, and very
importantly, through her original portrayal of a female saint, Baudonivia
furnishes us with the first extant sacred biography written by a woman
who has left us her name. Indeed, her *vita* of Saint Radegund is at the beginning of medieval women's biographic tradition—"in praise of women
worthies"—which culminates in Christine de Pizan's monumental historical work, *The Book of the City of Ladies*. Baudonivia's life provides us
with the unique opportunity to examine female perceptions, ideals, and
values of this early period. It is, then, this *vita secunda*, studied against
a background of Fortunatus's work as well as the writings of Gregory of
Tours, that is of particular value to those interested in women's history.

Problems and   Although there has been a great deal of interest
Possibilities   and scholarship in the area of hagiography over
                     the years, until approximately the last two decades
scholars had discredited the historical value of saints' lives. The hypercritical tradition in regard to hagiography can be found in a number of
studies by French scholars. For example, in his work on Saint Martin
of Tours, E. C. Babut claimed that most of the *Vita Martini* was an
"anthology of unbelievable facts of diverse sources . . . most of which
without doubt have come from fiction, plagiarism, or from a hundred-
fold exaggeration." According to Babut, the life of Saint Martin was "a
tissue of untrue tales [or lies]." [65] Ferdinand Lot, in his classic work *The
End of the Ancient World and the Beginnings of the Middle Ages*, provided
another critical attack on this genre: "The study of the lives of saints of
the East and West (there are thousands of them) has in store for us great
critical difficulties and also painful literary disappointments. Very few of
these *vitae* are sincere and have real emotion. The vast majority of them
are abominable trash. Hagiography is a low form of literature like the
serial novel in our own days." [66] In another work, Lot observed that the
lives of Breton saints were "entirely devoid of historical value." [67]

More recently, Frantisek Graus, in his introduction to hagiographic
studies, has qualified these early attacks by arguing that "the legends

are certainly not 'historical works' in the sense of the nineteenth century; they are rather 'literature,' and more particularly propaganda literature."[68]

Over the years, however, historians have generally demonstrated a profound mistrust of the lives of saints. Some of the more serious complaints leveled against hagiographic sources include the often substantial time lapse between the redaction of a life and the events it purported to record; the uncritical approach and analysis of the hagiographers; the incompetence of style accompanied by blatant plagiarism from earlier saints' lives or borrowings from the Bible; problems of authenticity and the attribution of the actions of a well-known saint to an unknown or spurious figure; invention of false information; distortion of events, actions, and virtues; the use of vague, abstract types and pious generalities rather than individualized depictions and particular details; and the incorporation of *topoi*, legends, and popular fantasy. Scholars are also warned of the critical problems surrounding the transmission of the *vitae* and the added difficulties involved in various interpolations and editions. Thus dismissing the dossiers of the holy dead as primary sources unworthy of serious historical study, scholars have restricted their use of saints' *vitae* to providing unusual anecdotes, incidental information, or notes that could then be gathered to support "real" historical evidence.[69]

It appears that with the development of the annales school, the growing interest in social history and the history of mentalities, and the adoption of a more sympathetic approach to the understanding of history, an increasing number of scholars have taken a serious second look at saints' lives. In his review of Delehaye's classic study, *Sanctus*, Marc Bloch, for example, underscored the great potential that saints' lives afford historians in their perceptions of "l'esprit humain."[70] Especially over the last two decades, historians have discovered the *vitae* of saints to be extremely rich as sources of both "intentional evidence" and "unintentional evidence," that is, evidence that is revealed in the sources rather than evidence that was intended to be communicated, or "evidence of witnesses in spite of themselves."[71] Saints' lives are now considered by many scholars as reliable sources of "factual information" and particulars of local history as well as of popular ideas, beliefs, and the collective mentalities of the period. Nevertheless, while there has been a recent proliferation of excellent historical and interdisciplinary studies on saints in medieval society, studies following in the tradition of the annales school, the emphasis of many of these works has been on male sanctity or the institution of canonization.[72] Few of these studies have concentrated specifically on the development of female sanctity or sainthood and gender in medieval society. Also, the scholars who have focused on female sanctity or have integrated the study of women saints into their general works on medieval sanctity have been mainly concerned with the central and late Middle Ages—the period from the twelfth or thirteenth through the fifteenth centuries. [73]

Therefore, the dossiers of saints have been recently recognized as an invaluable source for the study of women in the medieval church and society. They are especially useful for the early medieval period, when documentation is scarce enough for the study of traditional male-oriented, political history but frustratingly absent for the reconstruction of women's lives and experiences. Thus, despite their complexities, problems, and dangers, the immense possibilities and promise afforded by the lives of saints far outweigh their disadvantages.

The sheer numbers alone, the hundreds of female and male saints' *vitae* for this period, allow us to study on a macrolevel women in medieval society. Through a collective study of these sources, we can look at gender relations and compare the experiences of the *mulieres sanctae* with those of their male contemporaries. The lives provide us with the unique advantage, not available in any other sources of the period, to observe broad changes across the centuries and geographic boundaries in regard to female and male sanctity. Through the collection of rough statistical data—through a type of "nimbus" or "halo count"—enough information is available to form a rather crude but accurate evaluation of some of the following: shifts in the typology of sanctity; the density and distribution of female saints; sex ratios of saints; geographic disparities in the selection of *mulieres sanctae*; social and economic status; and demographic information, including, for example, family size, age of first marriage, and data on longevity and sanctity.

However, some of the most fascinating and little-known information that can be gleaned from the *vitae* consists of unique details: data that is not at all easily categorized and is essentially unquantifiable. These details frequently appear in the *vitae* as accidental or incidental facts. This type of hagiographic information falls into the category of unconscious or "unintentional evidence." As historical data, it is perhaps often more reliable than other kinds of "intentional" evidence found in the *vitae*, in that these details are not central to the eulogistic or propagandist purposes of the hagiographer. As such, they are perhaps less likely to be exaggerated or purposefully falsified. Thus, through a collective treatment of these inadvertent or accidental details, patterns frequently emerge that shed new light on many aspects of the medieval female experience.

The *vitae* are especially useful for providing insights on women and the early medieval family. Since it was through the irregular powers and landed wealth of the family that noblewomen of this early period could achieve a certain visibility leading to sanctity, the saint's family was of central importance to the hagiographer.[74] The *vitae* thus provide information on the saint's parents and her noble genealogy. (It is interesting that during this early period we find several instances in which all of the members of a family came to be recognized as saints.) The lives sometimes describe the economic status of the family, especially noting the great generosity of the saint and her relatives in making donations to the church. The *vitae* also provide glimpses into many details of everyday family life, including, for example, information on marriage, friendship within marriage, sexual practices, problems of infertility, childbirth, cesarean sections, naming of infants, care of premature infants, infanticide, abandonment of infants, child abuse, adolescence, incest, stepmothers, mother-daughter relationships, sibling bonds, economic independence of women, domestic roles, violence toward women (attempted rape, wife beating), repudiation or separation, widowhood, death, burial, and other topics.

However, since the majority of women saints of this early period were recruited from the cloister, the *vitae* offer a unique glimpse into the female monastic experience. (Some of the details provided by the hagiographers can be used to complete the basic information found in monastic *regulae*, charters, and chronicles.)[75] The lives, for example, describe the actual "founding" of monasteries, recruitment practices and problems, admission policies, vows, size of communities, organization of double monasteries and affiliated houses (as well as the relationships between nuns and monks), monastic administration, role of the abbess, adoption of monastic rules, and policies of enclosure. The lives include precious information about monastic churches, the arrangement of the cloister and its buildings, along with descriptions of special funerary churches or community cemeteries. They discuss the activities of the female communities, noting monastic curricula and education, reading, manuscript illumination, needlework and painting, the *laus perennis*, care of the sick, and charity work. In addition, the *vitae* tell of the dress of female religious, tonsure of nuns, hygiene, diet, along with ascetic practices of fasting and sleep deprivation, which were frequently carried to extremes by these spiritual athletes.[76]

The lives are also informative sources for the economic history of female monastic communities. They provide information on the constitution of landholdings and on agricultural and commercial activities, data that is, again, often confirmed by charters, diplomas, and so forth. Some of the *vitae* include evidence used to validate landholdings and privileges of monasteries as well as their possession of relics. Other lives emphasize the role of the patron saint in inspiring the generosity of the faithful to give landed estates to churches or monasteries, or they relate the saints' miraculous intervention in the retrieval of usurped properties and their "just" punishment of usurpers. The *vitae* also tell of the invasions and their devastating effects on female monastic life. Some lives describe growing poverty, famine, and plagues, with the decimation and ultimate dissolution of entire female communities.

Another area in which the *vitae* and *miracula* provide fascinating details is that of female nonconformity or "deviant" behavior. In some cases, these activities appear perhaps rather bizarre or even repulsive to the modern reader. The lives describe, for example, instances of women adopting various creative strategies in defense of their virginity, including those of "self-disfigurement" and feigned illness and insanity. A few of the *vitae* (in the "virago" tradition) portray examples of "bearded" holy women, or *mulieres religiosae*, disguised as men—wearing male dress with short hair or tonsure—in order to experience lives denied them as women or as a means to maintain their virginity. There are instances of women's covert attempts to enter male monasteries, or sanctuaries (forbidden to females), and of the subsequent miracles that they brought about or the severe punishment that they allegedly suffered for their audacious behavior. The *vitae* describe women continuing to foster pagan beliefs and observances. There are also accusations found in the saints' lives of various moral improprieties, such as incest between brothers and their saintly sisters, the breaking of vows of virginity as well as enclosure by recalcitrant nuns, and the determined attempts by nuns at "abbessicide." The active role of the *mulieres sanctae* in the acquisition of relics, including their direct involvement in the actual "furta sacra," or "theft" of the remains of the holy dead, are also described in some detail in the *vitae*.

While some of these "saintly excesses" might appear alien and irrational to us today, they reflect the range of nonconformist behavior that was regarded as "appropriate" for only the elite members of the heavenly kingdom. It is interesting to note in this context that, while the authors of the *vitae* stressed edification and imitation as their primary purpose, in some lives a problematic distinction was inferred or specifically made between *imitanda* and *admiranda*; that is, as Richard Kieckhefer has noted, the expected response of the reader was to copy the saint's exemplary behavior (when it was within the realm of socially approved behavior), while the saint's "abnormally" excessive deeds or virtues—her inimitable extremes—were only to excite admiration or wonder.[77] These deeds were therefore not to be imitated literally by the faithful but to be followed at a respectful distance.

The *miracula* of the saints' lives are also especially rich in data for the study of popular mentalities and the belief in the miraculous intervention of the holy dead. The miracles frequently furnish extraordinary descriptions of physical and mental illnesses as well as medical beliefs and practices, miraculous cures, and exorcisms. In addition, the *miracula* tell of those seeking the saint's assistance at her cult center and therefore provide invaluable data on gender, class, and age of the pilgrims along with their specific illnesses.[78]

Nevertheless, despite their incredible wealth as a historical source, the *vitae* must be used with caution. Scholars should not attempt to claim for the lives of saints a greater degree of historical accuracy than they warrant. As a source, they provide indirect rather than direct evidence: therefore, approximate rather than absolute conclusions should be drawn from the data. Since saints' lives did not remain static but changed with ecclesiastical and societal perceptions and needs, scholars should study, when possible, a series of lives for the same saint. They should then apply textual criticism to the *vitae* in order to see how the matter itself was transformed over time. They need to test each life for internal consistency of fact and language. Also, like most of the sources from this period, the *vita* presents only a single perspective and is incomplete in itself. Thus, to explore patterns in female sanctity and women's roles, expectations, and values within the broad context of culture and society, one needs to examine the lives collectively rather than study a single *vita* in isolation. In addition, the information of the *vitae* can often be supplemented by other hagiographic information, that is, calendars, martyrologies, liturgies, panegyrics, and homilies. However, this information is further strengthened when it is checked for external consistency or conformity against other sources of the period. Therefore, for the most complete and successful reconstruction of the female experience in the early medieval church and society, hagiographic literature should be used in collaboration with other contemporary historical sources, such as chronicles, canon and secular laws, penitentials, monastic *regulae*, cartularies, correspondence, treatises, archaeological and epigraphic evidence, and iconography. And, indeed, through this collective approach one finds, for example, that many of the behavioral modes and strategies attributed to female saints—previously dismissed by scholars as wildly implausible, mere hagiographic exaggeration, fantasy, or *topoi*—are reinforced or further corroborated as "real" contemporary behavior.

However, despite these various strategies, which attempt to extrapolate useful historical data from the *vitae* and to supplement it with other contemporary sources, one constantly needs to be reminded that saints' lives are ultimately reflections of the mind-set and world of the hagiographer. Therefore, as Kieckhefer has noted, one cannot assume in all cases that the information or data described in the *vitae* necessarily refers to specific social realities. Rather, as works of propaganda, the lives reflect the hagiographers' intense views of these realities, their own (sometimes skewed) personal visions of sanctity and society. Therefore, on one level the *vitae* frequently tell us as much or perhaps even more about the mind-sets of the hagiographers and their world, the ideas and stereotypes prevalent in their own society, than factual information about the saint. [79]

It is, then, in this context that one must ask how trustworthy the *vitae* are as evidence for women's experiences and lives. And how does one interpret them? Since the majority of saints' lives were written by men —medieval clerics—are the lives of female saints merely reflections of their world and their notions and fantasies of ideal women, or do they describe "real" women's roles and the religious and social expectations of women of the period?[80] Briefly, the very nature of sainthood required that the *mulieres sanctae* be somewhat atypical women. Through their aristocratic birth and exercise of autonomy and power, they formed an elite group who were singled out for their religious dedication and zeal. While the lives of these holy heroines do not seem to have been fully coterminus with the experiences of religious women in general, it appears that especially during the early stages of conversion to Christianity, when the nobility played a central role, there were a great many aristocratic women with more power and visibility in the church and society than usual. They were then rewarded for their leadership roles in the church by being elevated to sainthood. These female saints and their *vitae* therefore provided society with some idea of the ideals and the kind of life being practiced by this very special spiritual elite. However, churchmen in turn "used" the female saints and their lives for their own ends. The church endorsed these female symbols of virtue as *exempla*,

whose behavior was then to be emulated and, if possible, adopted by
especially the women of the Christian community. Through this means,
the church hoped to inspire a certain religious conformity and to mold
"social copies."[81] Thus, through the use of saints' lives, churchmen reinforced their own concepts of ideal female behavior. They attempted to
shape and control women and female sexuality by dictating how women
should think and behave. On this level, the *vitae* might be viewed as
oppressive tools utilized by the clergy to control or restrict women's
activities and visions.

Nevertheless, one also finds "multivalent messages" in female saints
as religious symbols and in the *vitae*.[82] As Clarissa Atkinson has noted,
these sacred symbols can be used "at different times by different persons
for totally different needs."[83] Women with religious leanings seemed
to have learned what they wanted to learn from the *vitae*, and they
frequently took some liberties in creatively adopting these behavioral
models to their own specific situations and needs. Thus, in addition to
serving as vehicles of ecclesiastical and societal control, saints' lives provided a variety of remarkable roles and experiences for the female imagination to act upon. Women seemed to have a special sympathy as well
as admiration for the concerns and achievements of the *mulieres sanctae*.
They inspired women with new possibilities for their own lives of spiritual perfection. They provided active strategies and roles that could be
used to transcend the social and ecclesiastical restrictions of the period.

As *exempla* of holy behavior, the *vitae* of saints therefore seem to have
profoundly influenced the lives of religious women and men in medieval society. The lessons of the female saints' lives were not lost on the
mulieres religiosae of the period. In his *History of the Kings*, William
of Malmesbury, for example, noted that Saint Cuthburga "embraced
the profession of holy celibacy from the perusal of Aldhelm's book on
virginity."[84] (As previously noted, this treatise contains an important
collection of the lives of virgin saints.) An example of the profound influence the lives of saints could exercise on medieval women can be found
in the *vita* of Saint Radegund. We learn that as a young child she was
very much moved by the lives of the martyrs and often "played at" being
a saint. (It was in her later life, when martyrdom was not forthcoming,
that she inflicted on herself various austerities and corporal punishments
as a type of self-martyrdom.)[85]

The author of the *vita* of Saint Salaberga, founder and abbess of Saint
Jean of Laon (d. ca. 665), notes that her saintly virtues "imitated" the
humility, charity, and moral goodness of the noble Saints Melania and

Paula, whose lives were written by Saint Jerome. The blessed Salaberga also repeated the behavior of others, including "imitata" Helena, the mother of Constantine, with the mortification of the flesh of her limbs, disdain of the worldly, and acting as a submissive servant of God. [86]

It is interesting to note the continuity in the influence of saints' lives on women in the modern world. Dorothy Day, one of the founders of the Catholic Worker, describes how in their childhood she, her sister, and a friend would "practice being saints." In her autobiography, *The Long Loneliness,* she writes: "I don't remember what we talked about, but I do remember one particular occasion when she [her friend, Mary Harrington] talked to me about the life of some saint. I do not know which saint it was, and I cannot remember any of the incidents of the life; I only remember my feeling of lofty enthusiasm, and how my heart almost burst with desire to take part in such high endeavor . . . I was filled with natural striving, a thrilling recognition of the possibilities of spiritual adventure." [87]

Our hagiographic sources, then, are especially rich in providing an indirect index of social and ecclesiastical values, collective mentalities, and commonalities of female experience in the medieval world. The *vitae* also furnish a wide variety of unique details on women's lives found in no other sources of the period. As a source, they still remain relatively unexplored. They present a myriad of possibilities for research in women's history. We need to study the *vitae* collectively in light of the complex relationships between the ideal models proposed by the clerical hagiographers and the collective mentalities and social and political structures of this early period.[88] We need to approach these lives in a sympathetic yet critical manner. We need to ask new questions and make an imaginative effort in our reexamination of these sources. The old yellowed parchments of the thousands of *vitae,* transcribed by the Bollandists in their monumental sixty-seven volume *Acta Sanctorum,* still have a great deal to tell us about the varied experiences and images of women in the medieval church and society, if we are willing to make the effort and take the time to listen.

NOTES

1. There has been a proliferation of studies on sanctity over the past twenty years. A select listing of some of the more recent major works includes: Vauchez, *La Sainteté en occident* (extensive bibliography); Delooz, *Sociologie et canonisations;* Brown, *Cult of Saints;* Gajano, *Agiografia altomedioevale* (extensive anno-

tated bibliography); Graus, *Volk, Herrscher, und Heiliger;* Poulin, *L'Idéal de sainteté dans l'Aquitaine carolingienne;* de Gaiffier, *Études critiques d'hagiographie;* de Gaiffier, *Recueil d'hagiographie;* Weinstein and Bell, *Saints and Society;* Goodich, *Vita perfecta;* Kieckhefer, *Unquiet Souls;* Wilson, *Saints and Their Cults* (extensive annotated bibliography); Ward, *Miracles and the Medieval Mind;* Patlagean and Riché, *Hagiographie, cultures, et sociétés;* Bekker-Nielsen et al., *Hagiography and Medieval Literature.* See the bibliography for additional works.

2. Delehaye, *Les Légendes hagiographiques,* p. 2; see also pp. 1–13, 79–102. (This work has been translated as *Legends of the Saints;* see pp. 3–11, 55–68.)

3. Attwater, preface to Delehaye, *Legends of the Saints,* p. xviii.

4. Delooz, *Sociologie et canonisations,* pp. 5–25.

5. Delehaye, *Les Légendes hagiographiques,* p. 2.

6. Roisin, *L'Hagiographie cistercienne,* p. 274; Mecklin, *Passing of the Saint,* pp. 62–63.

7. "Minus licet periti scholastica, sed magis studere volumus patere aedificationi plurimorum" (Prologue, *Vita Domnae Balthildis Reginae* 2.A.1.482).

8. Rudolf, "Life of St. Leoba," p. 205.

9. See, for example, Graus, *Volk, Herrscher, und Heiliger;* Prinz, *Frühes Mönchtum im Frankenreich,* especially the following chapters: "Die Selbstheilgung des frankischen Adels in der Hagiographie" (pp. 489–93), "Heiligenvita— Adel—Eigenkloster" (pp. 493–95), "Ein neues hagiographisches Leitbild" (pp. 496–501), "Kult und adeliges Heiligengrab" (pp. 502–3). See also de Gaiffier, *Études critiques d'hagiographie,* pp. 463–68; Wilson, *Saints and Their Cults,* pp. 33–34; Poulin, *L'Idéal de sainteté dans l'Aquitaine carolingienne,* p. 126

10. See Ward, *Miracles and the Medieval Mind;* Wilson, *Saints and Their Cults,* pp. 26–31; Roisin, *L'Hagiographie cistercienne,* p. 77.

11. Murray, *Reason and Society,* pp. 386–93.

12. Roisin, *L'Hagiographie cistercienne,* p. 126.

13. Van der Essen, *Etude critique,* pp. 309–11. The author of the *Vita Berlindis* also writes: "Non enim immerito haec virgo ab illis debet honorari quibus et ipsa in hac vita consanguinitate vel familiaritate coniucta fuit, vel qui ex eius parentela genealogiam ducant, vel qui eius atque maiorum illius famulatui obnoxii, obsequiis eius deservierunt. Indigena namque istius loci atque domina fuit" (p. 265, cited by Van der Essen, *Étude critique,* p. 311).

14. Poulin, *L'Idéal de sainteté dans l'Aquitaine carolingienne,* pp. 120–21.

15. Kieckhefer, *Unquiet Souls,* p. 14.

16. Aldhelm, *De virginitate,* pp. 14, 51, 59.

17. *Vita Sanctae Geretrudis,* p. 453, or *Vita Aldegundis prima,* chap. 18. See also Van der Essen, *Étude critique,* p. 221; however, he notes the stereotypic character of this formula in hagiographic literature and suggests that we not attach too much importance to these statements.

18. McNamara, "Legacy of Miracles," p. 37.

19. de Gaiffier, *Etudes critiques d'hagiographie,* p. 424.

20. *Vita Sanctae Geretrudis*, p. 453.

21. Van der Essen, *Étude critique*, pp. 221–23.

22. *Vita de S. Aldegunde*, pp. 651–52.

23. de Gaiffier, *Études critiques d'hagiographie*, p. 425.

24. Hucbald, Prologue to the *Vitae Rictrudis Sanctimonialis Marchianensis*, pp. 91–94; Hucbald, *Vita S. Rictrudis*, pp. 488–503; *Vita Aldegundis, abbatissae Malbodiensis*, pp. 79–90; *Vita Aldegundis prima*, pp. 315–24. See also Van der Essen, *Étude critique*, pp. 225–28, 260–65; de Gaiffier, *Études critiques d'hagiographie*, pp. 426–27, discusses the prestige of professional hagiographers "à la mode."

25. de Gaiffier, *Études critiques d'hagiographie*, p. 425.

26. Delehaye, *Les Légendes hagiographiques*, p. 69.

27. The authorship of the *Life of Saint Willibald* (d. ca. 786) and the *Life of Saint Wynnebald* (d. ca. 761) has been attributed to a nun of the Monastery of Heidenheim (*Bibliotheca hagiographica latina* 2:1288, 1297). Also, the *Passion* in meter of Saint Gengulfus or Gangolfus (d. ca. 760) was written by Hrotswitha of Gandersheim (ibid., 1:498). (Among the writings of the twelfth-century Saint Hildegard of Bingen are the *Life of Saint Rupert* [ninth century] and the *Life of Saint Disibodus* [seventh century?] [ibid., 2:1071, 1:333]).

28. Roisin also notes this pattern in *L'Hagiographie cistercienne*, p. 10.

29. See, for example, the letters of Saint Jerome in *St. Jerome*. Letter 23, to Marcella, consoles her for the loss of a friend, Lea, and praises Lea's holy behavior (pp. 341–42); letter 24, to Marcella, describes the model behavior of the virgin Asella (pp. 42–43); letters 38 and 39, to Marcella and Paula, praise Blaesilla's saintly austerities (pp. 47–54); letter 66, to Pammachius, praises the life and virtues of his deceased wife, Paulina (pp. 134–40); letter 108, to Eustochium, written to console her on the death of her mother, Paula, is a long and very interesting panegyric describing the events of Paula's saintly life (pp. 195–212); letter 27, to Principia, provides a saint's life of the holy woman Marcella; letter 130, to Demetrias, summarizes this woman's exemplary life in Rome and Africa (pp. 260–72). See also Palladius, *Lausiac History*. This work, written in the early fifth century (419–20), is one of the most important sources for the history of early monasticism in Egypt, Palestine, Syria, and Asia Minor. Palladius devotes a great deal of attention to the lives of women and their pursuit of spiritual perfection. He notes, for example, "I must also commemorate in this book the courageous women ["manly women"] to whom God granted struggles equal to those of men, so that no one could plead as an excuse that women are too weak to practice virtue successfully" (chap. 41, p. 117). Gregory the Great, *Dialogorum*, PL, 77, lib. IV, cap. 13, 340–41 (Galla); cap. 15, 344–45 (De transitu Romulae ancilla Dei); cap. 16, 348 (here Gregory praises the holy life of his saintly aunt, Tharsilla); cap. 17, 348–49 (Musa).

30. Odilo of Cluny, *Vita Sanctae Adalheidis Imperatricis*, p. 354.

31. Roisin, *L'Hagiographie cistercienne*, p. 124.

32. Talbot, *Anglo-Saxon Missionaries in Germany*, p. 152.

33. Nelson, "Queens as Jezebels," p. 46 n. 83.

34. de Gaiffier, *Etudes critiques d'hagiographie*, p. 476.

35. Ibid., pp. 431–37, 499–502.

36. Talbot, *Anglo-Saxon Missionaries in Germany*, p. 206; Goodich, *Vita perfecta*, p. 63.

37. Talbot, *Anglo-Saxon Missionaries in Germany*, pp. 205–6.

38. "A clericis et sanctimonialibus congregationis Deo dilectae famulae beatae Rictrudis rogitatus apponere novum ad conscribendum gesta ipsius naatorumque eius calamum, diu multumque renisus sum, vel quia meam quantulamcumque scientiolam tantae imparem materiei noveram, vel quia, tanto transacto tempore, nulla certae relationis de his scripta videram vel audieram, veritus, ne forte dubia pro certis vel falsa pro veris assererem. Cumque renitenti mihi quaedam historiarum exemplaria suis ostenderent concordantia dictis, de cetero illis, quorum non contemnendae videbantur personae, mihi fidem facientibus, quod haec quae referebant eadem olim tradita litteris fuerint, sed insectatione Northmannicae depopulationis deperierint" (Hucbald, *Vitae Rictrudis Sanctimonialis Marchianensis*, pp. 93–94).

39. Bertha, *Vita Adelheidis, abbatissae Vilicensis*, p. 756.

40. Odilo of Cluny, *Vita Sanctae Adalheidis Imperatricis*, p. 353.

41. See, for example, Dronke, *Women Writers of the Middle Ages*, p. 66. Here he comments on the topos of feminine weakness in the writings of the "strong voice of Gandersheim," Hrotswitha of Gandersheim.

42. Talbot, *Anglo-Saxon Missionaries in Germany*, p. 153 (italics mine). This same type of "apology" or submissive *topos* can be found in several of the prefaces of the tenth-century works of Hrotswitha of Gandersheim. For example, in one of her prefaces she writes: "To think that you, who have been nurtured in the most profound philosophical studies and have attained knowledge in perfection, should have deigned to approve the humble work of an obscure woman! You have, however, not praised me but the Giver of the grace which works in me, by sending me your paternal congratulations and admitting that I possess some little knowledge of those arts the subtleties of which exceed the grasp of my woman's mind." She also hopes that through her work "the Creator of genius may be the more honoured since it is generally believed that a woman's intelligence is slower." In Hrotswitha's preface to her poetical works, she states (as Dronke notes, "with tongue in cheek"): "Although prosody may seem a hard and difficult art for a woman to master, I, without any assistance but that given by the merciful grace of Heaven (in which I have trusted, rather than in my own strength), have attempted in this book to sing in dactyls." In a preface written to Gerberg, Hrotswitha describes the special vulnerability of her situation as an author: "At present I am defenceless at every point, because I am not supported by any authority. I also fear I shall be accused of temerity in presuming to describe in my humble uncultured way matters which ought to be set forth with

all the ceremony of great learning. Yet if my work is examined by those who know how to weigh things fairly, I shall be more easily pardoned on account of my sex and my inferior knowledge, especially as I did not undertake it of my own will but at your command" (*Plays of Roswitha*, pp. xxviii–xxx, xxxii–xxxiii, xxxv; Dronke, *Women Writers of the Middle Ages*, p. 66).

43. See, for example, "Biographies spirituelles: moyen âge," pp. 1646–56.

44. An interesting example of both the uncomfortable presence of *detractores* and the use of miracles as evidence of sanctity can be found in the virtues of Saint Gertrude of Nivelles. One of the nuns of Nivelles was confronted by the blatant skepticism of a noblewoman named Adula, who openly voiced her doubts in regard to the efficacy of this female saint. The nun tried to defend her patron saint with promises of Saint Gertrude's posthumous intervention on her feast day. It was then only through the working of a personal miracle on the anniversary of the saint at Nivelles (i.e., the restoring to life of the son of the skeptic after he had drowned in the convent's well) that the woman became convinced of Saint Gertrude's supernatural powers. See *De virtutibus Sanctae Geretrudis*, pp. 469–71. See also McNamara's comments in "Legacy of Miracles," p. 50.

45. Kemp, *Canonization and Authority*, pp. 29, 38–39.

46. Fortunatus, *De vita Sanctae Radegundis*.

47. Baudonivia, *De vita Sanctae Radegundis*. See also Coudanne, "Baudonivia."

48. Baudonivia, *De vita Sanctae Radegundis*, p. 378.

49. For a discussion of the relationship between these *vitae*, see Fontaine, "Hagiographie et politique," esp. pp. 114–15.

50. Coudanne, "Baudonivia," pp. 47–48.

51. Baudonivia, *De vita Sanctae Radegundis*, pp. 377–78.

52. Aigrain, *Sainte Radegonde*, pp. viii–ix.

53. Aigrain, *L'Hagiographie*, pp. 302, 161.

54. Delaruelle, "Sainte Radegonde," p. 69.

55. Graus, *Volk, Herrscher, und Heiliger*, p. 409–11.

56. Fontaine, "Hagiographie et politique," esp. pp. 136–37.

57. Ibid., p. 132.

58. "Quod fecit illa in orientali patria, hoc fecit beata Radegundis in Gallia," (Baudonivia, *De vita Sanctae Radegundis*, p. 388). Fontaine, "Hagiographie et politique," p. 135.

59. Baudonivia, *De vita Sanctae Radegundis*, p. 388. See also Wemple, *Women in Frankish Society*, pp. 184–85.

60. Baudonivia, *De vita Sanctae Radegundis*, p. 388.

61. Fontaine, "Hagiographie et politique," p. 132.

62. Ibid., pp. 137–39.

63. Wemple, *Women in Frankish Society*, p. 183.

64. Ibid., p. 184.

65. Babut, *Saint Martin de Tours*, pp. 108–9. For a discussion of this early

hypercritical attitude toward saints' lives, see Sulpicius Severus, *Vie de Saint Martin*, pp. 173–74.

66. Lot, *End of the Ancient World*, pp. 162–63.

67. Lot, *Mélanges d'histoire bretonne (VIe–XIe siècles)*, p. 97, cited by Wilson, *Saints and Their Cults*, p. 1.

68. Graus, *Volk, Herrscher, und Heiliger*, p. 39.

69. See, for example, Roisin, *L'Hagiographie cistercienne*, p. 209. Also, for a general overview of the problems in working with early saints' lives, see "Biographies spirituelles: moyen âge," pp. 1646–56. For an excellent discussion of the historical value of saints' lives and the use of new methodologies and analyses, see Sulpicius Severus, *Vie de Saint Martin*, pp. 171–210; de Gaiffier, "Mentalité de l'hagiographe médiéval"; Weinstein and Bell, *Saints and Society*, pp. 1–18. See also Van der Essen, *Etude critique*, pp. ix–xi, and Schmitt, "Note critique."

70. Bloch, review of Delehaye's *Sanctus*, cited by Vauchez, *La Sainteté en occident*, p. 1.

71. Bloch, *Historian's Craft*, pp. 61–62. Bloch notes in his discussion of sources of early periods, such as the lives of saints, that "because history has tended to make more and more frequent use of unintentional evidence, it can no longer confine itself to weighing the explicit assertions of the documents. It has been necessary to wring from them further confessions which they had never intended to give" (p. 89).

72. See above, n. 1, for a listing of some of the recent major studies on medieval sanctity and women saints. For comments on the tradition of the annales school and women's history, see Schulenburg, "Clio's European Daughters," pp. 44–47, and Stuard, "Annales School and Feminist History."

73. The major studies that discuss female sanctity or gender and sainthood include those of Vauchez, Bynum, Kieckhefer, Roisin, Weinstein and Bell, Goodich, and Bolton. The focus of these works is on the central and late Middle Ages.

74. See, for example, McNamara and Wemple, "Power of Women"; Wemple, *Women in Frankish Society*, pp. 27–123; Leyser, *Rule and Conflict*, pp. 49–73; Herlihy, *Medieval Households*, pp. 29–111. See also Theis, "Saints sans famille?"; Vauchez, " 'Beata Stirps.' "

75. See, for example, Roisin, *L'Hagiographie cistercienne*, p. 277.

76. For a discussion of the phenomenon of religious women's fasting, see the fascinating studies by Bynum, *Holy Feast and Holy Fast*, and Bell, *Holy Anorexia*.

77. Kieckhefer, *Unquiet Souls*, pp. 13–14.

78. See Ward, *Miracles and the Medieval Mind*; Finucane, *Miracles and Pilgrims*; McNamara, "Legacy of Miracles"; Heinzelmann, "La Littérature hagiographique latine"; Rouche, "Miracles, maladies, et psychologie de la foi."

79. Kieckhefer, *Unquiet Souls*, p. 5.

80. For a thoughtful discussion of the problem of sacred image and social reality, see Atkinson, Buchanan, and Miles, *Immaculate and Powerful*, pp. 1–14.

81. Mecklin, *Passing of the Saint*, pp. 62–63.
82. Atkinson, Buchanan, and Miles, *Immaculate and Powerful*, p. 5.
83. Ibid.; Atkinson, " 'Your Servant, My Mother,' " pp. 139, 164.
84. William of Malmesbury, *History of the Kings*, p. 29 n. 5.
85. Fortunatus, *De vita Sanctae Radegundis*, pp. 365–66, 373.
86. *Vita Sadalbergae, abbatissae Laudunensis*, p. 64.
87. Day, *Long Loneliness*, p. 25.
88. Vauchez, *La Sainteté en occident*, p. 1.

BIBLIOGRAPHY

Primary Sources

Aelfric. *Aelfric's Lives of Saints*. Ed. W. W. Skeat. Early English Text Society, nos. 76, 82, 94, 114. 2 vols. London, 1881.

Aldhelm. *De laudibus virginitatis*. In *Patrologia latina*, ed. J. P. Migne, 88:103–62.

———. *De virginitate*. In *Aldhelm: The Prose Works*, ed. and trans. Michael Lapidge and Michael Herren, pp. 51–132. Totowa, 1979.

Baudonivia. *De vita Sanctae Radegundis, Liber 2*. MGH Script. rer. mer. 2:377–95.

Bede. *A History of the English Church and People*. Trans. Leo Sherley-Price. Harmondsworth, 1955.

Bertha. *Vita Adelheidis, abbatissae Vilicensis*. MGH Script. 15:754–63.

Bibliotheca hagiographica latina: Antiquae et mediae aetatis. 2 vols. and supplement. Brussels, 1898–1901, 1911.

Christine de Pizan. *The Book of the City of Ladies*. Trans. Earl Jeffrey Richards. New York, 1982.

De virtutibus Sanctae Geretrudis. MGH Script. rer. mer 2:464–74.

Fortunatus, Venantius. *De vita Sanctae Radegundis*. MGH Script. rer. mer. 2:364–77.

Gregory of Tours. *The History of the Franks*. Trans. Lewis Thorpe. Harmondsworth, 1974.

Hrotswitha. *The Plays of Roswitha*. Trans. Christopher St. John. New York, 1966.

Hucbald. *Vitae Rictrudis Sanctimonialis Marchianensis, Prologus*. MGH Script. rer. mer 6:91–94.

———. *Vita S. Rictrudis*. AASS, 12 maii, 3:81–89.

———. *Vita S. Rictrudis*. Acta sanctorum Belgii selecta 4:488–503.

Jerome. *St. Jerome: Letters and Select Works*. Ed. Philip Schaff and Henry Wace. Select Library of Nicene and Post-Nicene Fathers of the Christian Church, 2d ser., vol. 6. New York, 1893.

Odilo of Cluny. *Vita Sanctae Adalheidis Imperatricis.* In *Bibliotheca Cluniacensis,* ed. Martinus Marrier and Andreas Quercentanus, pp. 354–69. Brussels, 1915.

Palladius. *The Lausiac History.* Trans. Robert T. Meyer. Westminster, 1965.

Rudolf. "The Life of St. Leoba by Rudolf, Monk of Fulda." In *The Anglo-Saxon Missionaries in Germany,* ed. and trans. C. H. Talbot, pp. 205–26. New York, 1954.

Sulpicius Severus. *Vie de Saint Martin.* Ed. and trans. Jacques Fontaine. Sources Chrétiennes, nos. 133, 134. 2 vols. Paris, 1967–68.

Talbot, C. H., ed. and trans. *The Anglo-Saxon Missionaries in Germany.* New York, 1954.

Vita Aldegundis, abbatissae Malbodiensis. MGH Script. mer. rer. 6:79–90.

Vita Aldegundis prima. Acta sanctorum Belgii selecta 4:315–24.

Vita Berlindis. Acta sanctorum Belgii selecta 5:264–71.

Vita de S. Aldegunde. AASS, Jan., 3:649–70.

Vita Domnae Balthildis Reginae. MGH Script. rer. mer. 2:477–508.

Vita Sadalbergae, abbatissae Laudunensis. MGH Script. rer. mer. 5:40–66.

Vita Sanctae Geretrudis. MGH Script. rer. mer. 2:453–64.

Secondary Sources

Aigrain, René. *L'Hagiographie.* Paris, 1953.

──── . *Sainte Radegonde (vers 520–587).* In *Les Saints.* 2d ed. Paris, 1918.

Atkinson, Clarissa W. " 'Your Servant, My Mother': The Figure of Saint Monica in the Ideology of Christian Motherhood." In Atkinson, Buchanan, and Miles, *Immaculate and Powerful,* pp. 139–72.

Atkinson, Clarissa W., Constance H. Buchanan, and Margaret R. Miles, eds. *Immaculate and Powerful: The Female in Sacred Image and Social Reality.* Harvard Women's Studies in Religion Series. Boston, 1985.

Babut, E. C. *Saint Martin de Tours.* Paris, 1912.

Baker, Derek, ed. *Medieval Women.* Studies in Church History, Subsidia 1. Oxford, 1978.

Bekker-Nielsen, H., et al. *Hagiography and Medieval Literature: A Symposium.* Odense, 1981.

Bell, Rudolph. *Holy Anorexia.* Chicago, 1985.

"Biographies spirituelles: moyen âge." In *Dictionnaire de spiritualité,* ed. M. Viller, 1:1646–56. Paris, 1937.

Bloch, Marc. *The Historian's Craft.* Trans. Peter Putnam. New York, 1959.

Brown, Peter. *The Cult of Saints: Its Rise and Function in Latin Christianity.* Chicago, 1981.

──── . "The Saint as Exemplar in Late Antiquity." *Representations* 1, no. 2 (Spring 1983): 1–25.

————. "Women's Stories, Women's Symbols: A Critique of Victor Turner's Theory of Liminality." In *Anthropology and the Study of Religion*, ed. Frank Reynolds and Robert Moore, pp. 105–25. Chicago, 1984.

Bynum, Carolyn Walker. *Holy Feast and Holy Fast: The Religious Significance of Food to Medieval Women*. Berkeley, 1987.

————. *Jesus as Mother: Studies in the Spirituality of the High Middle Ages*. Berkeley, 1982.

Bynum, Caroline Walker, et al. *Gender and Religion: On the Complexity of Symbols*. Boston, 1986.

Chance, Jane. *Woman as Hero in Old English Literature*. Syracuse, 1986.

Collins, Richard. "Observations on the Form, Language, and Public of the Prose Biographies of Venantius Fortunatus in the Hagiography of Merovingian Gaul." In *Columbanus and Merovingian Monasticism*, ed. H. B. Clark and Mary Brennan, pp. 105–31. BAR International Series, Oxford, 1981.

Coudanne, Louise. "Baudonivia, moniale de Sainte-Croix et biographe de Sainte Radegonde." In *Études mérovingiennes*, pp. 45–51. Poitiers, 1953.

Day, Dorothy. *The Long Loneliness*. New York, 1952.

de Gaiffier, Baudouin. *Etudes critiques d'hagiographie et d'iconologie*. Subsidia Hagiographica, no. 43. Brussels, 1967.

————. "Hagiographie et historiographie." In *La Storiografia altomedievale* 1:139–66. Settimane di studio del centro italiano di studi sull'alto medioevo, no. 17. Spoleto, 1970.

————. "Mentalité de l'hagiographie médiéval d'après quelques travaux récents." *Analecta Bollandiana* 86 (1968): 391–99.

————. *Recueil d'hagiographie*. Subsidia hagiographica, no. 61. Brussels, 1977.

Delaruelle, Etienne. "Sainte Radegonde, son type de sainteté et la chrétienté de son temps." In *Études mérovingiennes*, pp. 64–74. Poitiers, 1953.

Delehaye, Hippolyte. *The Legends of the Saints*. Trans. Donald Attwater. New York, 1962.

————. *Les Légendes hagiographiques*. 2d ed. Brussels, 1906.

Delooz, Pierre. *Sociologie et canonisations*. Collection scientifique de la faculté de droit de l'Université de Liège, no. 30. Liège, 1969.

Dronke, Peter. *Women Writers of the Middle Ages: A Critical Study of Texts from Perpetua (203) to Marguerite Porete (1310)*. Cambridge, 1984.

Dunbar, Agnes B. C. *A Dictionary of Saintly Women*. 2 vols. London, 1904–5.

Finucane, Ronald C. *Miracles and Pilgrims: Popular Beliefs in Medieval England*. Totowa, 1977.

Fontaine, Jacques. "Hagiographie et politique de *Sulpice Sévère* à Venance Fortunat." *Revue d'histoire de l'eglise de France* 62, no. 168 (1976): 113–40.

Gajano, Sophia Boesch, ed. *Agiografia altomedioevale*. Bologna, 1976.

Glasser, Marc. "Marriage in Medieval Hagiography." *Studies in Medieval and Renaissance History*, n.s., 4 (1981): 3–34.

Goodich, Michael. "Ancilla Dei: The Servant as Saint in the Late Middle Ages." In *Women of the Medieval World: Essays in Honor of John H. Mundy*, ed. J. Kirschner and S. F. Wemple, pp. 119–36. Oxford, 1985.

———. "The Contours of Female Piety in Later Medieval Hagiography." *Church History* 50 (1981): 20–32.

———. *Vita perfecta: The Ideal of Sainthood in the Thirteenth Century.* Stuttgart, 1982.

Graus, Frantisek. *Volk, Herrscher, und Heiliger im Reich der Meroqinger: Studien zur Hagiographie der Merowingerzeit.* Prague, 1965.

Heinzelmann, Martin. "Une Source de base de la littérature hagiographique latine: Le Recueil de miracles." In Patlagean and Riché, *Hagiographie, cultures, et sociétés,* pp. 235–57.

Herlihy, David. "Did Women Have a Renaissance?: A Reconsideration." *Mediaevalia et Humanistica,* n.s., 13 (1985): 1–22.

———. *Medieval Households.* Cambridge, Mass., 1985.

Kemp, Eric W. *Canonization and Authority in the Western Church.* London, 1948.

Kieckhefer, Richard. *Unquiet Souls: Fourteenth-Century Saints and Their Religious Milieu.* Chicago, 1984.

Leyser, K. J. *Rule and Conflict in an Early Medieval Society: Ottonian Saxony.* London, 1979.

Lot, Ferdinand. *The End of the Ancient World and the Beginnings of the Middle Ages.* Trans. Philip Leon and Mariette Leon. 1931. Reprint. New York, 1961.

McLaughlin, Eleanor, and Rosemary Reuther, eds. *Women of Spirit: Female Leadership in the Jewish and Christian Traditions.* New York, 1979.

McNamara, Jo Ann. "A Legacy of Miracles: Hagiography and Nunneries in Merovingian Gaul." In *Women in the Medieval World: Essays in Honor of John H. Mundy,* ed. J. Kirschner and S. F. Wemple, pp. 36–52. Oxford, 1985.

———. "Living Sermons: Consecrated Women and the Conversion of Gaul." In *Peace Weavers,* vol. 2 of *Medieval Religious Women,* ed. John A. Nichols and Lillian Thomas Shank, pp. 19–37. Kalamazoo, Mich., 1987.

McNamara, Jo Ann, and Suzanne Wemple. "The Power of Women through the Family in Medieval Europe, 500–1100." In *Clio's Consciousness Raised: New Perspectives on the History of Women,* ed. Mary Hartman and Lois W. Banner, pp. 103–18. New York, 1974.

Mecklin, John M. *The Passing of the Saint: A Study of a Cultural Type.* Chicago, 1940.

Millinger, Susan. "Humility and Power: Anglo-Saxon Nuns in Anglo-Norman Hagiography." In *Distant Echoes,* vol. 1 of *Medieval Religious Women,* ed. John A. Nichols and Lillian Thomas Shank, pp. 115–28. Kalamazoo, Mich., 1984.

Murray, Alexander. *Reason and Society in the Middle Ages.* Oxford, 1978.

Nelson, Janet. "Queens as Jezebels: The Careers of Brunhild and Balthild in Merovingian History." In *Medieval Women,* ed. Derek Baker, pp. 31–77. Studies in Church History, Subsidia 1. Oxford, 1978.

Patlagean, E., and P. Riché, eds. *Hagiographie, cultures, et sociétés, IVe–XIIe siècles.* Paris, 1981.

Petroff, Elizabeth A., ed. *Medieval Women's Visionary Literature.* New York, 1986.

Poulin, Joseph-Claude. *L'Idéal de sainteté dans l'Aquitaine carolingienne d'après les sources hagiographiques (750–950).* Quebec, 1975.

Prinz, Friedrich. *Frühes Mönchtum im Frankenreich: Kultur und Gesellschaft in Gallien, den Rheinlanden und Bayern am Beispiel der monastischen Entwicklung (4. bis 8 Jahrhundert).* Munich, 1965.

―――. "Heiligenkult und Adelsherrschaft im Spiegel merowingischer Hagiographie." *Historische Zeitschrift* 204 (1967): 529–44.

Riché, Pierre. "Note d'hagiographie mérovingienne: *La Vita S. Rusticulae.*" *Analecta Bollandiana* 72 (1954): 369–77.

Roisin, Simone. *L'Hagiographie cistercienne dans le diocèse de Liège au XIIIe siècle.* Louvain, 1947.

Rouche, Michel. "Miracles, maladies, et psychologie de la foi à l'epoque carolingienne en France." In Patlagean and Riché, *Hagiographie, cultures, et sociétés,* pp. 319–32.

Schmitt, Jean-Claude. "Note critique: La Fabrique des saints." *Annales: Economies, sociétés, civilisations* 39, no. 2 (1984): 286–300.

Schulenburg, Jane Tibbetts. "Clio's European Daughters: Myopic Modes of Perception." In *The Prism of Sex: Essays in the Sociology of Knowledge,* ed. Julia A. Sherman and Evelyn Torton Beck, pp. 33–53. Madison, Wis., 1977.

―――. "Female Sanctity: Public and Private Roles, ca. 500–1100." In *Women and Power in the Middle Ages,* ed. Mary Erler and Maryanne Kowaleski, pp. 102–25. Athens, Ga., 1988.

―――. "The Heroics of Virginity: Brides of Christ and Sacrificial Mutilation." In *Women in the Middle Ages and the Renaissance: Literary and Historical Perspectives,* ed. Mary Beth Rose, pp. 29–72. Syracuse, 1986.

―――. "Sexism and the Celestial Gynaeceum—from 500–1200." *Journal of Medieval History* 4 (1978): 117–33.

―――. "Women's Monastic Communities, 500–1100: Patterns of Expansion and Decline." *Signs* 15, no. 2 (1989): 261–92.

Stoeckle, Maria. *Studien über Ideale in Frauenviten des VII–X Jahrhunderts.* Munich, 1957.

Stuard, Susan Mosher. "The Annales School and Feminist History: Opening Dialogue with the American Stepchild." *Signs* 7, no. 11 (1981): 135–43.

―――, ed. *Women in Medieval History and Historiography.* Philadelphia, 1987.

Theis, Laurent. "Saints sans famille? Quelques remarques sur la famille dans le monde franc à travers les sources hagiographiques." *Revue Historique* 255 (1976): 3–20.

Van der Essen, L. *Étude critique et littéraire sur les "vitae" des saints mérovingiens de l'ancienne Belgique.* Louvain, 1907.

Vauchez, André. " 'Beata Strips': Sainteté et lignage en occident." In *Famille et parenté dans l'occident médiéval,* ed. Georges Duby and Jacques Le Goff, pp. 397–406. Rome, 1977.

———. *La Sainteté en occident aux derniers siècles du moyen âge d'après les proces de canonisation et les documents hagiographiques.* Rome, 1981.

Wallace-Hadrill, J. M. *The Frankish Church.* Oxford History of the Church. Oxford, 1983.

Ward, Benedicta. *Miracles and the Medieval Mind: Theory, Record, and Event, 1000–1215.* Philadelphia, 1982.

Weinstein, Donald, and Rudolf M. Bell. *Saints and Society: The Two Worlds of Western Christendom, 1000–1700.* Chicago, 1982.

Wemple, Suzanne Fonay. "Female Spirituality and Mysticism in Frankish Monasteries: Radegund, Balthild, and Aldegund." In *Peace Weavers,* vol. 2 of *Medieval Religious Women,* ed. John A. Nichols and Lillian Thomas Shank, pp. 39–53. Kalamazoo, Mich., 1987.

———. "Sanctity and Power: The Dual Pursuit of Early Medieval Women." In *Becoming Visible: Women in European History,* ed. R. Bridenthal, C. Koonz, and S. Stuard, pp. 130–51. 2d ed. Boston, 1987.

———. *Women in Frankish Society: Marriage and the Cloister, 500 to 900.* Philadelphia, 1981.

William of Malmesbury. *The Church Historians of England.* Vol. 3, *The History of the Kings of England.* Trans. J. Sharpe, rev. by J. Stevenson. London, 1854.

Wilson, Stephen, ed. *Saints and Their Cults: Studies in Religious Sociology, Folklore, and History.* Cambridge, 1983.

COINAGE IN THE NAME
OF MEDIEVAL WOMEN

Alan M. Stahl

 woman's right to place her name on coins was a major component of her right to reign. Coinage was perhaps the most conspicuous public activity of any medieval ruler, and the appearance of a woman's name on coinage was a concrete and widespread recognition of her actual governance. Unlike documents, which were often intended for archival storage and were limited in accessibility to the literate sector of the population, coins were immediately and widely disseminated; they were the only product of governmental activity with which virtually the entire population was familiar. While charters and other documents could be issued by people in a wide variety of status groups and might bear the names of many supporting individuals, medieval coins bore only the name of a person recognized as exercising public authority over a territory. While it must be admitted that the acknowledgment of a woman on coins as a ruler does not imply that she made the actual decisions of governance, the same consideration must also apply to many male hereditary rulers. The name that appeared on the coinage belonged to one whom a common individual would consider the ruler. The extent to which women were able to get their names on coins is an important index of the extent to which their right to political power was recognized by contemporaries of all classes. ❡ The practices governing who could issue and sign coins in the Middle Ages were as varied as those relating to any other medieval right or privilege. Under the Roman Empire, only those who bore the title of Augustus or Caesar could appear on the obverse of a coin, while family members and favorites occasionally appeared on the reverse. This practice was maintained in the Byzantine empire and was also adopted by the Carolingians. In the medieval German empire, however, minting privileges were frequently granted out, often along with market and toll rights. Thus, numerous towns, bishoprics, and monasteries received imperial minting rights, as did many dynasties of dukes, counts, and other categories of lordship. These minting rights could be further leased out or exercised jointly by treaty, but they always remained an attribute of public power; no individual who could not be said to govern in some sense could put his or her name on coins. In the former Carolingian lands that did not come under the Ottonian empire, minting rights appear to have devolved upon seigneurial dynasties with no formal grants or conditions. By the twelfth century, when petty coinage became a universal feature of medieval life, scores of dynasties in France and the Low Countries issued distinctive coinages. In the monarchies that ringed the old Carolingian heartlands, coinage was almost exclusively a regalian right. Thus in England, Sweden, Bohemia, Hungary, Serbia, and Castile, coinage was usually in the name of the reigning monarch, with only occasional examples of minting by vassals or churches. In the Islamic lands, coinage bore the name of the ruler responsible for its content, with occasional recognition of local subrulers and of higher religious authorities.

In all of these cases, with the exception of religious and communal coinages, the transmission of minting rights was dynastic, that is, from parent to child or other kinsperson. The preferred sequence was from father to son or sons, but few dynasties were as lucky as the Capetians in having an unbroken string of sons over many generations. Even then, the inheriting son was not always of sufficient age or ability to exercise his coining and other rights, and at least a temporary regency might be necessary. When no son survived his father, a choice often had to be made between admitting a daughter into the succession or passing the dynastic rights to a collateral branch. In the Merovingian and Carolingian periods, it was an established rule that no woman could enter into the line of succession or transmit such rights.[1] But in the eleventh century the principle of female inheritance of fiefs became established both within the empire and in surrounding lands.[2] That a woman could enter into the line of succession to a fief or even a crown is not to say that she herself could exercise the concomitant rights in her own name. A married woman might simply be a reference point in the transfer of title from her father to her husband, entering into the exercise of power little more than when she served as a medium to transmit succession from her husband to her son. Though a theoretical distinction was often made between a fief that a man held by right of his own inheritance and one that he gained by marriage, such a distinction is often difficult to discern in actual practice.[3]

In a preliminary survey, I have found about a hundred women whose names appear on coins of the period A.D. 500–1500. A few appear simply as consort to their husband, with no apparent independent claim to power. Many were widows or regents to minor sons; these two categories were frequently combined. The greatest number inherited their rights to coinage from their fathers, though most exercised them only in periods before, between, or after marriage. The only group of women who exercised minting rights specifically as women was the series of abbesses of imperial convents, whose minting rights extended from the tenth century through much of the modern age. Coins minted under the authority of medieval women rarely had specifically feminine iconography; the images on medieval coins were usually indicative of origin and denomination rather than the issuer. The real evidence for a woman's recognition as ruler is the appearance of her name on the obverse legend of the coin, the traditional position for the statement of the minting authority. Selected examples of medieval coinages in the name of women can illustrate many of the vicissitudes and conflicts involved in the transmission of political power to women. [4]

The Roman practice of conferring the title of Augusta on the wife of the emperor was not automatic in the Byzantine empire and did not usually lead to her appearance on the coinage. An exception was Sophia I in the sixth century, whose status as niece of Theodora shored up the claim of her husband, Justin II, nephew of Justinian. She appears, however, only on the bronze coinage and is not named (fig. 1). An analogous later coin is a bracteate (a one-sided penny) of Gelnhausen of Frederick Barbarossa, on which the imperial couple is portrayed, but only the emperor is identified (fig. 2). The count of the Brandenburg March, Albrecht the Bear, also put his wife's image on a bracteate (fig. 3).

A few medieval women based their minting claims on their status as widow of a childless ruler. In Gelderland, Mary of Brabant, widow of Renaud III, minted gold florins in her castle of Oyen in the late fourteenth century as "ducissa" of Gelderland at the same time as Matilda, the half sister of her late husband, issued coins as "Dux" (figs. 4, 5). In a tangled dispute over the succession to Luxembourg in the mid-fifteenth century, Elizabeth of Gorlitz, niece of the late duke, based her claim against the heir presumptive, brother of the duke, on an engagement of the duchy in lieu of dowry for her marriage to Antoine of Burgundy. After her husband's death at Agincourt, Elizabeth issued coins as duchess, but only before and after her brief second marriage, during which period her new husband's name replaced hers on the coinage (fig. 6).

Most widows whose names appeared on coins exercised power as regents for minor sons. In Byzantium in the late eighth century, Irene appeared with her son Constantine VI on the obverse of solidi, with three imperial predecessors on the reverse (fig. 7). After she had had her son killed, she reigned alone for five years, during which period she appeared alone on both the obverse and reverse of coins (fig. 8). When Ogotai, son of Genghis Khan, died in A.D. 1241, his widow, Turakina, not only issued coins in her own name as regent but also secured the succession of the son she preferred rather than the one designated by her late husband (fig. 9). On one of the earliest and most beautiful of Renaissance portrait coins, Bona of Savoy placed her image as regent for her seven-year-old son, Gian Galeazzo Maria Sforza, duke of Milan (fig. 10). Her regency was supplanted in 1480 by the boy's uncle, Ludovico il Moro, who eventually took the throne for himself.

The majority of women whose names appear on medieval coins inherited minting rights as the daughter of a ruler with no surviving sons. One who superseded male heirs was the thirteenth-century Radiyyah, whose father, the sultan of Delhi, designated her as his successor over two brothers (fig. 11). She reigned for three years, unveiled and diademed, and died after capture while directing her armies from the back of an elephant. Theodora, daughter of the Byzantine emperor Constantine VIII, was pulled from a convent to act as co-Augusta during her sister Zoe's regency for an adopted son (fig. 12). After the death of Zoe and her husband, Theodora reigned alone. Between these two periods of coinage bearing women's names, however, the Byzantine coinage bore the sole name of Zoe's husband, Constantine IX.

It was a common occurrence that a woman's inheritance of coinage rights meant only that her husband's name would replace that of her father. If the heiress was married at the time of her inheritance, her name might never appear; otherwise, she might sign her coins only before her marriage. Mary of Anjou inherited the crown of Hungary from her father, Louis I; it was only in the three years before her marriage to Sigismund of Luxembourg that her name appeared on Hungarian coins (fig. 13). Of the many women who regained rights to their minting inheritance after its exercise by a husband, the most famous was undoubtedly Eleanor of Aquitaine. Coins were issued for her realms of Aquitaine and Poitou in turn by Louis of France, Henry Plantagenet, and finally Richard the Lionhearted; it was only when Richard became king of England in 1189 that Eleanor minted deniers in Aquitaine bearing her title, "ducissa," though not her name (fig. 14). In 1109, the infanta

Urraca, already a widow, succeeded her father to the kingdom of Castile. Her second husband, Alfonso of Aragon, may have minted coins during their brief marriage, but in the thirteen years she ruled alone, she not only minted coins with her name and image but also granted minting privileges to the monastery of Sahagun (fig. 15).

A royal heiress who had to face much more opposition in securing her succession was Matilda of England, daughter of Henry I and known as the empress from her first marriage to the emperor Henry V. Though she was recognized as the heiress by her dying father and his barons, she was ultimately denied coronation by her nephew Stephen, who based his claim on succession through his mother. In the period of contested rule from 1135 to 1154, Stephen succeeded in controlling the royal administration but ultimately agreed to recognize Matilda's son as his successor. Thus the principle of succession through a woman was recognized, while actual female rule was denied. In the period from 1139 to 1142, Matilda issued coinage from her strongholds in the central and western country of England. She signed these coins as "imperatrix" and "comitissa," never "Anglorum domina," as she did in some of her charters. Her lack of real control of royal administration was reflected in her coinage, which was struck from few, crudely engraved dies and imitated in appearance that of Stephen (fig. 16).

An heiress often had to seek the aid of a neighboring ruler to secure her inheritance. When Baldwin IX of Hainaut died a year after becoming the first Latin emperor of Constantinople in 1204, he left behind him two daughters, who succeeded to his home territories of Flanders and Hainaut. Johanna reigned for four decades without signing any coins, to be succeeded in 1244 by her younger sister, Margaret, already twice a widow. Margaret's groat depicting a knight on horseback was one of northern Europe's first high-denomination silver coins (fig. 17). William of Holland, who bore the title of king of the Romans in opposition to Frederick II, tried to strip Margaret of her fiefs for failure to provide military relief, but under the arbitrage of Saint Louis, her lands and coinage were restored to her for her lifetime, to be divided at her death between the sons she had by each of her two husbands.

The coinage of the Frankish principality of Achaia in Greece in the late thirteenth and early fourteenth centuries illustrates some of the complexity that could enter into the questions of women's succession. When William of Villehardouin faced death with only a minor daughter to deal with his many enemies, he signed a treaty with Charles of Anjou to enfief his principality to the crown of Sicily. During Isabelle's minority, Charles minted as prince of Achaia. On her marriage to Florent of Hainaut, the suzerain renounced his title to the couple on the condition that, if Florent were to predecease Isabelle, she would reign alone or marry a husband of his choice. The name of Florent thus replaced that of Charles on the plentiful coinage of Achaia. On Florent's death, the coinage took on the name of Isabelle as princess (fig. 18). She later married, without her suzerain's consent, Philip of Savoy, and his name appeared next on the coinage. After many disputes and settlements, Isabelle and Philip renounced in favor of a succeeding Angevine suzerain, who ruled and coined in Achaia until their daughter Matilda was of marriageable age. Matilda received her inheritance under terms similar to those applied to her mother, and the next coinage bore the name of her husband, Louis of Burgundy, followed by her own name during her widowhood (fig. 19) and then that of John of Gravina, the husband imposed on her by her suzerain.

Other numismatic solutions were possible in the case of a married heiress. After the death of four brothers and a nephew, Constance I pressed her claim to the kingdom of Sicily with the assistance of her husband, the emperor Henry VI. His name appeared on the gold coins, hers alone on the bronze, and both names on the common billon pennies (fig. 20). The arrangement of shared appearance on the coinage was revived in Sicily a century later when Constance II, the last of the Hohenstaufen dynasty, appeared on the coinage with her husband, Peter of Aragon (fig. 21).

The most famous sharing of the coin imagery by a medieval couple is undoubtedly the facing portraits of Ferdinand and Isabella on the Spanish doubloon and other gold denominations (fig. 22). Each monarch had brought a kingdom into the marriage, and the coinage reflected an equal contribution to the rule. The coins of Catherine of Foix reflect the difference in practice in the two lands she ruled: in Bearn her coinage bore her name alone (fig. 23), while in Navarre she appeared, in imitation of the coins of Spain, with her husband, Jean d'Albret (fig. 24).

Few medieval women put their names alone on their coinage while married. Eleanore of Vermandois inherited her county from her sister, who had put her husband's name on the coinage. Eleanore maintained her own name in the center of her pennies during at least some of her five marriages (fig. 25). She donated her lands to Philip Augustus, and they were joined to the French crown on her death in 1214. Johanna of Anjou was named successor to the crowns of Provence and Naples as well as the titular kingdom of Jerusalem by her uncle Robert I of Anjou in 1343. She needed to enlist the support of the local nobility in a dispute with her first husband over her right to rule; during this period her name appeared on the coins. Her second husband, Louis of Taranto, had no lands of his own, and his name joined hers on the coins (fig. 26). During her succeeding two marriages and all periods of widowhood, the coins bore only her name (fig. 27). In the next century, Johanna II of Durazzo succeeded to the throne of Naples after a twenty-nine-year reign by her childless brother. Despite the fact that her husband, James of Bourbon, kept her imprisoned, the coins bore her name alone (fig. 28). Her supporter Alfonso V of Aragon, however, did issue Neapolitan coinage as "regine defensor." Mary of Burgundy was the only child of Charles the Bold and inherited much of the Netherlands in the late fifteenth century. Her name appeared alone on the coinages (fig. 29); it was only after her death that the name of her husband, Maximilian of Austria, appeared on coins of the Low Countries, and then it was as advocate for their son Philip the Handsome.

The only continuous, regular minting by women in the Middle Ages, and perhaps in all of world history, was in the nine imperial convents of Germany that enjoyed minting privileges.[5] These convents, closely allied to ruling families, received their coinage rights along with markets and tolls in the Carolingian and Saxon periods. The abbesses had the rights to set the standards and appearance of the coinage and to farm out production or even lease out the minting rights for specified time periods. These issues are the only series of medieval coins in which the development of a specifically feminine iconography can be traced. But, like other ecclesiastics who exercised temporal powers, abbesses had to rely on lay advocates for many public transactions and often found themselves in conflict over the exercise of rights. Twelfth-century bracteates of the convent of Quedlinburg that show a layman alongside an abbess or replacing her probably reflect such conflicts (figs. 30, 31). Though most were of limited circulation, certain issues of imperial convents appear to have been minted in significant quantities, such as the groschen of Hedwig, abbess of Quedlinburg at the end of the fifteenth century, which were modeled on the coins of her father, Frederick the Good of Saxony, and circulated with those of her brothers Albert and Ernest (fig. 32).

The claim of abbesses to coinage rights was clearly supported by feudal law. In most other cases of coinage by medieval women, however, politics and circumstance seem to have been as important as statute or custom in establishing their rights. General principles governing the circumstances under which a woman's name might appear on medieval coins are impossible to formulate categorically. What can be affirmed is that there clearly were many cases in which a woman's claim to power was a more important consideration for the purpose of coinage validation than was her gender.

APPENDIX

This is a preliminary listing of coinages of Europe, Byzantium, and Islamic lands from A.D. 500 to 1500 which bear the name of a woman. The references are to standard numismatic works, which, in most cases, contain complete descriptions of the legends and types of the coins and some explanation of the circumstances of their minting. I would welcome references to additional examples.

BOHEMIA

EMMA, ca. 988: Cach, *Njestarší České Mince*, vol. 1, nos. 144–45.
EUFEMIA, 1087–95: Cach, vol. 2, nos. 379–80.

BYZANTIUM

IRENE, 790–802: Grierson, *Catalogue of the Byzantine Coins*, pp. 336–47.
THEODORA I, 843–56: Grierson, p. 452.
ZOE I, 913–20: Grierson, p. 526.
ZOE II AND THEODORA II, 1028–56: Grierson, pp. 707–31.
EUDOCIA, 1067–71: Grierson, pp. 778–80.
ANNA OF SAVOY, 1341–47: Bertelè, "Giovanna (Anna) di Savoia," pp. 206–21.

CAROLINGIAN EMPIRE

ANGILBERGA, 866–72: Longpérier, "Louis II et Angilberge," pp. 364–67.
EMMA, ca. 980: Dumas, "Emma Regina," pp. 405–13.

ENGLAND

CYNETHRYD, WIDOW OF OFFA, 796: Keary, *Catalogue of English Coins*, p. 33.
MATILDA, 1139–42: Mack, "Stephen and the Anarchy, 1135–1154," pp. 85–88.

FRANCE

Aquitaine
ELEANOR, 1137–1204: Poey d'Avant, *Monnaies féodales de France* 2:78–79; Dieudonné, *Monnaies féodales françaises*, p. 217.

Arleux
> BEATRICE OF SAINT-POL, 1325–37: Poey d'Avant, 3:441; Dieudonné, p. 197.

Artois
> MATILDA, 1302–29: Poey d'Avant, 3:7; Dieudonné, p. 80.

Bearn
> CATHERINE OF FOIX, 1483–1516: Poey d'Avant, 3:169–70; Dieudonné, pp. 90–91. See also under Navarre.

Blois
> JOHANNA OF CHATILLON, 1279–92: Poey d'Avant, 1:234.

Brittany
> ANNE, 1488–91: Poey d'Avant, 1:184–91; Dieudonné, p. 129.

Château Meillant
> MARGARET OF BOMÈS, 1282–1323: Poey d'Avant, 1:298.

Elincourt
> MARY OF BRITTANY, 1317: Poey d'Avant, 3:420; Dieudonné, p. 198.

Fauquembergues
> ELEANORE, 1290–1326: Poey d'Avant, 3:408–10.

Flanders
> MARGARET OF CONSTANTINOPLE, 1244–80: Gaillard, *Recherches sur les monnaies des comtes de Flandres*, pp. 54–55. See also under Hainaut.
> MARY OF BURGUNDY, 1477–82: Dieudonné, p. 191. See also under Gelderland.

Narbonne
> ERMENGARDE, 1143–92: Poey d'Avant, 2:265–66.

Navarre
> JOHANNA I, 1274–84: Poey d'Avant, 2:176; Dieudonné, p. 88.
> BLANCHE, 1425–41: Poey d'Avant, 2:178–79; Dieudonné, pp. 88–89.
> CATHERINE OF FOIX, 1484–1512: Poey d'Avant, 2:181–83; Dieudonné, p. 91. See also under Bearn.

Nevers
> MATILDA II, 1257–67: Poey d'Avant, 1:315; Dieudonné, p. 300.
> YOLANDA, 1270–71: Caron, *Monnaies féodales françaises*, p. 107.

Provence
> JOHANNA OF ANJOU, 1343–82: Poey d'Avant, 2:327–31; Dieudonné, p. 344. See also under Naples.

Rodez
> CECILE, 1302–19: Poey d'Avant, 2:327–31.

Tonnerre
> MARGARET OF BURGUNDY, 1262–1308: Poey d'Avant, 3:226–27; Dieudonné, pp. 138–39.
>
> ELEANORE OF SAVOY, 1304: Poey d'Avant, 3:227; Dieudonné, pp. 138–39.

Vermandois
> ELEANORE, 1183–1214: Poey d'Avant, 3:385; Dieudonné, p. 330.

Vierzon
> BLANCHE OF JOIGNY, ca. 1250: Poey d'Avant, 1:290.
>
> MARY OF BRABANT, 1303–30: Poey d'Avant, 1:291–92.

GERMAN EMPIRE

Brabant
> JOHANNA, 1355–1406: de Witte, *Histoire monétaire des comtes de Louvain* 1:136–82.

Brunswick-Grubenhagen
> MARGARET OF SAGEN, 1463–81: Fiala, *Münzen und Medaillen der Welfischen Lande*, pp. 21–22.

Eschwege (convent)
> JUDITH, ca. 1150: Hess, "Eschweger Brakteaten," p. 120.
>
> GERTRUDE, 1180–90: Klein, "Münzen der Stauferzeit," p. 134.

Essen (convent)
> SOPHIA OF GLEICHEN, 1259–89: Saurma-Jeltsch, *Die Saurmasche Münzsammlung*, col. 71.

Falkenburg and Borne
> IDALIA OF SALM, 1398–1400: J. Menadier, "Die Münzen der Jülicher Dynastengeschlechter," p. 474.

Gandersheim (convent)
> LUITGART, ca. 1130–51: Gaettens, "Zur Münzgeschichte der Abtei Gandersheim," p. 63.
>
> ADELHEID IV OF SOMMERSCHENBURG, 1151–84: Gaettens, pp. 62–63.

Gelderland
> ELEANORE, 1343–44: Van der Chijs, *De munten der Nederlanden* 2:31–32.
>
> MATILDA, 1371–79: Van der Chijs, 2:44–46.
>
> MARY OF BRABANT, 1371–79: Van der Chijs, 2:46–52.
>
> MARY OF BURGUNDY, 1477–82: Van der Chijs, 2:91–94. See also under Flanders.

Hainaut
> MARGARET OF CONSTANTINOPLE, 1244–80: Chalon, *Recherches sur les monnaies des comtes de Hainaut*, pp. 28–33. See also under Flanders.

Margaret II, 1345–56: Chalon, pp. 66–69.

Jacqueline of Bavaria, 1417–33: Chalon, pp. 97–101. See also under Holland.

Herford (convent)

Eilicke, 1170–1217: Grote, "Die Münzen von Herford," p. 357.

Hildegund of Otgenbach, 1374–1409: Grote, pp. 380–87.

Holland

Jacqueline of Bavaria, 1417–33: Van der Chijs, 6:319–27. See also under Hainaut.

Lorraine

Berthe, 1189: Saulcy, *Recherches sur les monnaies*, pp. 241–47.

Luxembourg

Elizabeth of Gorlitz, 1415–51: Weiller, *Les Monnaies luxembourgeoises*, pp. 89–94.

Marburg-an-der-Lahn

Sophia, 1248–60: Klein, 1:135.

Megen

Elizabeth, 1418: Van der Chijs, 8:42–43.

Nordhausen (convent)

Cecilia, 1140–60: Klein, 1:137.

Quedlinburg (convent)

Adelheid II, 1063–95: Cappe, *Beschreibung*, p. 17.

Agnes I, ca. 1108: Cappe, pp. 17–20.

Gerburg, 1113–37: Cappe, pp. 20–22.

Beatrix II, 1138–60: Klein, 1:143.

Adelheid III, 1161–84: Klein, 1:143.

Agnes II, 1184–1203: Cappe, pp. 31–38.

Sophia, 1206–25: Cappe, pp. 38–41.

Beatrix III, 1224–30: Cappe, pp. 42–45.

Hedwig of Saxony, 1458–1511: Saurma-Jeltsche, *Die Saurmasche Münzsammlung*, col. 104.

Rummen

Johanna of Wezemaal, 1464–74: Van der Chijs, 8:265–71.

Saxony

Adelheid, 991–95: Dannenberg, *Die deutschen Münzen* 1:450, 2:701–17, 3:830–58, 4:958–66.

Silesia-Liegnitz-Brieg

Anne of Teschen, 1364–67: Saurma-Jeltsch, *Schlesische Münzen*, p. 3.

Zwolle
> ADELA, ca. 1017: Dannenberg, 2:615.

GREECE

Achaia
> ISABELLE OF VILLEHARDOUIN, 1297–1301: Schlumberger, *Numismatique de l'Orient Latin*, pp. 293–97.
> MATILDA OF VILLEHARDOUIN, 1316–18: Schlumberger, pp. 299–301.

Cyprus
> CHARLOTTE OF LUSIGNAN, 1458: Schlumberger, p. 171.
> CATHERINE CORNER, 1473–89: Schlumberger, pp. 172–74.

HUNGARY

> MARY, 1382–95: Huszar, *Münzkatalog Ungarn*, pp. 91–92.

IRAN

Sasanian empire
> BURAN, 630–31: Kuntz and Warden, "Gold Dinar," pp. 133–35.

ISLAM

Delhi
> RADIYYAH, 1236–40 (A.H. 634–37): Thomas, *Chronicles of the Pathan Kings*, pp. 104–6.

Egypt, Mamluk
> SHAJAR AL-DURR, 1250 (A.H. 648): Balog, *Coinage of the Mamluk Sultans*, p. 6.

Iran, Salghurid
> ABISH, 1263–87 (A.H. 662–86): Hennequin, *Catalogue des monnaies musulmanes*, pp. 615–17.

Kirman, Atabegs
> QUTLUGH TURKAN KHATUN, 1278–79 (A.H. 677): Markow, *Inventarny Katalog Musulmanskich Monet*, p. 435.

Mongols
> TURAKINA, 1241–44 (A.H. 639–42): Lane-Poole, *Catalogue of Oriental Coins*, pp. xiii, 5.
> SATI-BEG, 1339–41 (A.H. 739–41): Lane-Poole, pp. xx–xxi, 103–6.

ITALY

Forli

CATERINA RIARIO SFORZA, 1488–99: *Corpus Nummorum Italicorum* 10: 623–24.

Lucca

GIUDITTA, 970–1002: *Corpus Nummorum Italicorum* 11:65–66.

Milan

BIANCA MARIA VISCONTI, 1466–68: Crippa, *Le monete di Milano*, pp. 180–85.

BONA OF SAVOY, 1476–80: Crippa, pp. 232–42.

Naples

JOHANNA I OF ANJOU, 1343–82: Pannuti and Riccio, *Le monete di Napoli*, pp. 22–25. See also under Provence.

JOHANNA II OF DURAZZO, 1414–35: Pannuti and Riccio, pp. 33–35.

Savoy

IOLANDA LUIGIA, 1496–99: *Corpus Nummorum Italicorum* 1:135.

Sicily

CONSTANCE I, 1189–98: Spahr, *Le monete siciliane dai Bizantini*, pp. 146–81.

CONSTANCE OF ARAGON, 1209–13: Spahr, *Le monete siciliane dai Bizantini*, p. 192.

CONSTANCE II, 1266–1300: Spahr, *Le monete siciliane dagli Aragonesi*, pp. 3–7.

MARY, 1377–1402: Spahr, *Le monete siciliane dagli Aragonesi*, pp. 52–58.

SPAIN

Castile

URRACA, 1109–26: Heiss, *Descripción general* 1:5–6.

BEATRICE OF PORTUGAL, 1383: Heiss, 1:75–76.

ISABELLA, 1474–1504: Heiss, 1:114–38.

Navarra. *See* France

Urgel

TERESA OF ENTENÇA, 1314–27: Botet y Sisó, *Les Monedes catalanes* 1:149, 156–57.

NOTES

The commentary section of this paper was originally presented at the Seventh Berkshire Conference on the History of Women, Wellesley College, 1987. I would like to express here my thanks to the many colleagues who have offered advice and bibliographical orientation, especially to Constance H. Berman, who shared with me the text of her paper "Women, Coinage, and Inheritance in Medieval France," presented at the 1986 Southeast Medieval Association conference. The illustrations of coins are identified in the text and have references in the Appendix. All are in the collection of the American Numismatic Society, New York, and are reproduced with its permission.

1. Ganshof, "Le Statut," p. 54.
2. Thieme, "Die Rechstsstellung," p. 357; Gilissen, "Le Statut," p. 279.
3. Shahar, *Fourth Estate,* pp. 146–47.
4. References for the coinages of individual women are in the Supplement, below, arranged by country.
5. For a discussion of the minting of these convents, see D. Menadier, "Das Münzwesen," and Stahl, "Monastic Minting."

BIBLIOGRAPHY

Balog, Paul. *The Coinage of the Mamluk Sultans of Egypt and Syria.* American Numismatic Society Numismatic Studies, no. 12. New York, 1964.

Bertelè, T. "Giovanna (Anna) di Savoia, Imperatrice de Bisanzio." *Atti dell'Istituto Italiano di Numismatica* 6 (1930): 206–21.

Botet y Sisó, Joaquim. *Les Monedes catalanes.* 3 vols. Barcelona, 1908–11.

Cach, František. *Njestarší České Mince.* 2 vols. Prague, 1970–72.

Cappe, H. Ph. *Beschreibung der Münzen des . . . Stifts Quedlinburg.* Dresden, 1851.

Caron, E. *Monnaies féodales françaises.* Paris, 1882.

Chalon, Rénier. *Recherches sur les monnaies des comtes de Hainaut.* Brussels, 1848.

Chijs, P. O. van der. *De munten der Nederlanden van de vroegste tijden tot aan de Pacificatie van Gend.* 9 vols. Haarlem, 1851–66.

Corpus Nummorum Italicorum. 20 vols. Rome, 1910–43.

Crippa, Carlo. *Le monete di Milano dai Visconti agli Sforza.* Milan, 1986.

Dannenberg, Hermann. *Die deutschen Münzen der sächsischen und fränkischen Kaiserzeit.* 4 vols. Berlin, 1876–1905.

de Witte, Alphonse. *Histoire monétaire des comtes de Louvain, ducs de Brabant.* 3 vols. Antwerp, 1894–99.

Dieudonné, A. *Monnaies féodales françaises.* Vol. 4 of *Manuel de numismatique française,* by A. Blanchet and A. Dieudonné. Paris, 1936.

Dumas, Françoise. "Emma Regina." In *Actes du 8ème Congrès International de Numismatique*, ed. H. A. Cahn and G. Le Rider, pp. 405–13. Paris, 1976.

Fiala, Edward. *Münzen und Medaillen der Welfischen Lande: Das Alte Haus Braunschweig, Linie zu Grubenhagen.* Prague, 1906–7.

Gaettens, Richard. "Zur Münzgeschichte der Abtei Gandersheim im 12. und 13. Jahrhundert." *Blätter für Münzfreunde und Münzforschung* 24 (1959): 53–64.

Gaillard, Victor. *Recherches sur les monnaies des comtes de Flandres.* Ghent, 1857.

Ganshof, François. "Le Statut de la femme dans la monarchie franque." In *La Femme*, pp. 5–58. Recueils de la Société Jean Bodin pour l'histoire comparée des institutions, vol. 12. Brussels, 1962.

Gilissen, Jean. "Le Statut de la femme dans l'ancien droit belge." In *La Femme*, pp. 255–321. Recueils de la Société Jean Bodin pour l'histoire comparée des institutions, vol. 12. Brussels, 1962.

Grierson, Philip. *Catalogue of the Byzantine Coins in the Dumbarton Oaks Collection.* Vol. 3. Washington, 1973.

Grote, H. "Die Münzen von Herford." In Grote, *Münzstudien* 8:343–420. Leipzig, 1877.

Heiss, Aloïs. *Descripción general de las monedas hispano-cristianas.* 3 vols. Madrid, 1865–69.

Hennequin, Gilles. *Catalogue des monnaies musulmanes de la Bibliothèque nationale.* Vol. 5. Paris, 1985.

Hess, Wolfgang. "Eschweger Brakteaten." *Hessiche Heimat* 24 (1974): 116–23.

Huszar, Lajos. *Münzkatalog Ungarn von 1000 bis Heute.* Munich, 1979.

Keary, C. F. *A Catalogue of English Coins in the British Museum.* Vol. 1. Anglo-Saxon Series. London, 1887.

Klein, Ulrich. "Münzen der Stauferzeit." In *Die Zeit der Staufer*, ed. Reiner Haussher, 1:108–88 and vol. 2, pls. 93–127. Stuttgart, 1977.

Kuntz, Roger, and William B. Warden, Jr. "A Gold Dinar of the Sasanian Queen Buran." *American Numismatic Society Museum Notes* 28 (1983): 133–35.

Lane-Poole, Stanley. *Catalogue of Oriental Coins in the British Museum.* Vol. 6, The Coins of the Mongols. London, 1881.

Longpérier, H. de. "Louis II et Angilberge." *Revue Numismatique* 5 (1860): 364–67.

Mack, R. P. "Stephen and the Anarchy, 1135–1154." *British Numismatic Journal* 35 (1966): 38–112.

Markow, A. *Inventarny Katalog Musulmanskich Monet.* Saint Petersburg, 1897.

Menadier, Dorothea. "Das Münzwesen der Reichsäbtissinen im Mittelalter." *Zeitschrift für Numismatik* 32 (1915): 185–293.

Menadier, Julius. "Die Münzen der Jülicher Dynastengeschlechter." *Zeitschrift für Numismatik* 30 (1913): 423–529.

Pannuti, Michele, and Vincenzo Riccio. *Le monete di Napoli.* Lugano, 1984.

Poey d'Avant, Faustin. *Monnaies féodales de France.* 3 vols. Paris, 1858–62.

Saulcy, F. de. *Recherches sur les monnaies des ducs héréditaires de Lorraine*. Metz, 1841.

Saurma-Jeltsch, Hugo von. *Die Saurmasche Münzsammlung deutscher, schweizerischer und polnischer Gepräge*. Berlin, 1892.

——. *Schlesische Münzen und Medaillen*. Breslau, 1883.

Schlumberger, G. *Numismatique de l'Orient Latin*. 1878. Reprint. Graz, 1954.

Shahar, Shulamith. *The Fourth Estate: A History of Women in the Middle Ages*. Trans. Chaya Galai. London, 1983.

Spahr, Rodolfo. *Le monete siciliane dagli Aragonesi ai Borboni*. Palermo, 1959.

——. *Le monete siciliane dai Bizantini a Carlo I d'Angiò*. Zurich, 1976.

Stahl, Alan. "Monastic Minting in the Middle Ages." In *The Medieval Monastery*, ed. Andrew MacLeish, pp. 64–69. Medieval Studies at Minnesota, no. 2. Saint Cloud, 1988.

Thieme, Hans. "Die Rechtsstellung der Frau in Deutschland." In *La Femme*, pp. 351–76. Recueils de la Société Jean Bodin pour l'histoire comparée des institutions, vol. 12. Brussels, 1962.

Thomas, Edward. *The Chronicles of the Pathan Kings of Delhi*. London, 1871.

Weiller, Raymond. *Les Monnaies luxembourgeoises*. Numismatica Lovaniensia, no. 2. Louvain-la-Neuve, 1977.

COIN DESCRIPTIONS

1. Byzantium, Justin II and Sophia, 565–78, copper 40 nummi, Constantinople.
2. German empire, Frederick Barbarossa and Beatrix, 1156–84, silver bracteate penny, Gelnhausen.
3. German empire, Brandenburg, Albrecht the Bear and Sophia, 1123–70, silver bracteate penny.
4. German empire, Gelderland, Mary of Brabant, 1371–79, gold florin, Oyen.
5. German empire, Gelderland, Matilda, 1371–79, silver double groat.
6. German empire, Luxembourg, Elizabeth of Gorlitz, 1415–51, silver groat.
7. Byzantium, Irene and Constantine VI, 790–97, gold solidus, Constantinople.
8. Byzantium, Irene, 797–802, gold solidus, Constantinople.
9. Islam, Mongols, Turakina, 1241–44, silver dirham.
10. Italy, Milan, Bona of Savoy, 1476–80, silver testone.
11. Islam, Delhi, Radiyyah, 1236–40, silver tanka.
12. Byzantium, Zoe II and Theodora II, 1028–56, gold nomisma.
13. Hungary, Mary, 1382–95, gold florin.
14. France, Aquitaine, Eleanor, 1137–1204, billon penny.
15. Spain, Castille, Urraca, 1109–26, billon penny.
16. England, Matilda, 1139–42, silver penny.
17. France, Flanders, Margaret of Constantinople, 1244–80, silver groat.
18. Greece, Isabelle of Villehardouin, 1297–1301, billon penny.
19. Greece, Matilda of Villehardouin, 1316–18, billon penny.
20. Italy, Sicily, Constance I and Henry VI, 1189–98, billon penny.
21. Italy, Sicily, Constance II and Peter of Aragon, 1266–1300, silver tari, Messina.
22. Spain, Ferdinand and Isabella, 1474–1504, gold double excelente.
23. France, Bearn, Catherine of Foix, 1483–1516, gold ecu.
24. France, Navarre, Catherine of Foix and Jean d'Albret, 1484–1512, gold ecu.
25. France, Eleanore of Vermandois, 1183–1214, billon penny.
26. France, Provence, Johanna of Anjou and Louis of Taranto, 1343–82, silver sou coronat.
27. Italy, Naples, Johanna of Anjou, 1347–62, silver corona.
28. Italy, Naples, Johanna II of Durazzo, 1414–35, silver penny.
29. France, Flanders, Mary of Burgundy, 1477–82, silver double briquet, 1480.
30. German empire, Quedlinburg, Beatrix II, 1138–60, silver bracteate penny.
31. German empire, Quedlinburg, Adelheid III, 1161–84, silver bracteate penny.
32. German empire, Quedlinburg, Hedwig of Saxony, 1458–1511, silver groat.

1 O   1 R   2

3   4 O   4 R

5 O   5 R   6 O   6 R

7 O   7 R   8 O   8 R

9 O   9 R   10 O   10 R

11 O   11 R   12 O   12 R

13 O   13 R   14 O   14 R

15 O   15 R   16 O   16 R

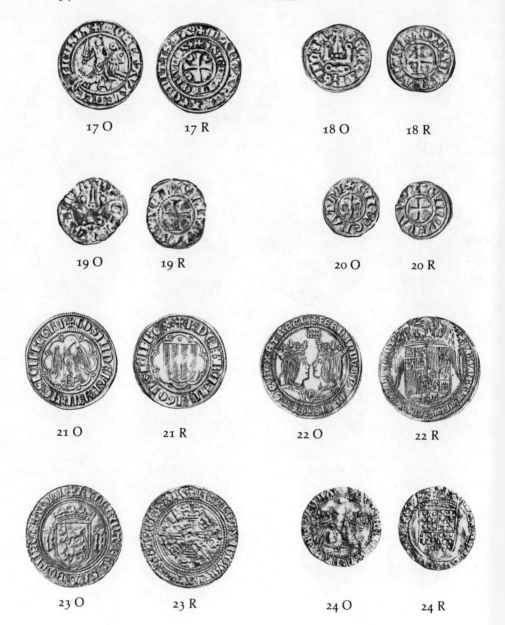

17 O   17 R   18 O   18 R

19 O   19 R   20 O   20 R

21 O   21 R   22 O   22 R

23 O   23 R   24 O   24 R

25 O   25 R   26 O   26 R

27 O   27 R   28 O   28 R

29 O   29 R   30

31   32 O   32 R

SOURCES ON MEDIEVAL WOMEN
IN MEDITERRANEAN ARCHIVES

Susan Mosher Stuard

ell, there is nothing on women in this archive." This flat assertion met a number of us who hoped to pursue research on women in the rich collections of southern Europe in the early seventies. Knowledgeable scholars were certain that our project on medieval women's history would never get off the ground. Women had not authored anything other than fragments of text, we heard, or women were rarely present in the charters, or "documents of practice," and then in such inconsequential roles that pursuing them would result only in wasted effort. In banding together to produce *Women in Medieval Society,*[1] a group of us investigated what could be found out about women in medieval archives. Legal records, wills, letters, and more surfaced, introducing us and our readers to a rich documentation. Found women account for the popularity of that volume. The records we used are now called up routinely, and women are frequently studied in Mediterranean archives. In the conviction that answers about the formation of our present gender system and women's position in the modern world lie in the study of the medieval era, historians consult medieval documents. And the sources have proven rich enough to reward the effort expended, provided, of course, that the researcher prove resourceful in applying deft methods to balky texts in order to squeeze the most out of them. ❡ Medievalists' undoubted advantage over our colleagues in ancient historical studies lies in the availability to us of a largely unexplored literature—the charters, or documents of practice. Medieval charters take up yards of space in the Mediterranean archives, and medievalists may compare what women did with what was said about women in a substantial number of cases. For this reason gender may be investigated and the lives of medieval women known in sufficient depth to explore the substantial change that occurred from the twelfth through the fifteenth centuries, when women's experi-

342

ence gave even earlier indication than men's to the profound nature of alterations demanded by a swiftly developing society. [2]

In this essay I plan to speak to three issues related to sources on medieval women: institutional affiliations of women (largely, but not always, ecclesiastical ones); familiar texts and what those often prized texts can tell us about women; and social history, or the possible construction of a prosopography of medieval women. I shall restrict myself to sharing some stories, but I hope the stories will help those planning research to think about what can be done when pursuing their own archival research on medieval women.

Traditionally, the best-known women of Europe's early centuries were holy women, who for the most part gained recognition from their institutional attachment to the church. In 1982 Mary Martin McLaughlin and Suzanne Wemple secured funding from the National Endowment for the Humanities to identify all medieval women's conventual houses. Because of the large number of women's orders and superior documentation available on them in the south, they chose to begin their study in Italy. The Italian project, compiled by Heath Dillard, continues, and the team has moved on to England. The project can supply computer-assisted information specifying when a house was founded, its donor, the order's approximate size, how long it survived, its published and unpublished literature, and particular members of renown. An invaluable starting point for research, the repertory reveals the extent of women's participation in religious, social, and cultural life through the medieval centuries. [3]

How little was understood about women's monastic orders may be illustrated by reference to a project that E. Ann Matter has begun. She has identified a very ancient and venerable house, Santa Maria alle Pertiche, which was a royally endowed convent founded by the Lombards in 675 in Pavia. It later moved, became a Cistercian house, and later a Cappucine order following the rule of Clare of Assisi. The house flourished as a spiritual center, attracting long-standing patronage from royal houses in Lombardy and visits from the likes of Queen Christina of Sweden. No published study has been made of the documents housed within the monastery in a private collection, nor has the most famous inmate of the house, Suor Maria Domitilla, a seventeenth-century visionary, received the attention of scholars. The life of Suor Maria Domitilla provides a corrective lesson on just how long the medieval mystic tradition survived within the institutional framework of conventual orders in Italy. In fact, Santa Maria alle Pertiche remained medieval in spirit for at least a thousand years, a remarkable institutional accomplishment. As for the convent itself, its rich private archives reveal how distorted a view of medieval religious development we have inherited because we have failed to count women's religious institutions among the powerful influences in the Mediterranean south. Knowing only what men have published about their own monastic orders, we have mistakenly placed the entire responsibility for many developments in religious life at men's doors. Our failure to take into account sister establishments of comparable importance has given us a distorted view of ecclesiastical, as well as social and cultural, life in such centers as Pavia and Milan. [4]

If unpublished, privately held records represent Matter's find, court records in the Florentine national archives provided Judith Brown with her information about Benedetta Carlini of Vellano, abbess of the Theatine nuns of Prescia. The Renaissance abbess whom Brown found gained the notoriety of a public trial in the sixteenth century and left a record of sufficient size and detail so that her biographer may recount the story of her rise to abbess within her order, her mystical experiences, and her downfall through the testimony of a nun implicating Benedetta Carlini in sexual acts. The procedure followed in Roman law cases has great benefit for a researcher since all the testimony of a trial was recorded and preserved with the court proceedings.[5] Perhaps the most important contribution of Brown's study lies in its assessment of community attitudes toward Benedetta Carlini's visions and alleged sexual misconduct. We learn about the lines that the community drew between acceptable spiritual impulses and the "immodest acts" that brought Benedetta Carlini to trial. Recorded women's lives provide us a unique entry point into the sensibility of an age, particularly in regard to how people of that age perceived gender.

Ecclesiastical court records provide rich sources. In Barcelona, the series of ecclesiastical court cases begins in 1301 and marches on until the twentieth century in unbroken sequence. For women in orders, laywomen who were donors, and all those whose lives gained the court's attention, such sequential ecclesiastical records prove to be a rich resource. [6]

Rudolph Bell and Donald Weinstein chose another path through the sources in order to learn about religious women and men and their expressions of their religious impulses. The authors approached the large corpus of literature on saints' lives, that is, medieval hagiography, with questions intended to classify those experiences found sufficiently holy to be recorded and forwarded to the Holy See at Rome as proof for canonization. Patterns emerge from their attempt at classification. When and by what behavior was a saint first recognized? Was sainthood gendered, at least in the minds of the contemporary beholder? Their study, *Saints and Society*, provides an example of how to extract general information about an age from a large, formulaic literature. This ought to prompt scholars to ask what other large collections lend themselves to comparable treatment. David Herlihy employed collected saints' lives to identify attitudes toward family and household in his recent study, *Medieval Households*. His use of material prompts a related question: may a known and often studied literature, such as hagiography, be turned to answering questions in other fields of inquiry, such as the investigation of economic or family life?

In fact, one rule of thumb that might well be applied to research in medieval archives is to identify fruitful sources and then think long and deeply about what questions might be addressed to them. In pursuing a deeper understanding of dynastic women's political power, may sigillographic evidence, that is, information gleaned from studying royal seals, be investigated?[7] As consorts, regents, or rulers, women employed seals on documents of state. These may reveal subtle clues on issues of power or jurisdiction that are difficult to assess using only textual evidence. In the same manner, coins may be used as evidence. According to Alan Stahl, over one hundred medieval women appear on coins.[8] What regalian rights descended to women or fell to them as consorts or as rulers in their own right? From minting activity both political and economic consequences extend outward into the world of state formation and economic development.

Certainly our known, prized, edited, and published texts, that is, the "classics" descending to us from medieval times, may be reexamined in the interests of inquiry about medieval women. In the 1960s Michael M. Sheehan turned what he knew of canon law and theology to two issues important for the history of medieval women: the property rights of married women and the church's position on what constituted a valid marriage. The decretals of Pope Alexander III (1159–81) provide a rich series of opinions on contested marriages. These cases were referred to the Holy See from throughout Christian Europe. Alexander's responses, despite their specificity, gained general validity as directives from the papal throne. Thus Alexander's insistence upon present consent (or future consent upon reaching the age of consent and consummation of the marriage) led to consent's becoming a woman's right by the last years of the twelfth century. This *ius novum* (new law) and the challenges to it over the centuries open up a window on women's legal position in the family. This is particularly important because the twelfth century's most eminent canon lawyer, Gratian (active from 1130 to 1150), attached importance to property, especially the wife's gift of dowry, for validating Christian marriage. Even if the Papacy subsequently disallowed property qualifications as criteria for a valid marriage, church law contained "an important series of texts associating *dos* (dowry) and *donatio propter nuptias* (groom's gift) with the proper constitution of the marital bond."[9]

While Pope Alexander III's decretals relied on Christian theology and precedent from the church fathers to arrive at conclusions, Gratian invoked classical antecedents for his arguments on women's legal incapacity to justify dowry funds passing through a woman to her husband once marriage was contracted. Gratian's rousing success in creating legal precedent for civil law in Italy and in influencing the designers of statute law in such city-states as Genoa, Siena, and Pisa assured the popularity of his revived classical notions about women's incapacity. Thus from Gratian to that other important canon lawyer, Pope Innocent III (1198–1216), and through Innocent to scholastic theologians in the thirteenth and fourteenth centuries, a restrictive gender system was reestablished in medieval letters and life.[10] For this reason the entire corpus of scholastic, humanist, and juristic writing of the late medieval and early Renaissance period is open to inquiry about the European gender system that arose in the twelfth and thirteenth centuries and gained steadily in power thereafter. A few of the texts have been examined, but the vast medieval and early Renaissance literature remains largely unexplored on the important question of thinking about gender.

Christiane Klapisch-Zuber, the French historian who with David Herlihy edited the *cadasto* of 1427, Europe's first census, asked entirely new questions about medieval literature because of what she learned from investigating census data. She was intrigued by the adoption of the Griselda myth from northern European sources (we find it, for example, in Geoffrey Chaucer's *Canterbury Tales*) in the art and literature of fourteenth- and fifteenth-century Florence. She learned that the popularity of the Griselda theme corresponded with changes in married women's property rights. She noted that by the late Middle Ages in Florence and in other northern Italian cities, women's marriage gifts to their husbands were given for the duration of the marriage but that husbands' gifts to wives only signified entry into a patrilineal line and were reclaimed by the lineage over a wife's lifetime. The author then associated the use of the Griselda myth, which emphasizes a wife's abject submission to her husband's will, with the steady erosion of women's property rights in marriage. The visual arts and literature allowed her to investigate how the deprivation of rights was explained through myth and story in bourgeois families. [11]

Diane Owen Hughes investigated the meaning of sumptuary legislation for women by reference to painting and fresco in Italian cities. Her major sources for study were more than fifty pieces of urban sumptuary legislation beginning in the twelfth century in Genoa. Her reference to visual art provided identifiable dates for the adoption of new fashions among affluent bourgeois Christian women, who often defied statutory limitations on their consumption and dress. [12] Readdressing the high tradition of Renaissance literature and painting, both Hughes and Klapisch-Zuber placed visual and textual information within their cultural and social context to reach conclusions.

When prized texts from the Middle Ages have been attributed to women, their authorship has often been disputed by medieval historians. One primary function of historians since the Renaissance has been the critical examination of medieval texts in order to detect forgery, spurious attribution, and alterations that may have occurred during the copying process. Nevertheless, when I began to examine the scholarship about Dame Trotula, physician at the University of Salerno in the eleventh century, I detected the operation of a criterion far different from that applied to cases where a man's authorship of texts was contested. [13] Historians of medicine simply could not accept the fact that a woman physician could have enjoyed an affiliation with a university in the eleventh century. The gynecological treatises attributed to Dame Trotula were therefore judged to be male-authored but assigned a woman's name out of delicacy, that is, a concern for women's modesty. This problem appeared to exist only among modern investigators. Through at least the fourteenth century medieval people had found no difficulty in accepting Dame Trotula as an authority on medical problems.

Fortunately, criticisms of the scholarship on the Trotula manuscripts reopened the question again. John Benton embarked on the arduous job of finding and comparing the manuscripts attributed to Trotula and subjected them to a new examination. Medieval manuscripts traveled, then and now, so this meant visiting Paris and Madrid as well as southern Italy, where they were allegedly written. Applying critical textual analysis has yielded interesting results. Benton argues that while the treatises *Trotula major* and *Trotula minor* may not have been written by Trotula, they have been attributed to a woman physician of that name (who taught at Salerno) because of her great fame. According to Benton, it appears quite likely that Trotula did author a major treatise on gynecology; moreover, the word "Trotta," which appears on the earliest known copy of the treatise, a copy now in Spain, is the name not of the treatise but of the woman author. [14]

The gynecological treatises of the Middle Ages have been taken as a field of study by some young historians; Monica Green, for example, is reinvestigating the question of Trotula's manuscripts. It is interesting to note that today's scholars bring different assumptions about gender to their research, if we compare them to those who wrote history of science and medicine in the late nineteenth and early twentieth centuries. [15] Many scholars today realize that some women were recognized as physicians in the medieval era. They have learned from the scholarship of Guido Ruggiero, for example, of documented cases where women served as physicians and were sanctioned in that professional role by Venetian civil authorities. [16] Also, recently trained historians recognize that the gender system, which would increasingly come to define who could and who could not affiliate with universities after the twelfth century, had a more tenuous hold on people's minds in the eleventh century. This increasing sophistication about changing medieval notions of gender supports a growing corpus of more reliable scholarship on women.

Clearly, scholars' basic assumptions about the course of women's history have changed markedly in the past dozen years. We no longer assume that in periods of so-called progressive change will women improve their condition. It is widely acknowledged today that women's history over the long term often followed a separate course from that taken by men even if men shared a common station in society or even the same family with the women in question. We know this because of the painstaking social reconstruction of medieval women's lives carried out through study of the charters, or documents of practice. Perhaps it is even more accurate to place that recent research at the juncture of rules and practice, because the conjunction of legal and religious proscriptions of women's roles and women's behavior as revealed in laws and charters has increasingly captured scholars' attentions. For a number of communities in the Mediterranean south, a prosopography of medieval women now takes its place alongside a prosopography of medieval men. For this reason our grasp of the social reality of that more remote time has increased significantly. Social history now illuminates the Balkan Peninsula, the Adriatic shores, Mediterranean France, and Spain as well as Italy. Nevertheless, Italian cities remain the best known in our scholarly literature.

[margin handwritten note: progressive Δ does not mean improvement of womens condition]

While medievalists enjoy the advantage of many charters over our colleagues studying ancient societies, we lack the wealth of long, uninterrupted series of documents that scholars studying early modern Europe take for granted. Peter Burke has recently assayed the literature of sixteenth- and seventeenth-century Italy in *The Historical Anthropology of Early Modern Italy*. He tells about the sources and how they may be used to classify people (use of the census materials, primarily) and study festivals, uses of insult or blasphemy, rates of literacy, patterns of consumption, rituals, religious life, and attitudes toward authority. The ambition of his program in cultural anthropology may not be so thoroughly realized for study of the centuries before 1500 because series of charters are more random and the rich surviving sources of wills and other related private records are seldom matched decade by decade with census data or civic records.

What medievalists may do is sample the literature. For example, Heath Dillard has promulgated and unpromulgated law at her disposal for studying medieval Spanish women. She does not have charters in any number, so the documents outside the laws available to her are often literary in nature: epics, novels, and the songs of courtly love. These tend to speak to the condition of women of elite status and not to that of the women from everyday walks of life, whom the author would like to investigate. Still, much can be reconstructed from the laws alone, and medievalists learn to use what is at hand.[17] Leah Lydia Otis encountered a more varied documentation for her study of urban prostitution in southern France. With archives allowing ever greater specificity of findings as the centuries progressed from the eleventh through the fifteenth, Otis accomplished a longitudinal study that charts major changes in attitudes toward prostitution, sexuality, and, through sexuality, women as a group. She looked at court cases involving prostitutes, traced some prostitutes in the charters, reviewed urban legislative initiatives in first licensing, then farming out, houses of prostitution for revenue purposes, and consulted literary works for references to prostitutes. A diversity of sources rounded out her picture of the steady institutionalization of prostitution in town life.[18]

Dusanka Dinić-Knežević proposed to write a history of the women of medieval Yugoslavia. Because she chose to feature the women of Dubrovnik (medieval Ragusa) and Serbia, Dinić-Knežević faced the problem many scholars encounter when reconstructing women's lives: she could write a fully detailed account of the women of Dubrovnik, but the code of Dusan and a few chronicles were her only major sources for information about Serbian women.[19] Her coverage is therefore skewed toward bourgeois life, and this proves true wherever prosopography is attempted around the Mediterranean basin. A few scholars have courageously addressed the question of the peasantry, but most of what we know of women concerns urban women. Still, Anageliki Laiou-Thomadakis has written an account of medieval Greek peasants,[20] and Barbara Kreutz has embarked upon a study of Sicilian peasants, with an emphasis on peasant women.

But researchers learn to be clever and to glean whatever there is from the preserved records and materials at hand. When Judith Herrin wrote "Women and Faith in Icons in Early Christianity," she knew she worked at a disadvantage. She had the church fathers and some Byzantine chronicle sources to consult but little else. She augmented these with preserved art and fragments, and even descriptions of early Christian art, from locales in the eastern Mediterranean region. To this she added evidence from archaeological finds, and she did not hesitate to consult and use graffiti, which can still be found around religious shrines. As the age grows more remote in time or place or the group studied farther removed from urban centers, the researcher is challenged to find materials that will yield answers.

While this walk about the Mediterranean indicates that scholarship on women in the region need not be restricted to northern Italy, it is nonetheless true that the women of northern Italy's towns remain the best documented and researched. This is not to say that continuous records exist for any northern Italian city for the entire medieval era. In fact, one can use the dates attached to scholarly investigations to fairly accurately assess when a community's archives begin and end. Medieval Genoa provides a case in point. The archives for Genoa support research on the twelfth century because remarkably full notarial registers of parishes have survived from that era, and in certain instances these may be set in the context of surviving civil legislation and then augmented by references to urban chronicles. But medieval Genoa's records do not remain full and varied for the later medieval centuries. By contrast, Pisa, its neighbor, supports research on the thirteenth century. After the silting up of Pisa's harbor and the decline of the city, which has been attributed to malaria, its records are less useful. Florence, on the other hand, has only a few surviving charters or, for that matter, civil records of any kind for the period before the Black Plague (1348–50). For the latter half of the fourteenth century and for the fifteenth century, the records are perhaps the most numerous and the most studied for all of Italy, with the possible exception of Venice.

This accounts for the tendency among medievalists to compare apples and oranges, that is, to occasionally use the history of a city like Genoa to sketch in twelfth-century history, then to shift to a documented thirteenth-century urban community, and to end using material on Florence from the fourteenth and fifteenth centuries. To the extent that each Italian city was unique in its evolution, this method misleads. On the other hand, certain longitudinal studies could not be undertaken unless the experience of more than one city-state were included. For the early era, for example, Diane Owen Hughes used Genoa and other Tyrrhenian Sea communities to understand the transition from bride-price to dowry in the twelfth century. She had sufficient evidence from the late eleventh and twelfth centuries to reach conclusions.[21] The current major study of dowry, undertaken by Julius Kirshner and Anthony Mohlo, is based on the fifteenth-century *monte delle doti* of Florence.[22] Precedents for this large study have been constructed through viewing Florentine and Bolognese juristic precedents in the fourteenth and fifteenth centuries, but questions about earlier practices must be referred to either what was found out about the seaports of western Italy by Hughes or what is known of Venice, whose archives can support research on thirteenth-century documents. There has been some nimble hopscotching from city to city in medieval social research.

This chronology assumes that the researcher will be content to learn about the twelfth and subsequent centuries. Research on the centuries prior to the twelfth and even on the early seventh and eighth centuries is possible by reference to the charters, but problems here abound. Still, almost all the charters from that remote time are available in edited and published collections. Northern Italy supplied by far the greatest number of these charters, and they have been published in the series Regesta chartarum italiae, although some others may be found in published monastic collections.[23] Unfortunately, however, no other region matches Italy in the number of extant charters. Some charters have survived in both France and Spain.[24] These charters have also been studied exhaustively as Europe's earliest, and therefore most precious, records of private lives. This does not mean that they cannot yield more information, particularly if a new question about women is addressed to them, but a researcher must conduct a thorough review of the secondary literature of this and the preceding century before claiming as original any new insight gleaned from them.

Perhaps the most famous document of the later medieval era, one that has become a reference point for all subsequent urban social history, is the Florentine *cadasto* of 1427. Florence preserved not only a massive *monte* on dowry but also a *monte* for tax purposes in the fifteenth century. This bundle of tax documents is our first major census in European history. With the help of computers, David Herlihy and Christiane Klapisch-Zuber produced a thorough, richly detailed study of the population of fifteenth-century Tuscany. Both urban and rural inhabitants as well as the land-tenure system and agriculture receive attention. This study serves as an extraordinary example of what medieval prosopography can tell us about women. It also serves as a research tool because its quantitative information is very rich and cannot be obtained for any other contemporary community. Almost all subsequently written social history draws basic information from this study: urban sex ratios, age at marriage for women and men, proportion of widows in urban populations, women in religious orders, comparative mortality rates, and more. This monumental work will clearly continue to serve as a basis for research, and a caution should therefore be issued. Those who use the detailed tables of this study should pause to read the text closely. The authors have been careful to qualify their conclusions based upon the limitations of the *cadasto* as a census document. The numbers constitute no absolute reference point. The highly skewed sex ratios in the study provide a case in point: unless these are understood in the context of reporting common to that day, they cannot be used to estimate the number of women and men in an age group. [25]

Working with notarial charters is rather like playing a game with no rules. Whereas the guidelines for textual analysis of medieval manuscripts are widely understood and accepted, the guidelines for working with notarial charters are imprecise. Two rules warrant mention, however. First, notarial charters must be understood in the context of a specific city and its customs, practices, and values. For example, were notariats centered in parishes or organized within a central chancellery? Second, paleography and formulas used by notaries must be mastered. While these follow certain general rules, paleography and abbreviations are best learned through visiting a specific archive and studying its charters, since both are prone to local variation. Once skill in reading charters has been gained, two approaches may be taken. First, the researcher may try to find a person, a family, a group, or an institution that might bear investigation. Second, if a number of charters are sufficiently formulaic in nature and available over a suitably long period of time, they may be compared. The first approach has already allowed us to "find" women, and a substantial increase in our understanding of the social life of cities has been the result. The latter, comparative approach yields numbers that have heretofore been largely unavailable for understanding the lives of women in the medieval period.

To illustrate the latter approach: while browsing in the Dubrovnik archives, I found some large volumes in a series named *Liber dotium* (*Book of Dowries*). My subsequent interest in what they first revealed to me prompts the use I have made throughout this essay of dowry to show changes in medieval women's legal and social condition. But the dowry records I first encountered were brief, three- to ten-line entries in the hand of the notary. I realized they were formulaic and terse, and while not all volumes survived and not all decades were covered, I could compare dowry awards among noble families of the town from the late thirteenth century to the fifteenth century. The increase in awards gave me a glimpse of private wealth and its accumulation in the centuries in which this city rose to prominence in Mediterranean trade. As it happened, no other comparable documents exist for assessing the extent of private wealth for these centuries. Statute laws could be compared to the series of dowries, and, with the help of extensive genealogies, which had been compiled for notable families, I was able to find an adequate basis for a longitudinal study. The numbers this study yielded have some validity because they can be set within the context of other known social facts about the community. Looking at changes in women's condition proved as revealing as looking at changes in men's social condition when it came to the important matter of assessing the increase in wealth of the community. [26]

How does a scholar go about getting started? A mentor helps. The women and men mentioned in this essay might be consulted. Learn about people who teach in North America and who use specific Mediterranean archives for their research. If you would like to learn about Rome, consult the work of Peter Partner, Robert Brentano, or Egmont Lee, all of whom have scoured Rome's archives.[27] Remember, a mentor can take you only where she or he has been. If you want to make a find, you may have to visit and investigate for yourself. Sabina Riemer, for example, decided to write her doctoral dissertation on medieval urban women in the thirteenth century; by traveling to Siena she was able to find the documents for her study. [28]

Next, learn the skills necessary to deal with charters or other documentary sources. Not only does using documents of practice require paleological skills and knowledge of Latin and Italian (or other appropriate vernacular languages) and of notarial formulas, but a scholar must subject charters to laws of evidence in a careful way as well. It is a mistake, for example, to assume that the special case that was litigated was routine. Good research depends upon a thorough understanding of the document and how it functioned in its time and place. Next, never assume that what was prescribed by authorities became common practice unless there is clear evidence for doing so. Yes, a historian may be safe in assuming that what was frequently condemned was also practiced, but again, the case must be made by the researcher through investigating context. Also, take a lesson from medievalists who remained avowedly interdisciplinary in their approach to history. The general rule among medievalists is that if it exists it should be consulted, whether it stands outside one's chosen discipline or not.

Remember as well that the lucky find happens to the informed mind. The Venetian archives are a fabled place to study social history because of the variety of records as well as the preservation of charters in series. When Stanley Chojnacki decided to use wills to understand whether noblewomen distributed their wealth in the same fashion as men of their families did, he decided to focus his research on one patrician clan. Strolling in the upper storage region of Santa Maria dei Frari, which houses the archives, he found a box of wills belonging to the noble Morosini clan. Why weren't these listed for scholars to study? The answer came back: they had not been probated. Chojnacki commented that it was unlikely that fourteenth- and fifteenth-century wills would ever be probated and asked if he could have a look at them anyway. These wills represented a genuine find, and they provide one important foundation for his subsequent social research.[29] Researching in Venice has supported other fortunate finds; Venetian records are so rich and varied that Patricia LaBalme and Guido Ruggiero have even been able to say something about medieval attitudes toward sexuality.[30]

An investigator can begin work this side of the Atlantic Ocean by consulting manuscripts in library collections here. The Library of Congress publishes a guide to collections of medieval manuscripts and updates it annually.[31] You may find it in the reference section of academic libraries. Some scholars find it useful to use microfilmed wills collected by the Church of Jesus Christ of Latter-Day Saints. A local Mormon congregation can provide a list of microfilmed wills from European archives, or you can write to their headquarters in Salt Lake City or in Washington, D.C. The same rules apply whether a scholar works with sources available here or visits Mediterranean archives: one must learn the context of the evidence to be able to interpret it properly.

In the last analysis, the sources are worth expending scholarly efforts. The question of women in the medieval period offers the researcher the opportunity to make an original contribution to scholarship; in other words, not all the answers are in—far from it. A ramble through Mediterranean archives, backed up with some serious research, may introduce you to a lifetime's occupation.

NOTES

1. Stuard, *Women in Medieval Society.*

2. Kelly, "Did Women Have a Renaissance?" see also the essays on the medieval era by Jo Ann McNamara, Suzanne Wemple, and Susan Stuard in Bridenthal, Koonz, and Stuard, *Becoming Visible.*

3. For information contact Mary Martin McLaughlin, R.D.3, Box 422, Millbrook, N.Y., 12545. The press release issued in 1986 states: "We have thus created, in effect, another research instrument enabling us to generate quantitative data on a number of important topics. Our data base also permits interim circulation of our results, pending completion of successive phases of our work."

4. E. Ann Matter, University of Pennsylvania, "Statement of Plans" for research, funded by the National Endowment for the Humanities, 1987–88.

5. Brown, *Immodest Acts.* Brown found the relevant texts listed under *Miscellanea medicea,* a signal for all would-be researchers that classification in archives can sometimes be misleading. On the value of Roman law procedure for historical analysis, see the introduction to LeRoy Ladurie, *Montaillou.*

6. These records are not published for the most part.

7. Brigitte Bedos Rezak delivered a paper at the Seventh Berkshire Conference on the History of Women: "Impression of French Medieval Women: The Sigillographic Evidence."

8. Stahl, "Women's Rights to Minting."

9. Sheehan, "Influence of Canon Law," p. 110. For a review of Alexander III's decretals, see Donahue, "Canon Law."

10. Gratian, *Decretum,* esp. c. 33. A manuscript of the Pisan statutes from the twelfth century is available in the United States: Pisa, *Constitutum legis; constitutum usus.*

11. See Klapisch-Zuber, "Griselda Complex."

12. Hughes, "Distinguishing Signs."

13. Stuard, "Dame Trot."

14. Benton, "Trotula."

15. See, for example, Green, "The *De genecia.*"

16. Ruggiero, "Status of Physicians," esp. pp. 170–71 and n. 9.

17. Dillard, *Women of the Reconquest.*

18. Otis, *Prostitution in Medieval Society.*

19. Dinić-Knežević, *Položaj zena u Dubrovniku*. This example serves to remind us that others are interested in and are writing the history of women. While many works appear in translation, such as Christiane Klapisch-Zuber's articles, some may be read only by learning a foreign language—in this instance Serbo-Croatian.

20. Laiou-Thomadakis, *Peasant Society*.

21. Hughes, "From Brideprice to Dowry."

22. Kirshner and Molho, "Dowry Fund and the Marriage Market."

23. See, for example, Petrucci, *Codice diplomatico del monastero benedettino di S. Maria di Tremiti*.

24. See, for example, Bernard and Bruel, *Recueil des chartes de l'abbaye de Cluny*; for early medieval Catalonia, see Merêa, *Estudos de direito hispanico medieval*.

25. Herlihy and Klapisch-Zuber, *Les Toscans et leurs familles*, translated and abridged as *Tuscans and Their Families*. The French edition is often better for the researcher because it is more detailed.

26. Stuard, "Dowry Increase and Increments in Wealth."

27. Partner, *Renaissance Rome*; Brentano, *Rome before Avignon*; Lee, "Foreigners in Quattrocento Rome."

28. Riemer, "Women in the Medieval City."

29. Chojnacki, "Patrician Women in Early Renaissance Venice," and "Dowries and Kinsmen in Early Renaissance Venice."

30. LaBalme, "Sodomy and Venetian Justice"; Ruggiero, *Boundary of Eros*.

31. Library of Congress, *National Union Catalogue of Manuscript Collections*, updated annually. Other valuable reference works include Kristeller, *Latin Manuscript Books before 1600* (this work is also updated); Thorndike and Kibre, *A Catalogue of Incipits of Medieval Scientific Writings in Latin*; and Bloomfield, *Incipits of Latin Works on the Virtues and Vices*. "Incipit" is the name given to the first word or phrase of a manuscript. There are also catalogs of collections at specific libraries; see, for example, Shailor, *Catalogue of Medieval and Renaissance MSS. in the Beinecke Rare Book and MS. Library*.

BIBLIOGRAPHY

Bedos-Rezak, Brigitte. "Impression of French Medieval Women: The Sigillographic Evidence (Twelfth to Fourteenth Centuries)." Paper presented at the Seventh Berkshire Conference on the History of Women, Wellesley College, June 1987.

Bell, Rudolph, and Donald Weinstein. *Saints and Society*. Chicago, 1983.

Benton, John. "Trotula, Women's Problems, and the Professionalization of Medicine in the Middle Ages." *Bulletin of the History of Medicine* 59 (1985): 30–55.

Bernard, Auguste, and Alexandre Bruel, eds. *Recueil des chartes de l'abbaye de Cluny.* 6 vols. Paris, 1876–1903.

Bloomfield, Morton W., ed. *Incipits of Latin Works on the Virtues and Vices,* A.D. *1100–1500.* Cambridge, Mass., 1979.

Brentano, Robert. *Rome before Avignon: A Social History of Thirteenth-Century Rome.* New York, 1974.

Bridenthal, Renata, Claudia Koonz, and Susan Stuard, eds. *Becoming Visible: Women in European History.* Boston, 1987.

Brown, Judith. *Immodest Acts.* New York, 1986.

Burke, Peter. *The Historical Anthropology of Early Modern Italy.* Cambridge, Mass., 1987.

Chojnacki, Stanley. "Dowries and Kinsmen in Early Renaissance Venice." In *Women in Medieval Society,* ed. Susan Mosher Stuard, pp. 175–98. Philadelphia, 1976.

——— . "Patrician Women in Early Renaissance Venice." *Studies in the Renaissance* 21 (1974): 176–203.

Dillard, Heath. *Women of the Reconquest.* Cambridge, Engl., 1984.

Dinić-Knežević, Dusanka. *Položaj zena u Dubrovniku u XIII i XIV veku.* Belgrade, 1974.

Donahue, Charles. "The Canon Law on the Formation of Marriage and Social Practice in the Later Middle Ages." *Journal of Family History* 8 (1983): 144–58.

Gratian. *Decretum.* Vol. 1 of *Corpus iuris canonici.* Ed. Emil Friedberg. Graz, 1955.

Green, Monica. "The *De genecia* Attributed to Constantine the African." *Speculum* 62, no. 3 (1987): 2299–2323.

Herlihy, David. *Medieval Households.* Cambridge, Mass., 1986.

Herlihy, David, and Christiane Klapisch-Zuber. *Les Toscans et leurs familles.* Paris, 1978.

——— . *The Tuscans and Their Families.* New Haven, Conn., 1985.

Herrin, Judith. "Women and Faith in Icons in Early Christianity." In *Culture, Ideology, and Politics,* ed. Raphael Samuel and Gareth Stedman Jones, pp. 56–83. London, 1982.

Hughes, Diane Owen. "Distinguishing Signs: Ear-rings, Jews, and Franciscan Rhetoric in the Italian Renaissance City." *Past and Present* 112 (1986): 2–59.

——— . "From Brideprice to Dowry in Mediterranean Europe." *Journal of Family History* 3 (1978): 263–96.

Kelly, Joan. "Did Women Have a Renaissance?" In *Becoming Visible: Women in European History,* ed. Renata Bridenthal, Claudia Koonz, and Susan Stuard, pp. 175–201. Boston, 1987.

Kirshner, Julius, and Anthony Molho. "The Dowry Fund and the Marriage Market in Early Quattrocento Florence." *Journal of Modern History* 50 (1978): 403–38.

Klapisch-Zuber, Christiane. "The Griselda Complex: Dowry and Marriage Gifts in the Quattrocento." In *Women, Family, and Ritual in Renaissance Italy,* trans. Lydia Cochrane, pp. 213–46. Chicago, 1985.

Kristeller, P. O. *Latin Manuscript Books before 1600.* 3d ed. New York, 1965.

LaBalme, Patricia. "Sodomy and Venetian Justice in the Renaissance." *Legal History Review* 42 (1984): 217–54.

Laiou-Thomadakis, Anageliki. *Peasant Society in the Late Byzantine Empire: A Social and Demographic Study.* Princeton, N.J., 1977.

Lee, Egmont. "Foreigners in Quattrocento Rome." *Renaissance and Reformation,* n.s., 7, no. 2 (1983): 135–46.

LeRoy Ladurie, Immanuel. *Montaillou: The Promised Land of Error.* Trans. Barbara Bray. New York, 1978.

Library of Congress. *National Union Catalogue of Manuscript Collections.* Updated annually.

Merêa, Paulo. *Estudos de direito hispanico medieval.* Coimbra, 1952.

Otis, Leah Lydia. *Prostitution in Medieval Society.* Chicago, 1985.

Partner, Peter. *Renaissance Rome, 1500–1559.* Berkeley, 1976.

Petrucci, Armando, ed. *Codice diplomatico del monastero benedettino di S. Maria di Tremiti.* Regesta chartarum italiae. Rome, 1960.

Pisa. *Constitutum legis; constitutum usus.* Beinecke Rare Book Library, 62 fols. Early thirteenth century.

Riemer, Eleanor Sabina. "Women in the Medieval City: Sources and Uses of Wealth by Sienese Women in the Thirteenth Century," Ph.D. diss., New York University, 1975.

Ruggiero, Guido. *The Boundary of Eros.* Oxford, 1985.

———. "The Status of Physicians in Renaissance Venice." *Journal of the History of Medicine and Allied Sciences* 36 (1981): 168–84.

Shailor, Barbara A. *Catalogue of Medieval and Renaissance MSS. in the Beinecke Rare Book and MS. Library.* Binghamton, N.Y., 1986.

Sheehan, Michael M. "The Influence of Canon Law on the Property Rights of Married Women in England." *Medieval Studies* 25 (1963): 109–24.

Stahl, Alan M. "Women's Rights to Minting in the Middle Ages." Paper presented at the Seventh Berkshire Conference on the History of Women, Wellesley College, June 1987.

Stuard, Susan Mosher. "Dame Trot." *Signs* 1, no. 2 (1975): 537–42.

———. "Dowry Increase and Increments in Wealth in Medieval Ragusa (Dubrovnik)." *Journal of Economic History* 41, no. 4 (1981): 795–811.

———, ed. *Women in Medieval Society.* Philadelphia, 1976.

Thorndike, Lynn, and Pearl Kibre, eds. *A Catalogue of Incipits of Medieval Scientific Writings in Latin.* Cambridge, Mass., 1963.

CONTRIBUTORS

BRIGITTE BEDOS-REZAK, a graduate of the Sorbonne and of the Ecole nationale des Chartes, is an associate professor of history at the University of Maryland at College Park. The social, cultural, and political implications of medieval seals are among her principal scholarly interests and have been the subjects of many of her articles and of her *Les Sceaux des villes*.

JACQUES BERLIOZ is a senior member of l'École Française of Rome, a research associate at the Centre National de la Recherche Scientifique, and he has prepared a critical edition of Etienne de Bourbon's *Tractatus de diversis materiis predicabilibus*.

JAMES A. BRUNDAGE specializes in the history of medieval law and the history of sexuality. A professor of history at the University of Kansas, he is also a life member of Clare Hall at Cambridge University, a fellow of the Royal Historical Society, and an associate editor of the *Journal of Medieval History*. His most recent work is *Law, Sex, and Christian Society in Medieval Europe*.

JOHN B. FREED, who studied at Cornell and Princeton, teaches at Illinois State University. He has published a number of articles about medieval Salzburg and two books, *The Friars and German Society in the Thirteenth Century* and *The Counts of Falkenstein: Noble Self-Consciousness in Twelfth-Century Germany*.

PENNY S. GOLD earned a doctorate in medieval studies at Stanford University. An associate professor of history at Knox College, she is the author of *The Lady and the Virgin: Image, Attitude, and Experience in Twelfth-Century France*. She is now retraining in the field of modern Jewish history.

DAVID HERLIHY is a professor of history at Brown University. He has published widely on social and demographic history, and his books include *Pisa in the Early Renaissance, Medieval and Renaissance Pistoia*, and *Medieval Households*. He has been president of the American Catholic Historical Association, the Medieval Academy of America, and the American Historical Association.

JENNY JOCHENS, professor of history at Towson State University, received her training in history and Old Norse literature at the universities of Copenhagen and Paris and at Johns Hopkins University. She has published widely on aspects of the lives of Old Norse women, and in 1987–88 she was the recipient of a fellowship from the National Endowment for the Humanities.

HELEN LEMAY is an associate professor of history at the State University of New York at Stony Brook. Her research has been centered on the twelfth-century philosopher and scientist Guillaume de Conches and on medieval scientific ideas on women and sexuality.

JANET SENDEROWITZ LOENGARD, who earned her Ph.D. at Columbia University, is a professor of history at Moravian College. She has published articles on medieval English legal history, and her edition of records of sixteenth-century London real estate litigation, *London Viewers and Their Certificates, 1508–1558*, was recently published.

JO ANN MCNAMARA is a professor of history at Hunter College of the City University of New York. She has published numerous articles on the subject of women in the Middle Ages, and her latest book is *A New Song: Celibate Women in the First Three Christian Centuries*.

MARIE ANNE POLO DE BEAULIEU belongs to the young generation of fellows of the Centre National de la Recherche Scientifique, where she has worked since 1986 under the direction of Jacques Le Goff. She has prepared an edition of the *Scala celi* of Jean Gobi.

JOEL T. ROSENTHAL is a professor of history of the State University of New York at Stony Brook. He received his degrees from the University of Chicago, and he has published on both Anglo-Saxon England and late medieval English society.

JANE TIBBETTS SCHULENBURG is a professor of history and of women's studies at the University of Wisconsin at Madison. She is the author of a number of articles on women saints and women in the medieval church and society. Her *"Forgetful of Their Sex": Female Sanctity and "Deviancy," ca. 500–1100* is forthcoming.

ALAN M. STAHL, who holds a doctorate in medieval history from the University of Pennsylvania, is curator of medieval coins at the American Numismatic Society, New York. His publications include *The Merovingian Coinage of the Region of Metz, The Venetian Tornesello: A Medieval Colonial Coinage,* and numerous articles on medieval numismatics and monetary history.

SUSAN MOSHER STUARD is a medieval historian concerned with social and economic questions. Her interest in women may be seen in the twin volumes that she has edited, *Women in Medieval Society* and *Women in Medieval History and Historiography.* She received her doctorate from Yale University and is currently a professor of history at Haverford College.

INDEX